Composite Artificial Intelligence

Scrivener Publishing
100 Cummings Center, Suite 541J
Beverly, MA 01915-6106

Leading-Edge Breakthroughs in Artificial Intelligence

Series Editor: Dr. S. Balamurugan (sbnbala@gmail.com)

The world is on the cusp of several breakthroughs in artificial intelligence (AI), rapidly transforming industries and the research field. The "Leading-Edge Breakthroughs in Artificial Intelligence" book series is dedicated to exploring the most pioneering developments in artificial intelligence. The series aims to highlight both theoretical and practical advancements, offering insights into several cutting-edge advancements in AI and how the same could be deployed to solve complex problems in fields such as healthcare, finance, manufacturing, robotics, marketing, energy management, agriculture, autonomous systems, and many more. It also addresses critical issues like AI governance, ethics, trust, security, transparency, and societal impacts, making it an essential resource for researchers, engineers, and industry leaders looking to leverage AI for future breakthroughs.

Publishers at Scrivener
Martin Scrivener (martin@scrivenerpublishing.com)
Phillip Carmical (pcarmical@scrivenerpublishing.com)

Composite Artificial Intelligence

Fundamentals, Challenges, and Applications

Edited by

T. S. Arun Samuel

Department of Electronics and Communication Engineering, National Engineering College, Tamil Nadu, India

L. Jerart Julus

Department of IT, School of Computer Science Engineering and Information Systems Vellore Institute of Technology, Vellore, India

P. Kanimozhi

Computer Science and Engineering, IFET College of Engineering, Tamil Nadu, India

T. Ananth Kumar

Computer Science and Engineering, IFET College of Engineering, Tamil Nadu, India

and

S. Balamurugan

Intelligent Research Consultancy Services (iRCS), Coimbatore, Tamil Nadu, India

Scrivener Publishing

WILEY

This edition first published 2026 by John Wiley & Sons, Inc., 111 River Street, Hoboken, NJ 07030, USA and Scrivener Publishing LLC, 100 Cummings Center, Suite 541J, Beverly, MA 01915, USA

For more information about Scrivener publications please visit www.scrivenerpublishing.com.

Wiley Global Headquarters
111 River Street, Hoboken, NJ 07030, USA

For details of our global editorial offices, customer services, and more information about Wiley products visit us at www.wiley.com.

The manufacturer's authorized representative according to the EU General Product Safety Regulation is Wiley-VCH GmbH, Boschstr. 12, 69469 Weinheim, Germany, e-mail: Product_Safety@wiley.com.

Library of Congress Cataloging-in-Publication Data

ISBN 978-1-394-39303-9

Cover image: Generated with AI using Adobe Firefly
Cover design by Russell Richardson

Set in size of 11pt and Minion Pro by Manila Typesetting Company, Makati, Philippines

Printed in the USA

10 9 8 7 6 5 4 3 2 1

Contents

Series Preface

This book discusses how multiple AI paradigms—such as symbolic reasoning, machine learning, and evolutionary computation—can be integrated to create more robust, adaptable, and intelligent systems for complex real-world problem-solving. The content of "Composite Artificial Intelligence: Fundamentals, Challenges, and Applications" is significant as it responds to the need to interleave diverse AI techniques—machine learning, symbolic reasoning, neural networks, evolutionary algorithms, etc.—to surpass the limitations of each and to create more intelligent, interpretable, and adaptive systems. Today, we live in an era characterized by complex problems that require multifaceted solutions. Composite AI opens up possibilities for developing robust, context-aware intelligent systems that can simultaneously reason, learn, and evolve. The book is relevant to the series of "Leading Edge Breakthroughs in Artificial Intelligence" because it defines a paradigm shift in how AI is develops and promotes interdisciplinary innovative next-generation AI systems that can tackle dynamic and high-dimensional real-world problems.

Dr. S. Balamurugan
Director, Intelligent Research Consultancy Services (iRCS), Coimbatore, Tamil Nadu, India
Series Editor - Leading Edge Breakthroughs in Artificial Intelligence

Preface

In the rapidly evolving landscape of artificial intelligence (AI), the demand for more adaptive, intelligent, and context-aware systems has led to the emergence of Composite Artificial Intelligence (Composite AI)—a paradigm that integrates multiple AI techniques to solve complex real-world problems with higher efficiency and intelligence. This book aims to serve as a comprehensive guide for students, researchers, and practitioners seeking to understand, develop, and apply composite AI systems.

Unlike traditional AI approaches that often rely on singular methodologies, composite AI combines symbolic reasoning, machine learning, data fusion, optimization algorithms, and cognitive computing to create solutions that mimic human-level decision-making more closely. From natural language processing and image recognition to biomedical diagnostics and social media analysis, composite AI is redefining what is possible in intelligent computing.

This book is structured into three parts:

Part I: Foundational Concepts and Emerging Trends in Composite AI lays the groundwork with key concepts, such as data fusion, language models, and early implementations of composite AI in pattern recognition.

Part II: Advanced Methods and Technical Challenges in Composite AI explores cutting-edge optimization techniques, bias mitigation strategies, and integration challenges, providing insights into the complexities of real-world AI development.

Part III: Real-World Applications of Composite AI in Healthcare and Beyond highlights practical implementations across diverse fields including healthcare, music recommendation, neurodiagnostic, and social systems—demonstrating the tangible impact of composite AI technologies.

Each chapter is authored with a balance of theoretical depth and practical relevance, supported by case studies, algorithmic frameworks, and experimental results where applicable. Whether you are an academic exploring new research direction, a student building foundational knowledge, or an industry professional applying AI to domain-specific problems, this book offers a holistic view of how composite AI is shaping the future of intelligent systems.

We hope this book will inspire further exploration, interdisciplinary innovation, and responsible deployment of AI in ways that benefit society at large. Finally, we extend our thanks to Martin Scrivener and the team at Scrivener Publishing for their efforts and guidance in bringing this work to fruition.

The Editors
December 2025

Acknowledgement

First and foremost, we are deeply thankful to the Almighty for granting us the strength, wisdom, and perseverance to complete this challenging and rewarding endeavor.

The preparation of this edited book has been a meaningful journey undertaken over several months. We extend our heartfelt gratitude to the "National Engineering College, India", "Vellore Institute of Technology (VIT), India" and "IFET College of Engineering, India", for their continuous support and encouragement have been instrumental in the successful realization of this work. We are profoundly grateful to our families, friends, colleagues, and well-wishers for their unwavering support and patience throughout this journey. Their belief in our mission kept us motivated through every phase of this work.

We sincerely thank all the contributors for their thoughtful research, insights, and willingness to be part of this volume. Their cooperation during the revisions and responsiveness greatly contributed to the overall quality and relevance of the book. We are also thankful to the reviewers, whose expert feedback and constructive suggestions played a crucial role in shaping and enhancing the final selection of chapters.

Lastly, we extend our heartfelt appreciation to our readers for their trust and interest. We hope this book proves to be a useful guide and an inspiration for scholars, professionals, and all those engaged in the evolving landscape of Artificial Intelligence.

Part I

FOUNDATIONAL CONCEPTS AND EMERGING TRENDS IN COMPOSITE AI

1

Data Fusion Techniques in Composite AI

S. Sowmyayani[1]*, D. Dhanya[2], J. Kavitha[3] and R. Roselinkiruba[3]

[1]*Department of Computer Science, St. Mary's College (Autonomous), Thoothukudi, Tamilnadu, India*

[2]*Dept of Artificial Intelligence and Data Science, Mar Ephraem College of Engineering and Technology, Malankara Hills, Elavuvilai, Marthandam, Tamilnadu, India*

[3]*Department of CSE, VelTech Rangarajan Dr. Sagunthala, R&D Institute of Science and Technology, Chennai, Tamilnadu, India*

Abstract

Nowadays, data is growing equivalent to or more than the population. At the same time, irrelevant and redundant data occupy more than the relevant ones. Considering these accounts, it is studied that data pre-processing needs special attention for any research to be more accurate. Also, it is necessary to group data according to the research. Hence, this chapter explores a few techniques that can be followed while using composite artificial intelligence (AI). A case study is elaborated to emphasize the need for data fusion and research fusion. An important and well-known Human Action Recognition (HAR) is embedded in Content-Based Video Retrieval (CBVR) to fully utilize composite AI's efficiency. It is achieved by combining a few deep learning models to create a HAR-CBVR system and the results (features) are fused in various ways. Experiments are demonstrated with various standard datasets and the results with fusion methods are compared with a few recent methods. The results proved that the inclusion of data fusion techniques works better than other methods.

Keywords: Composite AI, data fusion, deep learning, prediction

**Corresponding author*: sowmyayani@gmail.com

T. S. Arun Samuel, L. Jerart Julus, P. Kanimozhi, T. Ananth Kumar and S. Balamurugan (eds.) Composite Artificial Intelligence: Fundamentals, Challenges, and Applications, (3–32) © 2026 Scrivener Publishing LLC

1.1 Introduction

Big Data refers to integrating and analyzing vast quantities of complicated heterogeneous data. Applications for big data analytics offer thorough knowledge gleaned from the vast amount of data at hand. Health officials, physicians and patients will all gain more from the new information gleaned from big data analytics. The amount of data generated in numerical biomedical applications is increasing dramatically due to the rapid development of AI and social networks.

AI-powered predictions can enhance many services by identifying risks early, producing fresh perspectives, tracking the calibre of persons or nature and offering more effective options. Some issues in artificial intelligence are getting high throughput, integrating from several databases and using data mining techniques for high-dimensional data. This chapter provides additional information about big data fusion, or merging data from several databases, which helps policymakers make better decisions in their industry.

As individuals become increasingly open to participating in their own healthcare decisions, AI is becoming increasingly common in healthcare applications. Additionally, patients are more inclined to take the initiative to customize their medical care. More research is required because of the personalization of medical care and treatment. The field of mobile health is expanding and includes gadgets like ubiquitous smartphones, low-power body-area wireless networks, and miniature sensors. Composite AI can use predictive modeling to find people at high risk for particular diseases and recognize patterns. Estimating the chance of contracting an illness entails examining risk factors, medical history, genetic data, and even lifestyle information. This makes it possible to implement early diagnosis, proactive interventions, and customized preventative plans that have the potential to enhance health outcomes significantly.

In addition to storing all data in a publicly accessible, decentralized fashion while maintaining anonymity, blockchain offers several services, such as traceability, integrity, security, and non-repudiation. Data from multiple sources and forms, including structured and unstructured data, are integrated using composite artificial intelligence. By taking a comprehensive approach, all pertinent data are used, resulting in a more thorough and precise analysis.

By integrating several analytical methods, composite AI may extract more profound information from data. This improved data utilization makes more useful information for strategic planning and decision-making possible. Composite AI systems frequently use various data sources. Successful implementation depends on efficient data preparation. Preprocessing, cleaning, feature engineering, and integration are all included in this.

This book discusses some simple designs of data fusion in the internet age when the proliferation of data is becoming more widespread due to the enormous use of mobile devices and combining several sources of data into a single format that the composite AI system may utilize. Figure 1.1 shows the structure of composite AI.

The chapter is arranged as follows. The data fusion techniques in composite AI, their challenges, and their benefits are discussed in Section 1.2. The next section elaborates on the fusion technique with a clear application. Section 1.4 emphasizes the proposed algorithm with several experiments and analyses. The last section concludes the chapter with the path to future research.

1.2 Data Fusion Techniques in Composite AI

There are many ways to fuse data. A popular paradigm for classifying data fusion strategies is Dasarathy's classification [1], a well-known authority on data fusion. He grouped fusion techniques according to the relationship between data intake and output, i.e., data fusion, feature fusion, decision fusion, and hybrid fusion.

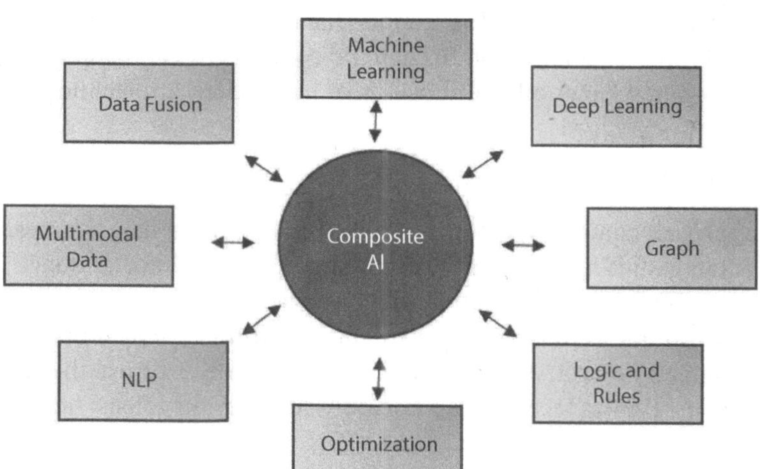

Figure 1.1 Composite AI.

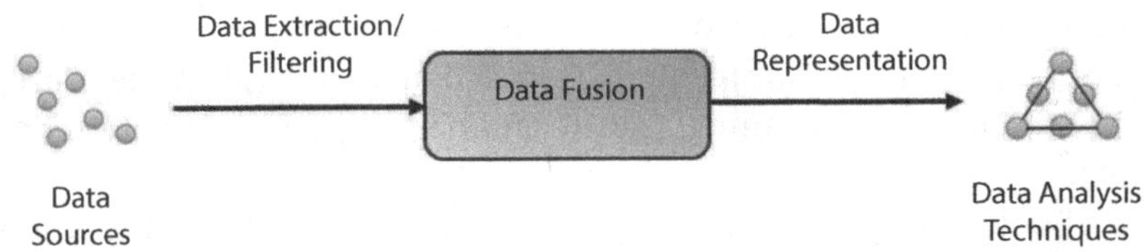

Figure 1.2 Data-level fusion.

1.2.1 Data Fusion

This approach aims to enhance the eminence, availability, or completeness of the data for further work. Figure 1.2 shows the data-level fusion. Typical techniques for data-level fusion consist of:

- Averaging fusion: This technique takes the mean value of the data from several sources to increase accuracy and lower noise. It works particularly well when sources have random variability and similar properties.
- Concatenation fusion: It combines raw data sequences from various sensors to create a longer sequence. This technique is frequently applied when sensors measure the same phenomenon from various angles. Concatenation is frequently used to enable thorough analysis of data from spectroscopy or image sensors. Several concatenation fusion methods include weighted averaging, Principal Component Analysis, Independent Component Analysis, etc.
- Fuzzy logic fusion: This method handles uncertainty by combining data based on fuzzy logic concepts. It can be helpful when sources offer ambiguous or insufficient information.

1.2.2 Feature Fusion

This approach combines features retrieved from several data sources. This may entail gathering pertinent features such as text, audio, or image from every data source and integrating them into a 1-D feature vector. The goal of this technique is to compile pertinent data from several sources into a form that can be utilized for further work. Figure 1.3 shows the feature-level fusion. Typical techniques for feature-level fusion consist of:

- o Features Concatenation: Concatenation combines features from various sources into a 1-D feature vector. When

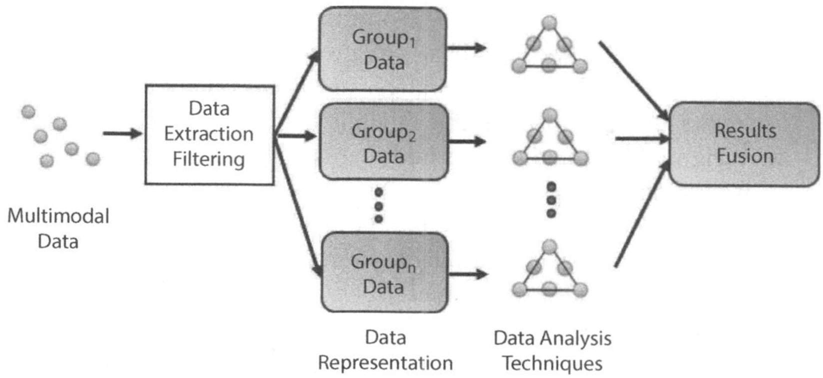

Figure 1.3 Feature-level fusion.

dimensions are comparable or features are the same, it works well.

- Feature selection: The pertinent features from each source are selected according to how crucial they are to the fusion process. By removing unnecessary or uninformative features, it lowers the dimensions. It enhances the fusion process by decreasing noise and increasing efficiency.
- PCA: The original features are turned into orthogonal features called principal components. It can lower the dimension of the data by collecting the greatest amount of variance in the data. It works well at mitigating multicollinearity and lowering the complexity of high-dimensional data.
- Wavelet Transform: By breaking them down into distinct frequency components, the wavelet transform obtains low-frequency and high-frequency intricacies of features. It identifies regional variances and patterns that other approaches might overlook. Applications involving image analysis and signal processing can benefit from it.

1.2.3 Decision Fusion

It is the process of combining judgments or outputs from several datasets to reach a conclusion or inference. Combining decisions from various classifiers, decision-making algorithms, or decision rules is one way to do this. It seeks to enhance the final decision's or inference's accuracy, dependability or robustness by combining the outputs of several datasets. The methods used in this type of fusion include:

- Majority voting: Choosing the option that receives the maximum votes allows decisions from several sources to be combined. It is helpful when sources are occasionally prone to errors and have comparable reliability.
- Weighted Voting: One method that is comparable to majority voting is weighted voting. Decisions are weighted differently in this case, depending on how reliable the source is. It lessens the impact of unreliable sources while increasing the influence of trustworthy ones.
- Plurality voting: It selects the option with the most votes. This method is useful if several classes have no obvious majority for one class.
- Expert opinion aggregate: It combines the opinions of multiple experts, each with specific knowledge. Making better decision stakes into account a range of viewpoints.
- The Bayesian Averaging Model: By computing the posterior distribution, it integrates choices made using Bayesian probability theory. It considers the degree of certainty and dependability of each dataset's viewpoint.
- Stacking: Combines the outcomes of several classifiers. The output of each classifier is used to teach a meta-classifier how to make the ultimate judgment.
- Consensus-based Fusion: By repeatedly improving choices until a consistent outcome is obtained, consensus-based fusion reaches agreement among sources. When sources give contradicting information, it works well.
- Evidence combination: Combines decisions based on uncertainty and evidence using Dempster-Shafer's theory. It is particularly helpful in situations where the information is vague or unclear.
- Fusion based on game theory: Examines how different sources interact to identify the most effective approach to decision-making. When sources have competing interests or goals, it can be helpful.

1.2.4 Hybrid Fusion

Combining two or more of the above-discussed fusion levels in a hybrid way is known as hybrid fusion. This can be feature-decision fusion, data-feature fusion, or the combination of the three fusions. Hybrid fusion methods can be customized for particular applications or situations and seek to capitalize on the advantages of several fusion methodologies.

1.3 Literature Survey

Many multidimensional datasets have been produced as a result of the introduction of inexpensive RGB-D cameras, and as a consequence, several multidimensional fusion-based HAR techniques have been developed. The majority of these techniques concentrated on combining various visual modes, which are discussed below.

The depth and RGB movies record 3D shape information and rich appearance, which complement and are useful for HAR. For more dependable HAR, early techniques concentrated on obtaining manually created features that capture spatiotemporal structural correlations from the RGB and the depth modalities. The previous work explores action recognition using deep learning models [2, 3]. The following deep learning techniques that combine these two data modalities are evaluated because deep learning architectures are now the main focus of research. A hybrid network comprising multi-stream CNNs and 3D Convolutional Long Short-Term Memory has been presented [4]. Action classification was then accomplished by fusing these features using canonical correlation analysis.

A generative framework [5], has investigated the feature distribution across the RGB and the depth videos. A cross-dimension discovery matrix has been created to complete the fusion and the resultant prediction has been given as input into a dimension correlation discovery network. Dhiman *et al.* [6], have developed a 2-stream network comprising a motion and a dynamic stream. Specifically, the motion stream provides classification scores after receiving a dynamic image.

Zhou *et al.* [7], have devised a decoupling and recoupling spatiotemporal feature extraction that disentangles the spatial and the temporal features to address the issue of tightly linked spatio-temporal representation modeling. The decoupled spatial and temporal networks have been created to learn the spatial and temporal features. The spatiotemporal relationships are then modeled using a re-coupling spatiotemporal network that consists of transformer blocks and a multi-scale layer. Lastly, information aggregation is carried out *via* a cross-modal adaptive posterior fusion technique. An inter-frame attention encoder processes RGB and its related depth data, which are subsequently fused by a mutual attention block in the transformer framework for egocentric HAR [8].

For action analysis, the RGB data's appearance information and the skeleton sequences' information on body posture and joint motion complement each other well. Several studies have looked into deep learning architectures to combine RGB and skeletal data. To execute HAR, Das *et al.* [9], have built an attention network on a 3D-CNN model using RGB input.

When calculating the spatio-temporal attention maps, they took into consideration the human body's topology [10]. The two-stream network created by Li *et al.* [11], is made up of three primary parts: the R(2+1)D network, which extracts RGB features, the Spatio-Temporal Graph CN, which extracts skeleton features and a guided block to improve the efficiency. Lastly, classification has been carried out using the score fusion technique.

A two-stream GCN network [12], has jointly aligned flow patches and skeleton data from RGB data. Skeletal data is represented as a 3D heatmap volume by RGBPose-Conv3D [13], which runs the video and the heatmap using a 2-stream 3D CNN.A high-framerate channel, two-pathway vision transformer, which consists of emphasizing temporal information and a path focusing on spatial data, has been recently developed by Jing and Wang [14], to merge RGB and skeletal data.

The skeleton data provides a concise yet useful representation for human behavior analysis [15]. Additionally, the performance of HAR when employed alone is limited by the noisy nature of skeleton data. HAR can benefit from the discriminative 3D shape and silhouette information that depth maps offer. To achieve more accurate HAR, early techniques have tried to merge manually created features that were taken from the depth sequences and the skeleton.

Zhao *et al.* [16], have used two 3D CNN streams that took as inputs depth data, motion maps and a 3D skeleton. Score multiplications were used to combine the classification results from these three networks. A three-stream 2D CNN has been created [17], to classify three distinct hand-crafted features that were taken from the depth and skeleton videos. Finally, a fusion module is used for final classification.

The audio data supplements the appearance and motion information in the visual data. HAR has developed various deep learning-based techniques that combine these two modalities. A temporal binding network that utilizes audio, image, and optical flow for HAR has been shown [18]. A temporal aggregation module is used after a three-stream CNN in the binding network. It fuses the multi-dimensional input with a window. According to their findings, the binding network performed better on the audio-visual HAR test than the temporal segment network.

The audio signals have been used to lessen temporal redundancy in videos [19]. Specifically, for effective HAR, this approach transfers the knowledge from a first network to a second network. The second network is a 2-stream model that uses the video clip's beginning frame and audio signal as input. It then goes through fusion, FC and softmax layers. A hierarchically integrated audiovisual representation architecture with slow and rapid video pathways that are interwoven with a quicker audio pathway at numerous layers has been presented [20].

Two training methodologies, hierarchical audio-visual synchronization and randomly skipping the audio pathway, have been introduced to train audio and video modalities. Alfasly *et al.* [21], have recently used a BERT model [22], to acquire the sentence-based knowledge of all labels in the audio and video datasets. They mapped each video label to*k* audio labels in a semantic audio-video label dictionary. Then, a dropout module has been suggested to choose the most appropriate audio modality embedding for every video. Lastly, the chosen audio and video modalities are combined for classification.

Another model that uses audio data to modify the video information in conjunction with the audio-in-fused recognizer has been designed to keep irrelevant data [23]. Similarly, a Relative Norm Alignment (RNA) loss [24], has been created to align visual and audio modalities for egocentric HAR. Additionally, a Multi-Modal Video Transformer (MMViT)has been created using the attention mechanism [25], across the three dimensions [26], for compressed video action identification.

For HAR, 2D inertial pictures and 3D video frames were fed into a 2D and 3D CNN, respectively, and score fusion outperformed feature fusion [27]. Several fusion approaches have been examined by developing various 2-stream CNNs, where the inertial signal is translated into an image [28–30]. A multi-dimensional transformer for action detection has been recently devised [31], in which transformers are used to describe the correlations between skeletal and acceleration data.

To execute HAR, the Wi-Fi, inertial and skeletal data are converted into a color image and fed into a CNN [32]. In the 3-stream architecture, gyroscopic, RGB, and skeletal data were processed using a 1D, 2D CNN and an RNN [33]. Several fusion strategies have been employed to predict the final class label; however, the best results were obtained by integrating information with canonical correlation analysis. WiVi, a two-stream architecture [34], utilized RGB and Wi-Fi frames for the CNN and C3D streams. A multi-dimensional fusion module has been created to perform HAR.

Adverb pseudo-labels in RGB movies have recently been used [35], for semi-supervised fine-grained HAR. Multi-modal GCNs were developed [36], to examine modality-aware multi-action relationships in text, audio, and RGB data. A video-audio-text transformer (VATT) was created to extract multi-modal representations by linearly projecting text, audio, and video data [37]. VATT is trained with noise contrastive estimation, which uses video-text and video-audio pairs and assesses the granularity of each modality. The study found that the majority of existing multi-modality approaches offer both advantages and disadvantages. Furthermore, it has substantial computational expenses. Thus, an effective multi-modality HAR approach must be developed.

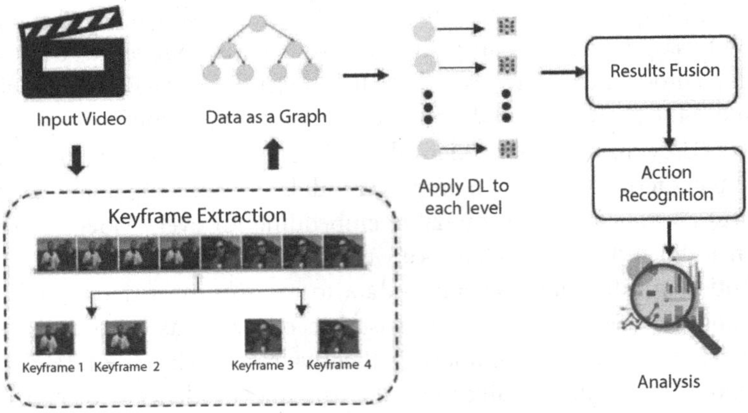

Figure 1.4 Architecture of the proposed action recognition methodology.

1.4 Proposed Methodology Using Composite AI

In this chapter, two major research areas are investigated. Human actions are recognized, and then embedded in content-based video retrieval. The complete architecture of the proposed HAR method is shown in Figure 1.4. The methodology consists of phases such as keyframe extraction, processing, fusion and recognition. All the phases are explained in the subsequent paragraphs.

1.4.1 Keyframe Extraction

There are temporal and spatial elements in every video. Each frame is used to extract spatial properties, while motion data is used to derive temporal features. A small number of keyframes are chosen from the input video rather than extracting spatial features from every frame, utilizing the Group of Pictures (GOP) technique in adaptive mode [38].

Using this strategy, the input video is partitioned into GOPs, rendering to the scene. Initially, the first and last frames are chosen as keyframes from each GOP. The small motion of objects (correlation) between frames is used to identify the scene (or GOP).This work makes use of the Pearson correlation coefficient (PCC), which is given as

$$PCC = \frac{\sum_{i=1}^{M}\sum_{j=1}^{N}(f(i,j)-f^m)(f_p(i,j)-f_p^m)}{\sqrt{\sum_{i=1}^{M}\sum_{j=1}^{N}(f(i,j)-f^m)^2(f_p(i,j)-f_p^m)^2}} \tag{1.1}$$

Where f and f_p are the frames whose correlations have to be calculated. f^m and f_p^m are the mean values of the former and latter frames. A PCC value of 0 indicates no connection, whereas a value of 1 indicates complete correlation. According to the analysis, there is no scene cut if the PCC value is less than 0.8. There is a cut if it is higher than 0.8. A few videos are experimented with to determine this value. The initial frame in all GOP is used as the keyframe following scene cutting.

1.4.2 Feature Extraction

The spatial and temporal information is recovered from keyframes and intermediate frames using two separate CNNs. 3D CNN is used to extract spatial data, while LSTM extracts temporal features. Only the most important proof of the acts under consideration can be found in the retrieved keyframes.

Spatial Feature Extraction:
According to the research from the literature, multi-fiber network (MFNet) achieved high-tech outcomes in the recognition of human actions. Therefore, to extract spatial characteristics, MFNet is used. This study aims to greatly boost 3D CNN efficiency inaction recognition. Hence, the focus is on the massive input tensors rather than breaking down the 3D convolution filters, which are the computational cost of 3D CNNs. In essence, each architectural unit is made up of several fibers and the sparsely coupled MFNet design makes use of lightweight, independent 3D convolutional networks.

Because the entire network is connected and N is the number of fibers used, the computational cost is lowered by around N times.

To improve information flow between fibers, a lightweight multiplexer module is utilized. It reroutes data between parallel fibers and is connected at the starting point of every residual block. Thus increases the total capacity of the model by allowing representations to be shared across multiple strands at minimal computational cost.

The advantages of MFNet can be summarized as:

1. When integrated into popular compact models, a highly effective MFNet architecture (whose efficacy is confirmed by testing it in a 2D CNN for image recognition) can improve performance.
2. MFNet is used to learn robust video representations at a computational cost that is approximately an order of magnitude lower than the high-tech 3D models at the moment.

No additional augmentation is required to use it because the input keyframes' size has already been adjusted to the MFNet input size. The final FC layer of MFNet is used to extract spatial characteristics. Let $f_{spatial}$ represent the MFNet feature set. This feature set has the following dimensions: $t \times C \times H \times W$, where t varies in size based on the number of keyframes, C - number of channels, H and W - feature's height and width respectively.

Table 1.1 shows the 2D MFNet architecture. The spatiotemporal MFNet is designed according to the ResNet-34 paradigm, although it has a different number of channels to use, less GPU RAM when processing movies. More specifically, the succeeding layers have more channels than the initial convolution layer (Conv1). This is because the feature maps in the first few layers have high resolutions and take up much more GPU memory than those that follow (Conv2-5) during training and testing.

Temporal Feature Extraction:
LSTM is used to extract temporal information from the intermediate frames. The backbone network of LSTM is GoogLeNet, which has a 224 × 224 input size.

As a result, this step does not involve data augmentation. An LSTM model is produced by incorporating a bidirectional LSTM layer into GoogLeNet. Low-level features are those that are taken from the final FC layer of the LSTM.

Table 1.1 Architecture of 2D MFNet architecture.

Layer	#Channel	Output size	Stride
Input	3	224 x 224	
Conv1 **Max Pool**	16	112 x 112 56 x 56	(2, 2) (2, 2)
Conv2	96	56 x 56	(1, 1) (1, 1)
Conv3	192	28 x 28	(2, 2) (1, 1)
Conv4	384	14 x 14	(2, 2) (1, 1)
Conv5	768	7 x 7	(2, 2) (1, 1)
AvgPooling		1 x 1	

The Attentive Correlated Temporal Feature (ACTF) [39], is calculated using linear and bilinear temporal features. The bilinear technique is used to identify the correlation between frames within a specified region of subsequent frames. This phase yielded an ACTF of $f_{temporal}$. With n being the number of keyframes, then the feature set's size is $n \times C \times H \times W$. Every video sequence has a temporal feature set that is larger than its spatial feature set.

1.4.3 Implemented Fusion Technique and Classification

There are differences in the magnitude of the temporal and spatial elements. As a result, concatenating the feature sets presents certain difficulties. To match the quantity of spatial characteristics, the temporal features compute the average feature set between two successive keyframes. The temporal and spatial features of a video sequence i can be represented as $f^i_{temporal}$ and $f^i_{spatial}$, where $size\left(f^i_{temporal}\right) > size(f^i_{spatial})$. These two features are united to create a spatiotemporal feature set $f^i_{spatio-temporal}$ and the size of the GoP is represented as $V = [m_1, m_2, \ldots, m_n]$, where n is the count of GoPs (i.e., size of $f^i_{spatial}$).

To construct spatiotemporal features, the number of keyframes is passed to feature fusion. A multi-SVM classifier can be used to classify this feature. The procedures for all these techniques are provided in Algorithm 1.1.

Algorithm 1.1 Proposed Feature Extraction with Fusion and Recognition.

Input: Dataset D
Output: Accuracy
Steps:

1. For every video V in D
   //Calculate Keyframes
   1.1 $K_f = f_1$
   1.2 For each frame f_p and f_{p+1} in V
      1.2.1 Calculate PCC using Eq. (1.1)
      1.2.2 If $PCC > 0.8$
         Add f_{p+1} to K_f
         Add intermediate frames to I_f
      1.2.3 End
   1.3 End
2. End
3. Extract $F_{Spatial}$ using MFNet in K_f
4. Convert I_f to feature vectors

5. Add LSTM layers to GoogLeNet
6. Extract low-level features from the fully connected layer of LSTM
7. Calculate $F_{Temporal}$ by extracting ACTF
8. j=1
9. For every feature f in $f^i_{spatial}$
   9.1 Obtain $V[j]$ from $f^i_{temporal}$
   9.2 Calculate mean of $V[j]$ to get $\sigma_{temporal}$.

$$f_{spatio-temporal} = [f\sigma_{temporal}]$$

   9.3 Obtain $f^i_{spatio-temporal}$ by concatenating $f_{spatio-temporal}$ row-wise.
10. End

//Classification

11. Classify using multiSVM Classifier

1.4.4 Proposed CBVR System

The classic CBVR method comprises two stages: training and testing. During training, the videos are divided into individual shots, whose features are retrieved and stored in a database. During testing, features from the query video are extracted. Each feature in the features database corresponds to these features. The output includes all of the corresponding video clips.

The HAR mentioned in the subsection is combined into the proposed retrieval system. Initially, the videos are separated into a set of scenes using the keyframe extraction technique. The spatial (f_s) and temporal (f_t) properties are obtained from keyframes and intermediate frames, respectively. The proposed HAR system generates both spatial ($SC_{spatial}$) and temporal ($SC_{temporal}$) scores. These ratings are combined to get a class score for each video. In a CBVR system, the fused scores are saved in the features dataset D_f. The spatial and temporal features of a particular query scene are fused and matched with all of the features in D_f using Euclidean Distance (ED) measurements, which is given as

$$ED = \sum_{i=1}^{n} \sqrt{\sum_{i-1}^{n} \left((f_s, f_t)_{pi} - (f_s, f_t)_{qi} \right)^2} \tag{1.2}$$

Where $(f_s, f_t)_{pi}$ is the spatio-temporal features obtained from D_f and $(f_s, f_t)_{qi}$ is the spatio-temporal features obtained from the query scene. All the matching videos are recovered from the dataset. Algorithm 1.2 shows the proposed HAR-CBVR method.

Algorithm 1.2 Proposed HAR-CBVR Method.

Input: Video Dataset D, Query video frames Q
Output: Retrieved video frames R_f, Score
Steps:
//HAR

1. For each video in D
   1.1 Identify Keyframes K_f and intermediate frames I_f using Step 1 in Algorithm 1.1.
2. End
3. Extract (f_s, f_t) are from K_f and I_f using MFNet and LSTM respectively.
4. The above step produces the scores $(SC_{spatial}, SC_{temporal})$.
5. Score = mean $(SC_{spatial}, SC_{temporal})$

//CBVR

6. Store (f_s, f_t) obtained in Step 3 in a dataset D_f.
7. For a given query scene Q, Obtain (f_s, f_t) using Steps 1 to 3.
8. Match the query features with all the features in D_f using ED of Eq. (1.2)
9. The frames whose features are matched are obtained as R_f.

Figure 1.5 shows the HAR-CBVR system that is being suggested. Each action's score in the HAR system is determined by its features. The features are combined and saved in a dataset in the CBVR system. Spatio-temporal features retrieved from the query scene are compared with the feature dataset using Euclidean distance.

1.5 Experimental Results

Both methods are tested onHMB51 [40], KTH [41], and the UCF Sports Action [42], dataset (see Table 1.2). The HMDB51 has multifaceted actions

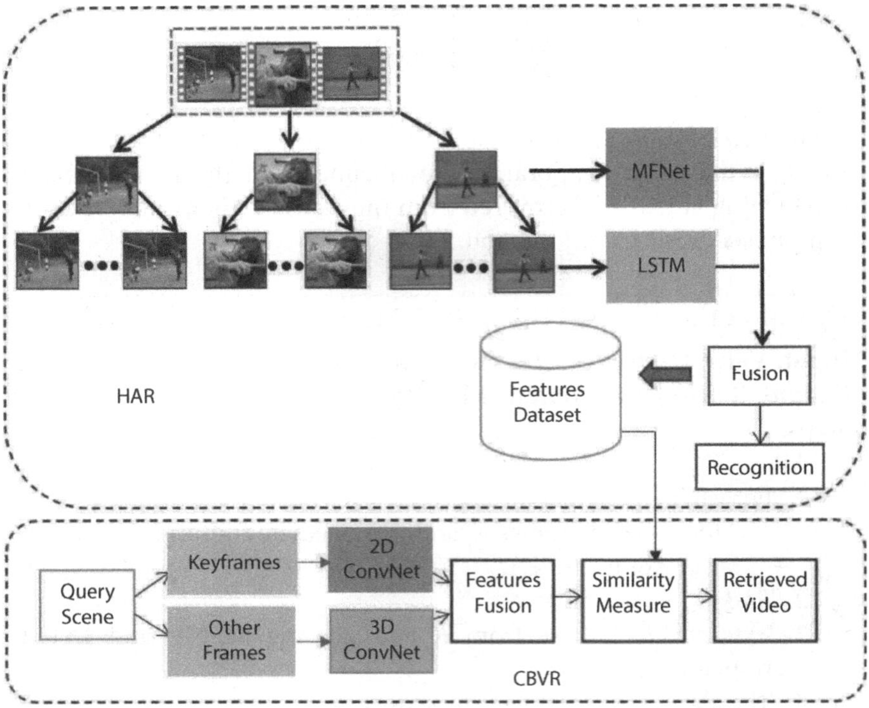

Figure 1.5 Proposed HAR-CBVR network.

Table 1.2 Details of experimented datasets

Property	HMDB51	KTH	UCF sports
# Action Classes	51	6	10
# Video Clips	6766	600	150
Resolution	320 x 240	160 x 120	720 x 480
Frame Rate	30 fps	25 fps	-

of 6766 videos, while the KTH and UCF Sports datasets consist of only 6 and 10 actions, respectively. The datasets are partitioned into 80-20 ratio for training and testing.

1.5.1 Implementation Details and Performance Measures

Table 1.3 shows the hyperparameters for both networks. The performances of both methods are evaluated separately. The HAR system is measured

Table 1.3 Hyper-parameters of MFNet and LSTM.

Model	MFNet	LSTM
Mini Batch Size	16	16
Dropout	0.8	0.5
Learning Rate	0.001	0.0001
GradientThreshold	-	2

Table 1.4 Performance metrics used in HAR and CBVR systems.

Metrics	Formula
Precision	$Precision = \frac{TP}{TP + FP}$
Recall	$Recall = \frac{TP}{TP + FN}$
F-Score	$F_m = 2\frac{Precision * Recall}{(Precision + Recall)}$
Sensitivity	$\text{Specificity} = \frac{\text{TN}}{(\text{FP} + \text{TN})}$
Accuracy	$Acc = \frac{TP + TN}{TP + TN + FP + FN} \times 100$

*True Positive (TP), True Negative (TN), False Positive (FP), and False Negative (FN)

using accuracy and the CBVR system is measured using precision, recall, F-score, and sensitivity values. The formula for each metric is shown in Table 1.4. Table 1.5 displays the visual findings produced by the proposed HAR-CBVR system. The table displays only a few frames from the retrieved findings, although all of them relate to the HMDB51 dataset.

The retrieved results are almost identical to the query frame, as Table 1.6 demonstrates. The output from the suggested HAR system is represented by the classes in Table 1.5. As a result, for a given query scene, the

Table 1.5 Results obtained by the proposed HAR-CBVR system.

Keyframe in query video	Class	Retrieved results (shown only a few frames)
	Chew	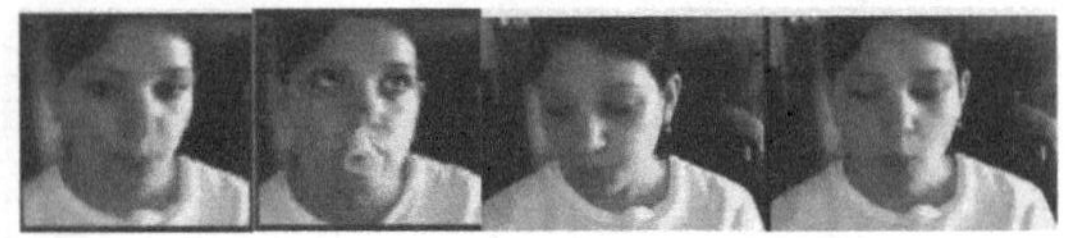
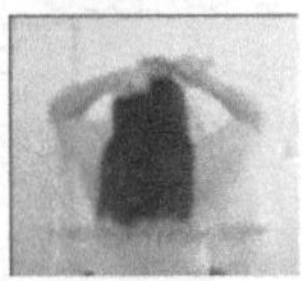	Brush hair	
	Cartwheel	
	Catch	

Table 1.6 Accuracy obtained by the proposed HAR system.

Method	Measure	HMDB51	KTH	UCF sports
Proposed HAR	Accuracy (%)	97.2	98.9	99.5
Proposed HAR-CBVR	Precision (%)	73.2	74.6	75.2
	Recall (%)	73.8	74.8	74.9
	F-Score (%)	73.2	73.6	75.4
	Sensitivity (%)	71.7	74.8	75.48
	Accuracy (%)	73.6	75.79	75.9

suggested HAR-CBVR system can determine the class and retrieve related movies from the dataset. Table 1.6 indicates that the suggested HAR system achieved outcomes of more than 90% across all datasets. All planned HAR-CBVR system measures are between 71% and 75%. It is also noted that the accuracy of the CBVR is significantly lower than that HAR.

1.5.2 Comparison of Both Fusion Methods

Table 1.7 Comparison of proposed HAR method on the HMDB51 dataset.

Author, year	Method	Accuracy (%)
Khan *et al.* 2021 [43]	26L-DCNN	81.4
Patrick *et al.* 2021 [44]	GDT	72.8
Huang *et al.* 2022 [45]	Three Stream Network	96.88
Zhang *et al.* 2021 [46]	VidTr-L	74.4
Koniusz *et al.* 2022 [47]	SCK(I3D)	86.11
Wang and Koniusz, 2021 [48]	DEEP-HAL with ODF+SDF (I3D)	87.56
Mazari and Sahbi, 2024 [49]	3D CNN-M + TP	80.54
Li *et al.* 2021 [50]	NST	76.1
Perrett *et al.* 2021 [51]	TRX	75.60

(Continued)

Table 1.7 Comparison of proposed HAR method on the HMDB51 dataset. (*Continued*)

Author, year	Method	Accuracy (%)
Omi *et al.* 2022 [52]	Multi-Domain	75.62
Chen *et al.* 2023 [53]	2L-Attention-s3DResNet	72.6
Paramasivam *et al.* 2023 [54]	HARNet + KNN	91.58
Sowmyayani *et al.* 2024 [3]	STHARNet	89.9
Proposed Method	MFNet + LSTM	97.2

Table 1.8 Comparison of proposed HAR method on the KTH dataset.

Author, year	Method	Accuracy (%)
Khan *et al.* 2021 [43]	26L-DCNN	98.3
Abdelbaky and Aly, 2021 [55]	ST-VLAD-PCANet	93.33
Paramasivam *et al.* 2023 [54]	HARNet + KNN	97.58
Mishra *et al.* 2022 [56]	FEA + RBF-SVM	96.2
Rahnama and Mansouri, 2024 [57]	Kseq + GRU	95.38
Chakraborty and Mukhopadhyay, 2023 [58]	Spatiotemporal HRSNN	94.32
Guo and Wang, 2021 [59]	Spatiotemporal features DBN	90
Liu *et al.*, 2022 [60]	LSM	86.3
Alhakbani *et al.* 2023 [61]	VGG-16	98
Chen *et al.* 2023 [62]	OFPI	98.3
Sowmyayani *et al.* 2024 [3]	STHARNet	98.7
Proposed Method	MFNet + LSTM	98.9

The above HAR and HAR-CBVR systems are individually compared with a few recent methods. Table 1.7 compares the proposed HAR method with a few recent methods on the HMDB51 dataset. It is observed that Huang *et al.*'s method (2022), achieved 96.88% accuracy, which could not be overcome by other recent methods (2023 and 2024). However, the proposed method overcomes that method by a 0.4% increase in accuracy. Table 1.8 compares the proposed HAR method with a few recent methods on the KTH dataset.

It is studied that all the methods obtain above 90% accuracy, except Liu *et al.*'s method. It shows the simplicity of the KTH dataset. In the HMDB51 dataset, most of the values are below 80%. Due to the simplicity of the dataset, the proposed HAR method achieved an appreciable accuracy of 98.9%. Table 1.9 compares the proposed HAR method with recent methods on the UCF Sports dataset.

Table 1.9 Comparison of proposed HAR method on the UCF sports dataset.

Dataset/method	Method	Accuracy (%)
Khan *et al.* 2021 [43]	26L-DCNN	99.2
Abdelbaky and Aly, 2021 [55]	ST-VLAD-PCANet	90
Patrick *et al.* 2021[44]	GDT	95.2
Xiao *et al.* 2023 [63]	AMF	97.84
Zhou *et al.* 2023 [64]	CG-BiLSTM	98.75
Afza *et al.* 2021 [65]	Feature Fusion	99.3
Muhammad *et al.* 2021 [66]	Attention-based LSTM	96.76
Sowmyayani *et al.* 2024 [3]	STHARNet	99
Proposed Method	MFNet+LSTM	99.5

Table 1.10 Comparison of proposed HAR-CBVR method with other methods.

Method	HMDB51	KTH
Saoudi *et al.* 2021 [67]	72.37	-
Savran *et al.* 2021 [68]	-	71.3
Yoon *et al.* 2022 [69]	65.7	-
Sowmyayani *et al.* 2024 [3]	73.25	74.6
Proposed Method	73.6	75.79

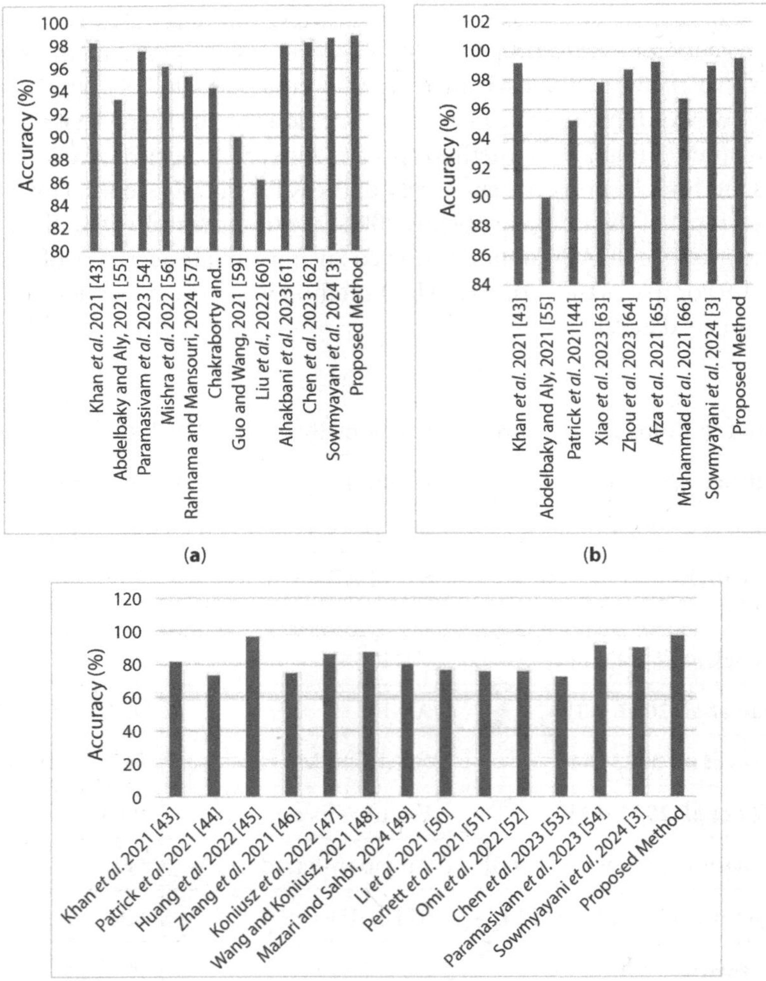

Figure 1.6 Graphs representing accuracy comparison of proposed method with recent methods (a) KTH dataset (b) UCF sports dataset (c) HMDB51 dataset.

Table 1.9 shows that all the methods achieve above 95% accuracy. The proposed method achieves only 0.5% less than 100%. Table 1.10 compares the proposed HAR-CBVR method with a few recent methods on the HMDB51 and KTH datasets. As the experimental datasets are widely used for action recognition, there is no proper method to compare the CBVR method on these datasets. Table 1.10 infers that our method achieves appreciable accuracies than other methods on HMDB51 and KTH datasets. Figure 1.6 compares the proposed method with recent methods.

1.5.3 Analyses of All the Proposed Methods

The proposed strategy is evaluated by examining the significance of spatial and temporal variables independently using varying network models. Tables 1.11 and 1.12 demonstrate the analyses used to assess the suggested approaches' correctness.

According to Table 1.11, the two-stream network outperforms individual streams in terms of accuracy across all datasets. When only spatial ConvNets are utilized, the accuracy is significantly worse. For spatial

Table 1.11 Accuracy of the proposed HAR-CBVR systems for various network models.

Dataset/ network	Spatial ConvNets	Temporal ConvNets	Two stream	Proposed method
HMDB51	72.10	73.5	74.96	97.2
KTH	72.6	73.5	75.4	98.9
UCF Sports	74.9	75.3	76.9	99.5

Table 1.12 Average accuracy study of various pre-trained networks.

Dataset/network	HMDB51	KTH	UCF sports
GoogleNet	73.6	73.3	75.95
VGG16	74.5	74.3	75.4
BN-Inception	74.69	75.78	76.8
Proposed Method	97.2	98.9	99.5

Table 1.13 Comparison of fusion techniques.

	Accuracy (%)		
Pooling	**HMDB51**	**KTH**	**UCF sports**
Mean Pool	97.2	98.9	99.5
Min Pool	95.6	97.5	98.3
Max Pool	96.4	98.1	99

and temporal ConvNets, the most widely used GoogLeNet and VGG16 are employed; Table 1.12 displays the average outcomes.In Table 1.12, the BN-Inception network model outperforms GoogLeNet and VGG16 in terms of accuracy. The following part emphasizes the integration of temporal and spatial data. Mean, minimum, and maximum pooling are used. The results of these three fusions are presented in Table 1.13.

It shows that the mean pool approach obtains higher accuracy on all the datasets than the max and min pools. As a result, the suggested method's architecture incorporates a mean pool for feature fusion, MFNet for spatial feature extraction, and LSTM+ACTF for temporal feature extraction.

1.6 Conclusion

In this chapter, two major applications, namely HAR and CBVR, are integrated using composite AI. The results of two network models are fused to obtain the classification score. There are challenges like incompatible size, datatype, etc., when combining data features. Overcoming those challenges and the results are combined in the HAR method. The obtained fused feature score retrieves related videos for the given query video. Three standard datasets are experimented with different hyperparameters. The efficacy of the suggested method is demonstrated by comparing it to recent methods. The HAR approach improves accuracy slightly on three datasets. The analysis is carried out on data feature fusion and several pre-trained network models. It is proven that the proposed network model works better than other compared models.

AI disclosure statement: The author acknowledges the use of AI-based tools for minor language editing or grammatical correction. However, all intellectual contributions, analyses, and conclusions presented in this chapter are entirely the author's own.

References

1. Dasarathy, B.V., Sensor fusion potential exploitation-innovative architectures and illustrative applications. *Proc. IEEE*, 85, 1, 24–38, 1997.
2. Sowmyayani, S., Vivek, V., Arulpandy, P., Tamilselvi, S., Frame Differencing Based Temporal Feature Extraction in Human Action Recognition. *J. Comput. Anal. Appl. (JoCAAA)*, *33*, 05, 549–557, 2024.
3. Xu, X., Zhou, S., Xu, H., Wu, Z., Advancing urban hub planning: A bibliometric analysis of concepts, effects evaluation, and spatial design. *Land Use Policy*, 152, 107507, 2025.

4. Wang, H., Song, Z., Li, W., Wang, P., A hybrid network for large-scale action recognition from rgb and depth modalities. *Sensors*, 20, 11, 2020.
5. Wang, L., Ding, Z., Tao, Z., Liu, Y., Fu, Y., Generative multi-view human action recognition, in: *ICCV*, 2019.
6. Dhiman, C. and Vishwakarma, D.K., View-invariant deep architecture for human action recognition using two-stream motion and shape temporal dynamics. *TIP*, 29, 2020.
7. Zhou, B., Wang, P., Wan, J., Liang, Y., Wang, F., Zhang, D., Lei, Z., Li, H., Jin, R., Decoupling and recoupling spatiotemporal representation for rgb-dbased motion recognition, in: *CVPR*, 2022.
8. Li, X., Hou, Y., Wang, P., Gao, Z., Xu, M., Li, W., Trear: Transformer-based rgb-d egocentric action recognition, in: *TCDS*, 2021.
9. Das, S., Dai, R., Koperski, M., Minciullo, L., Garattoni, L., Bremond, F., Francesca, G., Toyota smarthome: Real-world activities of daily living, in: *ICCV*, 2019.
10. Kumar, K.S., Abirami, K., Helen Sulochana, C., Ananth Kumar, T., Sunday, A.A., Morris, C., Multimodal Spatial-Temporal Prediction and Classification Using Deep Learning, in: *Spatiotemporal Data Analytics and Modeling: Techniques and Applications*, pp. 89–114, Springer Nature Singapore, Singapore, 2024.
11. Li, J., Xie, X., Pan, Q., Cao, Y., Zhao, Z., Shi, G., Sgm-net: Skeleton-guided multimodal network for action recognition. *Pattern Recognit.*, 104, 2020.
12. Cai, J., Jiang, N., Han, X., Jia, K., Lu, J., Jolo-gcn: mining joint-centered light-weight information for skeleton-based action recognition, in: *WACV*, 2021.
13. Duan, H., Zhao, Y., Chen, K., Lin, D., Dai, B., Revisiting skeleton-based action recognition, in: *CVPR*, 2022.
14. Jing, Y. and Wang, F., Tp-vit: A two-pathway vision transformer for video action recognition, in: *ICASSP*.
15. Liu, J., Shahroudy, A., Wang, G., Duan, L.-Y., Kot, A.C., Skeleton-based online action prediction using scale selection network. *TPAMI*, 42, 6, 2019.
16. Zhao, C., Chen, M., Zhao, J., Wang, Q., Shen, Y., 3d behavior recognition based on multi-modal deep space-time learning. *Appl. Sci.*, 9, 4, 2019.
17. Rani, S.S., Naidu, G.A., Shree, V.U., Kinematic joint descriptor and depth motion descriptor with convolutional neural networks for human action recognition, in: *MATPR*, 2021.
18. Kazakos, E., Nagrani, A., Zisserman, A., Damen, D., Epic-fusion: Audiovisual temporal binding for egocentric action recognition, in: *ICCV*, 2019.
19. Gao, R., Oh, T.-H., Grauman, K., Torresani, L., Listen to look: Action recognition by previewing audio, in: *CVPR*, 2020.
20. Xiao, F., Lee, Y.J., Grauman, K., Malik, J., Feichtenhofer, C., Audiovisual slowfat networks for video recognition, *arXiv preprint arXiv:2001.08740*, 2020.
21. Alfasly, S., Lu, J., Xu, C., Zou, Y., Learnable irrelevant modality dropout for multimodal action recognition on modality-specific annotated videos, in: *CVPR*, 2022.

22. Devlin, J., Chang, M.-W., Lee, K., Toutanova, K., Bert: Pre-training of deep bidirectional transformers for language understanding, arXiv preprint arXiv:1810.04805, 2018.
23. Zhang, Y., Doughty, H., Shao, L., Snoek, C.G., Audio-adaptive activity recognition across video domains, in: *CVPR*, 2022.
24. Planamente, M., Plizzari, C., Alberti, E., Caputo, B., Cross-domain first person audio-visual action recognition through relative norm alignment, *arXiv preprint arXiv:2106.01689*, 2021.
25. Dosovitskiy, A., Beyer, L., Kolesnikov, A., Weissenborn, D., Zhai, X., Unterthiner, T., Dehghani, M., Minderer, M., Heigold, G., Gelly, S., An image is worth 16x16 words: Transformers for image recognition at scale, in: *ICLR*, 2021.
26. Chen, J. and Ho, C.M., Mm-vit: Multi-modal video transformer for compressed video action recognition, in: *WACV*, 2022.
27. Wei, H., Jafari, R., Kehtarnavaz, N., Fusion of video and inertial sensing for deep learning–based human action recognition. *Sensors*, 19, 17, 2019.
28. Ahmad, Z. and Khan, N., Human action recognition using deep multilevel multimodal (M2) fusion of depth and inertial sensors. *IEEE Sens. J.*, 20, 3, 2019.
29. Ahmad, Z. and Khan, N., Cnn based multistage gated average fusion (mgaf) for human action recognition using depth and inertial sensors. *IEEE Sens. J.*, 2020.
30. Pham, C., Nguyen, L., Nguyen, A., Nguyen, N., Nguyen, V.-T., Combining skeleton and accelerometer data for human fine-grained activity recognition and abnormal behaviour detection with deep temporal convolutional networks. *Multimed. Tools Appl.*, 2021.
31. Ijaz, M., Diaz, R., Chen, C., Multimodal transformer for nursing activity recognition, in: *CVPR Workshop*, 2022.
32. Memmesheimer, R., Theisen, N., Paulus, D., Gimme signals: Discriminative signal encoding for multimodal activity recognition, *arXiv preprint arXiv:2003.06156*, 2020.
33. Imran, J. and Raman, B., Evaluating fusion of rgb-d and inertial sensors for multimodal human action recognition. *JAIHC*, 11, 1, 2020.
34. Zou, H., Yang, J., Prasanna Das, H., Liu, H., Zhou, Y., Spanos, C.J., Wifi and vision multimodal learning for accurate and robust device-free human activity recognition, in: *CVPRW*, 2019.
35. Shi, Z., Liang, J., Li, Q., Zheng, H., Gu, Z., Dong, J., Zheng, B., Multi-modal multi-action video recognition, in: *ICCV*, 2021.
36. Akbari, H., Yuan, L., Qian, R., Chuang, W.-H., Chang, S.-F., Cui, Y., Gong, B., Vatt: Transformers for multimodal self-supervised learning from raw video, audio and text. *NeurIPS*, 2021.
37. Doughty, H. and Snoek, C.G., How do you do it? fine-grained action understanding with pseudo-adverbs, in: *CVPR*, 2022.
38. Sowmyayani, S., Rani, J., Arockia, P., Adaptive GOP structure to H. 264/AVC based on Scene change. *ICTACT J. Image Video Process.*, 5, 1, 2014.

39. Xu, Y., Yang, J., Mao, K., Yin, J., See, S., Exploiting Inter-Frame Regional Correlation for Efficient Action Recognition. *arXiv preprint arXiv:2005.02591*, 2020.
40. Kuehne, H., Jhuang, H., Garrote, E., Poggio, T., Serre, T., Hmdb: a large video database for human motion recognition, in: *2011 International Conference on Computer Vision*, IEEE, pp. 2556–2563, 2011.
41. Schuldt, C., Laptev, I., Caputo, B., Recognizing human actions: a local svm approach, in: *Proceedings of the 17th International Conference on Pattern Recognition, 2004. ICPR 2004*, vol. 3, IEEE, pp. 32–36, 2004.
42. UCF Sports Website, http://crcv.ucf.edu/data/UCF Sports Action.php.
43. Khan, M.A., Zhang, Y.D., Khan, S.A., Attique, M., Rehman, A., Seo, S., A resource conscious human action recognition framework using 26-layered deep convolutional neural network. *Multimedia Tools Appl.*, 80, 28, 35827–35849, 2021.
44. Patrick, M., Asano, Y.M., Kuznetsova, P., Fong, R., Henriques, J.F., Zweig, G., Vedaldi, A., On compositions of transformations in contrastive self-supervised learning, in: *Proceedings of the IEEE/CVF International Conference on Computer Vision*, pp. 9577–9587, 2021.
45. Huang, R., Chen, C., Cheng, R., Zhang, Y., Zhu, J., Human action recognition based on three-stream network with frame sequence features, in: *2022 7th International Conference on Image, Vision and Computing (ICIVC)*, 2022, July, IEEE, pp. 37–44.
46. Zhang, Y., Li, X., Liu, C., Shuai, B., Zhu, Y., Brattoli, B., Chen, H., Marsic, I., Tighe, J., Vidtr: Video transformer without convolutions, arXiv [cs.CV], 2021.
47. Koniusz, P., Wang, L., Cherian, A., Tensor representations for action recognition. *IEEE Trans. Pattern Anal. Mach. Intell.*, 44, 2, 648–665, 2022.
48. Wang, L. and Koniusz, P., *Self-supervising Action Recognition by Statistical Moment and Subspace Descriptors*, Association for Computing Machinery, pp. 4324–4333, 2021.
49. Mazari, A. and Sahbi, H., Deep multiple aggregation networks for action recognition. *Int. J. Multimed. Inf. Retr.*, *13*, 1, 9, 2024.
50. Li, J., Wei, P., Zheng, N., Nesting spatiotemporal attention networks for action recognition. *Neurocomputing*, 459, 338–348, 2021.
51. Perrett, T., Masullo, A., Burghardt, T., Mirmehdi, M., Damen, D., Temporal-relational crosstransformers for few-shot action recognition, in: *Proceedings of the IEEE/CVF Conference on Computer Vision and Pattern Recognition, Virtual*, 19–25 June 2021, pp. 475–484.
52. Omi, K., Kimata, J., Tamaki, T., Model-Agnostic Multi-Domain Learning with Domain-Specific Adapters for Action Recognition. *IEICE Trans. Inf. Syst.*, 105, 2119–2126, 2022.
53. Chen, B., Meng, F., Tang, H., Tong, G., Two-Level Attention Module Based on Spurious-3D Residual Networks for Human Action Recognition. *Sensors*, 23, 1707, 2023.

54. Paramasivam, K., Sindha, M.M.R., Balakrishnan, S.B., KNN-based machine learning classifier used on deep learned spatial motion features for human action recognition. *Entropy*, *25*, 6, 844, 2023.
55. Abdelbaky, A. and Aly, S., Two-stream spatiotemporal feature fusion for human action recognition. *Vis. Comput.*, *37*, 7, 1821–1835, 2021.
56. Mishra, O., Kavimandan, P.S., Kapoor, R., Modal Frequencies Based Human Action Recognition Using Silhouettes and Simplicial Elements. *IJE Trans. A Basics*, 35, 45–52, 2022.
57. Rahnama, A. and Mansouri, A., Temporal Relations of Informative Frames in Action Recognition, in: *2024 13th Iranian/3rd International Machine Vision and Image Processing Conference (MVIP)*, 2024, March, IEEE, pp. 1–5.
58. Chakraborty, B. and Mukhopadhyay, S., Heterogeneous Recurrent Spiking Neural Network for Spatio-Temporal Classification. *Front. Neurosci.*, 17, 994517, 2023. [CrossRef].
59. Guo, Y. and Wang, X., Applying TS-DBN Model into Sports Behavior Recognition with Deep Learning Approach. *J. Supercomput.*, 77, 12192–12208, 2021. [CrossRef].
60. Liu, C., Wang, H., Liu, N., Yuan, Z., Optimizing the Neural Structure and Hyperparameters of Liquid State Machines Based on Evolutionary Membrane Algorithm. *Mathematics*, 10, 1844, 2022. [CrossRef].
61. Alhakbani, N., Alghamdi, M., Al-Nafjan, A., Design and Development of an Imitation Detection System for Human Action Recognition Using Deep Learning. *Sensors*, *23*, 24, 9889, 2023.
62. Chen, D., Zhang, T., Zhou, P., Yan, C., Li, C., OFPI: Optical Flow Pose Image for Action Recognition. *Mathematics*, *11*, 6, 1451, 2023.
63. Xiao, L., Cao, Y., Gai, Y., Khezri, E., Liu, J., Yang, M., Recognizing sports activities from video frames using deformable convolution and adaptive multiscale features. *J. Cloud Comput.*, *12*, 1, 167, 2023.
64. Zhou, T., Tao, A., Sun, L., Qu, B., Wang, Y., Huang, H., Behavior recognition based on the improved density clustering and context-guided Bi-LSTM model. *Multimed. Tools Appl.*, 1–8, 2023, https://doi.org/10.1007/s11042-023-15501-y.
65. Afza, F., Khan, M.A., Sharif, M., Kadry, S., Manogaran, G., Saba, T., Ashraf, I., Damaševičius, R., A framework of human action recognition using length control features fusion and weighted entropy-variances based feature selection. *Image Vision Comput.*, 106, 104090, 2021, https://doi.org/10. 1016/j.imavis.2020.104090.
66. Muhammad, K., Ullah, A., Imran, A.S., Sajjad, M., Kiran, M.S., Sannino, G., de Albuquerque, V.H.C., *et al.*, Human action recognition using attention-based LSTM network with dilated CNN features. *Future Gener. Comput. Syst.*, 454 125, 820–830, 2021b.
67. Saoudi, E.M. and Jai-Andaloussi, S., A distributed content-based video retrieval system for large datasets. *J. Big Data*, 8, 1, 1–26, 2021.

68. Savran Kızıltepe, R., Gan, J.Q., Escobar, J.J., A novel keyframe extraction method for video classification using deep neural networks. *Neural Comput. Appl.*, 1–12, 2021.
69. Yoon, H. and Han, J.H., Content-based video retrieval with prototypes of deep features. *IEEE Access*, *10*, 30730–30742, 2022.

2

Composite AI in Natural Language Processing: A Paradigm Shift in Understanding and Generating Human Language

Narendran M.[1*], M. Beema Meharaj[2], D. Diana Julie[3], Sowmya Banala[4], G. Umadevi[5] and A. Devi[6]

[1]*Department of Computer Science and Engineering, Sona College of Technology, Salem, Tamil Nadu, India*
[2]*Department of Information and Technology, KCG College of Technology, Chennai, Tamilnadu, India*
[3]*Department of Artificial Intelligence and Data Science, KIT-Kalaignarkarunanidhi Institute of Technology, Coimbatore, Tamilnadu, India*
[4]*Cybersecurity Engineer, BMW, Charlotte, NC, USA*
[5]*Department of Computer Science and Engineering, AGNI College of Technology (Autonomous), Chennai, Tamilnadu, India*
[6]*Department of ECE, IFET College of Engineering, Villupuram, Tamilnadu, India*

Abstract

Natural language processing (NLP) has improved a great deal, but there exist roadblocks such as understanding contexts, processing in different languages, and reasoning on complex data. Composite AI, which combines a variety of AI paradigms such as machine learning, deep learning, symbolic AI, and hybrid systems, provides a solution for these challenges. Composite AI boosts NLP solutions such as sentiment analysis, document comprehension, summarization, chatbots, and machine translation using the power of various paradigms.

This chapter delves into the role of composite AI in NLP and its underlying facets, such as using deep learning for representation learning, symbolic AI for logical reasoning, and statistical and combined knowledge-based models. Apart from this, case studies provide evidence of its applicability in industries such as

**Corresponding author*: naren0812@gmail.com

T. S. Arun Samuel, L. Jerart Julus, P. Kanimozhi, T. Ananth Kumar and S. Balamurugan (eds.) Composite Artificial Intelligence: Fundamentals, Challenges, and Applications, (33–64) © 2026 Scrivener Publishing LLC

legal document processing, medical bots, and content moderation. Although new opportunities come along, there exist barriers to data integration, computation efficiency, and ethics, such as explainability and bias. Future directions, such as quantum computer integration and multi-language NLP, signal a favorable trend.

The chapter focuses on highlighting the position of composite AI as a cutting-edge NLP approach, being a guide for practitioners and experts alike on leveraging its capability in solving complex language-related issues and making human-computer communication more effective.

***Keywords*:** Composite AI, natural language processing, deep learning, symbolic AI, hybrid models, machine translation, sentiment analysis, multilingual NLP

2.1 Introduction to Composite Artificial Intelligence (AI)

Artificial Intelligence (AI) is today not a tool humans use in film, it is a premise for critical decision-making in medicine, industry, and daily living. Beyond current AI, though, what is there? The interesting key is composite AI. Composite AI is here to solve the matter of traditional AI models, which businesses and innovators continuously face despite its widespread usage and speeding growth of AI technology. Composite AI is not just an advancement, it is a revolution in technology, combining different AI strategies in delivering end-to-end intelligence solutions [1]. By 2025, composite AI shall have revolutionized our data-to-technology relationship as a whole [2]. In building smarter and adaptive systems, this new process interweaves a variety of AI strategies, such as knowledge graphs, Natural Language Processing (NLP), and Machine Learning (ML).

2.1.1 What is Composite AI?

Composite AI is a new revolution in relation to other traditional forms of AI. The solutions using AI for a specific issue in the past made utilization of a solitary AI model. This solution is fine for simple issues, but it won't be fine for solving complicated issues. Composite AI, as presented by Dynatrace [3], is a divergence of this narrow solution by merging various forms of causal, predictive, and generative forms of artificial intelligence. Through this merger, a solution based on intelligence, which is more detailed and holistic, can be achieved. This solution provides solutions for various aspects of a job or a problem in a multi-aspect, all-round solution. Composite AI tries to solve a variety of different problems by merging a variety of different forms of analytical methods, such as

- Natural language processing (NLP)
- Machine learning/Deep learning
- Computer vision (CV)
- Descriptive statistics
- Multiple knowledge

Composite AI is capable of attaining holistic intelligence solutions by taking advantage of each of its respective AI models' strengths. Through this, it is achievable for it to overcome individual AI models' intrinsic drawbacks and provide a better and combined solution.

2.1.2 Why Composite AI is Important?

There are several fundamental aspects contributing to the growing significance of composite AI. Figure 2.1 illustrates the several fundamental aspects contributing to the growing significance of composite AI.

- The traditional AI is focused on a given set of tasks, but composite AI is a blend of various AI technologies such as ML, DL, and NLP.
- The combined AI can be enhanced in its reliability and precision by leveraging different AI methods as it is a combination of different AI methods.

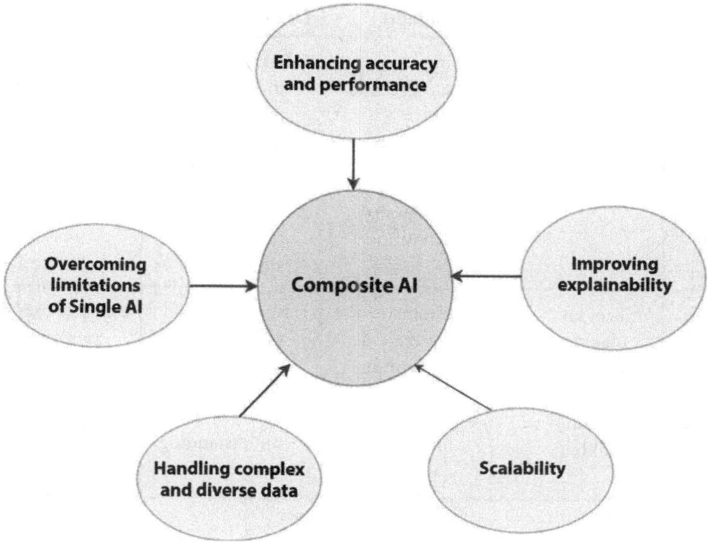

Figure 2.1 Significance of composite AI.

- The capability of combined AI in aggregating data from different AI practices results in improved comprehension and interpretation of complicated scenarios, which is highly valuable in a variety of industries, such as medicine, finance, and customer support.
- The flexibility and adaptability of composite AI are improved by dynamically reconfiguring its constituent parts in relation to a given set of a problem's requirements, which makes it more flexible than traditional AI systems.
- Retail, finance, and manufacturing companies, among others, who have composite AI, can provide suggestions and come up with a cutting-edge, creative solution that provides an edge in the market.

Some of these are among the major capabilities or properties of composite AI for addressing complex problems.

Comparison of Composite AI with other AI Approaches

The comparison between composite AI with other AI approaches are summarized in Table 2.1.

Table 2.1 Comparison of composite AI with other AI.

Approach	Definition	Advantages	Drawbacks	Composite AI advantage
Traditional AI	Rules set by a domain expert	1. Simple to comprehend and troubleshoot.	1. Difficult to handle dynamic unstructured or data.	Flexibility and adaptability ensue when data-driven reasoning is coupled with rule-based reasoning.
		2. Best for non-determine	2. Not adaptable to new situations.	
ML	Utilizes an algorithm for pattern analysis and decision-making.	1. Automatic pattern recognition	1. Necessitates extensive datasets.	Enhance explainability by using a variety of different methods that provide various levels of exposure.
		2. Appropriate for organized datasets.	2. Difficulty in understanding.	

(*Continued*)

Table 2.1 Comparison of composite AI with other AI. (*Continued*)

Approach	Definition	Advantages	Drawbacks	Composite AI advantage
DL	It uses deep networks to describe complex patterns and attributes of data.	1. It allows for large dimensional data processing, like images and audio.	1. Requires high computational cost	It works best when it is coupled with another AI solution for solving complex problems.
		2. Best feature extraction	2. Need large volume of data.	
RL	Learning by navigating an environment in a quest for maximum reward.	Suitable for sequential decision-making	1. Prolonged training time.	It can be combined with optimization or supervised learning strategies for enhanced learning efficiency and stability.
			2. Difficulties in sparse reward contexts.	
			3. Instability	

The primary goals of this chapter are:

1. Presenting an in-depth summary of composite AI and its applicability in NLP.
2. Demonstrating how a combination of AI techniques can perform better than individual techniques.
3. Presenting case studies and actual implementations
4. Outline challenges and avenues for future research in this interdisciplinary field.

2.2 Role of Composite AI in NLP

While we continue in the year 2030, composite AI is being made increasingly visible, particularly in business and industries [4]. The widespread applicability of AI technology in industries is making it obvious that there is a limit to standalone AI systems in solving complex situations. With a number of different artificial intelligence technologies being combined in a platform, composite AI is a great solution for the given issue. NLP systems can improve contextual understanding, adaptability, and accuracy using composite AI. In this section, we will discuss the advantage of using Composite AI along with its concerns.

2.2.1 Challenges in NLP that Composite AI Addresses

NLP faces various challenges due to the complexity and diversity of human language. Some of the important challenges are given below.

2.2.1.1 Word Sense Disambiguation

Human language is rich and complex, and there are a variety of human languages. Human language is in abundance in thousands of human languages on this earth, each of which includes its own vocabulary, grammar, and culture nuances. Human language is very ambiguous. Words and phrases have a variety of different meanings based on contexts. The term "bank" can be a finance institution or a river bank. Thus, to address this kind of issue, composite AI combines deep learning (for example, a transformer for contextual embeddings) and symbolic AI (for example, rule systems or a knowledge graph) in such a manner as to be capable of solving ambiguity such as word meaning ambiguity.

2.2.1.2 Handling Diverse Data Types

NLP is typically active in complicated environments in which various forms of data, such as text, audio, and video, have an intermixed relationship, hence making it easier for various modalities to intercommunicate. In voice assistants, NLP translates spoken content (audio) in a bid to infer valuable text, detect intent, and provide verbal responses, making it easier for all-round communication. In video subtitling systems, NLP plays a vital role in interpreting content in an auditory format and synchronizing it with visuals in a manner that leads to understanding and accessibility for various audiences [5]. Such systems exemplify NLP's role in unifying various forms of data using combined AI, making it an integral part of multimodal communication technology.

2.2.1.3 Multi-Lingual and Cross-Lingual Processing

Creating models which can speak fluently in a number of languages or which can freely translate between languages is a hard achievement. Such models must have the capacity for translation among languages, as well as being culturally aware, in a tone, and in a given situation. The capacity for quickly adapting to different cultural and situation nuances, combined with a firm grasp of grammatical forms, idiosyncratic phrases, and conventions of regions, is all needed for this. The sophistication of the problem calls for complicated solutions such as composite AI, which allows unencumbered cross-lingual processing by combining neural machine translation systems for scale-up reasons along with symbolic AI for grammatical conventions and culture-specific nuances.

2.2.1.4 Handling Noisy and Unstructured Data

Much of real-world data, such as data on social media networks, chats, and end-user-created content, is naturally unstructured and noisy. The data in question is typically flawed by misspellings, grammatical mistakes, abbreviations, and non-uniform formats, making it difficult for traditional natural language processing algorithms to process it effectively. With these drawbacks, effective interpretation of text and producing valuable insights is being hindered. In an effort to derive valuable insights even from noisy inputs, composite AI makes use of effective preprocessing methods, data cleansing based on rule-based systems, and deep learning algorithms in an effort to generalize patterns. This allows valuable insights to be derived.

2.2.1.5 Sentiment and Emotional Analysis

Being able to interpret not just the literal meaning of language but an underlying current of emotion, such as elation, frustration, sarcasm, or empathy, is paramount for a number of complicated natural language processing solutions. Some of these solutions include fine-tuning customer support, psychological state diagnosis, and presenting users with content tailored for them. It is difficult for normal NLP algorithms, in particular, to find these levels of emotion since these algorithms aren't typically capable of sensing slight shades of tone, feelings based on situation, or variation based on culture.

Composite AI is a revolutionized solution which is based on a variety of different implementations of AI. Symbolic reasoning utilizes sentiment lexicons and tried-and-tested rules in an attempt to increase interpretation, and powerful algorithms for sentiment analysis identify more pervasive patterns of emotion. Deep networks identify embedded signals of tone and context, and symbolic reasoning is a process which is utilized in an attempt to increase interpretation. Composite AI can identify and interpret even highly complex patterns of emotion in language, thanks to its multi-dimensional solution. It ultimately results in systems of natural language processing, which can have a greater capacity for empathy, sensitivity, and perception of its environments.

2.2.1.6 Bias Detection and Mitigation

Natural language processing algorithms have a proclivity for learning embedded biases in data on which they have been trained. This can result in outputs being discriminant, unjust, and, in certain instances, unrepresentative. Such biases have a proclivity to occur due to imbalances in data representativeness, historical biases, and structural inequalities, which find expression in corresponding data sources. If left uncorrected, these can result in negative stereotyping and erode trust in artificial intelligence systems. This is especially so in such critical fields as hiring, medicine, and policing.

The integration of composite AI provides a powerful tool for addressing and minimizing these biases. The integration of statistical modeling allows for identifying and quantifying biases and, subsequently, for unveiling underlying trends which can result in biased results. At the same time, it encompasses symbolic artificial intelligence in enforcing bounds of fairness and defining lucid norms for just decision-making. Composite AI ensures NLP systems are not only more aware of possible biases but also able to counteract these proactively. This results in outcomes which are more just, more inclusive, and socially aware.

2.2.1.7 Low-Resource Language Processing

Most of these languages, especially those of smaller speakers or spoken in underrepresented areas, are hindered by a dearth of annotated datasets, which makes it difficult to create effective natural language processing models. With little data, it isn't easy to achieve such functions as categorization of text, machine translation, and sentiment analysis for these languages. This has resulted in a digital divide in accessing AI.

Composite AI bridges this gap using a blend of new strategies. Transfer learning is employed for learning from rich-resource languages, which allows models to perform well despite a minimal dataset. The similarity of language representations between languages is made easier due to cross-lingual embeddings, which in return facilitates enhanced understanding and generalization for low-resource languages. Apart from this, symbolic rules and domain-specific heuristics are incorporated in place of annotated data. This leads to the provision of organized advice and enhanced accuracy.

Thus, by addressing these issues, Composite AI is further refining NLP capabilities, which allows language systems to be smarter and more adaptive.

2.2.2 Benefits of Leveraging Multiple AI Techniques in NLP

Natural language processing can be highly improved using a number of different AI techniques. Some of these benefits have been enumerated here.

2.2.2.1 Greater Precision

A substantial increase in predictive capability is achievable when statistical modeling is coupled with rule-based reasoning. The firm logic and bounds of rule-based reasoning minimize errors and ensure results agree with expectations in real-world situations. Statistical modeling excels in trend discovery and inference based on data.

2.2.2.2 Heightened Contextual Awareness

The synergy between domain-specific understanding and machine learning helps algorithms grasp nuances of vocabulary and meaning in a given industry. With this collaboration, NLP systems can learn about differences in a given situation, for instance, legal or medical jargon, resulting in improved precision and relevancy.

2.2.2.3 Powerful Multimodal Analysis

Composite AI makes NLP able to interpret and integrate a wide variety of sources of input, for example, text, speech, and video. Functions of sentiment analysis and media transcription benefit from this capability in a quest for greater comprehension. In sentiment analysis, body language and tone of voice accompany written content, while in media transcription, speech and visuals enhance understanding.

2.2.2.4 Scalability Across Domains

With domain-specific ontologies and pre-trained models, hybrid systems can be generalized to various industries, for example, finance, education, medicine, and media. Hybrid systems can be flexible in a natural manner. NLP systems can address every industry-specific need, thanks to their adaptability, which also ensures it of keeping maximum levels of precision and efficiency.

2.2.2.5 *Explainability and Trust*

Integrating symbolic AI in composite AI systems makes interpretability and transparency easier. In critical applications such as medical care or legal reasoning, logical reasoning aspects play a vital role since they provide system-made decision explanations. This makes it easier to establish trust and reliability, which is of critical importance in such a scenario. NLP composite AI not only surpasses traditional limitations which have been associated with it, but it also establishes a new standard for what is being measured in terms of performance, flexibility, and language system user confidence. NLP composite AI not only surpasses traditional limitations which have been associated with it, but it also establishes a new standard for what is being measured in terms of performance, flexibility, and language system user confidence.

2.3 Fundamental Elements of NLP Composite AI

The major facets of NLP's composite AI contribute in a critical role towards grasping its power of transformation and its contribution in language processing [6]. In this component, DL for learning representations in solving human language complexity, there exist two critical facets. They are-

- Presentation learning using DL
- Symbolic AI for reasoning for logic
- and hybrid models

2.3.1 DL for Presentation Learning

Composite NLP based on DL is rooted in DL as its representational learning platform in an effort to help a computer comprehend and process language in an effective way at different levels of granularity. This can be achieved using methods of word embeddings. We shall detail this in the following section.

2.3.1.1 *Word Embeddings*

Word embeddings have a more critical role in NLP and make use of numerical representations of a word in a 2D space in an attempt to encode syntactic and semantic content. Word embedding is a language modeling process that converts words to vectors of real numbers. Words or sentences are identified by a term in a multi-dimensional space of vectors. Word embeddings may be developed using different methods, such as co-occurrence matrices, probability distributions, and neural networks. One of the major word embeddings in NLP is predictive embeddings, for instance, Word2Vec.

a) **Word2Vec:** NLP makes wide usage of a process known as Word2Vec [7]. This makes it possible for words to be embedded in a continuous vector space. The researchers at Google have come up with a tool, which is an attempt to reduce words to vectors of a large number of dimensions in a quest for maintaining semantic relations between words. In keeping in mind the underlying idea of Word2Vec, similar in meaning words must have similar vectors [8]. Word2Vec makes use of two different architectures:
   - Continuous Bag of Words (CBOW): Outputs the target word based on its context.
   - Skip-Gram: Predicts the context given the target word

b) **CBOW:** The current word is predicted given a window of context words by a CBOW model. Words corresponding to a given context are stored in an input layer, and a current word is stored in an output layer [9]. For each output layer word, there is a corresponding hidden layer in which we wish to represent its dimensions. The CBOW structure is shown in Figure 2.2.

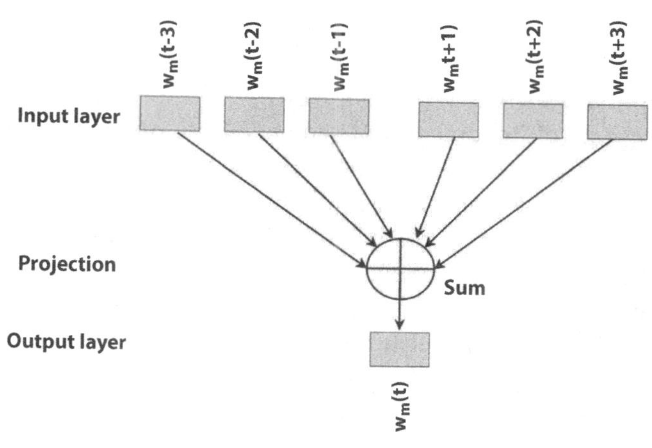

Figure 2.2 Architecture of CBOW.

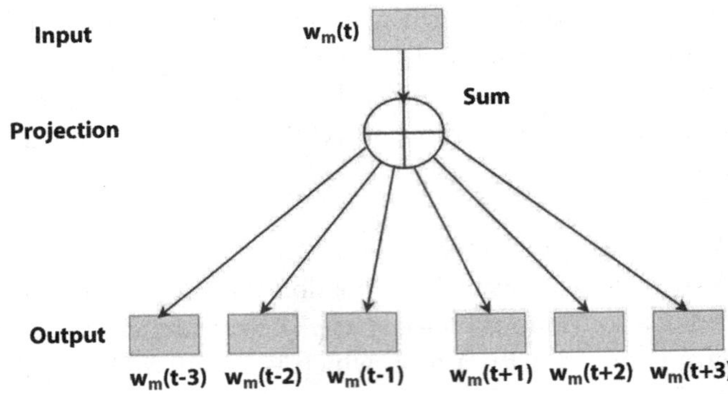

Figure 2.3 Architecture of Skip gram.

c) **Skip Gram:** Skip gram can predict the words in their current context in a given time window as shown in Figure 2.3. The current word is in the input layer, and the words composing its context are in the output layer [9]. Each input word is accompanied by a hidden layer that dictates the number of dimensions in which it is embedded.

2.3.1.2 Sentence and Document-Level Representations

A key contribution of NLP is a sentence and document scale language understanding. This is based on a foundation laid down by word embeddings such as Word2Vec and GloVe, which captured semantics on a world scale. Sentence and document representations generalize these on a wider variety of language forms and contexts. Such representations make it possible for robots to learn and understand language in a holistic manner, which makes it critical for operations such as summarization, sentiment, and question-answering.

The functions of document and sentence-level representations are to encode the meaning of entire sentences or documents in compact vectors of a given size. Besides capturing individual words, these vectors encode relations between these words, syntactic relations, and semantic content. For there to be effective representations on various levels, there is a necessity to address such issues as dependencies in contexts, grammatical variation, and polysemous term disambiguation [10]. One of the major methods in document and sentence-level representations is transformer-based models, which are explained in detail below.

A) Transformer based models

Transformers in NLP can be utilized quite well for document-level as well as for sentence-level representations owing to its mechanism of self-attention. With such a structure, it can process different granularities of text, ranging between a word and a large piece of text. For example, Bidirectional Encoder Representations from Transformers (BERT) can perform well in the case of sentence-level assignments. At the same time, BigBird is custom-made for processing large pieces of text, so it is well-suited for document-level representations.

(i) BERT

"Pre-trained language model" is a term widely used for BERT, which can subsequently be employed for processing language naturally *via* fine-tuning. The left and right contexts of a given input string are taken in parallel by BERT to create contextualized embeddings. BERT is a powerful system based on deep learning, which is widely being employed for a variety of NLP applications [11]. The reasons why BERT is a widely sought-after solution for NLP applications are given below.

1. BERT not only scans the sentence, but it also understands the meaning of each word in the sentence based on its context. Consequently, the BERT model is very well-liked for NLP tasks such as sentiment analysis, text classification, and named entity identification.
2. BERT is a pre-trained model and is well aware of a great amount of material in text prior to its training. Accordingly, it skips lengthy training, which is a big-time saver and enables us to start in NLP activities directly. In addition, fine-tuning can be done according to our requirements, which results in improved model performance.
3. BERT employs transfer learning, which enables experience developed under large-scale pre-training for utilization in a large number of activities, so there is no necessity to start anew. This is time-efficient on a large scale.

(ii) Architecture of BERT

We can represent long-range relations in a document using highly parallelized and computationally efficient mechanisms known as transformers [12]. The transformer structure is also used in BERT, which makes it able to support self-attention mechanisms and feedforward networks.

- Bidirectional Encoding: The past machines read in a direction, say, left to right. Contrarily, though, is a capability of BERT, which is termed bi-directionality, wherein it reads in a direction vertically along with a horizontal direction, i.e., left to right and right to left. With this, it is able to make a proper comprehension of each of its constituent words that lie in a phrase.
- Pre-Training and Fine-Tuning: Since it is trained on a large dataset of text, BERT can learn rich and contextualized word representations. BERT is highly flexible and powerful for a wide range of natural language processing tasks since we can fine-tune data that is already trained based on our requirements.
- Multi-Layer Stacking: Secondly, BERT is made up of a stacking of transformers. Hence, it is constructed on a large number of transformer layers on another. With this capacity, BERT is able to accumulate more complex and contextualized data.

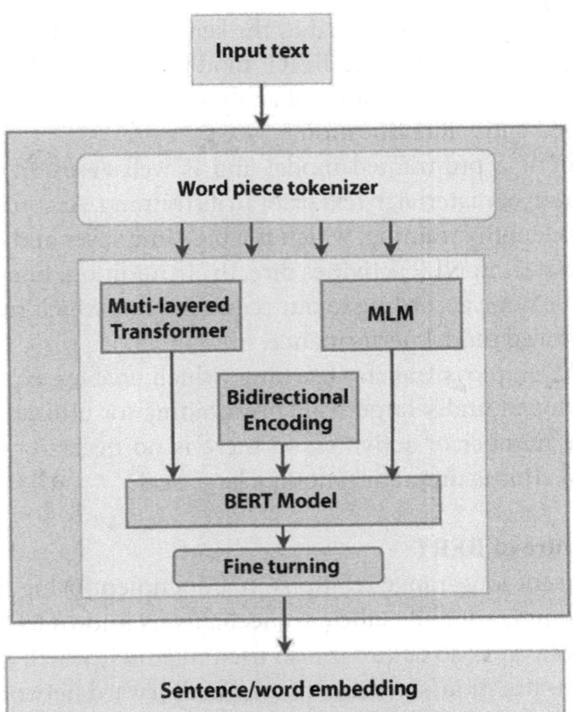

Figure 2.4 BERT model architecture [13].

- Embedding Layers: The process of Word Piece tokenization is followed in BERT. This involves splitting every word of the input phrase into a group of sub-word tokens.
- Masked Language Model (MLM): One of its other roles is its ability to detect masked words in a sentence. This is precisely why it is compelled to comprehend the contexts of a word in relation to its contexts. Figure 2.4 shows the architecture of BERT model [13].

For this BERT, its quadratic dependency is among its greatest constraints. Due to this dependency, its BERT-like model can process sequences of 512 tokens in parallel due to its full attention mechanism. In an attempt to evade this, Manzil Zaheer *et al.* [26], proposed adding a sparse attention mechanism in BigBird capable of processing sequences of lengths up to eightfold greater than what it is currently capable of processing using similar hardware.

2.3.2 Symbolic AI for Logical Reasoning

Symbolic AI can solve language nuances, so exactly straight out of the box— a tempting solution for NLP. Such systems can comprehend fine shades of language, which confuse statistical methods. This is made possible by a process known as disambiguation, a term whose meaning is based on its embedded and context-related information.

Businesses and programmers must consider the implications in a practical sense. Symbolic AI can achieve great outcomes utilizing smaller data sets and lower processing overhead than traditional machine learning NLP programs, which take a large amount of data for learning and processing. The symbolic AI system traditionally results in more precise and predictable language interpretation. This is not a matter of compromising on precision.

Following a process similar to solving math in steps, symbolic AI handles and communicates using distinct symbols, rules, and reasoning [14]. This human-like reasoning is simulated in this AI by using logic and structured data. Besides similar cognitive patterns of humans, this technology makes machines process data in an effort to aggregate data in large inter-related data networks. Additionally, this technology translates knowledge graphs into dynamic systems in an effort to uncover hidden patterns and valuable data. This is a much more powerful tool for navigating complex data environments in which explainability and accuracy count.

2.3.2.1 Fundaments of Symbolic AI

The major uses of symbolic AI consist of rule-based grammar checks and knowledge graphs for adding context. The use of these systems demonstrates symbolic thinking which can solve complex problems in a variety of industries.

a. Rule-based grammar checks: Tokenization and Its Role in Symbolic AI

Tokenization is a process that is mapped to rigid rule-governed patterns in symbol paradigms of AI to NLP. The process of dividing text based on given parameters such as punctuation, a space, or a set of given sequences of characters is part of this process [15]. The language processing is made predictable and consistent due to this process. The following example shows this process.

"Dr. Smith arrived at three o'clock in the afternoon, bringing her report."

Rules:

- Split at whitespace but retain punctuation with words.
- Treat abbreviations (like "Dr." or "p.m.") as single tokens.
- Recognize numbers and colons (e.g., "3:00") as cohesive units.

Output:

[\"Dr.\", \"Smith\", \"arrived\", \"at\", \"3:00\", \"p.m.\", \",\", \"bringing\", \"her\", \"report\", \".\"]

By ensuring that tokenization is in sync with grammatical patterns, this control makes grammar checks and semantic parsing more precise in their interpretation.

Advantages:

- Rule-based tokenization can give a guarantee of consistency for a wide variety of datasets and contexts. For example, it can ensure abbreviations and numbers are processed similarly without variation.
- The users can distinctly see why a solution is being proposed, since mistakes have been recognized based on concrete regulations.
- The learning benefit of grammar checks in language learning systems such as Grammarly is based on the premise that such programs apply rule-based methods of describing

grammatical errors using examples and reasoning, hence effectively helping learners.

Disadvantages:

- Rule systems have a hard time when facing creative language, which is a subtleness such as poetry, idiosyncratic language, or colloquial. The systems have a minimal margin for adaptability.
- Extending rule sets in support of all language differences, such as multi-language content and regional dialect, is a time-consuming process. This element is confronted by scalability.
- Restrictions on tokenization are too rigid and may misconstrue imprecise concepts. One case in point:

The phrase "the bank rose" (is it a riverbank or a financial institution?).
For such cases, context-specific models perform well in relation to solutions based on a set of rules.

b. Hybrid approaches in Future Grammer Check
Advanced technologies can surpass symbolic AI limitations by pairing them with machine learning. For example, first-time parsing can be made using rule-based tokenization. Followed by statistical models in an attempt to detect and disambiguate complicated errors, for example, homophones or verbs that have a contextual dependency. Thus, grammar checkers preserve their accuracy by constantly refining themselves in a great number of rapidly changing language environments. So, leveraging symbolic AI technologies such as rule systems and knowledge graphs, organizations can achieve exact, interpretable, and context-specific solutions in reasoning tasks [16]. Such technologies create a middle ground between data-centric and rule-centric solutions, opening doors for complex cognitive systems.

2.4 Case Studies and Use Cases of Composite AI in NLP

Composite AI is utilized in NLP for improved decision-making, language comprehension, and the generation of contextual insights. This is made possible using NLP in real-world scenarios. Some of the major implementations of these usages are discussed below.

2.4.1 Conventional AI and Virtual Assistants

The relationship between humans and machines has been transformed owing to the popularity of conversational AI and digital assistants in daily life. Such artificial intelligence systems can process, comprehend, and act on inputs in a human language, making it easier for them to provide unbroken experiences for customer care, home automation, and information systems.

Examples: Amazon Alexa, Google Assistant, and IBM Watson Assistant

Let us discuss these examples one by one.

2.4.1.1 Amazon Alexa

Amazon Alexa is a speech-enabled virtual assistant developed by Amazon Company. Alexa is a perfect example of how composite AI can enhance NLP in an effort to make interactions intelligent, context-aware, and seamless. With a blend of different artificial intelligence strategies, Alexa can take care of complex human interactions, delivering appropriate responses and streamlining tasks [17].

a) Composite AI in NLP for Alexa works?

To provide smart services, Alexa makes use of a variety of AI devices. With DL models like BERT, neural networks can detect intentions like "Play music" and extract critical data like location or time. This is a highly critical job that is being played by neural networks in intent recognition and slot filling. Preset and rudimentary actions like controlling smart home systems or setting an alarm clock are taken care of by systems based on rules, which ensures that actions are being completed in an effective and timely manner. Alexa can preserve context for a number of interactions and give appropriate replies due to the usage of a knowledge graph, which makes her a more effective multi-turn conversation manager. With the usage of deep learning models like Recurrent Neural Networks (RNNs), ASR converts spoken language and translates it into a written format. This process assures correct transcription of voices. NLU is a process that makes use of classifying the intentions of users and data extraction of a specific kind in interpreting queries of users. This process enables Alexa to process complex queries effectively. User satisfaction can be improved by the usage of personal experiences, which is made possible by ML, which personalizes replies based on users' preferences.

For example, when a customer asks Alexa for relaxing music, it plays. ASR translates the speech, NLU identifies the slot 'Genre: relaxing' and categorizes the intent as 'PlayMusic,' and it is the responsibility of the knowledge graph to correlate relaxing music with a set of playlists or artists. The action is taken using a rule-based system using the Amazon Music API. The responsibility of choosing a playlist based on customer preference is left to machine learning. The outcome is an experience that is frictionless but smart.

Composite AI for NLP in Alexa yields a number of different advantages, such as true intent recognition, job execution in a seamless manner, understanding in a given context, enhanced customer experience *via* personalization, and scalability, which enables Alexa to learn new customer requirements and new job functions. Alexa achieves powerful and intelligent NLP experience *via* composite AI strategies. Alexa is a market-leading conversational AI due to its capability of processing complex queries, delivering personal responses, and being contextually aware *via* a combination of neural networks, rule systems, knowledge bases, and ML.

2.4.1.2 Google Assistant

Similarly, Google Assistant makes use of Composite AI in a quest to comprehend user queries and process language naturally. Google NLP algorithms, for instance, such as LaMDA and BERT, support intent recognition, entity recognition, and generation of a response. For keeping track of multi-turn conversations in a given context, Google Assistant makes use of neural networks for voice recognition and knowledge bases. Rule-based reasoning provides for actions; for instance, reminders being set and occurring in a timely manner, and reinforcement learning improves personal suggestions based on a preference [18]. Google Assistant is able to provide accurate, live data on a variety of different topics since it is able to make use of powerful search functionality in Google.

Being able to take advantage of Google's powerful search functionality is one of the greatest aspects of Google Assistant. For this reason, it can access data on the web in real-time, making it capable of producing replies which are both appropriate and accurate. One such example is when an individual asks Google, "Hey, what is the best place for an Italian meal in the immediate vicinity?" The question is processed by Google Assistant, which considers a user's location, past search queries, and online ratings in an effort to provide a reply that is custom-made for a given individual.

Secondly, the multi-modal functionality of Google Assistant makes it capable of processing speech inputs and text inputs, making it suitable for usage on a wide array of gadgets, ranging from mobile handsets to smart speakers and wearables.

Integration of third-party apps and services is another capability that makes Google Assistant stand out. This is advantageous for businesses and consumers, as it gives a variety of Application Programming Interfaces (APIs), which assist in developing custom activities. For example, Google Assistant can be integrated into calendar apps for making appointments, managing smart home technology *via* Internet of Things solutions, and aiding in shopping *via* online buying apps.

The functionality of machine learning is taken a step further in personalization, wherein Google Assistant can learn experiences in the past in an effort to provide suggestions and support that is more appropriate for the situation of the users. For instance, it can remind users of daily routines, provide alternative directions in case of traffic, and give news reports based on users' surfing patterns. With such a degree of personalization, users have a higher engagement, and usage is made easier for users.

2.4.1.3 IBM Watson Assistant

The highly capable AI-powered digital helper IBM Watson Assistant is particularly tailored for business usage. To improve its conversational functionality, it makes use of a combination of rule-based NLP, deep learning, and symbolic AI, which are all combined under a term called composite AI. The Watson Assistant makes use of ML models for intent recognition and entity recognition [19]. For this, it makes use of pre-trained deep learning architectures such as transformers in an effort to interpret queries entered by users. The advantage of using rule-based logic is it makes it possible to maintain a set of predetermined steps, making it an excellent solution for customer support usage in which predetermined steps have to be followed.

Watson Assistant is able to maintain contextual understanding in all conversations based on its knowledge graphs, which allows it to have smarter and more insightful conversations. IBM Watson is also using Retrieval-Augmented Generation (RAG) strategies, which enable it to pull live data directly from unstructured and structured sources. This makes its responses more insightful and dynamic. Watson Assistant is a highly sought-after solution for enterprises in a wide variety of industries, such as banking, customer support, and healthcare, based on its enterprise security and regulatory support, which is a part of the solution. Business functions can be automated, and businesses can enhance business efficiency due to its integration capability with Customer Relationship Management (CRM), business analytics, and databases.

Using AI-driven conversation management and machine learning, for instance, Watson can interpret customer complaints, locate similar data in databases, and provide context-specific replies in a customer support chatbot. This is made possible owing to these technologies being combined. Through customer input analysis and subsequent adjustment of conversation models, Watson Assistant allows for mechanisms of reinforcement learning for enhanced answer precision over time. In addition, it can facilitate multi-modal interactions, which makes it capable of delivering speech, text, and chatbot interfaces for a hassle-free customer experience.

2.4.2 Healthcare Chatbots for Patient Interaction

A variety of Chatbots in medicine, which operate on composite artificial intelligence, are transforming accessible, individualized, and effective provision of medical care. The functions of these chatbots are to facilitate patient engagement and support in diagnosis and medical treatment by integrating different forms of artificial intelligence technologies among themselves [20]. The technologies consist of ML, NLP, knowledge graphs, and systems based on rules.

2.4.2.1 IBM Watson for Healthcare Case Study

To facilitate easier contact between medical practitioners and patients and supply vital health-related information, IBM Watson Assistant has been used in a number of different medical settings. In the Cleveland Clinic, for instance, medical questions, appointments, and advice based on a patient's signs and symptoms are responded to, scheduled, and made, respectively, by bots driven by Watson [21]. This is just a point in case. For input assessment, medical entity recognition, and return of replies, which is appropriate, it makes use of machine learning and natural language processing. Knowledge graphs support Watson's understanding of medical terms and medical conditions, which leads it to provide more accurate and contextually aware exchanges. The chatbot is also integrated with electronic medical records (EMRs), which allows it to have a patient's history and provide individualized recommendations. This facilitates easier provision of a lower amount of work for medical practitioners.

2.4.2.2 *Case Study: Ada Health – AI-Powered Symptom Checker*

An AI chatbot, Ada Health assists users in reaching a clearer understanding of their symptoms and possible health concerns. DL models and rule-based medical data are combined in an attempt to evaluate symptoms based on input provided by a user precisely [22]. The chatbot utilizes Bayesian inference algorithms in an attempt to evaluate probabilities of various diseases, and natural language understanding is utilized attempt to test patient reports of symptoms. In an attempt to give users individualized health evaluations and guidance on whether a medical visit is necessary, Ada Health searches colossal amounts of medical literature and patient case studies. Since it is embedded in a system of fuzzy logic, it can handle imprecise symptom descriptions, which makes it of greater utility in scenarios that occur in the real world when patients may not be able to characterize a situation suitably.

2.4.2.3 *Case Study: Babylon Health – AI-Driven Telemedicine Chatbot*

Babylon Health, a virtual healthcare assistant based on AI, provides tele-consultations, monitoring of health, and checks on symptoms among others. The intent recognition is managed by this chatbot using artificial neural networks, which ensures patient questions are well understood [23]. In addition, it makes use of rule-based AI in an effort to adhere to predetermined medical standards for assessing symptoms. The patient's symptoms can be analyzed using a Babylon Health chatbot, which is capable of making suggestions based on an urgent medical consultation, a visit to a doctor, or self-care. The additional context awareness is given by a chatbot using a knowledge graph. This makes it able to recall past experiences and medical histories in an effort to provide more appropriate suggestions. Patients can verbally report their symptoms owing to Babylon's speech-enabled chatbot.

2.4.3 Automated Content Moderation Systems

For purposes of making digital communication on various channels secure, appropriate, and regulatory-compliant, content moderation systems based on composite AI have a vital role. User content is examined and sifted in real-time by these systems on a blend of ML, NLP, DL, knowledge bases, and systems of rules [24]. Social network websites, online discussion boards, gaming networks, and business communication apps widely make use of these systems for content recognition, which is injurious, objectionable, and deceptive, along with making moderation just and accurate.

In this section, case studies of Facebook's AI content moderation system and OpenAI's AI content moderation API are to be discussed.

2.4.3.1 Case Study on Facebook's AI-Powered Content Moderation System

Meta, which owns Facebook, has developed an AI-powered content moderation system in a bid to moderate and supervise content made by users on its platform. Facebook deals with a humongous number of posts, comments, images, and videos given; it has billions of active users every day. Automated moderation is, hence, critical in keeping community standards in place *via* Facebook. Facebook utilizes composite AI in a quest to accomplish this.

A. Composite AI Techniques Used in Facebook's Moderation System

i. Deep Learning for Content Moderation in a Text Format

Text in posts, comments, and messages is processed using transformer-based models such as BERT and XLM-R in a quest for potentially dangerous content. Identification of hate speech, hurtful conversations, and bullying can be identified using sentiment analysis and hate speech recognition. NLP models possessing a perception of context search for geographic-specific language, slang, and instances of dangerous phrases in a quest for minimizing time in which mechanisms of detection can be circumvented. Through content moderation in different languages, translation models assist in ensuring cross-lingual moderation is being carried out.

ii. Computer Vision for Image and Video Moderation

Convolutional Neural Networks, now termed CNNs, are being utilized in an attempt to screen images for inappropriate, violent, or sexual material. For drug, gun, and other potentially dangerous images, object recognition algorithms are utilized. Identification and blocking of illegal images, for example, deepfake, can be made possible using facial recognition technologies. Automated screening of videos is utilized using which content violation frames are searched, which ensures dangerous imagery is eliminated even before being inspected by humans.

iii. Knowledge Graph for Contextual Comprehension

To assist in classifying content, Facebook maintains a content report knowledge graph. The job of AI models is to predict and deter all subsequent offenses by relating content that is being reported to historical patterns of similar offenses. The ability of knowledge graphs to identify relationships between sentences, words, and contexts makes them able to differentiate between policy violation, humor, and sarcasm.

iv. Rule-Based Filtering for Real-Time Moderation

Instant content filtering is achieved by using predetermined rules and pattern recognition. Words and phrases that have been recognized as violating Facebook policy are blocked by using automatic keyword screening. The use of threshold flagging ensures content is made accessible for study for determination by experts in case it meets predetermined risk factors.

v. Reinforcement Learning for Continual Improvement

To make it more precise, Facebook AI is constantly trained on human moderators' feedback. Reinforcement learning algorithms adjust the thresholds for categorization in line with shifting trends in content. The system adjusts automatically when new hate speech and new forms of disinformation come in.

vi. Moderation of AI-Powered Tools

While a great amount of first moderation is left in the hands of AI, human moderators are still hired by Facebook in a position to consider more complicated cases. AI may not comprehend humor, for example, or political language, so human interaction is needed in an attempt to make moderation more precise. A deeper understanding of a situation is reached by utilizing human input, making artificial intelligence more able to interpret nuanced or culturally based changes in content. If it is presented with uncertain situations that necessitate policy-directed decision-making, artificial intelligence flags content for human moderation. This is known as escalation handling.

B. The Impact of Facebook's AI Moderation System

- Automatic AI technology removes tens of millions of posts that violate policy before human users ever see them.
- In addition, over 95% of hate posts with offensive content were identified and deleted by AI prior to being identified by humans, based on reports in Facebook's Transparency Reports.
- In a bid to identify misleading content, the AI that screens for facts on Facebook checks data against reputable news sources.

- The dissemination of dangerous narratives can be prevented using labeling as misinformation and visibility reduction of content.
- Ai assists in enforcing Facebook's Community Guidelines in a uniform way in all of its regions and languages.
- Facebook promises it is in keeping with the laws of a respective region based on content standards depending on location.

C. Future Improvements and Advancements

- Multimodal AI, based on a combination of text, image, and audio processing, allows for greater depth of moderation.
- The Zero-Shot learning Models create a system for enabling AI to classify new instances of risky material based on prior unlabeled data.
- A variety of different AI inputs is being used in dataset refining in a quest for ethical AI systems to combat bias in moderation.

2.4.3.2 OpenAI GPT-Based Customer Service Chatbots Case Study

OpenAI created an AI content moderation API for identifying and filtering content that is hurtful, inappropriate, or in violation of a term of service on a large variety of digital media [25]. In pursuit of live content moderation, the application program interface (API) utilizes composite AI in an attempt to integrate ML, NLP, DL, and filtering based on a set of rules. In making moderation decisions, the system keeps online engagements on being secure, in line, and inclusive, along with minimizing cases of false positives and prejudice.

Chatbots powered by GPT and developed by OpenAI have revolutionized the customer support business by delivering interactions that are intelligent, automated, and resemble those of humans. These chatbots make use of composite artificial intelligence, which incorporates NLP, DL, sentiment analysis, reinforcement learning, and rule-based systems to manage client inquiries about their needs effectively. Chatbots that are based on GPT are used by businesses in a variety of sectors, including e-commerce, banking, healthcare, and telecoms, to improve the client experience, save operating costs, and guarantee service around the clock.

A. Composite AI Techniques in OpenAI GPT

i. NLP for Query Comprehension

User inputs are separated into understandable chunks *via* the process of parsing and tokenization. The process of identifying major data, such as customer name and order number, is called Named Entity Recognition (NER). User queries can be identified using intent recognition, such as following an order, requesting a return, and asking about a product.

ii. Machine Learning for Personalization

Chatbots developed based on GPTs can provide tailored suggestions based on learning experiences in past interactions. User data and past actions help in personalizing replies—adaptive responses are based on the mood and attitude of the customer.

iii. Emotion Recognition based on Sentiment Analysis

Depending on sentiment recognition in real-time, it is possible to identify a customer as neutral, satisfied, or annoyed. Emotion-aware responses can be employed by bots so that they can adjust tone, for instance, by being sympathetic to complaints and being cheerful when greetings are being responded to. If a negative sentiment is identified, human agents receive escalation triggers.

iv. Reinforcement Learning for Continual Enhancement

When it comes to reacting in the future, AI is trained on successful conversations as well as failed conversations. Feedback loops assist the chatbot in knowing which conversations went well and which conversations can be improved. The adaption is in real-time, depending on the action taken by a user.

v. Rule-Based Systems for Enforced Policy

To ensure corporate requirements such as eligibility for a refund and data security, predetermined actions are taken. Account authentication and complaint filing are a few of the actions instigated by automated systems. With switching between predetermined responses for questions in a predetermined format and responses formulated by GPT for unstructured conversations, hybrid AI systems can adapt to a variety of different scenarios.

B. Use Cases of GPT-Based Chatbots in Customer Service

i. E-Commerce & Retail (Shopify AI Assistant Case Study)

- The customer is able to locate merchandize, inquire about availability, and make a purchase *via* AI-powered chatbots.
- Order tracking that is automated decreases the amount of human involvement that is required.

- Increased sales and interest can result due to custom suggestions.

ii. Bank and Financial Services (Bank of America's Erica AI)

- Chatbots that GPT powers let clients inquire about their account balances, see their transaction histories, and get fraud warnings.
- The use of AI-driven financial advice assists clients in managing savings and assets.
- In addition to rendering timely service, secure authentication systems deter fraudulent behavior.

iii. Healthcare and Telemedicine (Example of Mayo Clinic AI Chatbot)

- Patients now screen for symptoms and make appointments using the help of AI-powered chatbots.
- The patient is provided with an initial medical opinion by virtual care assistants based on their apparent signs.
- Chatbots that are compliant with HIPAA safeguard the privacy and security of user data.

iv. Telecommunication and Internet Services (Example of Verizon's AI Chatbot)

- The users can solve connection issues using the assistance of AI-powered chatbots.
- The processing of payments and requests for billing is handled automatically.
- The customer retention can be improved by using suggestions for subscription plans.

v. Travel & Hospitality (Case Study: Expedia AI Assistant)

- AI chatbots assist travelers in the booking of flights, hotels, and the planning of itineraries.
- Presenting timely, live journey information and alerts enhances customer experience.
- The frustration of a customer can be reduced using automation of cancellation and return procedures.

C. Impact of GPT-Based Chatbots on Customer Support

- One can lower the operation costs by automating frequent questions.
- In addition, it simplifies human agents' work so that they can concentrate on more challenging matters.
- It is capable of managing a large number of consumer requests at the same time.
- Chatbots can have a large number of conversations, which can reach millions, using AI without human support.
- Round-the-clock support enhances the ability to reach clients all over the world.
- The minimizing of agent-dependent variability as a result of utilizing standard and appropriate responses.

D. Future Developments in Customer Service Using

- AI will recall past conversations more clearly, which will make discussion easier to comprehend.
- The voice chats shall be made possible using AI-powered chatbots for easier access.
- Future bots will have a wider capability for understanding and responding suitably to emotions.
- It can learn quickly in response to new queries, all without incurring retraining expenses.

2.5 Challenges and Future Directions

Throughout its current growth in NLP, composite AI is being confronted with a number of different challenges as well as opportunities. This chapter addresses major factors that shall guide directions for the future of composite AI in NLP, for example, technology restraints and ethics, as well as quantum computation improvements and multilingual NLP.

2.5.1 Challenges in Composite AI for NLP

- The NLP systems have to have large datasets of excellent quality, which have been well annotated.

- Various AI aspects, for example, ML, knowledge bases, and systems based on rules, require data integration that is seamless.
- The noisy, biased, or inconsistent data can have a detrimental effect on a model.
- The AI composite systems should have a great amount of computer capacity as it involves integration of DL, symbolic reasoning, and other AI.
- We have to apply Explainable AI (XAI) practices in a bid to develop observable, interpretable, and explainable AI systems.
- A great quantity of text data is required for NLP models, which raises concerns about data security and data privacy.
- The General Data Protection Regulation, Health Insurance Portability and Accountability Act, and other data regulations must be obeyed when processing and storing medical data, email communications, and user interactions.
- Federated learning, along with privacy-preserving AI, for example, differential privacy, is being researched for threat reduction purposes.

2.5.2 Future Trends in Composite AI for NLP

In spite of all these, there is a future for NLP composite AI, which is set to be influenced by substantial improvements in linguistics modeling, computer science, and robotics.

- The following will be accelerated using quantum computation, DL models, and NLP probabilistic reasoning.
- This technology advances all of these, including real-time translation, vocal recognition, and semantic search.
- It facilitates linguistics computations in a faster and more productive manner.
- In a bid to overcome language barriers and promote communication on a global scale.
- This is enabled by using DL, knowledge graphs, and systems of rules, which have the capability of surpassing the intrinsic limitations of low-resource languages.
- Multilanguage bots, artificially intelligent learning, and international corporations all have an interest.

- It gives transparency and ethical decision-making in AI-powered apps.
- Enabling enhanced trust and reducing bias in NLP systems *via* interpretable modeling.
- Critical in sectors such as healthcare, banking, and government, in which AI-made decisions can have an impact on outcomes of actual-world scenarios.
- To secure users' data, there is a greater emphasis on differentiated privacy and federated learning.
- In making advances in AI, there is a requirement to adhere to international regulations such as GDPR and HIPAA.
- Enables processing and communication of information using AI.
- Recommendation systems, virtual assistants, and sentiment analysis using artificial intelligence technologies will keep getting enhanced.
- The NLP models in improving interactions shall be able to comprehend users' intent, tone, and context more proficiently. This results in communication in AI-driven industries, which is inclusive, human-like, and more effective.

2.6 Conclusion

By combining many AI approaches, composite AI addresses the intricacies of human language and marks a paradigm shift in natural language processing. Together, deep learning, symbolic AI, and multi-model integration improve language comprehension and make it possible for NLP solutions to be more precise and contextually aware. By successfully reducing ambiguity, processing multilingual material, and combining data from several sources, this method creates NLP systems that are more reliable and scalable. Text summarization, sentiment analysis, medical chatbots, legal document analysis, and machine translation are just a few of the fields where Composite AI is being used practically. This chapter's case studies demonstrate its scalability and efficacy in resolving practical issues. However, despite its potential, obstacles like scalability limitations, high processing costs, and data integration continue to be major roadblocks to wider use.

The prospects of composite NLP AI in the future are favorable. The capability of quantum processing and multilanguage natural language processing will stretch possibilities beyond its current bounds. The more we make it a more capable tool, composite artificial intelligence will reduce human-to-computer communication gaps, enhance creativity, and drive NLP. Composite AI is a revolution, not an evolution. This paradigm is fueling the advancement of AI systems capable of understanding, interpreting, and generating human language of depth and precision beyond all expectations.

AI disclosure statement: The author acknowledges the use of AI-based tools for minor language editing or grammatical correction. However, all intellectual contributions, analyses, and conclusions presented in this chapter are entirely the author's own.

References

1. https://research.aimultiple.com/composite-ai/ accessed on 12/05/2025.
2. https://www.linkedin.com/pulse/composite-ai-comprehensive-guide-for2025-jade-mckinley-dfguc/ accessed on 18/05/2025.
3. https://joinwithcamilla.medium.com/composite-ai-a-comprehensive-guide-for-2025-de22a52739a1 accessed on 18/05/2025.
4. https://www.forbes.com/sites/robtoews/2024/03/10/10-ai-predictions-for-the-year-2030/ accessed on 20/05/2025.
5. https://www.prismetric.com/natural-language-processing-guide/accessed on 21/05/2025.
6. https://www.researchgate.net/publication/376506354_Advancements_in_NLP_The_Role_of_AI_in_Language_Understanding?channel=doi&linkId=657afbcb6610947889cc0c1e&showFulltext=true accessed on 20/05/2025.
7. https://medium.com/ask-anova/diving-into-word2vec-giving-meaning-to-words-in-nlp-7fee4a5d3324. accessed on 20/05/2025.
8. Suresh Kumar, K., Radha Mani, A.S., Ananth Kumar, T., Jalili, A., Gheisari, M., Malik, Y., Chen, H.-C., Moshayedi, A.J., Sentiment analysis of short texts using SVMs and VSMs-based multiclass semantic classification. *Appl. Artif. Intell.*, 38, 1, 2321555, 2024.
9. Preethi Krishna, P. and Sharada, A., Word Embeddings - Skip Gram Model, in: *ICICCT 2019 – System Reliability, Quality Control, Safety, Maintenance and Management. ICICCT 2019*, V. Gunjan, V. Garcia Diaz, M. Cardona, V. Solanki, K. Sunitha (Eds.), Springer, Singapore, 2020, https://doi.org/10.1007/978-981-13-8461-5_15.
10. Ding, N., Lin, Y., Liu, Z., Sun, M., Sentence and Document Representation Learning, in: *Representation Learning for Natural Language Processing*, Z. Liu, Y. Lin, M. Sun (Eds.), Springer, Singapore, 2023, https://doi.org/10.1007/978-981-99-1600-9_4.

11. Li, F., Shen, H., Mai, J., *et al.*, Pre-trained language model-enhanced conditional generative adversarial networks for intrusion detection. *Peer-to-Peer Netw. Appl.*, 17, 227–245, 2024. https://doi.org/10.1007/s12083-023-01595-6.
12. Zhang, Q., Ram, D., Hawkins, C., Zha, S., Zhao, T., Efficient long-range transformers: You need to attend more, but not necessarily at every layer. *arXiv preprint arXiv:2310.12442*, 2023.
13. https://www.geeksforgeeks.org/how-to-generate-word-embedding-using-bert/.
14. Kishor, R., Neuro-symbolic AI: bringing a new era of machine learning. *Int. J. Res. Publ. Rev.*, *3*, 12, 2326–2336, 2022.
15. Kovarik Jr., V.J., Cognitive research: Knowledge representation and learning, in: *Cognitive Radio Technology*, pp. 365–399, Newnes, 2006.
16. Lu, Z., Afridi, I., Kang, H.J., *et al.*, Surveying neuro-symbolic approaches for reliable artificial intelligence of things. *J. Reliab. Intell. Environ.*, 10, 257–279, 2024. https://doi.org/10.1007/s40860-024-00231-1.
17. Brill, T.M., Munoz, L., Miller, R.J., Siri, Alexa, and other digital assistants: a study of customer satisfaction with artificial intelligence applications, in: *The role of smart technologies in decision making*, pp. 35–70, Routledge, 2022.
18. https://research.google/blog/look-and-talk-natural-conversations-with-google-assistant/ accessed on 20/06/2025.
19. https://www.ibm.com/products/watsonx-assistant/artificial-intelligence
20. Clark, M. and Bailey, S., Chatbots in health care: connecting patients to information. *Can. J. Health Technol.*, *4*, 1, 2024.
21. Altamimi, I., Altamimi, A., Alhumimidi, A.S., Altamimi, A., Temsah, M.H., Artificial intelligence (AI) chatbots in medicine: a supplement, not a substitute. *Cureus*, *15*, 6, 2023.
22. https://www.skillademia.com/tools/ada-health/ accessed on 31/05/2025.
23. https://www.nsmedicaldevices.com/analysis/babylon-health-ai-health-services/.
24. Sun, H. and Ni, W., Design and Application of an AI-Based Text Content Moderation System. *Sci. Program.*, *2022*, 1, 2576535, 2022.
25. https://openai.com/index/upgrading-the-moderation-api-with-our-new-multimodal-moderation-model/ accessed on 02/06/2025.
26. Zaheer, M., Guruganesh, G., Dubey, K.A., Ainslie, J., Alberti, C., Ontanon, S., Pham, P., *et al.*, Big bird: Transformers for longer sequences. *Adv. Neural Inf. Process. Syst.*, 33, 17283–17297, 2020.

3

A Composite Artificial Intelligence Framework for Enhanced and Intelligent Word Recognition of Handwritten Hindi

R. S. Rampriya[1]*, Sabarinathan[2], SahayaBeni Prathiba[3], C. Renit[4], R. Arumuga Arun[5] and S. Bhuvana[1]

[1]*School of Computer Science Engineering and Information Systems, Vellore Institute of Technology, Vellore, Tamilnadu, India*
[2]*Department of Artificial Intelligence, Couger Inc., Tokyo, Japan*
[3]*Centre for Cyber Physical Systems, School of Computer Science and Engineering, Vellore Institute of Technology, Chennai, India*
[4]*Department of ECE, St. Xaviers Catholic College of Engineering, Kanyaumari, Tamilnadu, India*
[5]*School of Computer Science Engineering, Vellore Institute of Technology, Vellore, Tamilnadu, India*

Abstract

The Hindi Handwritten Intelligent Character Recognition (HICR) system digitizes handwritten Hindi text, enhancing accessibility, preserving cultural heritage, and improving efficiency in education and administration. It supports multilingual communication and modernizes various sectors by integrating advanced technology with linguistic diversity. This study uses the combination of two AI models to provide a novel method for handwritten Hindi word recognition: HindRoBERTa (A Hindi Robustly Optimized BERT Pretraining Approach) decoder and the Data-efficient Image Transformer (DeiT) encoder, within a Text Recognition Transformer (TROCR) framework. A vision transformer (ViT) model which is acted as encoder, obtaining the characteristics from handwritten Hindi input images. In the interim, a fine-tuned language model is acted as decoder on Hindi text, guaranteeing language-specific contextual indulgent. The proposed model is aimed to achieve better accuracy by compositing the mentioned models for

**Corresponding author*: rampriya.rs@vit.ac.in

T. S. Arun Samuel, L. Jerart Julus, P. Kanimozhi, T. Ananth Kumar and S. Balamurugan (eds.) Composite Artificial Intelligence: Fundamentals, Challenges, and Applications, (65–84) © 2026 Scrivener Publishing LLC

recognizing and transcribing handwritten Hindi texts. The experimental results validate the efficiency of this hybrid method and shows substantial progressions in recognizing complex handwritten Hindi scripts. [Code availability: https://huggingface.co/sabaridsnfuji/Hindi_Offline_Handwritten_OCR]

***Keywords*:** Composite artificial intelligence, handwritten hindi recognition, devanagari script digitization, vision transformer (ViT), HindRoBERTa, text recognition transformer (TROCR), character error rate (CER)/word error rate (WER), multilingual handwriting digitization

3.1 Introduction

Handwriting digitization has evolved as a cornerstone of the latest technological developments by integrating conventional practices with present digital resolutions. The forefront of this evolution is the Hindi Handwritten Intelligent Word Recognition (HHIWR) system which is a novel invention for converting handwritten Hindi characters into digital forms. This system is not only increasing the accessibility but also plays a major role in protecting cultural heritage and enhancing the productivity in sectors such as education and administration.

Handwritten text recognition is a method used to convert handwritten text into digital text automatically. Many applications like handwritten article digitization [1], postal automation [2], etc. are familiar research topic for decades. In [3], robust methods are introduced especially for small vocabulary size. Still, the area of handwritten Hindi text recognition has not been investigated much. In this work, the handwritten Hindi word recognition model is proposed with better accuracy. Nearly 662 million people around the world speak Hindi and it is the common Indic script [4]. Hindi is read from left to right. Different handwritten Hindi writings are given in Figure 3.1.

The most important benefit of HHIWR system is to provide support to visually challenged persons. The system permits access through screen readers or assistive technologies *via* the conversion of handwritten text

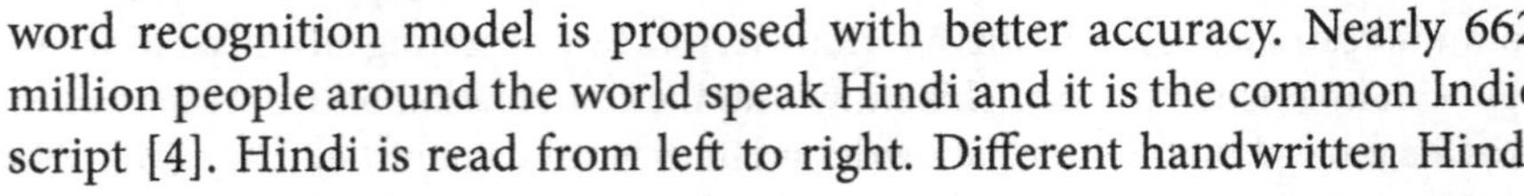

Figure 3.1 Examples of handwritten Hindi from modern writing.

into digital formats. This perspective is very important in a multilingual nation like India. Because, in India the handwritten works are used for communication and documentation by the majority of people. In addition, the HHIWR system plays a major role in the literacy writings and historical conservation in Hindi. The system can provide assurance of preserving rich cultural heritage of Hindi *via* digitization process. This kind of preservation will be helpful for education and research purposes.

Though many works have been done on Handwritten Text Recognition (HTR) for Latin- languages, HTR for Indian languages especially Hindi leads to challenge and diverse glitches. The Devanagari script is used to write Hindi in which it has various salient features of complexity. First, high level of character connectivity leads to complex ligatures that cannot be segmented easily. This is a vast challenge for algorithms that is used for character separation. Second, the existence of diacritical marks creates the process even more difficult for recognition. Proper recognition requires advance techniques for reliable proper identification. Third, Hindi script has a very large character set comprising of vowels, consonants, and combinations of two. Above all, it requires a robust model for HTR that clearly differentiate small visual differences and assigns right label to each character.

Moreover, human handwriting differs from person to person (see Figure 3.1); such type of natural variability also adds to the problem. That is, each person writing style differs from one another which is found by slant, pressure and speed. Based on factors such as paper used, tiredness and mood, there can be handwriting variations even with same author. These types of various challenges present in Hindi handwriting leads to considerable noise in the HTR process. Thus, it requires advance and robust deep learning model for molding and tolerating the above said variations.

Altogether, an efficient and accurate HTR for Hindi is a great prospective to transform many parts of society. To overcome the drawbacks of Devanagari script, two state-of-art artificial intelligence (AI) models are composited together. In which, one will act as encoder and the other will act as decoder. Vision Transformer (ViT) encoder and HindiRoBERTa decoder are the two AI models composite in a Text Recognition Transformer (TROCR) framework. ViT based encoder takes handwritten Hindi input images and identifies distinct features of scripts accurately. Meanwhile, the decoder uses a RoBERTa model trained on Hindi scripts to produce language specific context understanding [25]. This composition understands the linguistic context and provides more precious transcriptions of handwritten Hindi scripts.

3.2 Related Work

Basically, there are three methods used in handwritten Hindi word recognition system. In the first method, characters of a word image are divided into segments, and single symbol classifiers such as support vector machine (SVM) [7], artificial neural network (ANN) [5, 6] recognize individual characters. For instance, Roy *et al.* [8], applied image processing techniques such as form matching and morphological processing to partition images of words in the Indic language into three regions: bottom, middle, and higher. The middle zone was subsequently detected using Hidden Markov Models, while SVM were utilized for detecting the top and bottom zones. Eventually, results from all three zones were combined.

The second set of methods emphasizes building recognizers using segmentation-free methods that try to recognize the whole word or get an overall impression [9–11]. For instance, Shaw *et al.* [10], utilized image strips that were scanned by a sliding window from left to right using a chain-code directions histogram to extract feature vectors from word images. They proposed identifying handwritten Devanagari words employing a continuous density Hidden Markov Model (CDHMM). In an additional study, Shaw *et al.* [9], combined two feature vectors to present a unique method for comprehensive recognizing offline handwritten word images. However, because these approaches rely on predetermined lexicons, they fail in their capacity to identify a diverse lexicon.

The third group of techniques uses sequence modeling, which treats input and output as vector sequences and converts the handwritten text recognition problem into a sequence-to-sequence prediction challenge. This approach is commonly addressed by recurrent neural networks (RNN) [12, 13]. The goal of sequence-to-sequence models is to increase the likelihood that provided the input feature sequence, the output label would be predicted [14–16]. It solves the drawbacks of earlier approaches by enabling identification of variable-length lexicons and doing away with the requirement for explicit symbol segmentation. To recognize offline unconstrained wrote words by hand, for example, Garain *et al.* [9], suggested a recognition system that combines a connectionist temporal classification (CTC) layer with Bidirectional Long Short-Term Memory (BLSTM).

Adak *et al.* [14], created a handwritten text recognition system using a Convolutional Neural Network (CNN) in conjunction with LSTM and a CTC layer. Dutta *et al.* [15, 16] used a hybrid CNN-RNN model that build handwritten text recognizers for Telugu, Bengali, and Devanagari. A recognizer for eight Indic scripts—Bengali, Tamil, Malayalam, Kannada,

Gurumukhi, Odia, Gujarati, and Urdu—was developed by Santoshini *et al.* [17], utilizing a hybrid CNN-RNN and CTC layer in conjunction with a Spatial Transformer Network. A variety of data augmentations were also used to improve the recognizer's accuracy.

Transformer architectures were first created for natural language processing (NLP) problems and have since been adopted in deep learning [18]. These designs, in contrast to earlier techniques, determine the relationships between several elements in a sequence by using self-attention techniques. Because of their success in natural language processing, transformers have been extended into the field of vision, leading to the creation of Vision Transformers [19]. RNNs and CNNs are not required because these models divide images into a series of patches that are subsequently processed by the transformer. Originally created for Scene Text Recognition (STR), PARSeq [20], is a noteworthy development of the transformer architecture. This study improves handwritten recognition for Indic dialects using the PARSeq methodology.

3.3 Proposed Methodology

Figure 3.2 depicts an architecture for a handwritten text recognition system, the encoder is a ViT, while the decoder is a transformer based on HindRoBERTa. This model takes the best from Vision Transformers and strong text representation models to translate handwritten input images into equivalent text sequences. A handwritten Hindi word is given as input image. The input image is divided into small image patches which is a conversion mechanism belonging to ViT. After that, each image patch is flattened to form a vector. Now these flattened vectors are passed to patch embedding process which produce a higher-dimensional feature space. To maintain spatial structure of the image, patch embeddings are augmented with the positional embeddings. It ensures the special relationship between various regions of the image.

The proposed work uses the vision transformer model which acts as an encoder, and it is a pre-trained network model used for extracting features from handwritten images. The encoder passes the patch embedding to a series of transformer layers that contains multi-head attention and feed forward sublayers. These layers grab complex relationships and patterns present in the image patches. The encoder produces various feature vectors which is an abstract representation of each image patch. These feature vectors are denoted as H1, H2...H40 in the diagram, corresponding to the input patches.

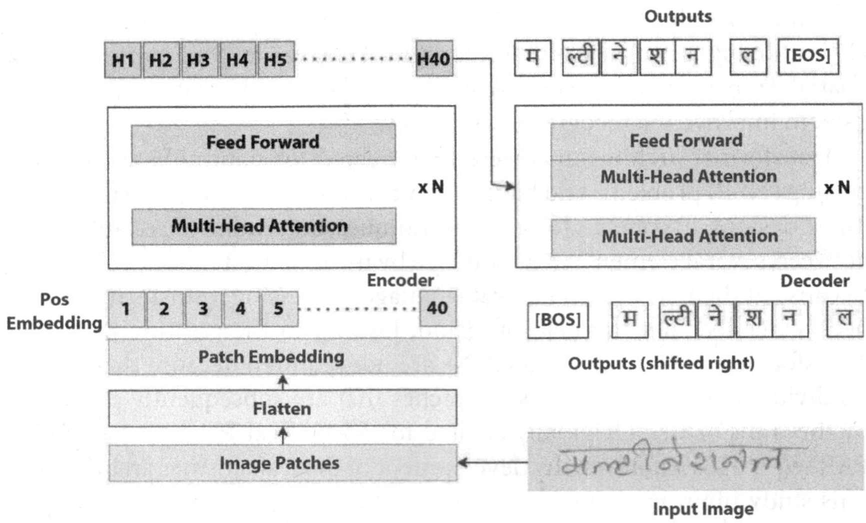

Figure 3.2 ViT-HindRoBERTa Architecture for Hindi Handwritten Intelligent Word Recognition (HHIWR) system.

The decoder, based on HindRoBERTa (a robustly optimized BERT pre-training approach), transforms the encoder's output features into a sequential text representation. The decoder takes two inputs: the encoded features from the ViT encoder and a sequence of tokens that represent the partially decoded output. The decoding process begins with a [BOS] (beginning of sequence) token, and the output tokens are shifted right during the decoding process to ensure autoregressive generation. The decoder applies self-attention to the output sequence for context modeling and cross-attention to the encoder's features to align text predictions with image features. It also includes feed-forward layers to refine the output representations further. The output tokens create a character sequence, ending with an [EOS] (sequence end) token. This sequence output is the text recognized from the handwritten input image.

The output of this structure is a sequence of characters that reproduces the input image's handwritten text. For instance, the system reads an image holding a word in Devanagari script and prints out the recognized text in sequence, producing one token at a time. This structure fits tasks such as handwritten text recognition in different languages and scripts. The synergy of ViT for extracting image features and HindRoBERTa for strong text decoding creates a formidable and versatile solution for visual information translation into text data.

3.3.1 Encoder - Vision Transformer

ViT is also a good image processor encoder, taking advantage of the transformer architecture originally designed to be deployed in natural language processing. As opposed to traditional CNNs, rather than presenting an image as an array of pixels, ViT presents it as a sequence of patches. It splits a given input image of dimension H×W×C into N P×P non-overlapping patches. These patches are transformed into 1D vectors, and then a learnable embedding matrix is used to project them linearly onto a lower-dimensional space. The resulting sequence of patch embeddings is augmented with a special class token; this retains spatial information by combining positional embeddings with total image information. The transformer encoder then receives the sequence. Figure 3.3 depicts the system architecture of vision transformer.

The ViT encoder consists of multiple layers of transformer blocks, each comprising a position-wise feed-forward networks (FFN) and the multi-head self-attention (MHSA) mechanism. MHSA mechanism computes attention scores by projecting the input sequence into query, key, and value matrices, then calculating the scaled dot-product attention. This allows the model to capture long-range dependencies and relationships between

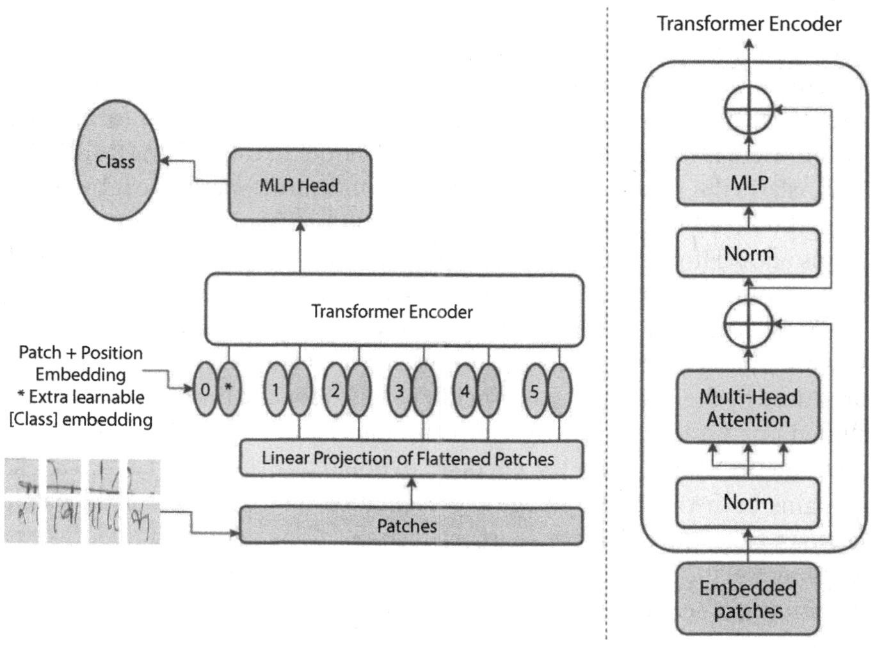

Figure 3.3 ViT (Vision Transformer) system architecture, derived from [24].

image patches. After being concatenated, the outputs from several attention heads are displayed again into the initial dimensional space. These outputs undergo additional processing by the FFN *via* two linear levels with a ReLU activation function, enabling complex transformations of the input features. Each block also incorporates layer normalization and residual connections, stabilizing the training process and enhancing gradient flow.

After passing through L transformer layers, the encoder produces a sequence of feature representations, where the class token summarizes global information about the input image, and the patch tokens capture localized features. This output can be passed to a decoder for tasks such as handwritten text recognition. ViT's ability to model global context through self-attention makes it particularly effective for complex image analysis tasks. It is also highly flexible, as it does not rely on fixed convolutional filters, and scalable, with pretrained models like ViT-Base-Patch16-224-in21k being fine-tuned for various downstream applications. These attributes make ViT a robust and versatile encoder for image-based tasks, as demonstrated in applications like handwritten text recognition using ViT-HindRoBERTa models.

3.3.2 Decoder –HindRoBERTa

An advanced transformer-based language model called HindRoBERTa (A Hindi Robustly Optimized BERT Pretraining Approach) works well as a decoder to provide textual outputs from encoded visual information. When used as a decoder in a multimodal model like ViT-HindRoBERTa, it translates the representations of visual inputs into coherent text by leveraging both self-attention and cross-attention mechanisms. These mechanisms allow HindRoBERTa to identify dependencies in the target text and map them well into the visual features delivered by the encoder.

Figure 3.4 shows the robustly optimized BERT pretraining architecture system. The decoder gets two main inputs: the visual feature embeddings produced by the Vision Transformer (ViT) encoder and the target sequence, shifted one position to the right during training to implement causal generation. The output from the encoder, denoted as $Z_{ViT} = [z_{cls}, z_1, z_2, \ldots z_N]$, contains both the global image representation (z_{cls}) and the local patch features (z_i). The decoder uses these features along with the target tokens to generate the output sequence step-by-step, beginning with a [BOS] (beginning of sequence) token and ending with an [EOS] (end of sequence) token.

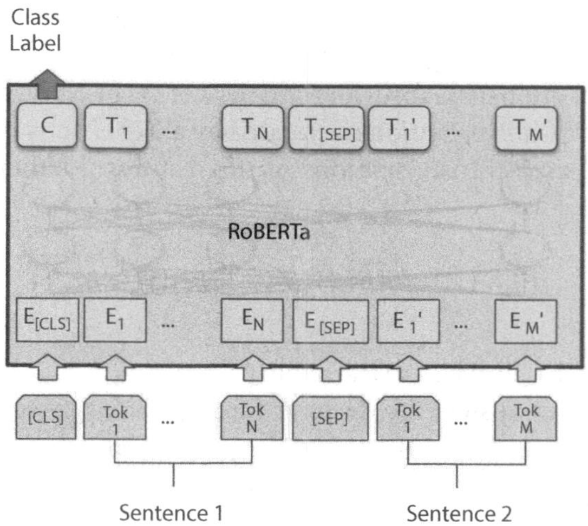

Figure 3.4 System architecture of HindRoBERTa, based on [26].

HindRoBERTa employs a **masked multi-head self-attention (MHSA)** mechanism to model relationships within the target sequence. This attention ensures that, at each decoding step, a token can only attend to previous tokens in the sequence. The attention scores are computed as:

$$A(Q,K,V) = S\left(\frac{QK^T}{\sqrt{D_k}} + M\right)V$$

Where A denotes attention, S means softmax, The target tokens are used to create the query, key, and value matrices Q, K, and V. A mask M stops future tokens from being attended to.

In addition to self-attention, the decoder uses **cross-attention** to integrate information from the visual features. For each token in the target sequence, the decoder computes attention over the encoder's output Z_{ViT}. The queries (Q) are derived from the target tokens; the encoder's outputs provide the values (V) and keys (K).

$$A(Q,K_{ViT},V_{ViT}) = S\left(\frac{QK_{ViT}^T}{\sqrt{D_k}}\right)V_{ViT}$$

This mechanism ensures that the decoder can align visual features with the textual output effectively. The outputs of the attention mechanisms are processed by position-wise feed-forward networks (FFNs). These networks apply two linear transformations separated by a ReLU activation function, enabling non-linear transformations of the features. Mathematically, the FFN is expressed as:

$$FFN(Z) = RELU(ZW_1 + b_1)W_2 + b_2,$$

where W1, W2, b1, and b2 are learnable parameters.

At every decoding step, the decoder forecasts the subsequent token by applying the softmax (sm) function to the output. Probability of the subsequent token can be considered as shown below:

$$P(y_t|Z_{ViT}) = sm(h_t, W_{out})$$

where, h_t represents the current hidden state of the decoder at time step t and W_{out} records the output vocabulary to hidden state.

During the training, the proposed model exploits cross entropy loss between ground truth and output tokens which is described in the equation below:

$$L = -\sum_{t=1}^{T} \log(P(y_t|y < t, Z_{ViT}))$$

where, T denotes the length of the target sequence. This loss ensures whether the proposed model develops the accurate sequences by aligning the encoded features with output textuals.

As a whole, ViT-HindiRoBERTa architecture is allowing to process and generate correct Hindi text sequences by utilizing both linguistic and visual cues. It has the capacity to handle dependencies and composite information from various modalities. This became a significant part of ViT-HindiRoBERTa for recongnizing Hindi handwritten text in digital format.

3.4 Experimental Result and Analysis

This section provides the experimental procedure like dataset collection, implementation details, evaluation metrics used to measure the performance of the proposed work with other state-of-art methods and result analysis. The result analysis provides an in-depth explanation of the results, including trends, comparisons of the proposed method with baseline methods, and observations of the performance of the proposed system.

3.4.1 Experimental Data

Only a small number of publicly available databases containing word or line-level labels are available for offline handwriting recognition using the Devanagari script. In Table 3.1, all publicly available offline handwriting datasets across all Indic scripts are included. Here, datasets with no ground truth data or just isolated segmented characters have been disregarded. It is evident that Indic datasets are far smaller than English datasets such as IAM [21], which contain over 100,000 annotated word pictures and 600 writers. A small number of Devanagari databases either exclusively include images from a limited specialized vocabulary, such as legal words [23], or employ a bespoke character annotation technique [22].

The IIIT-HWDev dataset has been utilized to get around these problems. The UTF-8-character encoding system, which is widely used on the

Table 3.1 Databases of handwritten documents for Indic scripts that are accessible. The modality used to create segmented labels for the dataset is referred to as the GT level in this context.

Dataset name	Language	#Writers	#Words	GT level
IIIT-HW-Dev	Devanagari	95k	12	Word
Tamil-DB [19]	Tamil	25k	50	Word
LAW [23]	Devanagari	27k	10	Word
RoyDB [22]	Devanagari Bangla	16k 17k	60 60	Word Word
CMATER [18]	Bangla	30k	40	Line
PBOK [17]	Kannada Oriya Bangla	29k 27k 21k	57 140 199	Page Page Page

internet, is used to annotate this information. The majority characters belong to this collection within UTF-8 Devanagari variety, giving a vocabulary comprising 9,540 Devanagari words. There are roughly an identical number of samples for every word in the lexicon in the database. There are eight fundamental unicode characters that make up every word in the dataset on average.

Twelve distinct people with varying ages and educational levels provided an overall of 95,381-word samples. The authors were allowed to write in their own way and using any pen they wanted. Forms with boxes were used to collect the data that were sufficiently spaced apart. A reference phrase image and each box included a place to write the word image that was presented. The collected data was digitized using a flatbed scanner and stored in JPEG format with 600 DPI colored resolution. The handwritten word pictures were extracted and labeled with the use of morphological techniques. Nevertheless, there was no manual correction of the segmentation. Figure 3.5 shows a sample of representative images from the collection.

To ensure that there is no writer intersection among the three groups, training, validation, and testing phases have been divided. There are around 70k, 12k, and 12k labeled word images in training, validation, and testing sets, which are coarsely considered as 70:15:15 ratio. The IIIT-HWDev dataset, which was presented in this study, will be openly accessible for scholarly research.

Figure 3.5 A selection of word images that belong to the IIIT-HW-Dev dataset. Various words authored by the same author are displayed in the first two rows. The identical word images written by various authors are displayed in the final two rows.

3.4.2 Implementation Details

The proposed framework was trained using a batch size of 254 on Nvidia GeForce GTX 1080 Ti GPUs used for over 160,000 iterations. Adam optimizer and a 1-cycle learning rate planner were used for pre-training. The whole pre-training and the majority of the trainings were conducted using the same parameters as the original BERT model: a patch size of 8×4, a permutation count of K=6, a dropout rate of 0.1, and a learning rate of 7e-4. The dataset informed the decision to limit the reasonable label length at 35 to account for important terms in subsequent inference. The amount of characters used for training varied by language, and the character set contained numerals, special symbols, and characters unique to each language.

There are two methods used to conduct training. The first method uses the dataset to train Devanagari scripts, using the SWA planner; a few iterations prior to training completion and the 1-cycle learning rate planner while on initial training. Transfer learning is used in the second method, where a hand written collection of Devanagari scripts is used to pre-train the model before it is trained on the dataset. After determining the least validation loss, three ideal model checkpoints were stored and evaluated on the dataset test set. According to the 70:15:15 ratio, the training, validation, and testing sets contain around 70k, 12k, and 12k labeled word images, respectively.

3.4.3 Evaluation Metrics

Word Error Rate (WER) processes each model's performance through separating the whole amount of words by the number of words that were improperly classified. When all of a word's characters are correctly predicted, the word is said to be correct; if not, it is said to be inaccurate. To compute the rate of errors at the character level, we also employed Character Error Rate (CER). The ratio of all errors to all forecasts is sometimes referred to as the error rate, or ER.

$$ERR = ES + ED + EI / EN$$

where the values for ES, ED, EI, and EN are the number of substitutions, deletions, insertions, and occurrences that belongs to the reference text, respectively.

The word level labels and images from the different datasets are used in all experiments, and the typical allocation intended for training, validation, and testing is followed. Compared to different models using the Character Error Rate (CER) and Word Error Rate (WER) measures—

$$CER = \sum \frac{\text{DistanceEdit (GT,PT)}}{\text{Characters}}$$

where GT stands for ground truth and PT for anticipated text and WER is well-defined as proportion of incorrectly transcribed words to all words.

3.4.4 Result Analysis

The character and word error rate values are the common measures for the HWR process, which are reported for word recognition in every experiment. The recognition outcomes of different CNNRNN hybrid architecture variations on the IIIT-HW-Dev dataset are displayed in Table 3.2. With exception of the final entry, all entries display outcomes in a lexicon-free deciphering configuration, meaning that deciphering is not limited to whichever specific collection of selected verses. Following are the lists of the different models along with their training methods:

- Mixed-SCNN-RNN: The IAM train set is pre-trained initially. It is then adjusted using a combination of the train set of IIIT-HW-Dev and generated data. It is finally optimized on the mentioned train set.
- Synth-SCNN-RNN: Prior to being fine-tuned on train set of IIIT-HW-Dev, the synthetic data is used to pre-train it.
- CNN-RNN: Train set of IIIT-HW-Dev is the sole one used for training.
- ViT-HindRoBERTa: Additionally, it has only been trained on train set of IIIT-HW-Dev.
- SCNN-BLSTM: Only the train set of IIIT-HW-Dev is used for training.

Table 3.2 shows that the ViT-HindRoBERTa module is successful for multi-writer handwriting recognition, since its inclusion significantly lowers WER. The synthetic data experiments provide empirical support for our fine-tuning approach. Using synthetic data is helpful in lowering WER, even though the cross-lingual transfer learning from English to Hindi only slightly lowers WER.

Table 3.2 Comparison of ViT-HindRoBERTa architectureword recognition performance on the IIIT-HW-DEV DATASET with other state of art models.

Model	CER	WER
CNN-RNN	43.56	16.23
SCNN-BLSTM	39.52	14.22
Synth-SCNN-RNN	29.21	12.12
Mixed-SCNN-RNN	15.27	6.21
ViT-HindRoBERTa	10.11	3.62

Figure 3.6 showcases examples of handwritten text in Devanagari script (Hindi) as input images and their corresponding predicted text outputs generated by the ViT-HindRoBERTa model. This visual representation highlights the model's capability to process handwritten text and accurately transcribe it into digital form. Each input image contains a unique handwritten word, which varies in complexity, writing style, and structure. Examples such as "समाप्ते" (Samāpte), "एटीवयियोर्टकि" (Aṭīviyōrṭik), and "हाल-फलिहाल" (Hāl-Philhāl) demonstrate the diversity of the input data. These variations in stroke thickness, spacing, and connectivity between characters present a challenge that the model seems to handle effectively.

The predicted words, as seen in the Figure 3.6, match the handwritten inputs with remarkable accuracy. The encoder ViT obtain features from

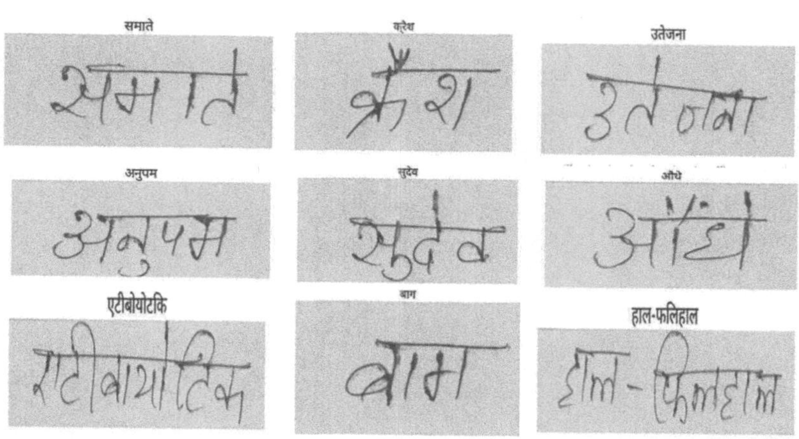

Figure 3.6 Visualisation of handwritten words are input images and digital words are the predicted words by ViT-HindRoBERTa model.

handwritten text and the decoder HindRoBERTa translates the obtained features into linguistic tokens. Thus, it produces digital text as output which is closely matched with the given handwritten Hindi input. Simple Hindi words like "बाग" (Bag) and "वाम" (Vam) are recognized easily. Also, complex Hindi word like "एटीवयिोरटकि" is recognized accurately, showing the robustness of the model. Additionally, the proposed model can consider the compound words and special characters. For instance, the word "हाल-फलिहाल," recognition proves the versatility of the proposed model.

Thus, the proposed work can be used as a valuable one across various applications such as scanning handwritten Hindi documents, searching and accessing archives of Hindi records. The proposed model can also be used in research and educational institutions to perform linguistic analysis, language learning, etc. Also, the proposed model has the ability to enhance accessibility for screen readers and other assistive technology.

Even with its outstanding performance, there's room for improvement and investigation. Experimenting with the model on a variety of handwriting styles, for instance, cursive or tilted penmanship, would assist in the assessment of its generalization skills. In the same way, determining its resistance to noisy inputs, like blurred or smudged handwriting, would enhance its applicability in realistic settings. Elaborating the model to identify handwritten text in other scripts used in India, like Bengali, Tamil, or Telugu, would further extend its uses and make it a powerful tool for multilingual handwritten text recognition.

At certain edit distance thresholds, the number of legal words that can be transformed from one valid word to another is presented for both datasets

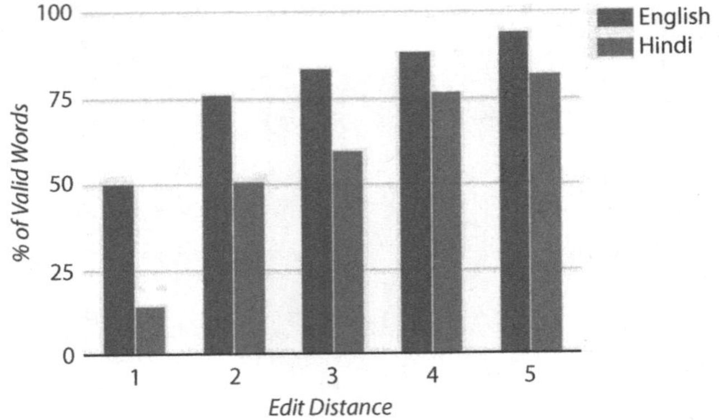

Figure 3.7 Proportion of Hindi and English words replaced with another acceptable word. Here, the English words are from the IAM dataset's lexicon, while the Hindi words are from the IIITHW-Dev dataset.

in Figure 3.7. It makes it plainly clear that Telugu words within our sample are more spread out than English words. The mean edit distance to convert a randomly picked valid words from the IAM database to other valid word is 6.14, whereas the IIIT-HW-Dev data set has an edit of 8.92.

3.5 Conclusion

Finally, the handwritten text recognition model based on ViT-HindRoBERTa showcases superior performance in transcribing handwritten Devanagari script accurately into digital format. Taking advantage of the Vision Transformer to identify visual features and HindRoBERTa for strong text generation, the model efficiently addresses handwriting style, complexity, and special character variations. Its precision in both simple and compound words makes it a good candidate as an effective tool for digitizing handwritings, enhancing access, and assisting linguistic research and education.

Yet, possibilities exist for further development and expansion. Upscaling the model's functionality to accept more heterogeneous handwriting styles, noisy data, and multiple scripts will further make it stronger and handier. Overall, this method is a significant breakthrough in handwritten text recognition., particularly for Hindi script-based languages, and promises promising practical prospects across multiple fields.

AI disclosure statement: The author acknowledges the use of AI-based tools for minor language editing or grammatical correction. However, all intellectual contributions, analyses, and conclusions presented in this chapter are entirely the author's own.

References

1. Rath, T.M. and Manmatha, R., Word spotting for historical documents, IJDAR, 2007.
2. Srihari, S.N. and Kuebert, E.J., Integration of handwritten address interpretation technology into the united states postal service remote computer reader system, in: DAS, 1997.
3. Milewski, R.J., Govindaraju, V., Bhardwaj, A., Automatic recognition of handwritten medical forms for search engines, IJDAR, 2009.
4. Usharani, S., Manju Bala, P., Rajmohan, R., Ananth Kumar, T., Pavithra, M., Data visualization for healthcare, in: *Intelligent Interactive Multimedia Systems for E-Healthcare Applications*, pp. 3–32, Apple Academic Press, 2022.

5. Labani, M., Moradi, P., Ahmadizar, F., Jalili, M., A novel multivariate filter method for feature selection in text classification problems. *Eng. Appl. Artif. Intell.*, 70, 25–37, 2018.
6. Alonso-Weber, J.M., Sesmero, M., Sanchis, A., Combining additive input noise annealing and pattern transformations for improved handwritten character recognition. *Expert Syst. Appl.*, 41, 18, 8180–8188, 2014.
7. Arora, S., Bhattacharjee, D., Nasipuri, M., Malik, L., Kundu, M., Basu, D.K., Performance comparison of svm and ann for handwritten devnagari character recognition. arXiv preprint arXiv:1006.5902, 2010.
8. Roy, P.P., Bhunia, A.K., Das, A., Dey, P., Pal, U., Hmm-based indic handwritten word recognition using zone segmentation. *Pattern Recognit.*, 60, 1057–1075, 2016.
9. Shaw, B., Bhattacharya, U., Parui, S.K., Combination of features for efficient recognition of offline handwritten devanagari words, in: *2014 14th International conference on frontiers in handwriting recognition*, IEEE, pp. 240–245, 2014.
10. Shaw, B., Parui, S.K., Shridhar, M., Offline handwritten devanagari word recognition: A holistic approach based on directional chain code feature and hmm, in: *2008 International Conference on Information Technology*, IEEE, pp. 203–208, 2008.
11. Kaur, H. and Kumar, M., On the recognition of offline handwritten word using holistic approach and adaboost methodology. *Multimed. Tools Appl.*, 80, 7, 11155–11175, 2021.
12. Graves, A., Liwicki, M., Fernández, S., Bertolami, R., Bunke, H., Schmidhuber, J., A novel connectionist system for unconstrained handwriting recognition. *IEEE Trans. Pattern Anal. Mach. Intell.*, 31, 5, 855–868, 2008.
13. Sankaran, N., Neelappa, A., Jawahar, C., Devanagari text recognition: A transcription based formulation, in: *2013 12th International Conference on Document Analysis and Recognition*, IEEE, pp. 678–682, 2013.
14. Adak, C., Chaudhuri, B.B., Blumenstein, M., Offline cursive bengali word recognition using cnns with a recurrent model, in: *2016 15th International conference on frontiers in handwriting recognition (ICFHR)*, IEEE, pp. 429–434, 2016.
15. Dutta, K., Krishnan, P., Mathew, M., Jawahar, C., Towards accurate handwritten word recognition for hindi and bangla, in: *Computer Vision, Pattern Recognition, Image Processing, and Graphics: 6th National Conference, NCVPRIPG 2017*, Mandi, India, December 16-19, 2017, Springer, pp. 470–480, 2018, Revised Selected Papers 6.
16. Dutta, K., Krishnan, P., Mathew, M., Jawahar, C., Towards spotting and recognition of handwritten words in indic scripts, in: *2018 16th International Conference on Frontiers in Handwriting Recognition (ICFHR)*, IEEE, pp. 32–37, 2018.
17. Gongidi, S. and Jawahar, C., iiit-indic-hw-words: A dataset for indic handwritten text recognition, in: *Document Analysis and Recognition–ICDAR*

2021: 16th International Conference, Lausanne, Switzerland, September 5–10, 2021, Springer, pp. 444–459, 2021, Proceedings, Part IV 16.

18. Vaswani, A., Shazeer, N., Parmar, N., Uszkoreit, J., Jones, L., Gomez, A.N., Kaiser, L., Polosukhin, I., Attention is all you need. *Adv. Neural Inf. Process. Syst.*, 30, 2017.
19. Dosovitskiy, A., Beyer, L., Kolesnikov, A., Weissenborn, D., Zhai, X., Unterthiner, T., Dehghani, M., Minderer, M., Heigold, G., Gelly, S., *et al.*, An image is worth 16x16 words: Transformers for image recognition at scale. arXiv preprint arXiv:2010.11929, 2020.
20. Bautista, D. and Atienza, R., Scene text recognition with permuted autoregressive sequence models, in: *European conference on computer vision*, Springer, pp. 178–196, 2022.
21. John, A., Singh, S.K., Adimoolam, M., Ananth Kumar, T., Dynamic sorting and average skyline method for query processing in spatial-temporal data. *Int. J. Data Sci.*, 6, 1, 1–18, 2021.
22. Roy, P.P., Bhunia, A.K., Das, A., Dey, P., Pal, U., HMM-based indic handwritten word recognition using zone segmentation, PR, 2016.
23. Jayadevan, R., Kolhe, S.R., Patil, P.M., Pal, U., Database development and recognition of handwritten devanagari legal amount words, in: ICDAR, 2011.
24. Dosovitskiy, A., Beyer, L., Kolesnikov, A., Weissenborn, D., Zhai, X., Unterthiner, T., Dehghani, M., Minderer, M., Heigold, G., Gelly, S., *et al.*, An Image Is Worth 16x16 Words: Transformers for Image Recognition at Scale. arXiv 2020, arXiv:2010.11929.
25. Liu, Y., Ott, M., Goyal, N., Du, J., Joshi, M., Chen, D., Levy, O., Lewis, M., Zettlemoyer, L., Stoyanov, V., RoBERTa: A Robustly Optimized BERT Pretraining Approach. *ArXiv* abs/1907.11692, 2019.
26. Singh, S., RoBERTa: A Robustly Optimized BERT Pretraining Approach, 2023. https://www.labellerr.com/blog/roberta-a-robustly-optimized-bert-pretraining-approach/.

4

Machine Learning-Driven Optimization for Composite AI in Wireless Body Area Networks (WBAN)

Krishna Kumar M.[1]*, Pricilla Mary S.[2], James Nesaratnam R.[1] and Sharon Geege A.[2]

[1]*Department of Electronics and Communication, Grace College of Engineering, Mullakkadu, Thoothukudi, India*
[2]*Department of Electronics and Communication, National Engineering College, Kovilpatti, India*

Abstract

Nowadays, Wireless Body Area Networks (WBANs) are vital in healthcare—thanks to their ability to track patients' health status and handle medical data. Many have started to pay close attention to how Composite artificial intelligence (AI) is improving reliability, fighting against data theft, and boosting energy consumption in WBAN systems these days. This chapter investigates the helpfulness of machine learning-powered optimization techniques in overcoming challenges in WBANs, such as interference, changing channel fading, and few available sources of power. A combination of many AI models, including ML, DL, RL, and expert systems, in Composite AI allows this method to be adaptable for resolving these problems. The discussion sets out different ways to boost the performance of antennas, improve channel estimates, and enable flexible network arrangements. Besides, the role of models such as CNNs and RNNs in reducing signal loss and improving how efficiently data can be transmitted in healthcare is evaluated. Besides common AI methods, federated learning and neuro-symbolic AI are gaining fans because they nurture privacy and strong performance for distributed operations. This chapter looks into transfer learning and cross-domain learning, as they help the system respond appropriately to shifting patient groups and various conditions. Since artificial intelligence is gaining importance in medical systems,

**Corresponding author*: krishna18innet@gmail.com

T. S. Arun Samuel, L. Jerart Julus, P. Kanimozhi, T. Ananth Kumar and S. Balamurugan (eds.) Composite Artificial Intelligence: Fundamentals, Challenges, and Applications, (85–100) © 2026 Scrivener Publishing LLC

new cybersecure issues have appeared. Here, the chapter looks into AI-based ways of securing medical data, detecting any unusual activity, and forming federated security systems without compromising system speed. Overall, it considers future areas to explore, for example, quantum machine learning, bio-inspired computing, and edge AI, which would make WBAN systems in healthcare fully autonomous and capable of self-repairing.

Keywords: Data-driven optimization, today's neural networks, low-power computing systems, advanced encryption, AI methods that use quantum systems

4.1 Prelude

WBANs are gaining popularity in today's healthcare, since they provide continuous monitoring of patients' bodily functions using wearable and implanted sensors. The reason these technologies work well is that they support chronic illness care and help provide remote healthcare, especially since delivering data quickly and accurately is important for both doctors' decisions and patient recovery [1]. Besides, adding AI and Machine Learning to WBANs is boosting their data handling, detection of abnormalities, and optimization of their networks. The initial investigations on applying AI to wireless networks pointed out that they show more dependable data and faster responses [2]. Lately, there have been adjustments to AI in WBANs for tasks such as patient pre-screening, handling the power supply, and spotting unusual health conditions [3].

Today, WBANs are being managed advanced AI approaches that put together different methods such as ML, DL, RL, and expert systems, and this is a key progress [4]. A good example is how real-time analysis in healthcare uses digital twin models together with ML algorithms to represent the health of an individual patient [5]. At the same time, security methods based on AI, such as identifying anomalies and federated learning, seem capable of safeguarding important patient data without collecting and storing data at a single site [6]. The chapter gives a close look at these advancements, mainly focusing on ML-based optimizations that seek to enhance the performance, energy use, and dependability of antennas in WBAN. It discusses new areas, for example, using AI for security and managing networks, giving a true picture of the prospects and limits of contemporary expansion in cyber security. This chapter sees AI-based WBANs as part of the growing area of smart healthcare and highlights future topics to explore by analyzing the results of recent studies.

4.2 Architectural Framework of WBAN Integrated with Composite AI

Wireless Body Area Networks (WBANs) are vital for healthcare today, since they make it possible to regularly monitor patients' vital signs using sensor devices that can be placed anywhere in the body. Usually, a WBAN has a main node called the sink that merges the personal data, various wireless sensor nodes to obtain this information, and back-end units in the cloud or at the user's location [7].

AI has greatly improved the way WBAN infrastructures work. WBAN environments face many different challenges, and composite AI has already shown potential for solving them. This point is especially important to observe. The goal is to increase the flexibility of the network, reduce the energy it uses, boost the precision of information stored, and make the whole system more reliable.

A WBAN architecture that uses AI is made up of several phases that link together. Body temperature, pulse rate, and levels of activity are regularly observed by the sensors that are attached to the human body. All the data gathered is sent to a sink node that is close by. After gathering the information, the sink node sends it over to a cloud or edge-based data system.

Depending on the AI modules found in each phase, users can monitor their systems with better reliability and intelligence. It makes use of different AI approaches to carry out different functions [8]. It is easier to notice irregular findings and handle vast biomedical information utilizing machine learning models. The adoption of both Convolutional Neural Networks and Recurrent Neural Networks has shown great results when classifying complex signals such as ECG and EEG readings. By using Reinforcement Learning, the system can change its operational parameters to suit the present conditions in the network and the environment. Figure 4.1 showcases a hybrid AI integration for intelligent WBAN optimization.

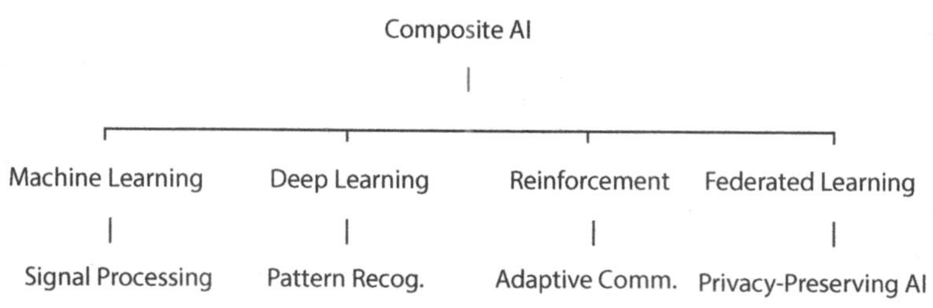

Figure 4.1 Hybrid AI integration for intelligent WBAN optimization.

AI frameworks within WBANs are steadily relying on techniques where data is not stored centrally to address issues with data privacy and security. They process data using each device's resources and yet make use of merged intelligence, cutting down the requirement to transmit important information through the internet. Since there are still difficulties involving computation and communication speed, these measures play a key role in protecting the system and its data. Components in WBAN architectures use several AI techniques to manage disturbed signals, decrease latency, and help the battery of wearables last longer. WBANs can identify issues when they occur, adjust to current needs, and use their resources efficiently, so they are easy to apply to managing healthcare around the clock

Table 4.1 Comparison of AI techniques in WBAN optimization.

AI technique	Application in WBAN	Advantages	Limitations
Machine Learning (ML)	Signal processing, anomaly detection, and patient monitoring	Efficient at recognizing patterns and processing large datasets	Requires labeled training data
Deep Learning (DL)	ECG/EEG classification, feature extraction, and predictive analytics	High accuracy in complex feature learning	Computationally expensive
Reinforcement Learning (RL)	Adaptive power control, dynamic resource allocation	Learns optimal policies for network efficiency	Requires large-scale real-time data
Federated Learning (FL)	Privacy-preserving AI models for WBAN devices	Decentralized learning ensures data privacy	High communication overhead
Neuro-Symbolic AI	AI-driven security mechanisms and logical reasoning	Enhances explainability of AI decisions	Still in early research stage

and at a distance [9]. Table 4.1 displays a comparison of AI techniques in WBAN optimization.

4.3 Machine Learning Models for WBAN Optimization

The reliability, intelligence, and success of Wireless Body Area Networks (WBANs) now mainly depend on machine learning. In WBANs, machine learning is used in streamlining systems' work and making predictions and discoveries of trends and patterns immediately. The kind of machine learning model chosen in a WBAN relies on the detailed issue the device is dealing with.

Many times, supervised learning is used to identify medical problems and note any changes in health. They are taught using labeled physiological data to spot unusual behaviors, for example irregular movements or different heartbeats. Such methods are very suitable for support vector machines (SVM) and decision tree- based models that can handle complex biomedical information. Whenever data is not or is little labeled, unsupervised learning provides useful alternatives [10].

Clustering methods may find out-of-sight patterns and link streams of data known to be alike, assisting in quick detection of potential health disorders before a label is used. They are important in continuous monitoring, since they allow the early detection of changes in patients, so medical staff can quickly act and help those under their care.

Reinforcement learning provides an additional opportunity for optimization, particularly in the management of network resources. WBANs frequently operate within constraints, including fluctuating wireless environments and restricted battery capacity. Reinforcement learning models can enhance decisions regarding energy usage, routing paths, and data transmission timing by allowing systems to learn optimal operational policies based on feedback from their environment. This adaptability is particularly advantageous in peripheral systems, as the quality of the signal can be unpredictable due to body movement and device positioning.

The integration of machine learning models into WBAN architectures presents specific challenges, despite these advantages. The complexity of algorithms that wearable and implantable devices can support may be restricted by their strict limitations on processing capacity and memory. Furthermore, it is imperative to prioritize the privacy and security of sensitive medical data during the training and operation of the model. Recent designs are increasingly incorporating lightweight models and decentralized learning approaches to resolve these issues, which involve local data processing on the device [11]. Figure 4.2 displays the machine learning's workflow for optimizing wireless body area networks.

In general, the integration of machine learning into WBAN systems has resulted in healthcare monitoring solutions that are more personalized,

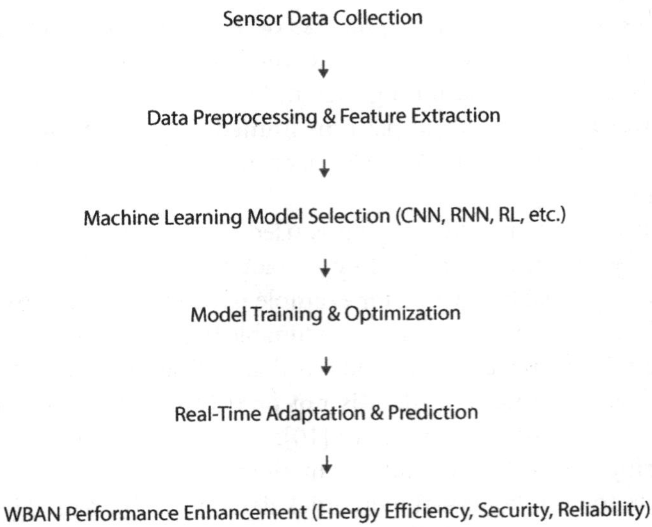

Figure 4.2 Machine learning workflow for optimizing wireless body area networks.

Table 4.2 Machine learning algorithms and their applications in WBAN.

ML algorithm	Application in WBAN	Advantages
Support Vector Machines (SVMs)	ECG signal classification	High accuracy, effective with small datasets
Random Forests	Multi-sensor activity recognition	Robust to noise, interpretable results
K-Means Clustering	Unsupervised anomaly detection	Efficient for large datasets
Recurrent Neural Networks (RNNs)	Predicting health trends (e.g., seizure detection)	Handles sequential data efficiently
Deep Q-Network (DQN)	Adaptive energy management	Self-learning and adaptable

efficient, and dependable. This proactive, patient-centered care is facilitated in both clinical and remote contexts by these intelligent networks, which continuously analyze physiological data and alter system parameters. Table 4.2 shows machine learning algorithms and their applications in WBAN.

4.4 Deep Learning for Signal Processing in WBAN

To provide effective patient care, WBANs count on continuous interpretation of signals obtained from the body, and this is where signal processing becomes very important. The previous way to do this job was to extract and classify features manually, but this took a lot of time and allowed for mistakes by the analyst. Even so, the arrival of deep learning has played a major role in upgrading the field by taking over learning features and making recognizing patterns more accurately [12].

Electrocardiograms (ECGs) and photoplethysmography waveforms (PPG) are categories of structured physiological signals for which convolutional neural networks (CNNs) are proven to work well among various artificial intelligence architectures in WBANs. They work exceptionally well at discovering the location of patterns in signals and, as a result, help accurately find blood oxygen changes or sudden variations in the heart's activity. Using CNNs, machines are capable of analyzing data in real time and making more accurate diagnoses than with normal approaches.

Recurrent neural networks (RNNs), particularly those that are designed for sequential data analysis, provide substantial benefits in the monitoring of physiological signals that exhibited temporal dependencies. RNNs are well-suited for the prognosis of imminent health events and the analysis of trends, as signals such as electroencephalograms (EEG) and continuous glucose measurements organically evolve over time. Their ability to retain contextual information from previous data points facilitates the identification of conditions such as abnormal glucose fluctuations or epileptic seizures. In addition to classification and prediction tasks, deep learning models also contribute to the improvement of signal quality in WBAN systems.

Autoencoder architectures, in particular, have shown potential for denoising and correcting signal distortions that are frequently caused by environmental interference or patient movement. Autoencoders can enhance the lucidity and reliability of the physiological information transmitted by restoring degraded data through the acquisition of compact and meaningful representations of input signals. This guarantees that healthcare providers obtain precise and actionable insights, regardless of the sensing conditions that are suboptimal [13].

Incorporating these models into implantable and peripheral devices poses practical obstacles, despite the evident benefits of deep learning. The complexity of models that can be deployed is restricted by high computational demands, memory limitations, and the necessity of low-latency processing. Consequently, developers frequently concentrate on neural network designs that are energy-efficient and lightweight, which are specifically designed for embedded systems.

Research continues to investigate methods for balancing model accuracy with device resource constraints, as the application of deep learning in WBANs continues to develop. It is anticipated that these developments will enhance the quality and dependability of continuous health monitoring, offering timely insights that facilitate proactive patient care in a diverse array of healthcare settings.

4.5 Security Challenges and AI-Based Solutions in WBAN

Because of the progress in WBANs, remote patient monitoring and healthcare are now more effective than ever. However, these advancements are linked with many security issues because patients' health information is still exchanged. Since WBANs use sensors that are everywhere and implantable, they are open to several cybercrimes like unauthorized data access, intercepting data, making counterfeit messages, and causing service disruption. Due to limited power in WBAN, it becomes challenging to apply straightforward security measures, so scientists need to look for better solutions [14].

Recently, AI has emerged as a good way to improve the security of WBANs. Using artificial intelligence, networks manage to respond to threats that are always evolving, unlike less flexible networks. In this case, models are able to identify unusual patterns that might mean someone is trying to break into the network by understanding the usual flow of data. Most of the time, these models are easy to change *via* machine learning and can detect threats as they appear and alter their thresholds depending on the situation. As a result, there is a drop in false alarms and threats are found easier.

The incorporation of AI-enhanced encryption mechanisms is a substantial improvement in the security of WBAN. These systems are capable of dynamically adjusting encryption parameters, including key length and refresh intervals, in response to real-time network activity and threat levels,

Table 4.3 Security threats in WBAN and AI-based mitigation.

Security threat	AI-based mitigation	Effectiveness
Data Eavesdropping	AI-powered encryption	High
Unauthorized Access	Biometric authentication (ECG/ Fingerprint-based)	Medium
Signal Jamming	RL-based frequency hopping	High
Malware Attacks	AI-driven anomaly detection	High

by integrating machine learning into key management practices. Furthermore, homomorphic encryption is acquiring popularity due to its capacity to facilitate computations on encrypted data without the necessity for decryption, thereby ensuring the privacy of data during processing.

Another promising remedy to privacy concerns in WBANs is Federated Learning (FL). In this method, machine learning models are collaboratively trained across multiple local WBAN nodes, with the exchange of only model parameters rather than actual patient data. This decentralized learning framework is particularly well-suited to healthcare applications, where it is imperative to maintain data confidentiality while simultaneously enabling accurate and responsive system behavior through collective model intelligence. Table 4.3 showcases the security threats in WBAN and AI-based mitigation.

Biometric authentication systems that are propelled by deep learning offer an additional layer of security for WBANs by facilitating continuous and non-intrusive user verification. These systems provide a more secure alternative to traditional password- or token-based methods by utilizing distinctive physiological signals, such as facial features or ECG patterns, to authenticate individuals. AI-driven solutions substantially diminish the probability of unauthorized access by utilizing their inherent biometric characteristics. Nevertheless, the implementation of AI for WBAN security is fraught with significant obstacles. The development of reliable and accurate models necessitates access to a variety of representative datasets, a task that is frequently challenging in healthcare contexts due to the stringent privacy regulations. Furthermore, the deployment of intricate AI algorithms may be impeded by the limitations of WBAN devices, including their limited processing capabilities and battery life. Therefore, the current research is concentrated on the development of AI models that are lightweight and the utilization of edge-computing techniques to facilitate real-time, efficient operation on devices with limited resources. In general, the integration of AI into WBAN security frameworks signifies a significant transition from static

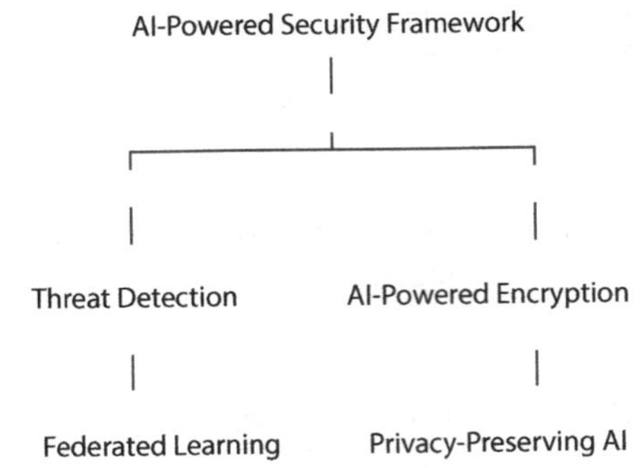

Figure 4.3 AI-powered security framework for protecting wireless body area networks.

protection mechanisms to intelligent, adaptive defense systems. These developments have the potential to create a healthcare monitoring infrastructure that is more resilient and privacy-conscious, and that is capable of addressing the changing nature of cybersecurity threats. Figure 4.3 holds AI-powered security framework for protecting wireless body area networks.

4.6 AI-Driven Antenna Optimization in WBANs

Data between implanted and wearable devices in WBANs is sent reliably—thanks to the presence of antennas. There is also a way that electromagnetic interference, movement, or a shortage of energy will lead to signal weakening and lower effective data transfer through communication. Thanks to its ability to adjust antenna performance in the present, machine learning (ML) finds an adaptable answer to these issues.

The way energy is used in a WBAN is close to being linked to how many sensor nodes are involved. It is clear from Figure 4.4 that using more sensor nodes makes the whole network consume more energy. It is noticeable that AI-enhanced WBANs need less energy than traditional WBANs. Adaptive transmission power control, dynamic duty cycling, and reinforcement learning-driven energy scheduling are mostly what have made this possible. Use of these methods makes it possible for organizations to manage energy consumption more smoothly and efficiently [14].

Looking at the results in Table 4.4, it's clear that traditional WBANs take 100 mW while AI-improved WBANs bring down the amount to 80 mW. When there are 20 nodes, the standard system requires 320 mW, but with AI-based methods, the network doesn't go over 210 mW, and this shows an energy saving of around 34%. Network efficiency is improved by using

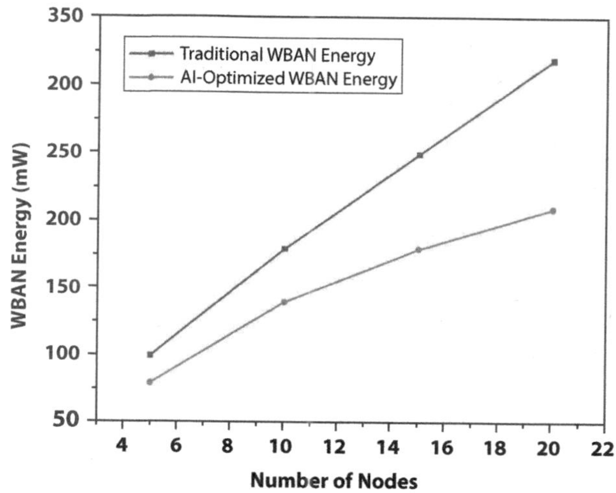

Figure 4.4 Energy consumption in WBANs with increasing nodes, comparing traditional and AI-optimized approaches.

Table 4.4 Energy consumption comparison in WBANs with and without AI optimization.

Number of nodes	Traditional WBAN energy (mW)	AI-optimized WBAN energy (mW)
5	100	80
10	180	140
15	250	180
20	320	210

AI tools to save unnecessary energy, keep networks working well, and optimize the speed of sending packets.

Application of AI to WBAN designs has allowed for great improvements in different basic metrics. Such advancements involve faster handling of security threats, less delay in communication, and a better signal that can be seen through the SNR levels. It is particularly important to have these modifications in healthcare applications because the data has to be transferred reliably and on time. Figure 4.5 shows AI-driven improvements in WBAN latency, SNR, and threat detection.

Decreasing the amount of time, it takes for data to be transmitted, is one of the most noticeable advantages when AI is introduced to WBANs.

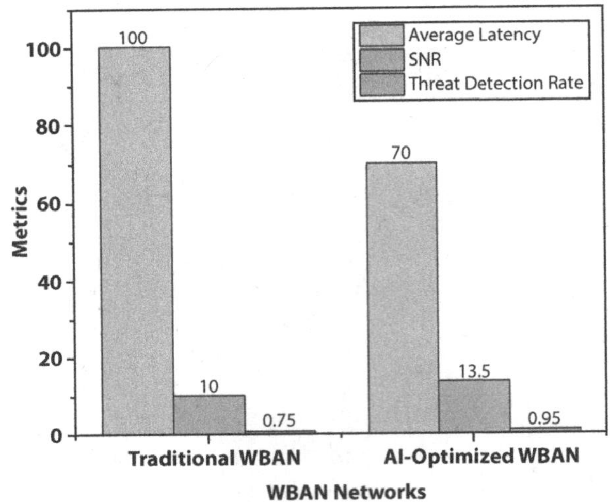

Figure 4.5 AI-driven improvements in WBAN latency, SNR, and threat detection.

Standard WBAN systems usually see delays caused by poor routing protocols, crowded networks, and static planning. Real-time monitoring of health problems can be difficult when there are delays, because such issues can put patients at risk. Meanwhile, AI-equipped WBANs change their routes and project network traffic patterns correctly. With the help of optimization techniques and machine learning, it has been shown that delay can be decreased from 100 to 70 milliseconds. As a result, the experience with the app has become significantly faster, such as checking real-time glucose and continuously reviewing one's ECG. Table 4.5 holds the data of AI-based reduction in WBAN data transmission latency.

AI is also very useful in ensuring that signals are clear and unbroken. WBAN antennas usually transmit information using a set beam pattern that does not adapt to body position, motion, or things around the body. This may decrease the strength of the signal, mostly in circumstances with a lot of interference. Techniques using AI, for example reinforcement learning for power control and deep learning for directing radio waves,

Table 4.5 AI-based reduction in WBAN data transmission latency.

Technique	Average latency (ms)
Traditional WBAN	100
AI-Optimized WBAN	70

Table 4.6 SNR improvement through AI-enabled antenna tuning.

Antenna type	SNR before AI (dB)	SNR after AI (dB)
Traditional Antenna	10	10
AI-Optimized Antenna	10	13.5

Table 4.7 Enhanced security threat detection in WBANs using AI.

Security technique	Threat detection rate (%)
Traditional Security	75%
AI-Driven Security	95%

can make adjustments on the fly according to the outside environment. That means, the SNR can improve a lot, going from 10 dB at the beginning all the way to 13.5 dB. Thus, communication is clearer and fewer mistakes happen when transferring data. Table 4.6 contains data of SNR improvement through AI-enabled antenna tuning.

AI also improves the safety of health data, as this is an important issue in any healthcare application. Conventional WBAN security protocols depend on definite rules, which sometimes makes them incapable of identifying new kinds of attacks. On the other hand, AI security relies on algorithms that learn all the time and adjust themselves to new dangers. They make use of context-aware anomaly classification, delegating threat analysis to federated learning, and using machine learning for spotting intrusions.

Being so, security issues are much easier for the system to detect and respond to over time, with the results proving to be 95% accurate or more, better than the 75% accuracy of legacy setups as shown in Table 4.7. For the safety of private and authentic patient records, such thorough protection is absolutely important. All in all, using AI in WBAN setups boosts the strength of healthcare monitoring and also improves communication and security in the system. Such improvements matter a lot as WBANs turn into self-sufficient and intelligent healthcare solutions.

4.7 Conclusion and Research Trajectories

As a result, the system can spot and handle security threats much more effectively, going from catching about 75% of them to more than 95% in

AI-enhanced situations. For ensuring the security of patient data, this level of protection is required during its transmission. All in all, using AI in WBAN not only boosts healthcare monitoring systems, but also optimizes the flow of information and protects it from threats. These advancements are very important because WBANs are getting more autonomous and intelligent over time. With the help of ML optimization, smart grids become much more flexible, efficient with energy, and able to transmit data without issues.

As a result, health professionals can get real-time predictions that assist in providing patient care. Both deep learning and reinforcement learning are used for better signal processing in the system and efficient allocation of resources when networks change. Future work in AI-driven WBANs aims to look at Quantum Machine Learning (QML) so that diagnostics can be completed quicker and more efficiently. Inspiration from natural mechanisms in AI systems leads to effective energy conservation at the sensor level, therefore, boosting battery life just as well as performance. Moreover, Edge AI can help make systems much quicker and less prone to delaying responses because data processing happens on edge gadgets.

Since these advanced AI systems are being used more in WBANs, it appears that entirely autonomous WBANs will be achievable in the future. Such changes will alter remote healthcare surveillance and also build WBANs into the main technologies of digital health in the future.

AI disclosure statement: The author acknowledges the use of AI-based tools for minor language editing or grammatical correction. However, all intellectual contributions, analyses, and conclusions presented in this chapter are entirely the author's own.

References

1. Wang, H. and Daneshmand, M., Artificial Intelligence (AI) Driven Wireless Body Area Networks, in: *Proceedings of the 2020 IEEE International Conference on Communications Workshops (ICC Workshops)*, pp. 1–6, 2020.
2. Wang, X., Han, Y., Zhang, C., Yang, K., Shen, X.(.S.)., Application of Machine Learning in Wireless Networks: Key Techniques and Open Issues. *IEEE Commun. Surv. Tutor.*, 21, 4, 3072–3108, 2019.
3. Wang, X., Zhang, C., Shen, X.(.S.)., Toward Intelligent Network Optimization in Wireless Networking: An Auto-Learning Framework. *IEEE Wirel. Commun.*, 26, 3, 76–83, 2019.

4. Peng, M., Fang, Y.(.M.)., Zhang, H., Artificial Neural Networks-Based Machine Learning for Wireless Networks: A Tutorial. *IEEE Commun. Surv. Tutor.*, 21, 4, 3039–3071, 2019.
5. El-Adwai, E., *et al.*, Wireless Body Area Sensor Networks Based Human Activity Recognition. Nature Scientific Reports, 2024.
6. Nawaz, A., *et al.*, A Novel Methodology for Patient Prescreening Using Wireless Body Area Networks. *J. Med. Artif. Intel.*, 7, 1–15, 2024.
7. Kalyanaram, S., *et al.*, AI-Enhanced Optimization Algorithm for Body Area Networks in Intelligent Wearable Patches for Elderly Women's Safety, in: *Wearable Devices, Surveillance Systems, and AI for Women's Wellbeing*, pp. 52–80, 2024.
8. Alsheikh, M.A., Niyato, D., Lin, S., Tan, H.P., Han, Z., A Survey on Machine Learning-Based Performance Improvement of Wireless Networks: PHY, MAC, and Network Layer. *Electronics*, 10, 3, 318, 2021.
9. Punj, R. and Kumar, R., Technological aspects of WBANs for health monitoring: a comprehensive review. *Wirel. Netw.*, 25, 1125–1157, 2019.
10. Suresh Kumar, K., Radha Mani, A.S., Ananth Kumar, T., Jalili, A., Gheisari, M., Malik, Y., Chen, H.-C., Moshayedi, A.J., Sentiment analysis of short texts using SVMs and VSMs-based multiclass semantic classification. *Appl. Artif. Intell.*, 38, 1, 2321555, 2024.
11. Taleb, H., Nasser, A., Andrieux, G., Charara, N., Motta Cruz, E., Wireless technologies, medical applications and future challenges in WBAN: A survey. *Wirel. Netw.*, 27, 8, 5271–5295, 2021.
12. Yaghoubi, M., Ahmed, K., Miao, Y., Wireless body area network (WBAN): A survey on architecture, technologies, energy consumption, and security challenges. *J. Sens. Actuator Netw.*, 11, 4, 67, 2022.
13. Albahri, O.S., Zaidan, A.A., Zaidan, B.B., Hashim, M., Albahri, A.S., Alsalem, M.A., Real-time remote health-monitoring Systems in a Medical Centre: A review of the provision of healthcare services-based body sensor information, open challenges and methodological aspects. *J. Med. Syst.*, 42, 1–47, 2018.
14. Filipe, L., Fdez-Riverola, F., Costa, N., Pereira, A., Wireless body area networks for healthcare applications: Protocol stack review. *Int. J. Distrib. Sens. Netw.*, 11, 10, 213705, 2015.

Part II

ADVANCED METHODS AND TECHNICAL CHALLENGES IN COMPOSITE AI

5

AI-Driven Hybrid Ant Colony and Golden Jackal Optimization Algorithm for Lung Disease Prediction and Classification

Karthikeyan A.[1*], Pradeep S.[1], Boorneush M.[1] and Dhivya P.[2]

[1]Department of Electronics and Communication Engineering, SNS College of Technology, Coimbatore, India
[2]Department of Electronics and Communication Engineering, Bannari Amman Institute of Technology, Sathyamangalam, Erode, Tamil Nadu, India

Abstract
The number of lung disease cases is rising daily, yet no country has yet developed an effective solution. When the disease gets inside the body, it infects the respiratory system. Early diagnosis and screening programs help with lung disease management, which lessens the burden on healthcare systems. Promising techniques have been presented by recent studies; they are applicable in the current pandemic scenario. In terms of genuine positive rate, they do not, however, yield results that are satisfactory. Better optimization techniques are also needed to increase precision rate while minimizing the time duration of prediction. To overcome this issue, the suggested method created a hybrid optimization algorithm – the Ant Colony Optimization Algorithm combined with the Golden Jackel Optimization Algorithm – which utilizes a lung image to forecast the severity of lung disease. The lung disease dataset is utilized as the initial input, and is pre-processed by dataset logic to identify the age of the patient, whether this is a male or a female affected with dataset history like fever, cough, and lung infection; this is mentioned in the different criteria. The best features are chosen using the proposed hybrid optimization algorithm (ACO+GJO). The implementation is experimented using MATLAB 2013A. The research is done on the suggested ACO+GJO system, and it shows that it can outperform existing systems such as filtering of test images, pre-processing of test images, segmentation and feature extraction,

**Corresponding author*: karthikeyan1686@gmail.com

T. S. Arun Samuel, L. Jerart Julus, P. Kanimozhi, T. Ananth Kumar and S. Balamurugan (eds.) Composite Artificial Intelligence: Fundamentals, Challenges, and Applications, (103–124) © 2026 Scrivener Publishing LLC

and classification of the test especially in terms of f-measure, recall, sensitivity, accuracy, and precision.

***Keywords*:** Ant colony optimization, golden jackal optimization, machine learning, lung disease, pre-processing, segmentation, classification, prediction

5.1 Introduction

Lung cancer is a dreadful disease. Most of the patients die, and it is proven in medical records. The International Agency for Research on Cancer (IARC) mentioned in the year 2022 that almost 2.5 million people recovered from lung cancer, and more than 1.8 million people died from the disease. Most of the lung cancer patients were chain tobacco smokers, and approximately 85% of all cases were identified by the World Health Organization (WHO).

The rapid progression and specific rates associated with lung cancer highlight the results and are needed for accuracy, early diagnosis, and effective treatment. Medical images mainly from X-ray and CT scan diagnoses of early detection of lung infection, add to lung cancer, pneumonia, and emphysema fibrosis, are updated through computational techniques like image enhancement, segmentation, and feature extractions – the types of techniques to improve the robustness and measure the early observations of these infections.

The pre-processing methods enhance the quality and reduce the noise. The overall result can be obtained by using a statistical median filter. The non-linear image enhancement methods are used to observe the reduced noise through edge computational techniques in medical images for quality and clarity, and diagnosis is made using computer aided design.

For different enhancement parameters, we use a statistical median filter like PSNR and MSE to reconstruct the images through compression or denoising techniques, providing accurate accounts of infections that occur in diseases that are identified.

Segmentation is a critical stage in medical diagnosis. In this phase, we utilize Local Binary Active Contour Integration (LBACI) for better segmentation accuracy using the parameters Jacquard and Dice, which are used to measure the similarities between two sets or models, ensuring that the segmented image accurately represents the diseased area. The segmentation output accurately highlights abnormalities within the lungs, facilitating the differentiation between similar disease types and supporting feature extraction for further analysis. Feature extraction is essential for converting segmented image data into quantifiable attributes, which are then utilized for classification. After obtaining segmented images, this study applies hybrid classification techniques.

After obtaining segmented images, this study applies hybrid classification techniques, combining Golden Jackal Optimization (GJO) with Ant Colony Optimization (ACO), to classify the most important process for enabling efficient feature selection and improving classification accuracy. Classification algorithms are typically used to categorize data (e.g., medical images, patient symptoms) into disease classes (e.g., healthy, pneumonia, tuberculosis, etc.).

Golden Jackal Optimization (GJO) is a relatively new optimization algorithm inspired by the hunting strategies and social behavior of golden jackals, and Ant Colony Optimization (ACO) is an optimization algorithm inspired by ants' behavior to find optimal solutions; both categorize patient data for disease diagnosis. This hybrid methodology will improve accuracy, specificity, and sensitivity.

Lung disease is a leading cause of morbidity and mortality worldwide, affecting millions of people annually. The complexity of lung diseases, such as chronic obstructive pulmonary disease (COPD), lung cancer, pneumonia, and pulmonary fibrosis, poses significant challenges to timely diagnosis and effective treatment. Earlier results and predictions, as well as a set of result classifications, improve the outcomes of patient results, thereby reducing cost, improving health condition, and saving the life of the patient. Research communities focus on improving the diagnostic tool with Artificial Intelligence and Machine Learning techniques by using advanced datasets and algorithms in identifying patient result patterns to produce accurate diagnosis predictions.

In the past few years, using powerful tools and metaheuristic algorithms has emerged to solve the computational problems in various domains like healthcare. New approaches are utilized – Ant Colony Optimization (ACO) is inspired by the behavior of ants and has the ability to find out computational optimal solutions to carry out exploration and research contributions through data mining, feature selection, and the scheduling allocation process; Golden Jack Optimization (GJO) is inspired by hunting behavior and uses relative datasets of convergence capability and dynamic performance through multidimensional role distribution among GJO mechanisms that sort out the computational complexity of real problems.

This research carries a supervised algorithm that optimizes the impacts of Ant Colony Optimization and Golden Jackal Optimization to specify the location to complete the task of lung disease infection diagnosis and methods. The primary exploration technique of this hybrid approach is to pull up the performance of capabilities of algorithms. ACO improves the search optimization to analyze Regions of Interest (ROI). In a few scenarios, results are stuck with premature convergence or get stuck in local search and local optima. By implementing these two approaches, our proposed supervised algorithm aims to achieve faster convergence, enhanced accuracy, improved robustness, and accurate prediction to identify the detection of different complex datasets to predict lung diseases.

After the implementation of different complex datasets proven by clinical imaging, the graphical result datasets are matched with lung diseases. Algorithm techniques identifying the feature classification and accurate decision making are combined to build an ACO and GJO-supervised model, enabling high-dimensional performance to reduce noise observed with medical data; both algorithms establish the accuracy, sensitivity, computational efficiency, and specificity of results.

Furthermore, the integration of ACO–GJO provides a hybrid architecture framework designed with computational intelligence and analytical intelligence proved by clinical observations to predict accurate results. It is an optimal goal to predict lung diseases in different patterned interventions.

5.2 Literature Survey

Nowadays, lung disease is a major illness for patients. In fact, the lack of early diagnosis and observations has markedly increased patient suffering and survival difficulty and decreased patient reliability rates. A technique called Machine Intelligence (MIFH) is designed to observe lung disease, according to Gupta, A. *et al.* [1]. By analyzing the improved given framework of MIFH, improved observations can be made for both healthy individuals and lung patients. In order to categorize cases, predict lung diseases, and predict healthy people, MIFH uses the properties of FAMD to train machine learning predictive models. Gudadhe, M. *et al.* [2] provided evidence that MIFH was comparable to a variety of current baseline procedures. Based on performance standards and input predictive models, MIFH improves the system's efficacy and provides the most useful answer, with feasibility taken into consideration, which can aid doctors and radiologists in properly diagnosing lung patients.

In Kavitha, M. *et al.* [3] and K Sivanantham *et al.* [19], the hybrid model achieved a lung disease prediction accuracy of 88.7% based on test results.

In the interface, we integrated a Decision Tree Algorithm and Random Forest methods to predict lung conditions using the user's input parameters.

M. Abdar *et al.* [4] introduce data mining algorithms that can predict a patient's likelihood of contracting a lung condition. In terms of model accuracy, KNN, SVM, and neural networks outperformed KNN, SVM, and C5.0 Decision tree, and varied clinical practitioners can readily understand their recommendations.

C. BouRjeily *et al.* [5] describe the procedure for sorting through a large amount of data to discover intriguing patterns and crucial information. The significance of random prediction evaluated various factors in predictions, including the ranges of its occurrences. The system looked at the transactions over time to find recurrent patterns in the product sequences, according to Kalimuthu, S. *et al.* [17]. It is crucial to establish a positioning for sequential mining in this industry, given that time dimension is a crucial component to consider while analyzing medical data.

U. Shafique *et al.* [6] conclude that Naive Bayes classification algorithms are the most accurate, with an accuracy of 82.914%. Data mining may effectively and correctly predict lung illness. The results of our thesis could be used as a tool to help establish more precise lung disease diagnosis. M. Shouman *et al.* [7] offer a strategy for methodically closing these gaps in lung disease diagnosis and treatment, and they investigate whether utilizing data mining techniques to analyze treatment data might yield results that are as reliable as those discovered while diagnosing lung disease patients. A few uses of data mining in the medical industry are listed by Barati, E., *et al.* [8]. We have focused on using data mining to treat skin diseases for the past 20 years. A difficult dermatological problem is erythemato-squamous disease diagnosis. It has been looked into in several studies that used dermatology databases. In this document, we've collected several of them and examined their results.

The SVM algorithm outperformed ANN for having stronger power and sensitivity, according to Ayatollahi, H *et al.* [9]. In general, it provided a more precise classification for CAD prediction. Khourdifi, Y. *et al.* [10] achieve additional data mining strategies suggested to raise the illness prediction's positive predictive value. They describe the steps to get accuracy scores of 99.65% with KNN and 99.6% with RF for the FCBF, PSO, and ACO optimized models. Shang, J. *et al.* [11] analyze the pros and cons of the pertinent techniques, provide guidance on how to apply them, and present several viewpoints on the potential future applications for epistasis detection techniques in Kalimuthu, S. [18].

The formula mentioned previously has positive outcomes for this reason, as demonstrated by Hsu, C. H *et al.* [12], who found that the average forecast accuracy was 94 and 95.4%, respectively. A different strategy is to identify the lung tumor using a decision tree and BPNN computation, which capitulates a successful result as contrasted to early calculations. Ma, Ling, *et al.* [13] show the trailed dataset of lung CT images where our predicted strategy consistently increased identification performance when compared to single classifiers. Irianto, B. G. *et al.* [14] talked about how to help users recognize patterns in lung illness and create a GUI application with form training and testing for image processing. Up to 80% of the time, the training images of a healthy lung and a lung cancer are accurate. The total accuracy of the results is 80%. G. Kaur *et al.* [15] explain that BPNN models outperform hybridization only. The accuracy of the suggested method is 99%, 98% when neural networks are used, and 89% when SVM is used. According to Prajapati, K. *et al.* [16], when used in conjunction with an efficient feature extraction method and a principal components analysis, the classifier performs rather well across all performance measures.

Given the generality of severe infection in lung diseases, including chronic obstructive pulmonary disease (COPD), an accurate diagnostic powerful tool approaches the classified infections like lung cancer and pulmonary infections, focusing on artificial intelligence (AI) optimization techniques. A new local search method is implemented with the help of metaheuristic exploration to observe several studies and clinical approaches in medical domains, especially for lung diseases prediction. ACO and GJO observations improved diagnostic precision.

ACO earlier diagnosis aims to find out optimal phenomenal performance based on research contributions, to observe large-scale optimization methods, to sort out feature selection datasets, to eliminate irrelevant and redundant attributes, to reduce computational complexity problems, and to provide enhanced inter-ability in healthcare data.

Golden Jackal Optimization (GJO) is a balanced trade-off between metaheuristic algorithms and inspires the cooperative traverse complex computational traditional algorithms to perform the different optimization models. Existing methods using design allocation and predictive performance recognized by AI models are induced directly with GJO applications to improve their convergence capabilities to improve computation optimization.

5.3 System Design

This research work focuses on a proposed hybrid algorithm and improved observation techniques to predict lung diseases. In this suggested system, an image processing technique is used for lung disease prediction. The research work aims to explore efficient and reliable lung image dataset; performance is improved by pre-processing, segmenting, extracting features, choosing features, and classifying features with optimization techniques. The data of lung images are obtained from "Kaggle and UCI web sources" for training and testing of classification.

Lung Nodules: 163 patients had lung nodules visible on their CT scans. We made use of nodular photos in two dimensions. Each nodule was histologically confirmed. Squamous cell carcinomas and adenocarcinomas were present in the malignant nodules. Hamartomas, tuberculomas, and organizing pneumonias were seen in the benign nodules. Figure 5.1 below explains the flow of the proposed system.

Preliminary processing: The first step of the proposed approach for lung disease prediction is pre-processing. It is a technique for turning sets of dirty data into collections of clean data. Every time data are collected from several sources; they are never processed, which makes analysis impossible. The raw file is then transformed into a readable format so that computers can comprehend it and employees across the organization may use it.

Before images can be employed for a model with trained dataset and inference, they must undergo pre-processing. This includes adjustments in size, color, and orientation, among other modifications. Additionally, effective model pre-processing can help reduce training time and accelerate

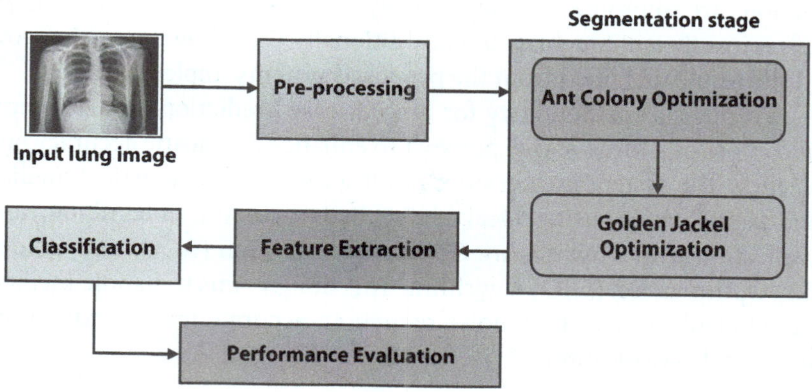

Figure 5.1 Schematic work flow of the proposed system.

inference, leading to improved overall performance. Here, the pre-processing is done by using the median filter.

Median Filter: In this proposed system for pre-processing, the median filter is used. To reduce the input noise, the image produced from the input side is sent to the pre-processing stage. It is used to reduce image noise in a manner akin to a mean filter. It performs a better job of keeping important details in the image than the mean filter does, though. The median filter is superior to the mean filter in two key ways:

- In comparison to the mean, it offers a more accurate approximation. The median won't be significantly affected by an unrepresentative pixel from a single neighborhood.
- Since the median must precisely reflect the value of one of the nearby pixels, it does not produce additional, irrational pixel values.

Feature Extraction: To make the input vector smaller, feature extraction is done. The input data must be reduced to a more manageable set of features before being represented. During the feature extraction process, fewer resources are required to effectively represent a substantial amount of data. It means converting the current features into a smaller, two-dimensional space. Feature extraction aims to decrease the original data set.

Image Classification: Image classification is a complicated process that depends on various factors. Here, some of the tactics, problems, and more picture order potential are discussed. Modern categorization techniques that are used to increase characterization accuracy will be the main focus. The raw pixel data can be influenced by factors such as the object's position, the background, ambient lighting, camera angle, and focus. These variations are so pronounced that simply averaging the RGB values of the pixels is insufficient for correction. Additionally, the following session covered the results obtained from the proposed system's implementation.

The proposed methodology for lung disease prediction and classification comprises a three-stage approach to enhance diagnostic accuracy and efficiency. The system includes image filtration using a statistical median filter, segmentation using local binary active contour integration, and classification with a hybrid Ant Colony Optimization (ACO) and Golden Jackal Optimization (GJO) algorithm. This design aims to handle medical imaging challenges such as noise reduction, accurate feature extraction, and optimal classification.

5.3.1 Image Filtration Using a Statistical Median Filter

The initial stage of the image extraction removes redundant noise from observed medical images to enhance the pre-processing methods and techniques. Retrieved medical image noises are reduced at subsequent conditions to monitor equipment conditions and patient movement. The median filter reduces noises and edging techniques.

5.3.2 Statistical Median Filter Process

- Each pixel in the image is considered, along with its neighboring pixels within a defined window size (e.g., 3x3, 5x5).
- The picture element values in this window are divided in ascending order.
- The average value of these divided pixels replaces the central pixel value.
- This process is repeated for all pixels in the image, resulting in a smoothed output that retains critical edges necessary for accurate segmentation and feature extraction.

The statistical average filter is particularly effective in reducing impulsive distortion, such as salt-and-pepper noise, without blurring critical boundaries that are essential for accurate segmentation.

5.3.3 Image Segmentation Using Local Binary Active Contour Integration

After noise reduction, image segmentation is performed using local binary active contour (LBAC) integration. This segmentation technique is chosen for its capability to accurately delineate complex and irregular boundaries in medical images, which is crucial for identifying regions of interest (ROIs) associated with lung diseases.

Local Binary Active Contour Approach:

- The algorithm initializes a contour around the ROI (e.g., lung region or lesion).
- The contour evolves iteratively by minimizing an energy functional that depends on image gradients, intensity variations, and predefined constraints.
- Unlike global methods, the local approach focuses on region-specific features, allowing for more precise boundary

detection even in images with varying intensities and low contrast.

- o The LBAC approach integrates both local and global image information to handle challenging cases such as overlapping structures, noisy edges, and subtle disease patterns.

The segmentation output serves as the input for feature extraction and classification, providing accurate boundary delineation that is critical for accurate disease prediction.

5.3.4 Classification Using Hybrid ACO and GJO Optimization Algorithm

The core component of the proposed system is the classification stage, which utilizes a hybrid optimization algorithm integrated with Ant Colony Optimization (ACO) and Golden Jackal Optimization (GJO). This hybrid approach leverages the reinforcement of algorithms to optimize better selection and improve classification accuracy.

5.3.5 Ant Colony Optimization (ACO)

ACO is motivated by the behavior of ant optimization and uses pheromone trails to find optimal solutions. In this context, ACO optimizes feature selection by identifying the most relevant features for lung disease classification.

- **ACO Algorithm Steps:**
  1. **Initialization**: Initialize a contrived population of ants, each representing a potential solution (subset of features).
  2. **Pheromone Update**: Place pheromone trails on features, with initial values reflecting their importance.
  3. **Solution Construction**: Ants design results and solutions by probably selecting features based on pheromone concentration and a heuristic value (e.g., feature importance score).
  4. **Evaluation**: Evaluate each solution using a classification metric (e.g., accuracy, sensitivity).
  5. **Pheromone Evaporation and Update**: Apply pheromone evaporation to reduce the influence of older trails, and update trails based on the performance of each ant's solution.

6. **Iteration and Convergence**: Repeat until a conclusion criterion is met (e.g., maximum repetition or convergence threshold).

ACO adequately shortens and reinforces the feature space and elevates the interpretability of the model, but it may suffer from premature convergence or stagnation in local optima. This limitation is addressed through integration with GJO.

5.3.6 Golden Jackal Optimization (GJO)

GJO is inspired by the cause of stalking the hunting behavior of golden jackals, which promotes an equalized trade-off of both manipulation and implication in caused spaces. It aggregates ACO by enhancing universal search capabilities.

- **GJO Algorithm Steps**:

1. **Formalization**: Formalize the population of golden jackals, representing each subset of candidate to sort out the solutions (feature subsets).
2. **Proposition**: Investigate and employ adaptive search mechanisms to explore different regions of the problem space, reducing local entrapment.
3. **Manipulation**: Gradually focus on problems and necessary efforts to manipulate their potential with regions identified during the abuse.
4. **Implying**: Update problem subset positions based on cooperative hunting strategies, adjusting different directions using adaptive rules.

The integration of GJO into the hybrid framework enhances the search capabilities of ACO, allowing the combined algorithm to escape local optima and achieve better global convergence.

5.3.7 Hybrid ACO-GJO Algorithm for Classification

The hybrid algorithm integrates the strengths of ACO and GJO to optimize feature selection and classification. The workflow is as follows:

- **Step 1**: Perform initial feature selection using ACO to identify relevant features based on pheromone trails.

- **Step 2**: Refine feature selection using GJO's exploration and exploitation mechanisms to optimize the feature subset further.
- **Step 3**: Trained datasets are used for the classification model (e.g., SVM, Neural networks), using the optimized feature subset.
- **Step 4**: Metrics and performance are effective such as accuracy, sensitivity, and specificity.
- **Step 5**: Iterate until a satisfactory classification performance is achieved.

5.4 Results and Discussion

This research work is about the obtained result and outcome of the proposed system of lung prediction based on image processing techniques.

Input Image: A component of data preparation and stages of data pre-processing involve the processing performed on raw data to make it ready for subsequent data processing tasks. The first phase in the data

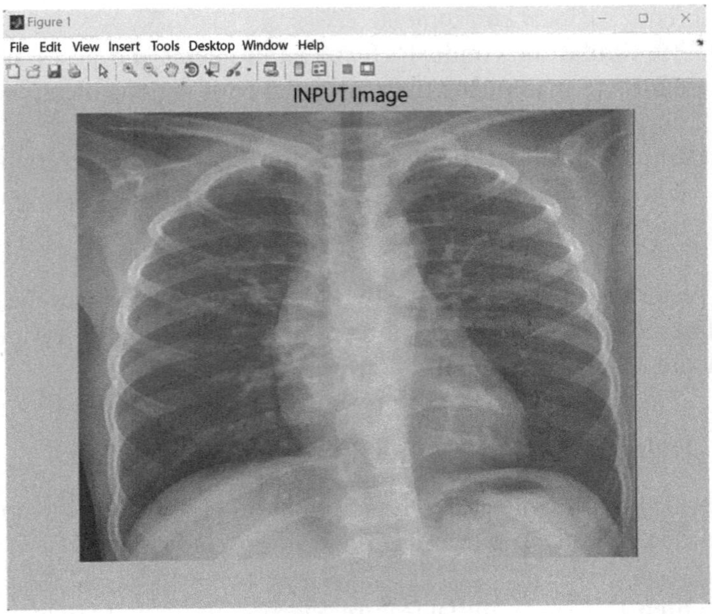

Figure 5.2 Input image for the proposed system.

mining process has historically been very important. The proposed system's input of a human lung image is shown in Figure 5.2.

Feature Extraction: The feature extraction process retains information from the original dataset while converting raw data into manageable numerical features. This approach generally yields better outcomes than using machine learning on the raw data directly. Based on Figure 5.2, the feature extraction is explained clearly. The feature-extracted result of our proposed system is collected and listed in Table 5.1 below.

Performance Evaluation: To calculate the efficacy of your trained ML models, performance evaluation measures are employed. This allows you to gauge how well the model is likely to perform on a previously unseen dataset. A confusion matrix provides a detailed summary of the performance of a classification method. Figure 5.3 shows the confusion matrix flow model and Figure 5.4 shows the confusion matrix of the proposed model.

True Positive (TP): Ground-based connecting box detections to perform well.
False Positive (FP): Detects the failing object and not to perform the operation.
False Negative (FN): Encircling the connected ground bounding boxes.

Table 5.1 Feature extraction result of extracted features.

Extracted Features											
0.4785	0.7751	52.1223	8.1348	0.1816	0.3582	1.3412	0.9464	0.9389	0.5325	26.9884	26.9086

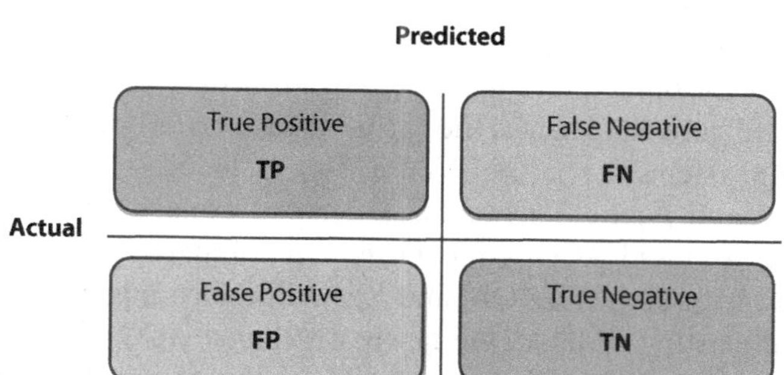

Figure 5.3 Confusion matrix flow model.

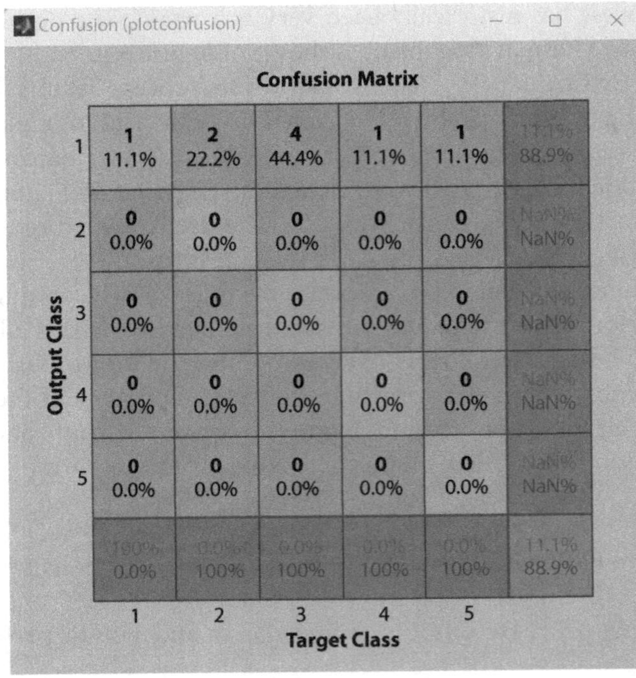

Figure 5.4 Confusion matrix of proposed system.

True Negative (TN): For object detection, a true negative (TN) result is meaningless since every image contains a large number of bounding boxes that are not supposed to be recognized.

5.4.1 Accuracy

The accuracy formula represents accuracy as a deviation from 100% based on the error rate. To calculate accuracy, we first need to determine the error rate, which is the observed value divided by the actual value, expressed as a percentage. Figure 5.5 displays the accuracy results for both the proposed and existing systems.

Table 5.2 and Figure 5.5 provide a detailed explanation of the accuracy of the proposed ACO+GJO strategy in comparison to the existing approaches, including DT, BOA, and RF. Outperforming all of the previously listed existing systems, the newly developed ACO+GJO algorithm for lung illness categorization achieves the greatest accuracy of 94.45%.

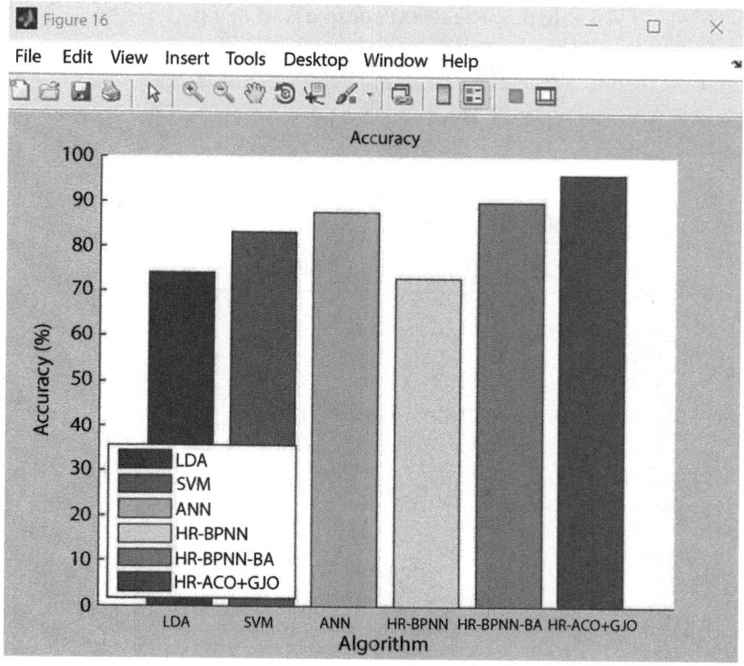

Figure 5.5 Accuracy output graph.

Table 5.2 Accuracy comparison result.

Algorithm	Accuracy (%)
Decision Tree	85.24
BOA	89.57
Random Forest	87.46
ACO+GJO	94.45

5.4.2 Precision

The degree of agreement between the various measures is indicated by the precision level. Ascertaining precision is possible by calculating the average deviation, which takes the mean of the inaccuracies in measurements.

The precision of the suggested approach ACO+GJO in relation to the current approaches such as, DT, BOA, RF is explained in detail in Table 5.3

Table 5.3 Precision comparison result.

Algorithm	Precision (%)
Decision Tree	84.47
BOA	86.26
Random Forest	87.38
ACO+GJO	92.66

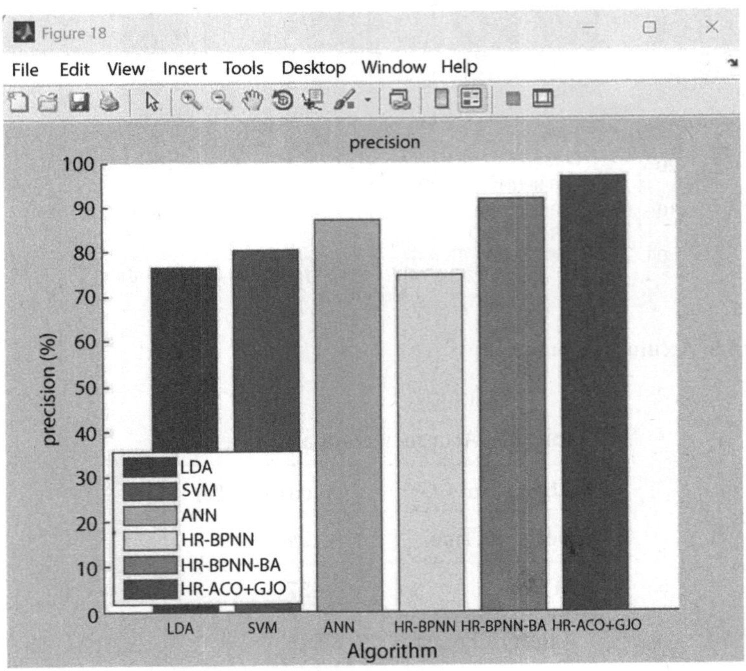

Figure 5.6 Precision output graph.

and the bar chart graph in Figure 5.6. The precision outcome for the newly constructed ACO+GJO algorithm for lung disease classification obtains the highest precision of 93.74%, and it outperforms all aforementioned existing systems.

5.4.3 Sensitivity

The sensitivity detects the ability ranges of the model to identify the positive cases out of all actual positive cases in the dataset.

The sensitivity of the suggested approach ACO+GJO in relation to the existing approaches such as, DT, BOA, RF is explained detail in the bar chart graph in Figure 5.7. The sensitivity outcome for the newly constructed ACO+GJO algorithm for lung disease classification obtains the highest sensitivity of 92.66%, and it outperforms all aforementioned existing systems.

In the healthcare industry, a number of ML-based image processing techniques, including Golden Jackel Optimization and Ant Colony

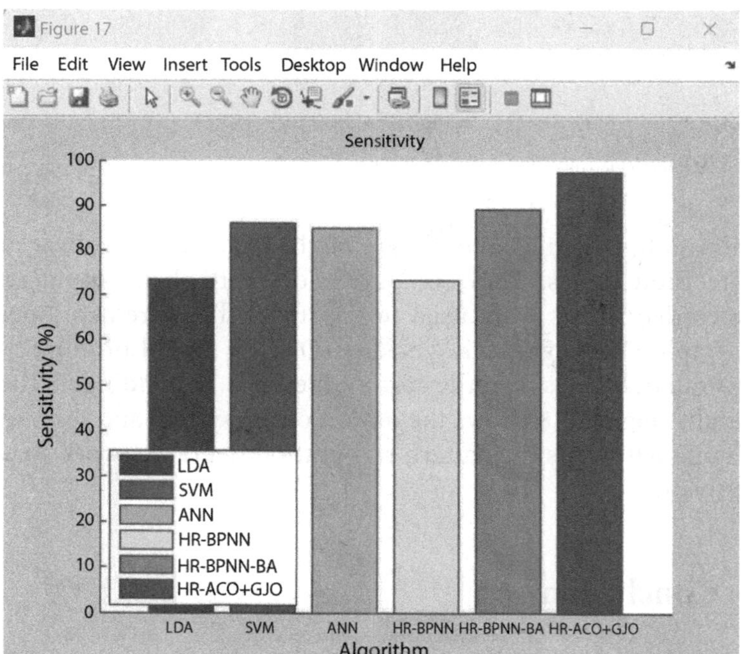

Figure 5.7 Sensitivity output graph.

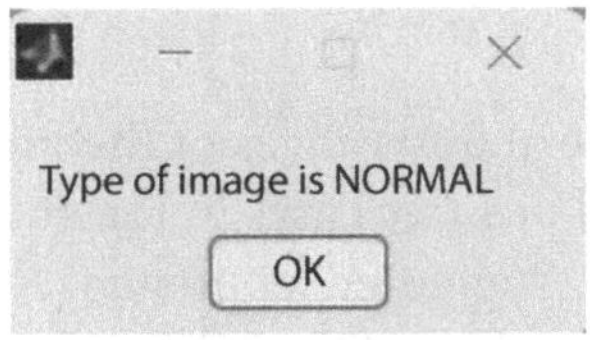

Figure 5.8 Disease type.

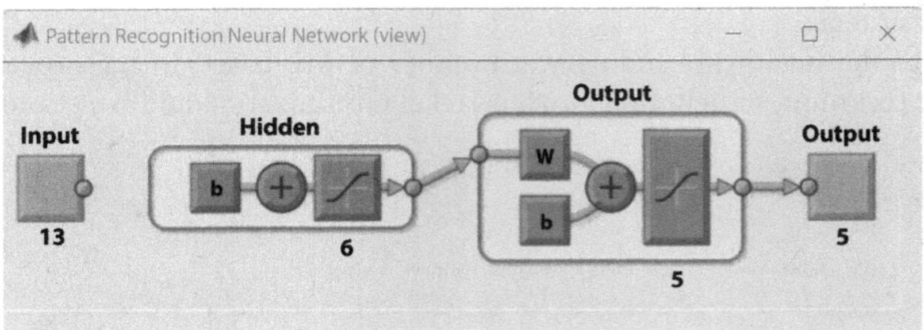

Figure 5.9 Pattern recognition neural network.

Optimization, are utilized to determine the f-measure, recall, accuracy, and precision values. They compute and record their output results. The recorded values were used to construct the aforementioned bar chart graph. Our suggested hybrid ACO+GJO model produces superior overall outcomes than the current methods, depending on the output results. Figure 5.8 shows the output of the system and disease type and Figure 5.9 shows the pattern recognition neural network structure respectively.

5.5 Conclusion

Lung diseases have been leading causes of death over a few years, underscoring the critical need for early identification everywhere. Pulmonologists will be able to diagnose these conditions more precisely with the use of computer-assisted lung disease forecasting tools. Eliminating key attributes that are no longer required improves their classification performance while significantly lowering classification expenses. Based on an optimization method inspired by the way certain animals search for food and their concept of collective life, the proposed ACO+GJO was developed.

The suggested strategy outperforms the present one with an f-measure of 92.16%, recall of 91.42%, accuracy of 94.45%, and precision of 93.74%.

5.6 Future Scope

In this research, we proposed a new approach to use lung input images for lung disease classification and prediction. Classifying various lung conditions utilizes more challenging datasets based on visual processing. Future study will concentrate on ML and DL methods in a medical healthcare environment. In terms of calculation, early detection, and very accurate diagnosis of lung disease, the suggested integrated ACO+GJO model is highly effective.

AI disclosure statement: The author acknowledges the use of AI-based tools for minor language editing or grammatical correction. However, all intellectual contributions, analyses, and conclusions presented in this chapter are entirely the author's own.

References

1. Gupta, A., Kumar, R., Arora, H.S., Raman, B., MIFH: A machine intelligence framework for lung disease diagnosis. *IEEE Access*, 8, 14659–14674, 2019.
2. Gudadhe, M., Wankhade, K., Dongre, S., Decision support system for lung disease based on support vector machine and artificial neural network, in: *2010 International Conference on Computer and Communication Technology (ICCCT)*, 2010, September, IEEE, pp. 741–745.
3. Kavitha, M., Gnaneswar, G., Dinesh, R., Sai, Y.R., Suraj, R.S., Lung disease prediction using hybrid machine learning model, in: *2021 6th International Conference on Inventive Computation Technologies (ICICT)*, 2021, January, IEEE, pp. 1329–1333.
4. Abdar, M., Kalhori, S.R.N., Sutikno, T., Subroto, I.M.I., Arji, G., Comparing Performance of Data Mining Algorithms in Prediction Lung Diseases. *Int. J. Electr. Comput. Eng.*, 5, 6, 2088–8708, 2015.
5. BouRjeily, C., Badr, G., Hajjarm El Hassani, A., Andres, E., Medical data mining for lung diseases and the future of sequential mining in medical field, in: *Machine Learning Paradigms*, pp. 71–99, Springer, Cham, 2019.

6. Shafique, U., Majeed, F., Qaiser, H., Mustafa, I.U., Data mining in healthcare for lung diseases. *Int. J. Innov. Appl. Stud.*, 10, 4, 1312, 2015.
7. Shouman, M., Turner, T., Stocker, R., Using data mining techniques in lung disease diagnosis and treatment, in: *2012 Japan-Egypt Conference on Electronics, Communications and Computers*, 2012, March, IEEE, pp. 173–177.
8. Barati, E., Saraee, M.H., Mohammadi, A., Adibi, N., Ahmadzadeh, M.R., A survey on utilization of data mining approaches for dermatological (skin) diseases prediction. *J. Sel. Areas Health Inf. (JSHI)*, 2, 3, 1–11, 2011.
9. Ayatollahi, H., Gholamhosseini, L., Salehi, M., Predicting coronary artery disease: a comparison between two data mining algorithms. *BMC Public Health*, 19, 1, 1–9, 2019.
10. Khourdifi, Y. and Bahaj, M., Lung disease prediction and classification using machine learning algorithms optimized by particle swarm optimization and ant colony optimization. *Int. J. Intell. Eng. Syst.*, 12, 1, 242–252, 2019.
11. Shang, J., Wang, X., Wu, X., Sun, Y., Ding, Q., Liu, J.X., Zhang, H., A review of ant colony optimization based methods for detecting epistatic interactions. *IEEE Access*, 7, 13497–13509, 2019.
12. Hsu, C.H., Manogaran, G., Panchatcharam, P., Vivekanandan, S., A new approach for prediction of lung carcinoma using back propagation neural network with decision tree classifiers, in: *2018 IEEE 8th International Symposium on Cloud and Service Computing (SC2)*, 2018, November, IEEE, pp. 111–115.
13. Ma, L., Liu, X., Song, L., Zhou, C., Zhao, X., Zhao, Y., A new classifier fusion method based on historical and on-line classification reliability for recognizing common CT imaging signs of lung diseases. *Comput. Med. Imaging Graphics*, 40, 39–48, 2015.
14. Irianto, B.G., Mak'ruf, M.R., Titisari, D., Identification of lung cancer using a back propagation neural network. *TELKOMNIKA Indones. J. Electr. Eng.*, 16, 1, 91–97, 2015.
15. Kaur, G. and Singh, H., An Intelligent System for Lung Cancer Diagnosis Using Fusion of Support Vector Machines and Back Propagation Neural Network. *Int. J. Sci. Res. (IJSR)*, 2013.
16. Prajapati, K., Patel, J., Pathak, K., Lung Diseases Using Deep Learning: A Review Paper. *Int. Res. J. Eng. Technol.*, 5, 2, 1694–16, 2018.
17. Kalimuthu, S., Naït-Abdesselam, F., Jaishankar, B., Multimedia Data Protection Using Hybridized Crystal Payload Algorithm With Chicken Swarm Optimization, in: *Multidisciplinary Approach to Modern Digital Steganography*, pp. 235–257, IGI Global, 2021.

18. Kalimuthu, S., Sentiment Analysis on Social Media for Emotional Prediction During LUNG Pandemic Using Efficient Machine Learning Approach, in: *Computational Intelligence and Healthcare Informatics*, p. 215, 2021.
19. Sivanantham, K., Kalaiarasi, I., Leena, B., Brain Tumor Classification Using Hybrid Artificial Neural Network with Chicken Swarm Optimization Algorithm in Digital Image Processing Application, in: *Advance Concepts of Image Processing and Pattern Recognition: Effective Solution for Global Challenges*, p. 91, 2022.

6

Removing Bias in Maritime Imagery: Advancing Gender Equality through Data-Driven Methods

Jordan Taylor[1] **and J. Padmapriya**[2*]

[1]*Project Harrison, California, USA*
[2]*AMET University, Chennai, India*

Abstract

The maritime industry exhibits a pronounced gender imbalance, with women comprising one to two percent of the global seafaring workforce. Despite international efforts to advance gender equality, underrepresentation persists. As a result, female seafarers face significant taxation as a result of unequal working conditions, namely social and psychological challenges at sea and ashore. Further, women encounter entry barriers such as limited access to decision-making roles, training programs, and a lack of female role models. Cultural norms and traditions in some countries can serve to exacerbate gender disparity by normalizing gender inequality. The United Nations 2030 Agenda for Sustainable Development is one of many global efforts to promote gender equality by creating fair workplaces. To enhance gender inclusivity, systemic policy reforms are required, including the introduction of mentorship programs and targeted recruitment initiatives, as advocated by organizations such as the International Maritime Organization. We posit that (1) innovative technologies such as computer vision can serve to quantify and visualize systemic challenges in gender equity and (2) that many existing vision models exhibit difficulty in identifying women that don personal protective equipment in a male-dominated environment. In this study, we collect images sourced from governmental and non-governmental organizations worldwide to reduce maritime-related gender bias through application of a convolutional neural network. The methodology involves three key steps: (1) preprocessing the images and converting them to visual embeddings, (2) analyzing these embeddings to detect

**Corresponding author*: padmapriya@ametuniv.ac.in

T. S. Arun Samuel, L. Jerart Julus, P. Kanimozhi, T. Ananth Kumar and S. Balamurugan (eds.) Composite Artificial Intelligence: Fundamentals, Challenges, and Applications, (125–150) © 2026 Scrivener Publishing LLC

patterns related to gender and roles, and (3) evaluating the results to identify potential biases. This approach is designed to avoid reliance on pre-trained or transfer models, ensuring that the analysis is tailored specifically to the maritime domain and avoids perpetuating biases present in generalist models. The United Nations emphasizes the significance of data-driven initiatives as effective instruments for the advancement of communities, industries, and nations. This research aims to facilitate a more sophisticated, data-driven comprehension of gender representation in the marine industry, thereby advancing the United Nations Sustainable Development Goal of fostering gender equality as an essential human right.

***Keywords*:** Gender equity, women workforce, computer vision, maritime industry, supply chain

6.1 Introduction

Nearly two million seafarers inhabit and operate maritime vessels. Seafarers, akin to medical professionals, are recognized as essential workers under European Union Regulation 2016/399 [1]. Due to the nature of their occupations, these workers remain invisible to the public and vulnerable to exploitation by shipowners and governments, as demonstrated during the Ukraine crisis and the early 2020s pandemic. Organizations such as the International Transport Workers' Federation and the International Maritime Organization exert considerable efforts to elevate awareness of seafarers and get public recognition and support for the essential responsibilities that mariners perform daily.

Nonetheless, female seafarers, constituting a small percentage of maritime professionals at sea, around 24,000 in total, encounter the greatest risk. Notwithstanding the initiatives of organizations like the International Women Seafarer's Foundation and the IMO's Women in Maritime Gender Program, women employed at sea face significant career obstacles and harassment. In 2023, Captain Jessica Ryals conducted a study that highlights the obstacles to gender equality, revealing structural and social constraints *via* interviews with women in the sector. Captain Ryals' study is significant as it is conducted by an active female senior officer, polls other female officers, and provides a clear and actionable framework for resolving gender imbalance.

As the maritime industry adopts swift technical breakthroughs, like artificial intelligence and autonomous vessel operations, experts are actively investigating whether these innovations will sustain existing gender inequities or generate new prospects for equity. These improvements additionally impact female marine professionals employed onshore in positions such as vessel operations, insurance, and ship brokerage. Women in port operations encounter substantial challenges, particularly as sustainability emerges as a pivotal concern in this sector [2]. Emerging AI technologies provide a systematic analysis of representation and obstacles.

Education and endorsement from shipping business leadership, coupled with enhanced rules to promote female empowerment, are essential for tackling gender imbalance in the marine sector. In a survey 195 of the 260 female seafarers surveyed reported experiencing some sort of bullying or harassment. Lyu and Li emphasize the significant underrepresentation of Chinese female sailors (0.13%), despite China ranking as the third-largest seafaring nationality overall. This difference is attributed to cultural impediments, including conventional perspectives on family responsibilities and childbearing, and advocates for educational and policy reforms to confront these biases [3]. Ojwala *et al.*, investigate hurdles and gender stereotypes in marine work in Kenya, employing surveys and interviews to reveal challenges such as restricted career advancement, widespread preconceptions, and adverse perceptions from male colleagues [4]. These findings highlight the convergence of gender bias and worker safety, stressing the imperative to rectify technical biases as automation and AI become more prevalent in maritime operations. The prevalence of harassment and bullying not only highlights the urgent need for equitable policies but also raises concerns about the potential role of biased technological tools in perpetuating unsafe environments if not deliberately designed to mitigate these issues.

Public awareness is a catalyst for modern maritime-related risk management and has resulted in the lowest level of waterborne mishaps in modern history [5]. Likewise, a key to gender equality in maritime trade is visibility. For example, the United Nations tracks sustainable development goals [6], using data-driven techniques to ensure a workable SDG roadmap.

Suresh *et al.* [7], investigated the connection between gender and stress levels among seafarers, focusing on how maritime characteristics disproportionately affect female sailors. A questionnaire administered to 124 female seafarers revealed a significant correlation between gender and stress, suggesting the need for strategies to improve the wellbeing and inclusivity of the maritime workplace.

Computer vision's ability to interpret visual data offers a powerful tool for identifying gender within the maritime context, providing valuable insights to inform policy-making. Building on this capability, this paper proposes developing a custom computer vision model to identify female seafarers, enabling more accurate tracking of sustainable development goals. Generalist vision models may perform poorly when trained on data that reinforce cultural biases — for example the assumption that a person wearing a hardhat and safety glasses onboard a vessel must be male. While generalist models are improving, this paper advocates for a specialized approach that can serve as a foundation for measuring female representation using networking tools [8]. Data can serve to highlight the urgency of addressing key issues, including anti-discrimination initiatives for women who work at sea.

Ametepey *et al.*, cite artificial intelligence as a positive catalyst for the empowerment of women in relation to sustainable development goal 5 [9]. Of note within the paper is artificial intelligence's ability to [identify] and [mitigate] discrimination, promoting equality through data analyses.

Addressing fairness in vision models began earnestly in the 2010s, when different algorithmic models were making their way out of research and academia and into the general public. Early models often assigned male pronouns to male-dominated professions: for example, doctors and pilots tended to be assigned male pronouns and nurses and flight attendants assigned female pronouns [10]. Despite vision model advancements, the removal of bias remains a concern in 2024. Further, bias is considered harmful when applied to a severely underrepresented group, as the effort involved in addressing these biases is generally left to the groups most affected. Generalist models may not be able to solve bias in all domains, particularly underrepresented domains. As such, the ability to lessen bias may lie with niche developers.

Gender bias within artificial intelligence is well documented. A comprehensive survey of bias in big language models was undertaken by the IRCAI under the aegis of UNESCO. The study highlighted the prevalence of gender bias in AI frameworks and emphasized the critical need for to mitigate these biases [11]. It identified the development cycle as a key factor contributing to unintended bias and the potential amplification of gender discrimination. Addressing this issue requires the involvement of multiple stakeholders, particularly governments, which should enact regulations to ensure the fair treatment of underrepresented groups.

Guilbeault *et al.*, investigate the overwhelming amount of visual content online, such as Snapchat, Instagram, and TikTok, which exacerbates gender bias. The study is notable for using a survey that relied, in part, on Googling images among thousands of roles. The study espouses the idea that bias can be reinforced by casually viewing images online, a behavior that is gradually supplanting text as a way people spend their time consuming media.

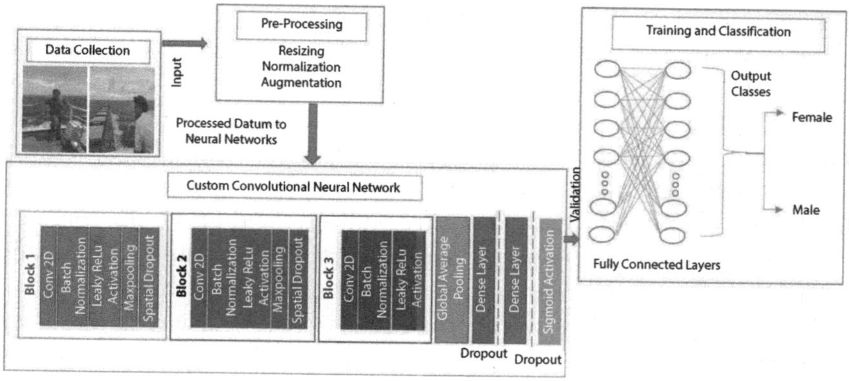

Figure 6.1 Framework of the proposed research.

Theite Krämer investigates the degree in which shipping companies adhere to the United Nations sustainability goals. Of note, the study observed that shipping companies partitioned seafarers and shoreside workers when addressing sustainability, and in the case of one of the largest shipping companies in the world seafarers were omitted from sustainability initiatives entirely. Hancock *et al.*, at the Alan Turing Institute in London ask the question whether technology in the maritime domain supports sustainability initiatives. An outcome of the study is to engage more directly with the communities affected by technology, or to better assess fairness and mitigate bias within such systems [12].

This effort herein aims to support organizations like the United Nations in measuring progress toward equitable goals while addressing three core challenges: working with limited datasets, operating in an under-studied field, and leveraging computer vision as a force for positive, equitable data collection. The proposed convolutional neural network framework is depicted in Figure 6.1.

6.2 Literature Review

To contextualize the challenges and opportunities associated with gender representation and technological bias, this literature review examines studies on gender inequality, biases in computer vision (CV) models, and strategies for mitigating these issues through targeted interventions. This paper explores three disparate subjects: gender bias, convolutional neural networks, and the management of vision models with limited training data. An exploratory, non-systematic literature review is divided into three sections: gender studies related to maritime professionals, bias in computer vision (CV) models, and research challenges associated with limited data.

a. Gender Studies for Female Maritime Professionals

Barahona-Fuentes *et al.* [13], points out that a gender gap within the maritime industry persists, and advocates for the need for agencies is needed to develop more effective gender equality policies." Şenburşa [14], conducts a survey of leading articles on gender in the maritime industry. Acejo and Abila [15], explore the role of gender within merchant shipping, focusing on the experiences of women in a traditionally patriarchal industry. Bhirugnath-Bhookhun *et al.* [16], focus on the leadership and socio-economic development of women in Eastern and Southern Africa's maritime sector, while investigating regional disparities. They discuss the various barriers to women in maritime, specifically recruitment, a dearth of female leadership, and male biases. A study by Osundiran and Tshehla explores the contributions of female seafarers to global trade, despite the persistent challenges they face. Through a structured questionnaire distributed to 50 female seafarers, the authors examine key challenges and motivations, providing insights into female representation in Angola, India, Indonesia, Kenya, Nigeria, and South Africa.

The authors elucidate female maritime professional's responsibilities into operational, navigational, health safety, communication, and leadership roles. Addressing the ongoing mariner shortage affecting both men and women, the study emphasizes the need to increase female representation in the maritime profession [17].

Tseng *et al.*, examined the challenges faced by female seafarers in Ghana, including gender-based discrimination, harassment, and limited career advancement opportunities. Using a qualitative case study design, the research conducted interviews with 20 participants and applied thematic analysis to uncover how a male-dominated industry culture and inadequate onboard facilities hinder women's progression. The findings bring to light a significant deficiency in research on the experiences of female seafarers in developing maritime states, highlighting the necessity of adopting focused measures to address these systemic concerns [18].

The research on gender disparity in Taiwan's marine sector investigated female sailors' views on policies, advantages, and obstacles. The study included comprehensive interviews with 30 seafarers (24 female, 6 male) to identify employment impediments, such as restrictive corporate rules and systemic biases ingrained in the male-dominated business culture. The research additionally observed how gender inequality influenced participants' reactions, mirroring the overarching problem of bias across the sector.

The research included practical ideas for overcoming these challenges, in accordance with United Nations Development Goals aimed at promoting gender equality in marine professions [19].

The persistent prejudice against women in nautical culture, stemming from the assumption that their presence brings misfortune aboard, was examined in the anthropological study [15]. This study comprises interviews with women mariners who recounted their good and negative experiences about gender bias. Leveraging Turkey's extensive nautical heritage, Captain Ayşe Aslı Başak, a co-founder of SheFarers and presently the Chief Executive Officer in the marine sector, analyzes the distinctive problems faced by women in both domestic and international shipping. Leticia Grimett, of the University of KwaZulu-Natal Natal, South Africa explores methods to eliminate discriminatory practices [20].

The gender imbalance in Tanzania's maritime industry with the least women participation as seafarers was addressed in the study. This study utilized descriptive research and prevalent literature review to highlight the causes such as lack of education and societal norms. Promoting women in maritime education and training and implementing policies to encourage their involvement in seafaring roles are emphasized and recommended. The confidence levels of women seafarers in Indonesia were examined in the research by using trust theory and statistical tools such as AHP and System Dynamics. Factors such as competence, integrity and benevolence were identified to influence trust while harassment and abuse were found to be the most significant factors eroding trust. The result in measuring the overall trust score was medium (63.68%) which highlighted the need for strategic policy reforms to enhance trust and support for women in the maritime sector.

Support for the National Rally (RN) by women began in 2012 and was influenced by Marine Le Pen's focus on women's policies [21]. Liberal language of rights and equality was reappropriated by Le Pen and this shift is paralleled by growing support for right-wing female politicians in both maritime and global contexts.

b. Gender Bias using Computer Vision

Results, from the Sustainable Action Conference 2024 (SAC 2.0) underscored how digitalization and artificial intelligence could help to advance sustainable development by stressing their potential to increase resource efficiency, climate action, and social inclusion and so improve resource economy. The results guaranteed moral application and governance structures to help reach the UN Sustainable Development Goals (SDGs).

The potential of artificial intelligence in achieving sustainable development goals was explored in *The Role of AI in Assessing and Achieving the Sustainable Development Goals (SDGs)* [22]. The study focused on key issues such as data bias, job automation, and transparency. It highlighted the importance of implementing significant measures and conducting further research to enhance AI's ethical impact on the SDGs. Sunny *et al.*, "Fairness and Bias Mitigation in Computer Vision: A Survey." arXiv preprint arXiv:2408.02464 (2024) [23]. Bias in computer vision arises from various sources, with dataset composition and image captioning as primary contributors. Algorithmic and architectural decisions further influence bias, as evidenced by studies on Vision Transformers (ViTs) and CNNs, which reveal architecture-specific dynamics in amplifying social biases [24]. Techniques like image augmentation and self-supervised learning contribute to this bias by reinforcing patterns within training data. Bhardwaj *et al.*, applied CNN with OpenCV to predict gender and estimate age by considering the necessary measures to encounter varied lighting conditions and other features through preprocessing. The research demonstrated a reasonable performance and highlighted the significant applications across various domains [25].

Diverse datasets such as Adience and UTKFace are considered to ensure variability in datasets for predicting gender and age. The datasets were preprocessed and augmented to have variability and applied CNN based method which resulted in high accuracies 96.32% for gender prediction. This research showcases the need for data variability in classification tasks for achieving enhanced performance. Alrashed *et al.*, applied gait analysis to determine gender by using CNN and SVM and also back tested the performance with varying hyperparameters. This study showcased the gait's potential as a behavioral identifier for determining gender by leveraging computer vision [26].

Tareef *et al.*, proposed an automated deep learning framework for human identity and gender classification using images. The hand image datasets were pre-processed to enhance the image resolution and applied the CNN model in determining gender and human identity; k-fold cross-validation was applied to measure the performance which resulted in 96.79% for gender classification [27]. Devash Kumar *et al.*, applied CNN for classifying gender and age in 8 different ranges and also addressing the requirement of huge computational resources. The study classified the images well while addressing the challenges of lighting and expressions. The classification resulted in better performance by using the Adience dataset and the research utilized cloud services for facilitating computation and dataset access [28].

Moreover, vision-language models trained on publicly available datasets tend to exhibit ethno-centric and gender-specific biases, often excluding lower-income groups with limited digital access. Current trends indicate that popular vision models may have exhausted available data for further training, underscoring the need for novel approaches to mitigate these biases and improve fairness across AI systems.

Bias mitigation may be more effectively addressed through architectural decisions guided by specialists rather than generalists, as domain-specific approaches can help mitigate risks for severely underrepresented groups, such as women in the maritime industry. Nonetheless, the prominence and recognition of specialist models have increased significantly since the 2010s. Torralba and Efros [29], first introduced the notion of dataset bias with relation to context— for example, what the subject is wearing (e.g., personal protective equipment). Zhang *et al.*, discussed representation bias using background objects such as a vessel [30]. Images of females working in industrial environments, particularly aboard vessels, are exceedingly difficult to source. Some are impossible: within the global merchant fleet, 30% of mariners are on tankships where cell phones and photography are prohibited due to explosive atmospheres.

The removal of bias in the presented context necessitates binary classification, rather than the elimination of gender-identifying annotations, as demonstrated in previous studies. This paper builds on binary gender classification, using it as a foundation while adhering to global data protection regulations without relying on supplementary annotative data.

c. Research Challenges

The rationale for employing a custom CNN stems from literature cautioning that transfer models may perpetuate biases inherent in pre-trained models. Architectural decisions in vision models for gender recognition are investigated by Mandal *et al.* [31], who explore the use of vision transformers and CNNS, measuring bias propagation based on design considerations.

Gender identification systems are classified by the European Union as high-risk artificial intelligence [32]. High risk artificial intelligence has the potential to amplify biases tied to sensitive protected attributes, such as race, gender, and ethnicity. Biases such as these can undermine sustainable development goals by reinforcing systemic inequalities. Generalist models, which handle vast amounts of data, face challenges when processing large sets of disparate images combined with annotated data, potentially leading to unwanted outcomes. Studies that point to measurement and selection of data that are applied to vision models is thus warranted. Shah *et al.* [33], survey the degree of bias across visual datasets and propose methodologies for quantifying and mitigating bias effects such as uneven class distribution.

Data augmentation is a proven method for reducing bias, particularly in scenarios involving occluded facial recognition, such as when personal protective equipment obstructs human features. Google's research on auto-augmentation demonstrates the value of dynamically altering images during training to address such challenges. Kim *et al.*, in their BiaSwap framework, focus on bias-specific attributes to reduce bias more effectively [34], while Ding *et al.*, propose innovative augmentation techniques powered by large language models, thereby reducing the need for additional data [35].

Computer vision is evolving rapidly. Advancements in data collection, transformer architecture, and large-scale pretraining have given rise to multimodal foundations models, which can simultaneously generalize and also exhibit remarkable capabilities in domain-specific tasks.

6.3 Methodology

Predicting gender from images has become a notable application of computer vision, particularly when datasets align with the relevant context. Existing research demonstrates the potential of CNNs for this task. Aryanmehr *et al.*, utilized OpenCV and CNNs to develop a real-time system for age, gender, and ethnicity prediction, achieving 89.45% accuracy using a large open-source labeled dataset. Similarly, hybrid models leveraging datasets like ImageNet have demonstrated enhanced performance compared to standalone CNNs, with applications spanning real-time surveillance, access management, and intelligent transportation systems. In the maritime domain, applying CNNs for gender prediction presents unique challenges due to visual similarities in personal protective equipment, such as hard hats, safety glasses, and coveralls, which obscure gender-related features. To address these complexities, this research proposes a custom CNN model designed specifically for the maritime context. The model is built to reduce reliance on pre-trained or transfer models, mitigating biases while effectively predicting gender within resource-constrained settings. This section outlines the research methodology, encompassing data collection, preprocessing, model architecture, hyperparameter optimization, and evaluation strategies. By leveraging a domain-specific approach, the study aims to refine computer vision techniques to address gender representation challenges within the maritime industry.

a. Data Collection
Sourcing high-quality images of underrepresented groups while adhering to European Union privacy laws pose significant challenges. As a result,

custom tools with annotated search functions are employed to identify women and men in industrial settings using publicly available datasets, including VGG Face, Insight Face, Labeled Faces in the Wild, and Kaggle's Face Recognition dataset. A total of 55,000 images are extracted from these datasets to create an image repository for drawing smaller, targeted training sets. Sample images are shown in Figure 6.2.

Seafarer nationalities are highly diverse: Filipinos constitute 13.3%, the largest group, followed by the Russian Federation at 10.5%, and China at 7.1%. Indonesia and India account for 7.6% and 6%, respectively. Ukraine represents 4%, while Greece, Japan, the United Kingdom, and Poland each contribute 1-2%. To ensure better representation of ethnic diversity within the global seafarer population, DemogPairs dataset is utilized.

Bias reduction is achieved by ensuring equal representation of women wearing personal protective equipment in the training dataset. Insight Face is used to expand the bounding box [x_min, y_min, x_max, y_max] by 40%, capturing equipment such as hard hats, safety glasses, ear protection, and coveralls. The expanded bounding box also includes contextual background elements like ships, angular metal structures, and water.

The dataset contains 55,000 generic facial images, evenly divided between male and female subjects. From this collection, 1,000 images each of women and men working in maritime and related industries, such as

Figure 6.2 Primary data collected.

factory workers, are selected. The selected images are labeled with gender to enhance the utility for model training. Data augmentation techniques are applied to expand the maritime-focused dataset, resulting in 10,000 curated images for training, 25% of which are domain-specific.

b. Data Preprocessing

Data preprocessing involves ensuring the inclusion of an adequate and representative dataset for the training, validation, and testing phases. Developing a custom vision model requires an interdisciplinary approach and specialized knowledge of the computer vision tool's objectives. A primary focus of data preprocessing is enhancing image quality to align with the system's goals. Prior to sourcing images, informal consultations with subject matter experts helped identify key image features and better understand the representation of women in maritime and industrial settings.

Specialized computer vision models are likely to play a significant role in future maritime applications. Some of the strongest cases for custom model development and implementation include domains like medical imaging, robotics, and agriculture. Image classification, object detection, and segmentation tasks remain central to advancing this field. For example, Insight Face is employed for object detection, and a bespoke convolutional neural network (CNN) is developed for a binary classification issue pertinent to the research. Additional improvements may include multi-label categorization, ensemble learning methodologies, and transfer learning to increase results.

The practicality of using computer vision models for statistical analysis, such as estimating the representation of women in maritime roles, is beyond the scope of this paper. While computer vision is a rapidly advancing field with diverse applications, its adoption varies significantly across industries. Sectors like healthcare and finance have made more substantial progress in implementation. However, despite the growing body of literature, the practical deployment of computer vision in high-risk AI applications remains limited.

A key driver of CNN efficacy is the availability of high-quality datasets. Sourcing GDPR-compliant images of women in maritime is particularly challenging. Despite these limitations, the study achieved 87% accuracy in custom CNN training, demonstrating the potential for specialized models. Expanding datasets, improving diversity, and leveraging synthetic data augmentation techniques could further enhance performance and applicability.

c. Image Resizing and Normalization

Images are resized to a resolution of 128128 pixels in order to standardize the input dimensions for training. Studies suggest that pre-trained transfer learning models such as ResNet 50, ResNet100 utilize 224X224 resolution images for better performance. Though pretrained models are not deployed in this instance, it could be surmised that performance improvement of about 10% could be seen using this data. This research utilizes the 128X128 resolution to strike a balance between computational efficiency and retaining the sufficient information for accurate predictions in the maritime domain. By dividing each pixel's intensity by 225, the pixel values of the images are brought down to the range of [0, 1].

d. Data Augmentation

Given the relatively small size of the source dataset, an aggressive augmentation strategy is adopted. Since the majority of images featuring women in maritime settings were captured in daylight, augmentation parameters used in this study are tuned to account for lighting variability to enhance model generalization.

The augmentation process involved the following image transformations: rotation range of 30 degrees, horizontal and vertical shifts of up to 20%, shear transformations of 20%, zoom in and out by 30%, and an aggressive brightness adjustment range of ±20%. Points outside image boundaries are filled using the nearest pixel value through the fill_mode parameter to complement the image augmentation process. Rescaling is applied to scale pixel values to the range [0, 1] to normalize the values. The validation split is set at an arbitrary 0.2, aligning with the model's training/validation/test data partition. The above parameters are selected for data variability while avoiding computational complexity and to demonstrate minimal impact on training loss. Additional augmentation is applied using a balance_training_data function, which augments random images from the minority class until it matches the majority class in size. The process involves counting images in each class, determining the target count, performing augmentation, and adding the generated images to the corresponding training, validation, and test sets. The diversity of the data through these augmentation processes will ensure better performance of the proposed custom CNN model and avoid overfitting which is a critical factor while dealing with limited size of data. Future research considerations include the use of featurewise_center, samplewise_center, and featurewise_std_normalization for enhanced preprocessing.

e. Labeling

Of the 30,000 images used, the dataset is split into equal classifications of male and female. However, a slight imbalance was introduced due to the inclusion of false positives (FPs) and false negatives (FNs), which accounted for approximately 5% of the total dataset. These FPs and FNs were gradually reintroduced into the training set to mitigate bias. Labeling of the images is handled by the binary classification framework and assigned the boolean values 0 and 1 to female images, and male images respectively. This binary labeling is underlying for training the custom CNN model to distinguish between female and male images in the maritime domain.

f. Dataset Splitting

During the training and validation, images are allocated 80% and 20% respectively. Test images are drawn from leftover, randomized images from the master image repository and represent 20% of the total training/validation set. For the purpose of positively ensuring no data leakage to the final test set, stratified splitting is adopted to ensure the balanced distribution of data. During the training, generators train_generator and val_generator contained such parameters as image size (128X128), batch size (64) and declaration of the binary and subset declarations.

g. Model Architecture

The proposed custom CNN model performs binary classification for gender prediction in maritime domain and the architecture is depicted in Figure 6.3. This research implementation utilizes Tensorflow 2.18 as a high-level application program interface for purposes of simplifying model deployment.

Three convolutional blocks are sequentially utilized, each with a progressively increasing number of filters (e.g. 32, 64, 128) to enhance feature extraction. Concurrently, the dropout rate is progressively increased across layers to prevent overfitting. The architecture concludes with two fully connected dense layers, and a final sigmoid function. Table 6.1 provides a detailed layer-by-layer summary of the architecture.

Values are derived from the hyperparameter search space defined for Keras Tuner, which includes the number of units in dense layers, dropout rates, and learning rate. A three-day optimization exercise is conducted to search the space and identify suitable hyperparameters. Resultant hyperparameters are found in Table 6.2.

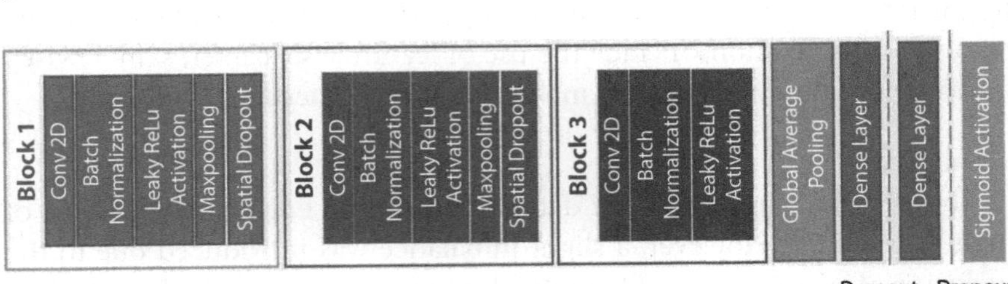

Figure 6.3 Custom CNN model architecture.

Table 6.1 Model architecture.

Layer type	Description
Input Layer	Input image with dimensions (height, width, 3)
Conv2D (Layer 1)	3x3 convolution filter, He initialization, padding
	Followed by batch normalization, LeakyReLU activation
MaxPooling2D (Layer 1)	2x2 max pooling layer to downsample spatial dimensions
SpatialDropout2D (Layer 1)	Dropout to prevent overfitting
Conv2D (Layer 2)	3x3 convolution filter, He initialization, padding
	Followed by batch normalization, LeakyReLU activation
MaxPooling2D (Layer 2)	2x2 max pooling layer to downsample spatial dimensions
SpatialDropout2D (Layer 2)	Dropout to prevent overfitting
Conv2D (Layer 3)	3x3 convolution filter, He initialization, padding
	Followed by batch normalization, LeakyReLU activation
GlobalAveragePooling2D	Averaging throughout the world to decrease geographical dimensions
Dense (Layer 1)	Fully connected layer with L2 regularization and ReLU activation
Dropout (Layer 1)	Dropout layer to prevent overfitting
Dense (Layer 2)	Fully connected layer incorporating L2 regularization and ReLU activation function
Dropout (Layer 2)	Dropout layer to prevent overfitting
Dense (Output Layer)	Final output layer with sigmoid activation for gender classification

Convolutional Layers

The first convolutional layer is configured with conv1_filter which consists of 112 filters and a kernel size of 3x3 to extract low-level local features specific to maritime environments. Features such as hard hats, safety glasses, and coveralls—key visual elements typically linked to maritime personnel are taken into account. Training stability is ensured through batch normalization where inputs to each layer are normalized. A LeakyReLU activation function is then applied to enhance the model's capability to capture subtle maritime-specific patterns that include gender-related visual cues. The spatial dimensions of the feature maps are reduced using a 2x2 max pooling layer. To further prevent overfitting, SpatialDropout2D is employed to randomly remove entire feature maps that exhibit significant similarity thereby reducing covariance.

The second convolutional layer is configured with conv2_filters that consist of 128 filters to further refine and extract higher-level features such as uniform patterns and pose variations relevant to the maritime context. Similar to the first layer, batch normalization is applied to stabilize training followed by a LeakyReLU activation function to enhance learning capabilities. A 2x2 max pooling layer is employed to reduce spatial dimensions while SpatialDropout2D is utilized to randomly drop highly similar feature maps by mitigating overfitting. These processes enable the model to focus on subtle differences between images such as variations in posture or equipment placement which may indicate gender-related attributes.

The third convolutional layer incorporates conv3_filters that consist of 160 filters. Batch normalization and a LeakyReLU activation function are used as in the preceding layers. However, instead of max pooling, GlobalAveragePooling2D is applied to aggregate global spatial features and reduce dimensionality. This adjustment allows the model to prioritize overall image representations such as the arrangement of visual elements across the entire frame which is a crucial consideration in maritime scenarios where gender-related distinctions are often subtle.

Fully Connected (Dense) Layers

The first dense layer is configured with dense1_units that comprises 224 neurons and utilizes the ReLU activation function to identify intricate patterns such as gender-related visual characteristics in maritime-specific features like hard hats, safety glasses, ear protection and coveralls, uniforms and body posture. Overfitting is mitigated through the application of L2 regularization which penalizes large weight values. Additionally, a Dropout layer with a rate of 0.5 is implemented to deactivate a random subset of neurons during training thereby enhancing generalization. The second dense layer is constructed similarly to the first that includes dense2_units which consist of 160 neurons and also employs ReLU activation along with L2 regularization. A Dropout layer with dropout4 is incorporated to further regularize the model by randomly deactivating neurons according to the minimal covariance thereby reducing the likelihood of overfitting to the training dataset.

Output Layer
The concluding layer comprises a thick layer including a solitary unit and has a sigmoid activation function. This setup is intended to generate an output that signifies the likelihood of the input image being classified as either male or female. This binary output is very appropriate for the gender classification task in a marine scenario.
Training Configuration
We use stochastic gradient descent (SGD) to train the models, and the batch size is set at 128 samples. The weight decay parameter is also set to 0.0005, and the momentum value is set to 0.9. One of the most important factors that contributes to the success of the model's learning process is the slight loss of weight. Specifically, the weight decay acts not only as a regularizer but also as a mechanism to reduce the model's training error.

For model compilation, the Adam optimizer is employed. This optimizer dynamically adjusts the learning rate based on training progress, thereby ensuring both efficient and stable convergence throughout the training process.

h. Hyperparameter Tuning
Hyperparameter tuning is evident in the model building to obtain optimal performance and the study proposed CNN hyperparameter tuning algorithm - HyperTuning SK algorithm for the image classification in constructions. The algorithm selected the optimal hyperparameters to obtain enhanced accuracy while classifying the images for binary tasks. Centiner proposed CNNTuner to optimize the CNN-based deep learning model to encounter the challenges in classification of fashion image recognition. This study utilized the Fashion MNIST dataset and applied Keras Tuner Tool to obtain better performance. Results proved that the hyperparameters applied on the dataset provided enhanced accuracy which explicits the effectiveness of the optimization approach. Ottoni *et al.*, proposed a methodology to tune the hyperparameters for data augmentation to meet the requirements of applying deep learning models for image classification. The study underwent 128 image transformations as part of data augmentation while focusing on vegetation recognition through logistic regression model; the model demonstrated the optimal performance with the application of data augmentation.

In this research, hyperparameter tuning is done using a convolutional neural network for binary classification of images for predicting gender in maritime context. The model incorporates regularization, dropout, and data augmentation during training. During tuning the same amount of training data, and initial parameters, and seed value are used for each training session to ensure consistency during training sessions.

Regularization and Callbacks

To mitigate overfitting and improve generalization, multiple regularization strategies are integrated into the model. L2 regularization is applied to the weights of dense layers which helps in minimizing the risk of overfitting by penalizing excessively large weight values, thereby encouraging a more generalized solution. Dropout layers are strategically placed across both convolutional and dense layers to deactivate a random subset of neurons during training. This strategy reduces the model's reliance on specific neurons and enhances its robustness against dataset noise.

The training process is further optimized with the implementation of three essential callbacks. EarlyStopping is employed to monitor the validation loss by halting the training process if no further improvement was detected, and restoring the model to its best-performing weights. ModelCheckpoint is utilized to save the model at its optimal validation performance by ensuring that the most accurate version was retained for deployment. Finally, ReduceLROnPlateau is used to dynamically decrease the learning rate when validation loss plateaued, and allowed for finer optimization and improved convergence during later training epochs. Table 6.2 demonstrates the various hyperparameters opted for tuning the proposed custom CNN model.

Keras Tuner is utilized to tune hyperparameters. Prior to Keras Tuner and similar tools such as Optuna, hyperparameter tuning was typically a laborious process. The Keras Tuner application program interface handles models with, "non-linear topology, shared layers, and multiple inputs and outputs." Since there is one input tensor and one output tensor, keras. sequential is utilized. To begin the search function, the shape of the sample is specified, in this case— it is 128 X 128 X 3.

Step #1. Define Search Space. A list of layers is passed using Kera Tuner's HyperParameters API and accessed using the layers attribute. Initial parameters are 32, 64, and 128 were used for dense layers. Three activation functions were tested (e.g., ReLU, sigmoid, and tanh). Dropout rate ranges were 0.1 to 0.5. Other parameters included number of convolutional layers, kernel size, and batch size. Learning rate is obtained but during tuning was dealt with separately using ReduceLROnPlateau during training.
Step #2. Start the Search. Three models are utilized: Random Search, Bayesian Optimization, and Hyperband. Bayesian is utilized for large search spaces with limited resources, and hyperband is utilized for longer training time. Hyperband proved to be optimal due to search space and training time during the testing period.
Step #3. Query the results. Logging is maintained during each trial session to record outcomes. A dedicated server performed the training sessions

Table 6.2 Hyperparameters.

Tuned hypermeters table			
Parameter	**Value**	**Parameter**	**Value**
conv1_filters	112	dropout2	0.5
dropout1	0.15	learning_rate	0.0005
conv2_filters	128	batch_size	64
dropout2	0.2	epochs	50
conv3_filters	160	image_size	64 x 64
dense1_units	224	validation_split	0.2
dropout3	0.5	rescale	0.00392
dense2_units	160	12_regularization	11: 0.0008, 12 0.001

over several days. Callbacks are used to save the best weights with accompanying checkpoints during training.

Step #4. Retrain Model. Hyperparameters are narrowed at 8-12 hour intervals.

Step #5. Tune model. Learning rates are tested using the ReduceLROnPlateau callback, while dropout rates are optimized using a custom layer implemented to accept dynamic rates.

6.4 Results and Discussion

This section provides a qualitative analysis of the custom CNN model's performance and discusses improvements and further optimizations to be taken into account in gender prediction within the maritime domain. The challenges encountered were limited availability of secondary data specific to the maritime context, the need to have diverse data, and the sparse scientific literature when identifying women in maritime domain using computer vision.

This research assesses the suggested model's performance based on accuracy, precision, recall, and F1 score. Furthermore, a confusion matrix is generated to analyze the true positive, true negative, false positive, and false negative values for the Female and Male classes.

Table 6.3 delineates the performance indicators of the suggested research, assessed utilizing a bespoke Convolutional Neural Network (CNN) model.

Table 6.3 Performance metrics of proposed research.

Metrics	Custom CNN model
TP (Z)	13039
TN (Z)	13038
FP (Z)	1962
FN (Z)	1961
Accuracy (%)	87.17
Precision (%)	87.44
Recall (%)	86.93
F1 Score (%)	87.19

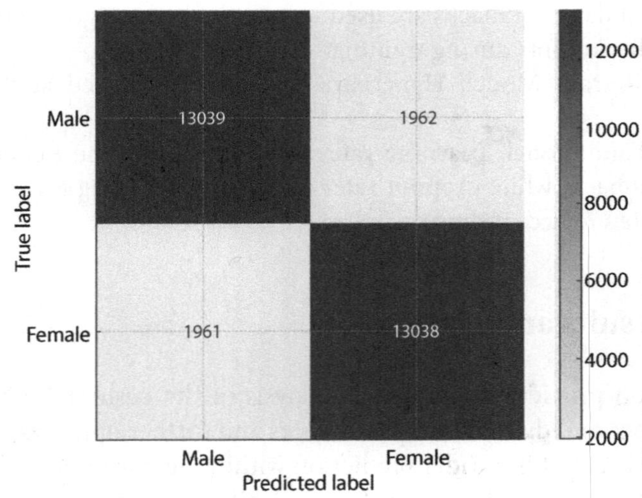

Figure 6.4 Confusion matrix for gender prediction.

The proprietary CNN model accurately identified 13,039 true positives and 13,038 true negatives, with both false positives and false negatives recorded at 1,962 as depicted in Figure 6.4. The findings yielded an accuracy of 87.17%, indicating the proportion of correctly categorized events relative to all forecasts. The accuracy, measured as the proportion of correctly predicted positives to the total expected positives, is 87.44%. The recall, representing the ratio of correctly identified positives to all actual positives, reached 86.93%. The F1 Score, which integrates precision and recall, is at 87.19%, signifying the model's dependable and effective performance.

b. Training and Validation Performance

Figure 6.5 illustrate the training and validation accuracy across epochs and Figure 6.6 illustrate the training and validation loss across epochs, offering significant insights into the model's learning behavior. The accuracy curves exhibit a consistent increasing trajectory, with the validation accuracy

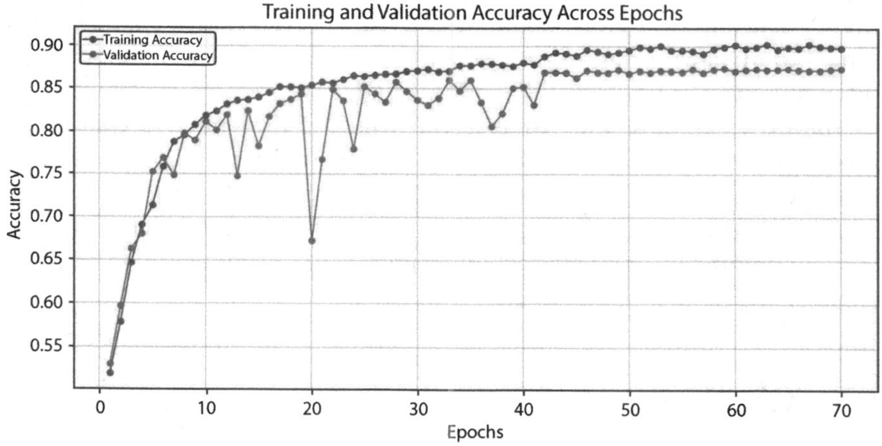

Figure 6.5 Training and validation accuracy across epochs.

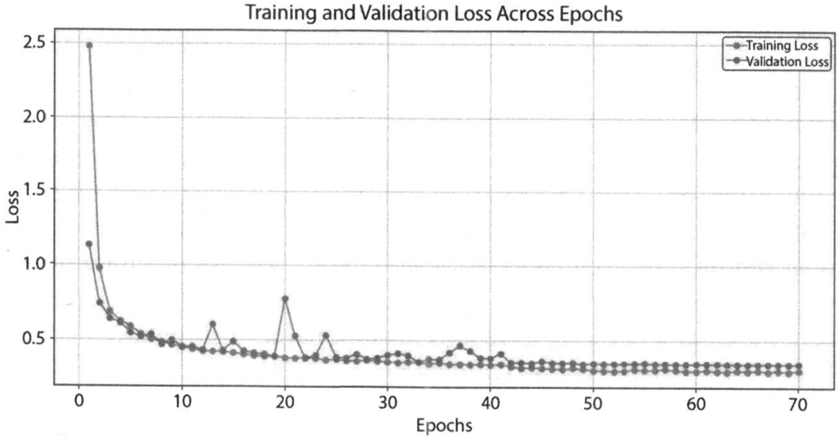

Figure 6.6 Training and validation loss across epochs.

stabilizing marginally towards the conclusion, signifying effective learning and convergence to an optimal solution. The loss curves for both training and validation demonstrate a steady drop with minimal divergence, indicating minimized overfitting and robust generalization ability. The robust association between the training and validation curves underscores the efficacy of the employed regularization techniques, such as L2 penalties and dropout layers, in alleviating overfitting and enhancing the model's performance.

The findings demonstrate that the proposed custom CNN architecture is highly effective for gender prediction in maritime settings by achieving impressive accuracy and strong generalization capabilities. The application of data augmentation techniques played a crucial role in enabling the model to manage variations in the dataset such as differences in lighting, orientation and scale.

The presence of subtle visual features related to gender in maritime images combined with environmental factors like lighting, angles and other conditions presented challenges for accurate classification. Incorporating additional feature engineering or integrating multi-modal data sources (e.g., combining images with textual metadata) has the potential to further enhance the model's ability to do its job.

6.5 Conclusion

Ninety percent of the world's tradable goods are transported over water. Many of the goods that we use, the food that we eat, and the energy we consume are carried aboard merchant vessels. The reason is cost: transportation of goods is 12-16 times more expensive by air than by sea. Rail is 3-4 times more expensive. Waterborne trade is the backbone of our global economy.

In 2015, the United Nations introduced a roadmap for Sustainable Development Goals (SDGs) to be achieved by 2030. These SDGs provide a "blueprint for peace and prosperity in the world" and emphasize that no one should be left behind, particularly those invisible to the broader global community. Women in maritime, an overwhelmingly underrepresented demographic, require heightened awareness and targeted policies to support the welfare of 28,000 female seafarers worldwide. Between 2015 to 2021, female representation among mariners increased by 45.8%, or a 6.5% annual growth rate, according to the International Maritime Organization's study on women in maritime. Progress is largely attributed to the tireless work and advocacy of women-led organizations. However, this growth should not be mistaken for gender equity: the maritime community must remain vigilant in addressing persistent disparities. This study demonstrates how gender-specific computer vision models can provide actionable insights into gender representation in maritime roles, supporting data-driven approaches to advance SDG 5. By refining vision models to suit domain-specific contexts, this research underscores the transformative potential of technology to address systemic inequities. While the model achieved an accuracy of 87.17%, it also highlighted the challenges of using biased generalist computer vision systems to recognize women in maritime contexts, emphasizing the need for tailored solutions.

Extensive media coverage and academic studies have underscored how questionable decision-making in the technology sector has led to flawed computer vision systems. Data-at-all-costs approaches have eroded public trust. Nevertheless, these challenges have driven significant regulatory progress, which includes the General Data Protection Regulations of the European Union and the Artificial Intelligence Act, which is considered to be a pioneering piece of legislation according to the European Parliament and Council of the European Union, from 2016. These regulations aim to enhance safety in high-risk AI applications and mitigate risks of unacceptable systems, such as China's social credit framework.

This research aligns with these regulatory advancements, showcasing how ethical, high-accuracy AI systems can be leveraged to support global equity initiatives. By addressing the limitations of generalist models and proposing custom solutions, this study provides a foundation for equitable innovation in high-risk domains. Challenges remain, particularly in sourcing high-quality images of underrepresented groups while complying with E.U. privacy regulations. The ethnic diversity of female seafarers—predominantly Filipinos, Russians, and Chinese—adds further complexity. However, expanding datasets, improving diversity, and leveraging synthetic data augmentation techniques present opportunities to enhance model performance and broader applicability.

This study aspires to serve as both a case study and a catalyst for further exploration of computer vision's applications within the maritime industry and beyond. By addressing the intersection of gender bias, technological innovation, and global policy, it advances understanding of SDG 5 while inspiring additional research and advocacy. Ultimately, this research underscores the critical role of tailored computer vision models in advancing equity and sustainability across industries. An EU-compliant Data Protection Impact Assessment (DPIA) was completed for this study. The dataset used to train the model was sourced from publicly available data. No additional annotated data beyond binary gender classification was processed, and in many cases, this classification was manually performed by the authors. The data, which was partially hand-curated and comprehensively sourced, was deleted upon the conclusion of the study.

AI disclosure statement: The author acknowledges the use of AI-based tools for minor language editing or grammatical correction. However, all intellectual contributions, analyses, and conclusions presented in this chapter are entirely the author's own.

References

1. Krystosik-Gromadzińska, A.M., During and After COVID-19: Seafarers Onboard, in: *Handbook of Research on the Future of the Maritime Industry*, pp. 377–399, IGI Global Scientific Publishing, 2022.
2. Kennard, A., Zhang, P., Rajagopal, S., Technology and training: How will deck officers transition to operating autonomous and remote-controlled vessels? *Mar. Policy*, 146, 1053265, 2022.
3. Solo, J. and Festin, M., Provider bias in family planning services: a review of its meaning and manifestations. *Global Health Sci. Pract.*, 7, 3, 371–385, 2019.
4. Ojwala, R.A., Buckingham, S., Neat, F., Kitada, M., Understanding women's roles, experiences and barriers to participation in ocean science education in Kenya: recommendations for better gender equality policy. *Mar. Policy*, 161, 1060005, 2024.
5. Mohsendokht, M., Li, H., Kontovas, C., Chang, C.-H., Qu, Z., Yang, Z., Decoding dependencies among the risk factors influencing maritime cybersecurity: Lessons learned from historical incidents in the past two decades. *Ocean Eng.*, 312, 1190785, 2024.
6. Hassani, H., Huang, X., MacFeely, S., Reza Entezarian, M., Big data and the united nations sustainable development goals (UN SDGs) at a glance. *Big Data Cognit. Comput.*, 5, 3, 28, 2021.
7. Suresh, A. and Krithika, M., Analysis of Stress Correlations between Gender Disparities in Ship Industry, in: *2024 10th International Conference on Communication and Signal Processing (ICCSP)*, IEEE, pp. 66–70, 2024.
8. Barnes, T.D., Strategies for improving gender diversity in the methods community: Insights from political methodologists and social science research. *PS Political Sci. Polit.*, 51, 3, 580–587, 2018.
9. Ametepey, S.O., Aigbavboa, C., Didibhuku Thwala, W., Addy, H., The impact of AI in Sustainable Development Goal implementation: A Delphi study. *Sustainability*, 16, 9, 3858, 2024.

10. Keles, U., Mansouri, B., Yazan, B., Perpetuation of gender bias in New Headway: A multimodal critical discourse analysis with a diachronic lens. *Pedagogy Cult. Soc.*, 31, 3, 379–401, 2023.
11. Arumugam, D., Govindaraju, K., Kumar Tamilarasan, A., AIIoT-based smart framework for screening specific learning disabilities, in: *Machine Learning for Critical Internet of Medical Things: Applications and Use Cases*, pp. 103–124, Springer International Publishing, Cham, 2022.
12. Kordzadeh, N. and Ghasemaghaei, M., Algorithmic bias: review, synthesis, and future research directions. *Eur. J. Inf. Syst.*, 31, 3, 388–409, 2022.
13. Barahona-Fuentes, C., Castells-Sanabra, M., Ordás, S., Torralbo, J., Female figures in maritime education and training institutions between 2009 and 2018: analysing possible impacts of gender policies. *WMU J. Marit. Aff.*, 19, 1, 143–158, 2020.
14. Şenbursa, N., A review of maritime women in the global arena. *J. Marit. Transp. Logist.*, 1, 1, 20–25, 2020.
15. Acejo, I.L. and S. Abila, S., Rubbing out gender: women and merchant ships. *J. Org. Ethnogr.*, 5, 2, 123–138, 2016.
16. Bhirugnath-Bhookhun, M. and Kitada, M., Lost in success: women's maritime careers in Eastern and Southern Africa. *Palgrave Commun.*, 3, 1, 1–10, 2017.
17. Pike, K., Wadsworth, E., Honebon, S., Broadhurst, E., Zhao, M., Zhang, P., Gender in the maritime space: how can the experiences of women seafarers working in the UK shipping industry be improved? *J. Navig.*, 74, 6, 1238–1251, 2021.
18. Tseng, P.-H. and Pilcher, N., Women seafarers in Taiwan: policies, benefits, challenges, and bias in the data, in: *Maritime Policy & Management*, pp. 1–17, 2024.
19. Shellock, R.J., Cvitanovic, C., Mackay, M., McKinnon, M.C., Blythe, J., Kelly, R., Van Putten, I.E., *et al.*, Breaking down barriers: the identification of actions to promote gender equality in interdisciplinary marine research institutions. *One Earth*, 5, 6, 687–708, 2022.
20. Grimett, L., The status of coastal marine tourism in KwaZulu natal in 2022. *Am. J. Ind. Bus. Manage.*, 12, 12, 1725–1760, 2022.
21. Fatimah, S., Usman, I., Kukuh Susilo, A., Mayangsari, A.S., Pratiwi, N.A., A Framework for Assessing Trust of Women Seafarers' Performance in Indonesia's Maritime Sector using Analytical Hierarchy Process and System Dynamics. *J. Marit. Res.*, 21, 2, 358–372, 2024.
22. Vinuesa, R., Azizpour, H., Leite, I., Balaam, M., Dignum, V., Domisch, S., Felländer, A., Daniela Langhans, S., Tegmark, M., Fuso Nerini, F., The role of artificial intelligence in achieving the Sustainable Development Goals. *Nat. Commun.*, 11, 1, 233, 2020.
23. Gebru, T. and Denton, R., Beyond Fairness in Computer Vision: A Holistic Approach to Mitigating Harms and Fostering Community-Rooted Computer

Vision Research. *Found. Trends® Comput. Graphics Vision*, 16, 3, 215–321, 2024.

24. Sunny, F.P., Taheri, E., Nikdast, M., Pasricha, S., A survey on silicon photonics for deep learning. *ACM J. Emerg. Technol. Comput. Syst.*, 17, 4, 1–57, 2021.
25. Islam, M.R., Uddin Ahmed, M., Barua, S., Begum, S., A systematic review of explainable artificial intelligence in terms of different application domains and tasks. *Appl. Sci.*, 12, 3, 1353, 2022.
26. Harris, E.J., Khoo, I.-H., Demircan, E., A survey of human gait-based artificial intelligence applications. *Front. Rob. AI*, 8, 7492745, 2022.
27. Tareef, A., Al-Dmour, H., Al-Sarayreh, A., An Automated Deep Learning Framework for Human Identity and Gender Detection. *J. Adv. Inf. Technol.*, 14, 1, 94–101, 2023.
28. Abdallah, A.M., Saif Rashed Obaid Alkaabi, A., Bark Nasser Douman Alameri, G., Hafsa Rafique, S., Shifa Musa, N., Murugan, T., Cloud network anomaly detection using machine and deep learning techniques—recent research advancements. *IEEE Access*, 12, 56749–567735, 2024.
29. Tommasi, T., Patricia, N., Caputo, B., Tuytelaars, T., A deeper look at dataset bias, in: *Domain adaptation in computer vision applications*, pp. 37–55, 2017.
30. Zhang, B., Karray, F., Li, Q., Zhang, L., Sparse representation classifier for microaneurysm detection and retinal blood vessel extraction. *Inf. Sci.*, 200, 78–905, 2012.
31. Mandal, A., Little, S., Leavy, S., Multimodal bias: Assessing gender bias in computer vision models with nlp techniques, in: *Proceedings of the 25th International Conference on Multimodal Interaction*, pp. 416–424, 2023.
32. Lütz, F., Gender equality and artificial intelligence in Europe. Addressing direct and indirect impacts of algorithms on gender-based discrimination, in: *ERA forum*, vol. 23, no. 1, pp. 33–52, Springer Berlin Heidelberg, Berlin/Heidelberg, 2022.
33. Shah, M. and Sureja, N., A comprehensive review of bias in deep learning models: Methods, impacts, and future directions. *Arch. Comput. Methods Eng.*, 32, 1, 255–267, 2025.
34. Kim, E., Lee, J., Choo, J., Biaswap: Removing dataset bias with bias-tailored swapping augmentation, in: *Proceedings of the IEEE/CVF International Conference on Computer Vision*, pp. 14992–15001, 2021.
35. Ding, B., Qin, C., Zhao, R., Luo, T., Li, X., Chen, G., Xia, W., Hu, J., Anh Tuan, L., Joty, S., Data augmentation using llms: Data perspectives, learning paradigms and challenges, in: *Findings of the Association for Computational Linguistics ACL 2024*, pp. 1679–1705, 2024.

7

Text-Based Analysis of Twitter Data with Machine Learning Models

N. Malathy*, G. Sharmila, R. Yuvarshini and R. Lavanya

Department of Information Technology, Mepco Schlenk Engineering College, Sivakasi, Tamil Nadu, India

Abstract

Our culture now shares new information on social media as a result of recent technological advancements. Throughout the pandemic, the use of social media services like Twitter has surged. The researchers developed a method to extract the negative, positive, and neutral attitudes from the Twitter Covid-19 dataset. The tweets were categorized using machine learning algorithms for that reason. A machine learning technique was utilized to label the tweets and the established framework is also deployed utilizing the lexicon-based technique to categorize the tweets as good, negative, or neutral. The approach is assessed using several performance metrics, such as accuracy, precision, recall, and F1-Score. Decision trees, random forests, Gaussian nave Bayes, and multi-nominal nave Bayes are examples of models that can be combined rather than built independently. By merging the models, we can improve accuracy using an NLP framework called BERT. It can parse language with "common sense" which is essentially like a human. By using the BERT framework, we get an increased accuracy of 94%. This value indicates that our proposed system can be able to classify the tweets of even a huge volume of datasets.

***Keywords*:** Sentiment analysis, Twitter, tweet classification, COVID-19

**Corresponding author*: malathy@mepcoeng.ac.in

T. S. Arun Samuel, L. Jerart Julus, P. Kanimozhi, T. Ananth Kumar and S. Balamurugan (eds.) Composite Artificial Intelligence: Fundamentals, Challenges, and Applications, (151–180) © 2026 Scrivener Publishing LLC

7.1 Introduction

7.1.1 Inspiration

The COVID-19 outbreak caused widespread fear. As a result, more people use Twitter to voice their ideas, raising awareness among the general public [1]. On social media, there was a tonne of updates in the shape of tweets, postings, etc. [2]. The primary information source during times like COVID-19 is this kind of update. The majority of people use Facebook and Twitter to express their feelings, ideas, and opinions. The widespread COVID-19 infection confused individuals, resulted in numerous fatalities, and instilled panic [6]. Through various social media platforms, the live people of the world replied to the pandemic and shared their perspectives. One of the social media outlets used during this time was Twitter. People from all around the world would tweet things with various emotions [6]. Numerous distractions and mental disorders were brought on by the fluctuating attitudes during the COVID-19 period. Public health has suffered greatly as a result of the pandemic. Tweets using the phrases "increased coronavirus," "death," "surge in cases," "impact on the Indian economy," and "second wave" convey feelings of fear and worry as well as have a detrimental effect [7]. The increased accessibility of numerous social media platforms makes it easier to discover the opinions of a diverse group of people. As a result, a significant volume of data, whether structured or not, is analyzed [3]. As a result, it is challenging to categorize the sentiment of tweets. As a result, the framework will extract, review, and categorize the data. Additionally, there is a chance for other viewpoints to proliferate as a result of public reactions to COVID-19 news on microblogging services [8]. To do that, machine learning using lexicon methods was used to extract the sentiment of the tweets. Extracting the sentiment even from a big dataset of tweets, expands the breadth. Thus, our study contributes to the understanding of which ML approaches for tweet classification work well and which do not [6]. The approach uses both tagging by ML methods and lexicon-based tweet sentiment analysis. Based on the tagged datasets, we built models using an ML technique. The models were then used to predict the intended outcome. The lexicon-based technique analyses the semantics of the words. The lexicon-based method determines the polarity of the data. An example would be positive, neutral, or negative. Supervised learning and lexicon-based techniques are utilized for automatic categorization. By removing tweets' semantic content, Valence Aware Dictionary and Sentiment Reason, a lexicon-adopted technique, can identify them [6]. The labeled tweets serve as the input for the ML approach.

Supervised machine learning methods including Gaussian Naive Bayes, Logistic Regression, Decision Tree, Multinominal Naive Bayes, Random Forest, Long Short-Term Memory, and Support Vector Machine use these tweets as input. The automatic classification of tweets is the primary purpose of the hybrid approach. The lexicon technique used in natural language processing and machine learning is both included in the hybrid approach. For the training to anticipate the intended results, these approaches require a sizable labeled dataset [9]. The BERT framework is used by the recently described approach to achieve a high accuracy rate. Its main goal is to use Transformer's bidirectional training, a well-known attention model, for language modeling [10]. BERT's ability to read text consecutively in both directions allows for this improved value. It is hence bidirectional. BERT's calculated accuracy value is 94% technique.

7.1.2 Related Work

Much research has recently focused on using sentiment analysis on microblogging platforms, including [8, 11], and [12, 13]. Due to the concentration of people's emotive datasets, Twitter has become popular [14]. Identifying useful and informative posts on social media plays a crucial part in understanding the situation during a crisis and a plague. Twitter provides a ton of data to be mined for extracting information, during the widespread pandemic called COVID-19. For instance, the analyses of numerous tweets looked at social media data to determine how the public felt about mask usage travel, and also immunization during the COVID-19 epidemic. We will treat these sentiment analysis researches as prime examples of Twitter knowledge analysis application cases. Generally speaking, there are three categories of emotions: negative, good, and neutral. Core sentiment categories are appropriate for brief matter knowledge, such as user tweets, according to studies [13, 16]. There exists another sub-classification that contains categories that include distinctive emotions of people, like joy, fear, anxiety, happiness, disgust, etc., which is the analysis of user emotions. More research, including [17, 18], has examined how people communicate their emotions on social media. Infodemiological study may be used to identify the primary effect in a given community because the word "infodemic" was developed to facilitate the spread of pandemic-related information online [19]. Furthermore, the topic modeling is a technique used to gather information on the spread of pandemics from tweets. Here, [20], the tweets from the countries like Brazil and the USA, are used to [21], look at COVID-19-related subjects. This study [22], also gathered data on the issue of the pandemic—a variety of symptoms, and ultimately

COVID-19's progression. Furthermore, the study [10], carefully examined tweets from roughly 183000 tweeters throughout a couple of months and concluded that COVID-19 had changed the behavior patterns of humans from a positive attitude to a negative attitude. According to the study, the fluctuation in attitudes throughout the pandemic led to mental problems. Figure 7.1 shows the various countries with most tweets.

The research [15], and [13], used information from the blogging platform named Weibo and gathered information about COVID-19 from the perceptions of people and also from the emotions that are extracted. The collection of information is the process of separating the majority of news from a huge collection of stories and information, using clustering methods like K-means based on the news headlines before identifying the news that is most closely related to the headlines as the day's most important news. The cc approaches are preferred for producing high-quality results because they are better suited than other methods for analyzing English texts [24]. Studies like [5], and [23], used tweets that had been manually tagged, which may have introduced human biases. On the other hand, objective tweet labeling is made possible by the hybrid system we present, which employs an automated Twitter labeling technique. We typically

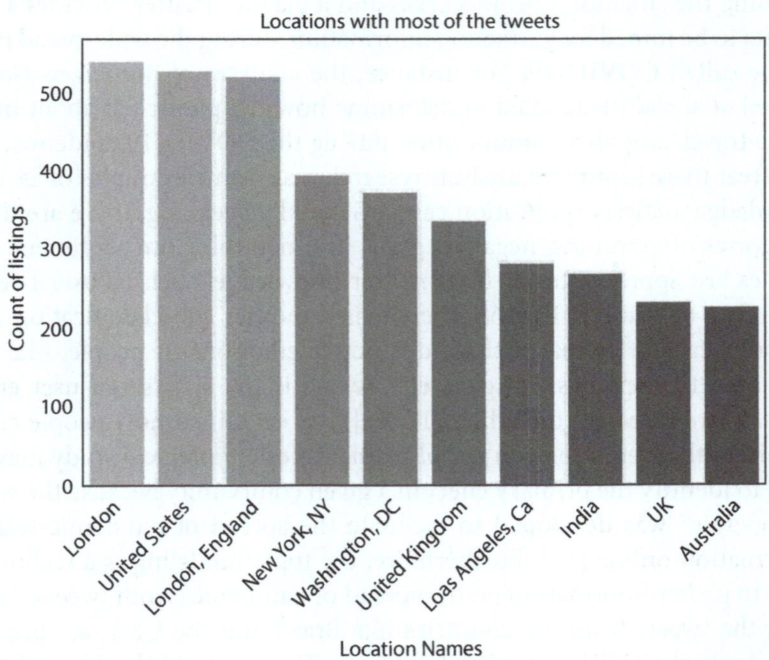

Figure 7.1 Countries with the most tweets [2].

notice that the studies [10, 13] were particularly focused on analyzing the sentiment of a specific place, like China and Australia. Comparable studies [23–25] conducted sentiment analysis for the United Kingdom, India, and the United Arab Emirates, respectively. In opposition, a data that includes tweets about the pandemic COVID-19 all over the world is used here. Furthermore, whereas we prefer to focus primarily on the COVID-19 pandemic, researchers like [10, 24, 26] performed an analysis of the sentiment to look at the diversity of events like government policies, readiness management, and separate programs. We perform multi-class analysis of the sentiment and the classification along with cc and Deep Learning techniques, the study [26], only considers the binary extraction of the sentiment and its classification. The work detects community among social networks. This study [10], used VADER for the extraction of both positive feelings and negative feelings, which is similar to our approach. But the extracted sentiments were neutral instead by assuming that a sizable cluster of people will be preferring tweets neutrally. Figure 7.2 represents the ratio of tweets from various countries.

In contrast to the study [8], which focused on analyzing tweets made after the lockdown, the dataset contains a range of COVID-19 data, including general insults among people, emotions, regarding the vaccination, preventive steps towards the spreading of the virus, policies of the government, and a ton of other information (see Figure 7.3). Whereas other recent research, such [26], waged the lexicon-based sentiment reasoning in VADER to get many tweets based on sentiments in the social media like Twitter, we used Crystal Feel, Text blob, and continuous neural network methodologies to examine sentiment from the tweets. The emotions expressed in the COVID-19 tweets are analyzed using Deep Learning and

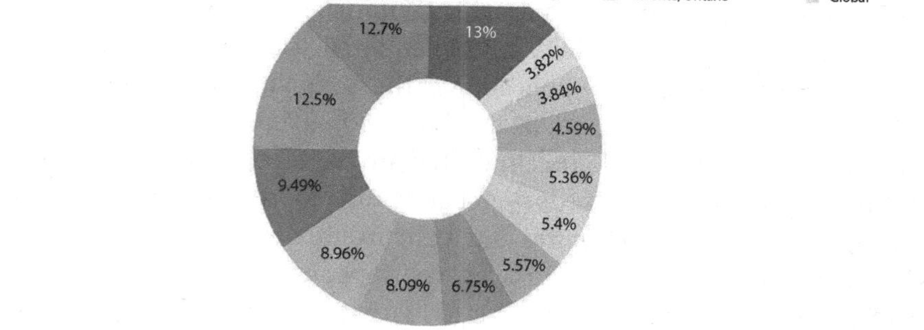

Figure 7.2 Ratio of tweets for different countries.

CC techniques, and we also used a combination of the lexicon-adopted VADER system and CC techniques to pull out and categorize the emotions. We have taken the content from Twitter based on the user account for analyzing the sentiment following the broad guidelines from [17, 18]. The objective of the study is to create a hybrid framework and to evaluate the same. For that, the NLP framework known as BERT, according to the most useful of our data, with a lexicon-based method like VADER, the BERT automatically analyze and categorize feelings about COVID-19 tweets. The accuracy rate is boosted by the BERT reading the data in a bi-directional format, and it also classifies the tweets using cutting-edge cc methods.

7.1.3 Contribution

This part advances knowledge in the area of COVID-19 tweets categorization by offering a special hybrid classification method that will improve knowledge to categorize the wide range of opinions expressed on microblogging websites. Our main contributions are listed below.

1) Using cubic centimeters, the created hybrid framework for the analysis of the sentiment and categorization from a beaux arts perspective. The newly disclosed innovative hybrid framework combines cutting-edge decilitre approaches for tweet classification with automatic lexicon-based sentiment analysis. It clears the hurdle of manual Twitter annotation, as shown by our hybrid architecture.

2) From a performance standpoint, we have used numerous performance analysis metrics, such as recall, accuracy F1 score, and precision to confirm the hybrid framework style justifications. It usually demonstrates how to analyze the most basic progressive cubic centimeter approaches using a variety of analysis metrics.

Our investigation into several cubic centimeter methods and how well they function concerning COVID-19 sentiment categorization advances knowledge of practical AI applications. The automatic sentiment classification makes it easier to understand how people feel about the COVID-19-related laws, rules, and guidelines that are required by the government. Acting swiftly is necessary during pandemics to control the pandemic through governmental measures and, concurrently, to reduce any unfavorable social emotions that could lead to disobedience and undermine the epidemic control actions. Caregivers, aid providers, and government representatives will monitor the sentiments of individuals expressing themselves through the vast amount of content accessible through social networks by using automatic hybrid sentiment categorization systems. For instance, the hashtag #antivax became a global protest in May 2020 while trending on Twitter. These inciting tweets have a direct correlation to the public's emotions, which generates enormous amounts of text-based emotional expression on social media. As the only sentiment analysis tool, VADER will likely fall short of processing these enormous text volumes. Consequently, we tend to suggest a novel hybrid of VADER with cubic centimeter methodologies which increase the significance of the data process for the analysis of sentiment. In our proposed design, VADER and cubic centimeter work best together because VADER supplies the label of the data and the knowledge type, which in turn gives the teaching of cubic centimeter procedures its inspiration. The intended hybrid approach will help inform the creation of guidelines and marketing campaigns to quickly notify the public of scientific truths. Also, the effort has been expanded to improve the accuracy of other models. The best outcome is produced by using the BERT framework. The best outcome is produced by the improved use of BERT. It might be a method that turns words into numbers. The ASCII text file BERT is. Being reachable could be quite beneficial. Since ASCII text file code encourages development by facilitating other researchers to easily apply your notions, numerous new developments in the machine learning industry are being pressed to be ASCII text files. This system is vital as machine learning models prefer inputs as numeric rather than string, therefore it formulates and turns words into numbers so you can train the models using the information that was initially text-based. When compared to other models, the BERT's bidirectional technique takes a little less time to train.

7.2 Objective

The prime aim of the proposed framework is to enhance the accuracy of the classification of the sentiment and to classify the larger datasets such as the COVID-19 dataset according to the sentiments in society. The hybrid approach, which combines NLP and ML methods based on lexicons, was employed to achieve automatic sentiment classification. Sentiment research on social network platforms including Twitter is primarily used to get insightful business information that will enhance overall business performance. We can quantify every mention and conversation using media sentiment analysis, as on Twitter. Every brand-related communication reveals significant consumer attitudes that can directly influence the overall business strategy. Furthermore, we also developed a Natural language processing framework called BERT. It is capable of reading the text or sentiments in both directions. This bidirectional property of the BERT framework has resulted in the best accuracy results, as it combines the modules to get an increased accuracy rate. It has been pre-trained using the text corpus and is an unsupervised language representation. Transformers, BERT employs a mechanism that detects concept-based links between words in a passage. A decoder is one of the mechanisms and is used to read the prediction, while an encoder is used to receive the input text. BERT is created so that the computer can determine a text's confusing language meaning by establishing the context around the text. The BERT's goal is to foretell the hidden word.

7.3 Classification of Tweets

7.3.1 Data Pre-Processing

Preparing information for future processing through any type of process is known as data pre-processing, which is a part of information preparation. There's a chance that the dataset's data won't be in a sentiment classification-friendly format. The data should be pre-processed as a result to make it suitable for sentiment categorization. There are numerous ways to perform the data preprocessing process.

7.3.1.1 Stop Word Removal

A stop word could be unremarkably utilized words that an inquiry engine has been configured to disregard, such as "the," "a," "an," or "in," both when categorizing entries for looking and when obtaining them as a result of an inquiry question. Further, we tend to eliminate using regular expressions, you can filter out special characters (*, $,!), URLs, user mentions (@), and hashtags (#).

7.3.1.2 Tokenization

Tokenization is a process by which a token is used to stand in for certain sensitive information, such as a Mastercard variety. Tokenization is often done to separate words or sentences. The terms "word tokenization" and "sentence tokenization" refer to the same process of breaking down a text into hot water sentences and dividing it into words using a separation strategy.

7.3.1.3 Lemmatization

Lemmatization produces what is known as a "lemma," which could be a word form as opposed to the stemmed-out root. The stemming technique yields inaccurate results. Forex: The term "battling" was changed to the meaningless "battl." Lemmatization is used as a result. Using this technique, a further check is produced by searching the lexicon for a word's base type. Lemmatization is used to economically produce the mil.

7.3.1.4 Stemming

By removing affixes from words, a technique called stemming can be used to extract the basic form of the words. The stem of the words intake, eats, and ingested is eat, thus it's kind of like pruning back a tree to its main branches. Stemming is a method used by search engines to categorize words. The area unit of the stemming algorithm is often rule-based. Once a term has been stopped using an excessive quantity, overstemming occurs. This could result in meaningless stems, where the word's entire meaning is obscured or ambiguous. University, universal, universities, and universe, for instance, are four nouns. An algorithmic computer that can resolve these four words has an edge over stemmed. As "univers" and "universities" stemmed, universal and universe also developed.

7.3.2 Feature Selection

The linguistics and grammar options are extracted by mistreatment of the text classification. Linguistics options ACCOMMODATE words. The syntactic feature includes "Unigrams," "Bigrams," and "n-grams." The algorithmic program is reworked using the vectorization technique from one price to a collection of values just once. The use of NumPy operations makes vectorization faster than the loop, which is a key factor in the decision. A dot is a vectorization instance. It operates more efficiently—thanks to NumPy. It executes internal operations using NumPy's optimizing function, which uses the two input numerical values directly rather than manually performing loop-based manual multiplication and summing. This inner product is additionally referred to as real. This performs the elementwise multiplication in it.

7.3.3 Sentiment Analysis

The length of the tweets and the proposed system model is given in Figures 7.3 and 7.4 respectively. Data are contained in the information set, and sentiment analysis is the process used to separate the dataset's positive, neutral, and negative sentiment types. Sentiment-containing content is represented

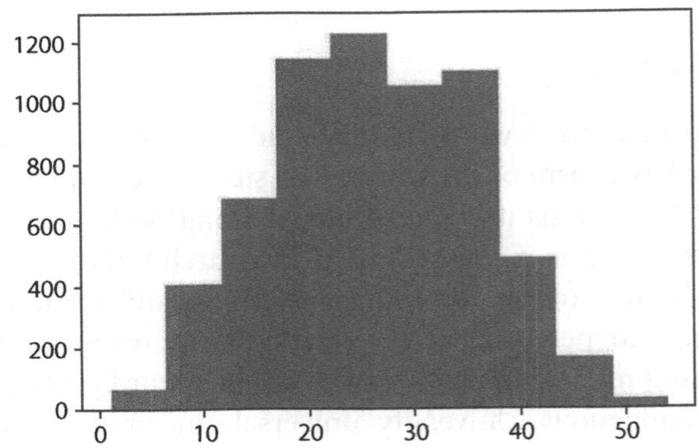

Figure 7.3 Length of the tweets.

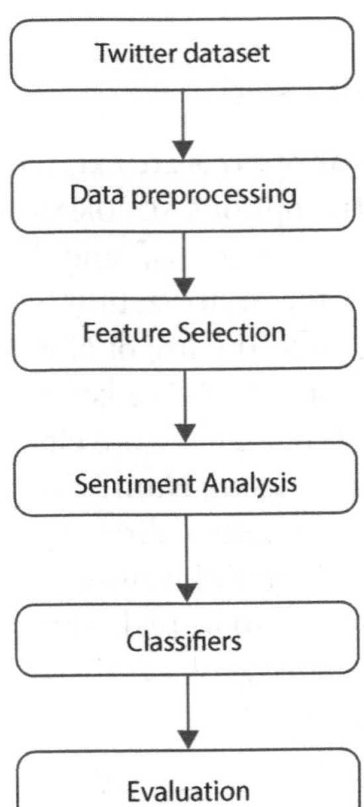

Figure 7.4 Proposed system model.

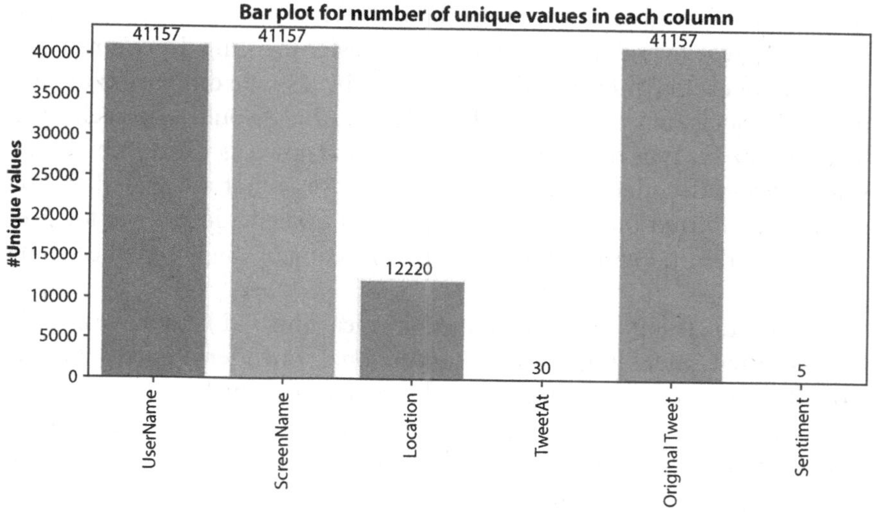

Figure 7.5 Number of unique values in each column.

by subjective components. In our system, VADER, a rule-based method, does sentiment analysis. By carefully selecting the wording used in the tweets, the VADER analyzes sentiment. Positive, negative, neutral, and compound sentiment polarity values are provided. When the value is more than or capable of 0.05, the values are indicated as optimistic; similarly, if the value is less than or capable of -0.05, the values are predicted as pessimistic; otherwise, the values are classified as neutral. When compared to approaches like language analysis, word count, and general research, VADER delivers a better result. That explains why VADER was mistreated for categorizing feelings. Figure 7.5 shows the number of unique values in each column.

7.3.4 Sentiment Analysis Using BERT

Bidirectional Encoder Representations, or BERT as it is known from the film Transformers, using the unlabeled text, pre-train deep bidirectional representations, is planned to learn collectively on each situation, both left and right. The result is– to create progressive models and it is utilized for a diversity of applications of NLP. The pre-trained BERT model is frequently improved with only 1 additional output layer. A model must be bi-directional to truly comprehend how a language operates. The objective of Masked Language Model (MLM) coaching is to secrete a term in every line and ask the computer program to identify the hidden word using the context of the hidden word. From then, BERT will be adopted based on the user's favorite and it is referred to as transfer learning. In contrast, the meaning of each word was only represented by a single dimension or slice in prior models such as GloVe and word2vec, which would map each word to a vector. This type of language processing is known as word embedding. Encoder and decoder are two of the mechanisms that are included. The encoder is utilized for reading the input text and the decoder is for predicting the result. Figure 7.6 shows the processing of single sentence using BERT.

In addition, there are models for transfer learning (TL) that have already been trained, including BERT (Bidirectional Encoder Representations from Transformers). By integrating the models for which a high accuracy rate can be attained, it incorporates sentiment categorization. There are 2 steps to it. The first step is the encoder and the second step is the decoder. The encoder is utilized to provide sentiment categorization using the inputs. The decoder is to sense the classification of the input sentence and gives the final output with a high accuracy rate. The transformer's input is processed using Equations 7.1 and 7.2.

The formula's Trans(.) indicates every transformer operation.

$$v_t = Trans(w_t x_a + b_t) \tag{7.1}$$

Here, v_t and x_a stand for the transformer input and output, respectively. The steps of the BERT model

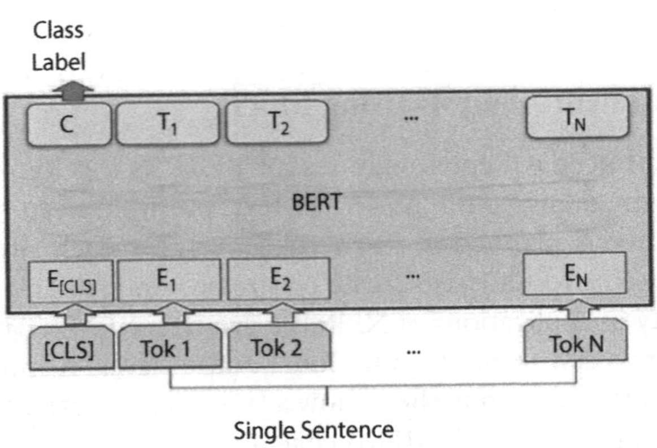

Figure 7.6 BERT processing of a single sentence.

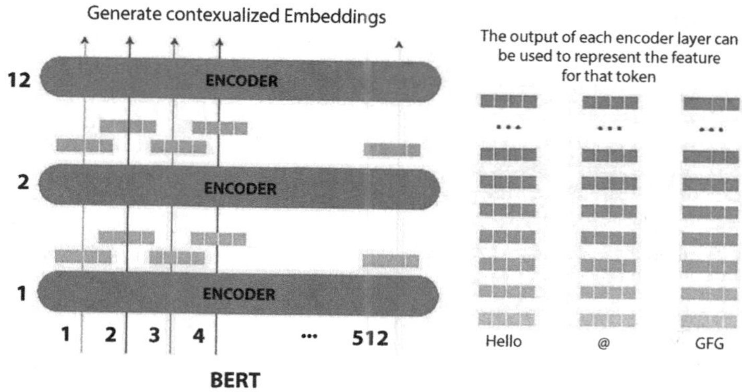

Figure 7.7 Encoder step in BERT.

$$z = Tokenization(Y) \tag{7.2}$$

When Y is present, the model's input is tokenized.

$$Z = Bert(Z)$$
$$Z = (Activation = RELU)$$
$$Z = (Dropout\ rate = 0.5)$$

Then, the tokenized input is given into the BERT model with the activation function as RELU and the dropout rate with values. The output of the BERT model is stored in Z. The encoder step is illustrated in Figure 7.7.

7.3.5 Labeling the Data

Before acting on the metric capacity unit techniques, the task is to label the tweets. The labeling of the tweets relies on sentiment values. When labeling the information, we tend to obtain the new dataset that includes text. stemmer, lemmatize, sentiment. We assign the optimistic tweets as zero, pessimistic tweets as two, and the unbiased tweets as one. The count for various sentiments is represented in Figure 7.8.

7.3.6 ML Model

The tweets' emotional content is classified as supported by the cubic centimeter techniques and deciliter techniques that are termed classifiers.

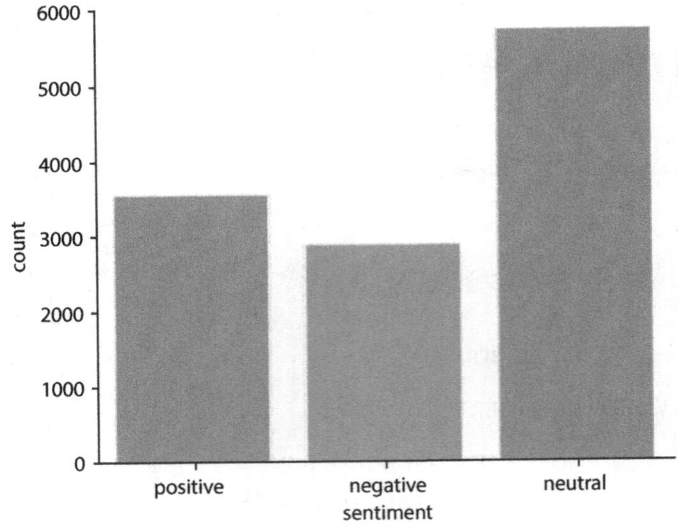

Figure 7.8 Count for sentiment analysis.

The classifier techniques that area unit utilized in this model area unit Gaussian NB, Multi-nominal NB, supplying regression, call Tree, Random Forest, LSTM, and SVM. A DT can be viewed as an illustration of nodes and branches, where nodes contain the classification-related attributes and branches include the values for those attributes. The text sentiment extraction method VADER can change how tweet contents are classified as good, negative, or neutral. VADER excelled at extracting emotions from microblogging sites with a 90% accuracy rate. The main classes for each of its subcategories are the +1, -1, and 0 sentiments (i.e., extremely optimistic, optimistic, unbiased, pessimistic, and extremely pessimistic). To achieve a high accuracy, the rate of the models is combined. Combining the models, by using an appropriate framework can improve the sentiment classification's level of accuracy. As a result, the NLP method known as BERT was employed. It is capable of reading the text or the sentiment in both directions, until the desired result is obtained. The BERT provides the best results for Natural Language Processing (NLP) tasks.

a) Decision tree:

Decision Nodes and branches make up trees. It is represented in Figure 7.9. The attributes are indicated by nodes. The value of the property that might result from the flaw is held by the branches. The entire dataset is contained in the foundation node. The foundation node is divided into several subsets, each of which has values for the most appropriate attributes. It creates

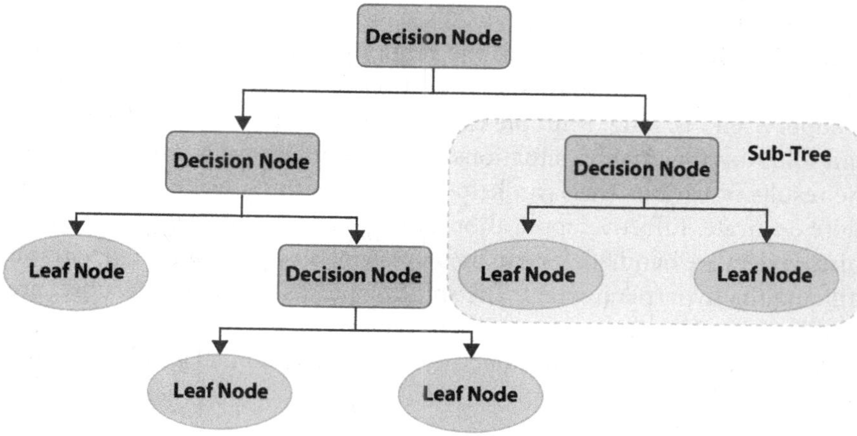

Figure 7.9 Decision tree model.

a decision tree that includes the most useful attribute. Another word for a techie is entropy. Entropy, which is the measure of randomness or uncertainty in knowledge, is denoted by the symbol E(s) for a finite collection of s. First, the formula given in Equation 7.3 is used to determine the entropy of the given model.

$$E(s) = \Sigma -P_i \, log_2 \, P_i \tag{7.3}$$

The likelihood of an event I occurring in a state node S, where S stands for "current state," is represented. T is the present situation (Information Gain) and X → selected quality Information gain, indicated by the symbol IG (T, X) for a set, is also known as Kullback-Leibler divergence. As a result of selecting a particular characteristic A, S indicates the actual change in entropy. Based on independent variables the variation in entropy is obtained. The formula given in Equations 7.4 and 7.5 determines the information gain for the model.

$$IG(T,X) = Entropy(T) - Entropy(T,X) \tag{7.4}$$

Another method for calculating the Gini index is

$$Gini = 1 - \Sigma(P_i^2\ ) \tag{7.5}$$

b) Random forest:

There are several choice trees in the random forest. To address the problems, Random Forest employs classification and regression. It is a method of supervised learning. Multiple classifier techniques can be combined to find solutions for complex situations. Calculating the average or mean from the results of various trees can help machine learning techniques become more accurate. Effective application of these techniques depends on how missing data are handled. It generates a reasonable prediction even without utilizing the hyperparameters. The splitting points of the node's subset are used to choose the feature at random. The work is illustrated in the Figure 7.10. Each feature's weight in a decision tree is determined as follows using Equations 7.6 and 7.7:

$$f_i = \frac{\Sigma_j \; node\ j\ splits\ on\ features\ i^{n_i}}{\Sigma_{k \in all\ nodes} \; ni} \tag{7.6}$$

The computed value can then be normalized by dividing by the total feature significance values to yield a number between 0 and 1:

$$Norm\ f_i = \frac{f_i}{\Sigma_{j \in all\ features} \; fi} \tag{7.7}$$

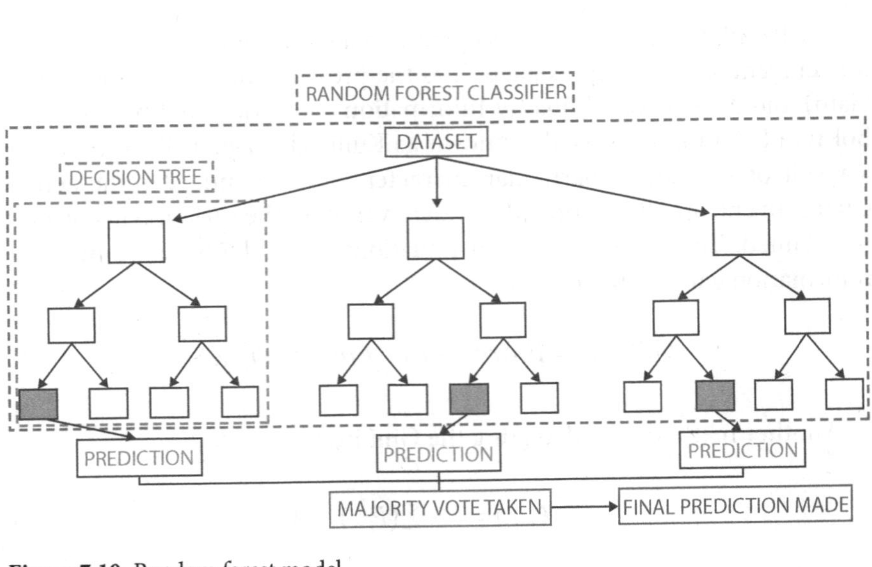

Figure 7.10 Random forest model.

On each tree, the significance value of the features is added up. Following that, the value is split by the whole amount of the trees. RF fi sub(i)= i-computed a feature's relevance using data from every tree in this model using Equation 7.8.

The normalized feature significance for I in tree j is given by Norm fi sub(ij), and T is the total number of trees.

$$RF\ f_i = \frac{\sum_{j \in all\ trees} norm\ fi}{T} \tag{7.8}$$

c) Logistic regression:

A supervised learning method called logistic regression calculates the likelihood of a binary event. Linear regression using continuous variables as results and logistic regression using discrete values as outcomes are the two primary categories of supervised learning techniques. Logistic regression delivers the results in discrete components as opposed to linear regression, which produces continuous values as a final output. Logistic regression produces distinct results as opposed to linear regression. Figure 7.11 shows the working model.

The straight line's equation is as follows: y represents the y-axis, b represents the intercept and $_X$ represents the x-axis given in Equation 7.9.

$$y = b_0 + b_1x_1 + b_2x_2 + \cdots \ldots b_nx_n \tag{7.9}$$

The only range for y in logistic regression is between 0 and 1. As a result, multiply the previous equation by (1-y) using Equation 7.10:

$$\frac{y}{1-y} \tag{7.10}$$

When y = 1, it applies to y = 0 and y = infinite. The range must be between -[infinity] and +[infinity], though. If we use the logarithm of the Equation 7.11, it becomes:

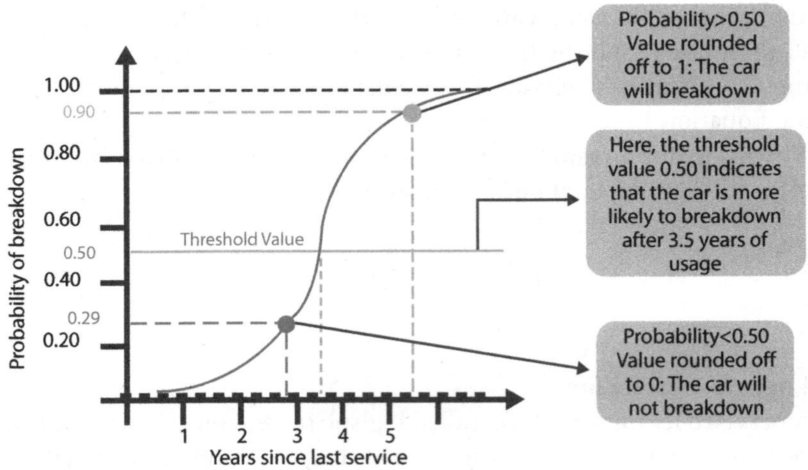

Figure 7.11 Logistic regression model.

$$\log[\frac{y}{1-y}] = b_0 + b_1x_1 + b_2x_2 + \cdots \ldots b_nx_n \tag{7.11}$$

d) Gaussian Naïve Bayes:

A probabilistic classification approach, the Gaussian Naive Bayes algorithm, is based on Bayes' theorem and operates under the assumption of feature independence. Naive refers to the use of the presumption that an object's alternatives are independent of one other gift inside the dataset. The performance decreases quickly with the expansion of the training set. Assuming that Xs have a normal or Gaussian distribution, then replace the normal distribution's probability density and refer to the model as Gaussian Naive Bayes and it is represented in Figure 7.12 and is computed using Equation 7.12.

$$p(x|y = c) = \frac{1}{\sqrt{2\pi\sigma^2}^{e} \, {}^{-(x-\mu)}/_{2\sigma^2}} \tag{7.12}$$

Sigma and mu are the continuous variable X's variance and mean as calculated for a certain class c of Y. The standard deviation and mean for every

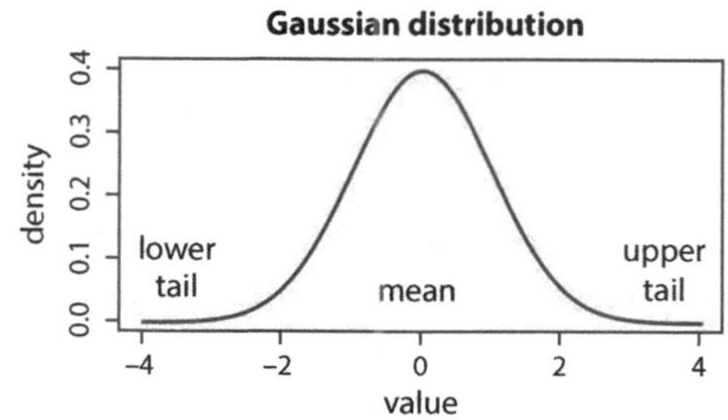

Figure 7.12 Gaussian Naïve Bayes model.

input variable for the class have to be saved including the probabilities for every class.

Mean(X) is equal to 1/n Sum(X), where X is the value of the input variable in the data and n is the number of instances. Standard Deviation(X) is calculated using the formula Standard Deviation(X) = sqrt (1/n * Sum), where n is the instances count, and xi is a particular x value.

e) Multinominal Naïve Bayes:

The Multinomial Naive Thomas Bayes rule could be a Bayesian learning approach standard in language process (NLP). The program tries to spot the tag of a text, like an associate email or a newspaper story, mistreatment of the Thomas Bayes theorem. It's easy and might be wont to forecast period applications. It's climbable. It will even handle monumental datasets with ease.

The formula for Multi-nominal NB is given in Equation 7.13.

$$p\left[\frac{A}{B}\right]=P\left(\frac{P(A\cap B}{P(B)}\right)=\frac{P(A)\div P\left(\frac{n}{A}\right)}{P(B)} \tag{7.13}$$

The likelihood of 1 event A occurring once another event B with some relationship to A has already occurred is termed probability using Equation 7.14.

$$P\left(\frac{A}{B}\right)=P\left(\frac{P(A\cap B}{P(A)}\right) \tag{7.14}$$

This expression is valid only when P(A) is greater than zero.

f) LSTM:

LSTM networks were designed specifically to beat the long dependency drawback two-faced by the continual neural networks. Cell states, a type of memory cell, govern the AN LSTM model's central function. Over time, the cell state stays in its current state. LSTMs have feedback connections that make them completely different from the normal feedforward neural networks. This property of LSTM allows the state to method the whole sequences of information. In addition to generating c(t) and h, Moreover, LSTM equations yield f(t), i(t), and c' (t). They are used internally by the LSTM (t). The lack of time dependency for the weight matrices (Wf, Wi, Wo, Wc, Uf, Ui, Uo, Uc) and biases (bf, bi, bo) indicates that these weight matrices do not vary from one step to the next. In other words, the same weight matrix area unit is utilized to calculate the outputs of several time-steps by using equations [7.15–7.20]. The working of LSTM is given in Figure 7.13.

$$f_t = \sigma_g(W_f * x_t + U_f * h_{t-1} + b_f) \tag{7.15}$$

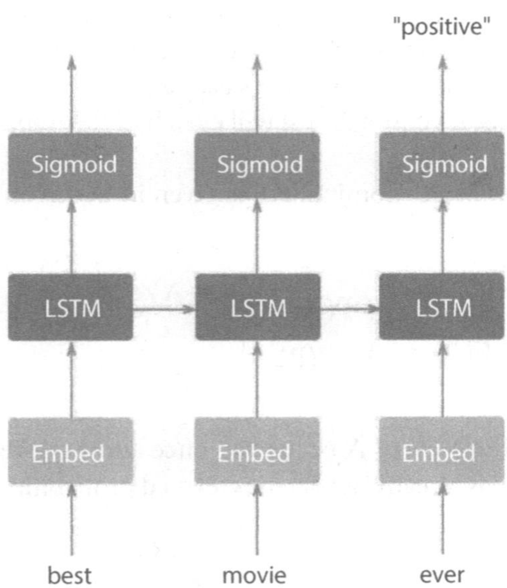

Figure 7.13 LSTM model.

$$i_t = \sigma_g(W_i * x_t + U_i * h_{t-1} + b_i) \tag{7.16}$$

$$o_t = \sigma_g(W_o * x_t + U_o * h_{t-1} + b_o) \tag{7.17}$$

$$c_t = \sigma_g(W_c * x_t + U_c * h_{t-1} + b_c) \tag{7.18}$$

$$c'_t = f_t . c_{t-1} + i_t . c'_t \tag{7.19}$$

$$h_t = o_t . \sigma_c(c_t) \tag{7.20}$$

the parameters used in it are:
f_t →is the forget gate
i_t →is the input gate
o_t →is the output gate
c_t →is the cell state
h_t →is the hidden state

g) Support Vector Machine:
Support Vector Machine, also referred to as SVM is a potential linear model for problems with regression and classification. The algorithmic rule creates a line or a hyperplane that splits the data into categories. SVM is an Associate in the Nursing algorithmic rule that takes the information as Associate in A line separating the inputs and outputs of the nursing profession categories if attainable. In line with the SVM algorithmic rule, we discover the locations in each category that are closest to the route. Currently, we frequently encrypt both the support vectors and the space between the road. Our objective is to increase this distance, which is known as the margin. The best hyperplane is one where the margin is greatest. In Associate in Nursing n-dimensional metric space, a hyperplane is a flat, n-1 dimensional set that separates the space into two independent parts. Fitting associate SVC implies tends to the square measure determination associate improvement downside. In other words, it tends to attempt to increase the margin between the hyperplane and also the support vectors of the various labels once the best margin and hyperplane have been found. We can use the subsequent equations to predict the label for a brand new information point and it is given in Figure 7.14.

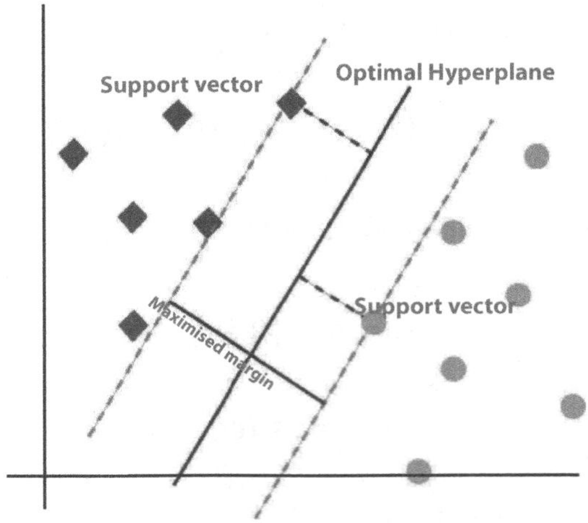

Figure 7.14 Support vector model.

$$w.x+b \geq 0 \text{ (label as 1)}$$

$$w.x+b < 0 \text{(label as -1)}$$

The bias is added when we take the dot product of the coefficient and the new point. We label the new point as label 1 if the outcome is greater than or equal to 0. Otherwise, if the outcome is less than 0, we label the new point with the label "-1."

7.4 Evaluation Metrics

7.4.1 Dataset

The dataset that we worked on for our proposed system is the COVID-19 dataset. The tweet about COVID-19 is taken from Kaggle.com [27]. Any other social media datasets can also be used to achieve the deliverables.

7.4.2 Performance Metric

a. Accuracy:

One metric that typically describes how the model performs across all areas is accuracy.

Accuracy = Divided by the total number of guesses, the number of right forecasts. It is computed using Equation 7.21.

$$Accuracy = \frac{TP+TN}{TP+TN+FP+FN} \tag{7.21}$$

Where TP, TN, FP, and FN stand for True Positives, True Negatives, and False Positives, respectively.

b. Precision

The quantitative relationship of correctly categorized positive samples (True Positive) to the full spectrum of properly classified positive samples is what defines precision and it is calculated using Equation 7.22.

$$Precision = \frac{TP}{TP+FP} \tag{7.22}$$

c. Recall:

Because of the magnitude relationship between the ranges of positive data which gets correctly categorized as positive and overall positive samples, the recall is determined. The recall gauges how well the model can identify promising samples. The more positive samples are found, the higher the recall. By victimization recall, one can do associate degree multiplied in accuracy; whereas, implementing at the side of the formula is given in Equation 7.23.

$$Recall = \frac{TP}{TP+FN} \tag{7.23}$$

d. F1-score:

The preciseness and recall measures are intended to be combined into one statistic by the F1 score. The rationale behind the incorporation of each preciseness-associated recall is to enhance the accuracy and potency to an extent. In most cases, the F1 score has been designed to figure well on unbalanced information using Equation 7.24.

$$f1-score\ k_i = 2 * \frac{precision\ k_i * recall\ k_i}{precision\ k_i + recall\ k_i} \tag{7.24}$$

7.4.3 Results

7.4.3.1 Labeling of Sentiment

According to this distribution, tweets about COVID-19 tend to be significantly longer than the 90-character average for all tweets. The severity and intensity of the COVID-19 epidemic, as well as the consequent inherent necessity of people to open up their emotions in greater depth on Twitter, are also to blame for the COVID-19-related tweets' relatively high character count. The volume of text that needs to be processed as a result of these lengthy tweets has increased significantly, necessitating machine-controlled sentiment analysis using cc. The lengthy tweets, on the other hand, are rich in information and will express nuanced feelings that are useful for learning about the sentiments of the social group. The following distribution is produced by the sentiment analysis using VADER. The number of tweets belonging to positive tweets is 3500, negative tweets with a count of 2900, and neutral tweets with a count of 5900. Thus, most of the sentiments were neutral, indicating a neutral opinion towards the pandemic. In the entire worldwide dataset, Figure 7.2 indicates the ratio of tweets in different locations. Among the given countries represented in the figure, London has recorded the highest number of tweets with a percentage of 11.7%. The least number of tweets were recorded in Global with the least percentage of 3.44%. Washington, DC recorded an average tweets ratio of about 8.07%. Figure 7.4 represents the number of unique values in the given Twitter datasets. It is represented by the bar plot where the number of unique values is plotted on the y-axis and the features or the column names are plotted on the x-axis. The username of the Twitter dataset contains a unique value of 41,157. The feature screenname and original tweets contain 41,157 which is equal to the username feature. The location contains 12,220 unique values. The dataset's sentiment feature has the fewest unique values among the Twitter datasets. This is how the labeling of the sentiment is done for the Twitter dataset. The word count and sentence count for neutral, positive, and negative tweets are given in Figures 7.15-7.19. Table 7.1 shows the sentiment classes with polarity score.

7.4.3.2 Performance of ML Models

For classification purposes, the dataset is split into training datasets and testing datasets. The entire dataset is divided into training and testing with a percentage of 70% and 30% respectively. For labeling the data, we use VADER and then the splitting of datasets proceeded. The testing of ML models was done on the testing datasets. Based on unknowable test data,

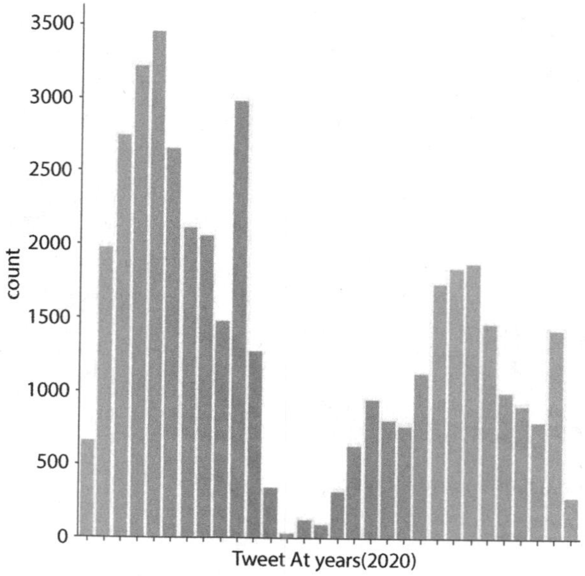

Figure 7.15 Count of tweets in the year.

all models are assessed. Thus, measuring the accuracy of the model is a good sign of judging the effectiveness of machine learning. VADER is used for sentiment analysis and labeling, as it has a high throughput of approximately equal to 4.8*10^3 tweets per second. It is used for achieving high processing speed in analyzing Twitter data. Table 7.2 represents the evaluation measure of scores for various model and their performances. The LSTM model has resulted in an increased accuracy rate of 90% when compared to other models like decision tree, random forest, Gaussian NB, Multinominal NB, logistic regression, and SVM. By combining various models to improve performance, we devised a technique called BERT. This BERT is used to get increased accuracy. The LSTM technique performed well than the other ML techniques. By working with BERT, we get an accuracy rate of 94% which is higher and more optimized than the other model that is computed.

7.5 Conclusion and Future Work

In particular, for classifying societal sentiments automatically on Twitter, the lexicon-based technique called VADER is used by which we combine the attitudes expressed in the tweets—positive, negative, and neutral—and categorize the COVID-19 tweets following these sentiments. We employed

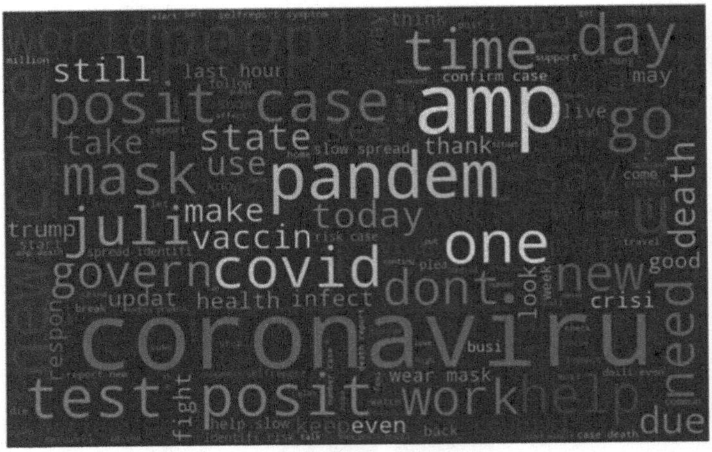

Figure 7.16 Word cloud for overall sentiments.

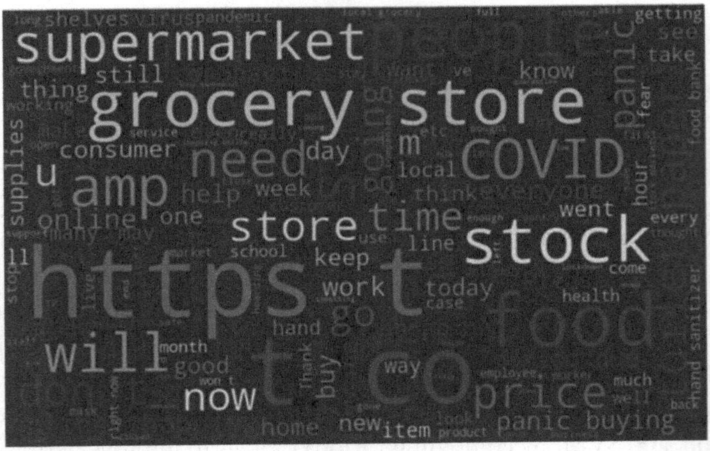

Figure 7.17 Word cloud for positive tweets.

various machine learning and natural language processing algorithms for the classification challenge. The LSTM has an accuracy of 90% for sentiment analysis. With training, the machine learning classifier has a fast processing speed of magnitude compared to the VADER technique. Overall, there's a huge quantity of text knowledge out there; however, if we wish to form task-specific datasets, we want to separate that pile into several various fields. And it tends to find you only a few thousand or a few hundred thousand examples of training that have been identified by humans. The NLP models based on deep learning require much greater amounts of data; after being trained on millions or billions of annotated coaching examples,

Figure 7.18 Word cloud for neutral tweets.

Figure 7.19 Word cloud for negative tweets.

Table 7.1 Sentiment classes with polarity score.

Text	Polarity	Compound	Sentiment
Trump never claims hoax claim effort	{'neg:0.0,'neu:0734,' pos':0.266}	0.257	positive
Cahng work gener recruit specif *via* recurit	{'neg':0.0,'neu':1.0, 'pos':0.0'}	0.0000	neutral

Table 7.2 Scores on the evaluation metrics for model performances.

Model	Accuracy	Precision	Recall	F1 score
Decision Tree	88%	75%	70%	71%
Logistic Regression	74%	77%	59%	61%
Multinominal NB	74%	58%	47%	43%
Gaussian NB	54%	79%	66%	68%
Random forest	87%	79%	66%	68%
LSTM	90%	78%	76%	77%
SVM	88%	84%	86%	85%
BERT	94%	90%	92%	93%

they see significant improvements. There are numerous techniques for coaching general-purpose language illustration models victimization of the big piles of unannotated text on the net. This approach leads to nice accuracy enhancements compared to other NLP techniques So, it gives the final output with a high accuracy rate of 94%.

In the future, the work can be increased to a further extent by applying various algorithms to get better performance for sentiment classification which might automatically classify the tweets even for the unstructured data. In the future, we would like to consider a wide range of sentiments such as fear, disgust, anticipation, trust, extreme pressure, etc., and the false prediction in some cases would be detected in the future to attain a high state of efficiency in the classification. Examining the interactions between the analysis and its manipulation is a significant area for future research.

AI disclosure statement: The author confirms that no artificial intelligence (AI)-generated content or AI-assisted writing tools were used in the preparation of this chapter (including summaries and the abstract). All text, analysis, and conclusions are the result of the author's original work.

Bibliography

1. Khan, R., Khan, R., Shrivastava, P., Kapoor, A., Tiwari, A., Mittal, A., Social media analysis with AI: Sentiment analysis techniques for the analysis of Twitter COVID-19 data. *J. Crit. Rev.*, 7, 9, 2761–2774, 2020.

2. Rajput, N.K., Grover, B.A., Rathi, V.K., Word frequency and sentiment analysis of Twitter messages during Coronavirus pandemic, Apr. 2020, [Online]. Available: arXiv:2004.03925.
3. Imran, A.S., Doudpota, S.M., Kastrati, Z., Bhatra, R., Crosscultural polarity and emotion detection using sentiment analysis and deep learning—A case study on COVID-19. *IEEE Access*, 8, 181074–181090, 2020, DOI: 10.1109/ACCESS.2020.3027350.
4. Krupse, A., Haberle, M., Kuhn, I., Zhu, X.X., Cross-language sentiment analysis of European Twitter messages during the COVID-19 pandemic, Aug. 2020, [Online]. Available: http://arxiv.org/abs/2008/12172.
5. Agarwal, A., Xie, B., Vovsha, I., Rambow, O., Passonneau, R., Sentiment analysis of Twitter Data, in: *Proc. Workshop Lang. Social Media*, pp. 30–38, 2011.
6. Xue, J., Chen, J., Hu, R., Chen, C., Zheng, C., Su, Y., Zhu, T., Twitter Discussions and Emotions About the COVID-19 Pandemic: Machine Learning Approach *J. Med. Internet Res.*, 22, 11, e20550, 2020. URL: https://www.jmir.org/2020/11/e20550 DOI: 10.2196/20550
7. Abbas, R. and Michael, K., COVID-19 contact trace app deployments: Learnings from Australia and Singapore. *IEEE Consum. Electron. Mag.*, 9, 5, 65–70, 2020. https://doi.org/10.1109/MCE.2020.3002490.
8. Yu, X., Zhong, C., Li, D., Xu, W., Sentiment analysis for news and social media in COVID-19, in: *Proc. 6th ACM SIGSPATIAL Int. Workshop Emerg. Manage. GIS*, Nov. 2020, pp. 1–4, doi: 10.1145/3423333.3431794.
9. Dey, A., Machine learning algorithms: A review. *Int. J. Comput. Sci. Inf. Technol.*, 7, 3, 1174–1179, 2016.
10. Towardsdatascience.com/bert-explained-state-of-the-art-language-model-for-nlp-f8b21a9b6270
11. Zhou, J., Yang, S., Xiao, C., Chen, F., Examination of community sentiment dynamics due to COVID-19 pandemic: A case study from Australia, Jun. 2020, [Online]. Available: http://arxiv.org/abs/2006.12185.
12. Li, S., Wang, Y., Xue, J., Zhao, N., Zhu, T., The impact of COVID-19 epidemic declaration on psychological consequences: A study on active Weibo users. *Int. J. Environ. Res. Public Health*, 17, 6, 2032, 2020 Mar 19. doi: 10.3390/ijerph17062032. PMID: 32204411; PMCID: PMC7143846.
13. Elbagir, S. and Yang, J., Twitter sentiment analysis using natural language toolkit and VADER sentiment, in: *Proc. IMECS*, pp. 1–5, 2019.
14. Bilgin, M. and Sentürk, I.F., Sentiment analysis on Twitter data with semi-supervised Doc2Vec, in: *Proc. Int. Conf. Comput. Sci. Eng. (UBMK)*, pp. 661–666, 2017, doi: 10.1109/UBMK.2017.8093492.
15. da Silva, N.F.F., Hruschka, E.R., Hruschka, E.R., Tweet sentiment analysis with classifier ensembles. *Decis. Support Syst.*, 66, 170–179, Oct. 2014, [Online]. Available: https://doi.org/10.1016/j.dss.2014.07.003.

16. Ghafarian, S.H. and Yazdi, H.S., Identifying crisis-related informative tweets using learning on distributions. *Inf. Process. Manag.*, 57, 2, 2020, Art. no. 102145. [Online]. Available: https://doi.org/10.1016/j.ipm.2019.102145.
17. Lagutina, K., Larionov, V., Petryakov, V., Lagutina, N., Paramonov, I., Shchitov, I., Sentiment classification into three classes applying multinomial Bayes algorithm, N-grams, and thesaurus, in: *Proc. 24th Conf. Open Innovat. Assoc. (FRUCT)*, pp. 214–219, 2019.
18. Singh, P., Singh, S., Sohal, M., Dwivedi, Y.K., Kahlon, K.S., Sawhney, R.S., Psychological fear and anxiety caused by COVID-19: Insights from Twitter analytics. *Asian J. Psychiatr.*, 54, Art. no. 102280, Dec. 2020, doi: 10.1016/j.ajp.2020.102280.
19. Mahsuda, N., Ananth, C., Farukh, Z., Fakhriddin, K., Iskandar, M., Ananth Kumar, T., Theoretical and Methodological Foundations of Virtualization of Social Services, in: *2023 International Conference on Advances in Computing, Communication and Applied Informatics (ACCAI)*, IEEE, pp. 1–6, 2023.
20. Garcia, K. and Berton, L., Topic detection and sentiment analysis in Twitter content related to COVID-19 from Brazil and the USA. *Appl. Soft Comput.*, 101, Art.no. 107057, Mar. 2021, doi: 10.1016/j.asoc.2020.107057.
21. Jang, H., Rempel, E., Roth, D., Carenini, G., Janjua, N.Z., Tracking COVID-19 discourse on Twitter in North America: Infodemiology study using topic modeling and aspect-based sentiment analysis. *J. Med. Internet Res.*, 23, 2, Art. no. e25431, 2021, doi: 10.2196/25431.
22. Boon-Itt, S. and Skunkan, Y., Public perception of the COVID-19 pandemic on Twitter: Sentiment analysis and topic modeling study. *JMIR Public Health Surveillance*, 6, 4, Art. no. e21978, 2020, doi: 10.2196/21978.
23. Whang, D. and Vosoughi, S., Dartmouth CS at WNUT-2020 task 2: Informative COVID-19 tweet classification Using BERT, in: *Proc. 6th W-NUT*, Dec. 2020, pp. 480–484, doi: 10.18653/v1/2020.wnut-1.72.
24. Alhajji, M., Al Khalifah, A., Aljubran, M., Alkhalifah, M., Sentiment analysis of tweets in Saudi Arabia regarding governmental preventive measures to contain COVID-19, to be published, doi: 10.20944/preprints202004.0031.v1.
25. Barkur, G., Vibha, Kamath, G.B., Sentiment analysis of nationwide lockdown due to COVID 19 outbreak: Evidence from India. *Asian J. Psychiatr.*, 51, Art. no. 102089, Jun. 2020, doi: 10.1016/j.ajp.2020.102089.
26. Samuel, J., Ali, G.G.M.N., Rahman, M.M., Esawi, E., Samuel, Y., COVID-19 public sentiment insights and machine learning for tweets classification. *Information*, 11, 6, Art. no. 314, Jun. 2020, doi: 10.3390/info11060314.
27. Available:https://www.kaggle.com/datasets/gpreda/covid19-tweets

8

Fingerprint Registration and Matching Based on Improved Convolutional Neural Network

Lakshmanan B.*, Selvakumar B., Kasthuri K., Nivashini S. and Swetha R.

Department of Computer Science and Engineering Mepco Schlenk Engineering College, Sivakasi, Tamil Nadu, India

Abstract

The problem of latent fingerprint matching is significant yet unresolved. As an essential step in fingerprint matching, registration of fingerprints has an important effect on recognition performance. Existing techniques for registering latent fingerprints mostly depend on identifying correspondences between minute details, and they will almost surely fall short if insufficient minutiae are retrieved due to a tiny fingerprint regions or noisy images. This work, represented an improved method for latent fingerprint registration based on human fingerprint patch alignment and matching; it assesses the spatial transformation between two fingerprints. The presented work is used to enhance recognition performance of the latent fingerprint with various challenging conditions like tiny regions, poor image quality, and severe distortion. In this proposed method, deep learning-based convolution neural networks (CNN) is adopted for feature extraction, descriptor extraction, and matching similarity score. In this presented work, we skip the minute detail extraction stage and use evenly sampled locations as critical points when we have a matched pair of fingerprints. Each pair of sampling points is then compared using the suggested patch alignment and matching procedure, which generates similarity and alignment parameter values. Finally, a collection of consistent correspondences has been identified using Oriented fast and Rotated Brief (ORB) detector and brute force. Experiments on two public high resolution fingerprint databases demonstrated the efficacy of fingerprint matching

**Corresponding author*: lakshmanan@mepcoeng.ac.in

T. S. Arun Samuel, L. Jerart Julus, P. Kanimozhi, T. Ananth Kumar and S. Balamurugan (eds.) Composite Artificial Intelligence: Fundamentals, Challenges, and Applications, (181–198) © 2026 Scrivener Publishing LLC

with a limited fingerprint region and a low-quality image. Multiple experiments on the NIST and NISTSD27 databases show that the suggested technique gives cutting-edge registration performance, especially in challenging applications.

***Keywords*:** Fingerprint matching, deep learning, convolutional neural network, latent fingerprint, similarity score

8.1 Introduction

Fingerprint identification has recently seen a rise in the use of automatic latent fingerprint feature extraction and matching to relieve the demand on fingerprint experts. Despite extensive research, the recognition performance of latent fingerprints with tiny effective regions, fuzzy or distorted images, is significantly inferior. Because of this, latent fingerprint matching still has a lot of space for development. Accurate fingerprint registration is essential for identification performance in latent fingerprint-matching algorithms.

The most common method used to build correspondences between images is minutiae-based techniques, which work on the principle of extraction of information from each fingerprint; then extract minutiae descriptors, then utilize these to locate reliable matches. It can be challenging to extract enough fine details from weak latent fingerprints. The estimated minutiae may be insufficient or in the wrong place or direction, if latent fingerprints have a tiny effective area or if background noise significantly distorts fingerprint images. The ability to identify offenders using latent fingerprints has been demonstrated in this work.

In this work, we presented improved convolutional neural network algorithm to tackle the various challenges faced by traditional approaches. The key contributions of the work are –

(a) Constructing deep learning architecture that effectively works for fingerprint matching
(b) Matching done within less computational time
(c) Working well for noisy images and providing good detection accuracy

8.2 Related Works

Zhiyuan He *et al.* [1], presented a network known as PFVNet; it only verifies a portion of a fingerprint. AlignNet spatial transformer network, which is a part of PFVNet, determines the affine transform parameters between the reference and query images. The rotating AlignNet technique performs effectively in large rotation angles due to its high rotation invariance properties. This work resulted in good performance but it fails to detect accurately for few cases like low quality images and tiny size. Hanzhuo Tan *et al.* [2], proposed deep neural networks which are used for 2D contactless fingerprint minutiae identification. This approach adapted atrous spatial pyramid pooling block. This method works very well for cross database and shows supremacy over other existing approaches.

Steven A. Groszetal [3], developed the contact to contactless fingerprint matching (C2CL)method. This framework consists of two stages (1) pre-processing algorithm, and (2) matching algorithm. In the first stage, the algorithm performs segmentation, enhancement, and scale the input image. In the next stage, it performs extraction of minutiae and texture features. The authors evaluated their method on three publicly available dataset and resulted False Acceptance Rate (FAR) value of 0.01%. Quang Nhat Tran and Jiankun Hu [4], presented the method named fingerprint matching for multi-filter method. This approach is a combination of EMCC and KNN-MPT method. Their approach performs well for publicly available dataset and shows improved detection performance. John Harvey *et al.* [5], proposed a statistical measure called biometric performance that is used to track the effectiveness of the biometric system over time. This approach is evaluated on large volume of fingerprint data collected over a different year.

Sheng Lan *et al.* [6], presented non-rigid registration techniques for distorted fingerprint matching images. In this work, the authors considered the direction information of fingerprints for matching. The authors suggested that spatial transformation details can be extracted using their approach. They evaluated their method on four publicly available fingerprint databases namely FCV2004, NIST, SD27, SD30, and Tsinghua distorted fingerprint database. Rudolf Haraksim *et al.* [7], discussed that fingerprint matching have significantly improved by adopting the growth model. This algorithm can effectively work for displacement of minutiae over different age interval of the individual.

Nadia Nedjah *et al.* [8], proposed skin elasticity tolerant algorithm (SETA) for biometric recognition. This approach uses minutiae and maximizes the matching score. The authors summarized their findings that SETA method is suitable for real time implementation of smart biometric card mechanism after mitigating the problem of data storage. Lei Shi *et al.* [9], presented a new end-to-end fingerprint matching approach for 2D contactless fingerprints called triplet network combined GAN.

The triplet network is employed for data augmentation and balancing, which reduces overfitting and improves robustness of the model. They evaluate their approach on PolyU and FVC2004 DB1 dataset.

Feng Liu *et al.* [10], discussed DeepPore ID method for learning a deep feature from a pore. Their approach resulted in a high recognition rate and tested on FMR1000 dataset. They utilized Euclidean distance as distance metric to find similarity between query and template fingerprint images. Their method works very well for small image size. Ram P. Krish *et al.* [11], proposed the algorithm which considered extended features like unusual / rare minutiae from latent fingerprint images for fingerprint identification process. They evaluated their method on SD27 database and this approach improves the fingerprint identification substantially compared to other existing approaches.

Zhe Cui *et al.* [12], proposed the framework consisting of two stages: (1) Siamese network, (2) encoder-decoder network. In the first stage, the network will perform feature embedding and in the second stage, it will perform regressing displacement field. The framework is trained *via* end-to-end manner. The authors designed the model which performs both registration and mosaicking. They model supremacy, and is evaluated on FVC2004, TDF and NIST SD27 databases. Yijie Xun *et al.* [13], presented CNN and support vector machine for automobile driver fingerprint recognition. Their approach alleviates the security problem and it can recognize the driver identity information in real time. These method results show model's superior performance in detecting illegal drivers.

In the work of Wei Jing Wong [14], multi-task CNN model was developed to recover ridge details from noisy fingerprint images. The model consists of two stages: (1) reconstruction phase and (2) orientation field phase. The framework shows significant improvement in enhancing image quality and matching accuracy. Zhao Zhang *et al.* [15], proposed fingerprint minutiae based on deep CNN. The author introduced multi-task learning algorithm to learn minutiae detection and its direction. The proposed approach effectively works on grayscale fingerprint images, and its supremacy is evaluated on publicly available benchmark datasets.

M. Ali *et al.* [16], presented two stage fingerprint pore detection. In the first stage, CNN is used to extract the pore features, and in the second stage it concentrates on precisely locating pore centroids for the detection of true or false pores in the fingerprint image. Their method works very well with improved performance compared to other methods. Suresh Kumar *et al.* [17], developed a method for pose estimation of latent fingerprints based on feedback approach. The method is fully automated and able to find potential poses in a progressive manner and weak friction ridge regions are enhanced based on iterative feedback mechanism. They evaluated their approach on NIST SD27 and MOLF DB4 latent fingerprint databases. Their method shows improved identification accuracy compared to other methods.

8.3 Dataset Description

The latent fingerprint is obtained from the NIST SD27 database [18].The NIST SD27 database contains 300 samples of latent fingerprints. In our experimental setup, 250 images are considered for training and 50 images are utilized for testing purposes. The latent fingerprint image has size of 800*768 pixels and it is shown in Figure 8.1. The rolled fingerprint is obtained from the NIST database. Each person's fingerprint has ten different samples in the fingerprint database. In rolled fingerprint, 800 images are considered for training and 150 images are considered for testing. The rolled fingerprint image in the NIST database is 512*512 pixels size and it is shown in Figure 8.2.

8.4 Proposed Work

In this work, the proposed work describes the various functional blocks of the architecture which consists of image pre-processing, registration, feature extraction, local patch alignment, descriptor extraction and matching. The block diagram of the proposed architecture is shown in Figure 8.3.

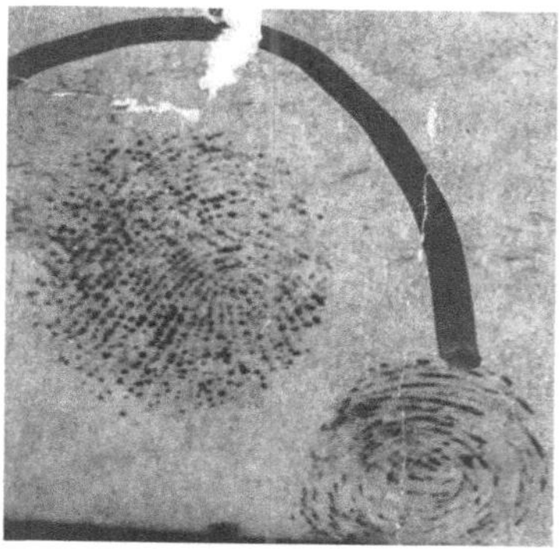

Figure 8.1 Latent fingerprint image in the NIST27 database.

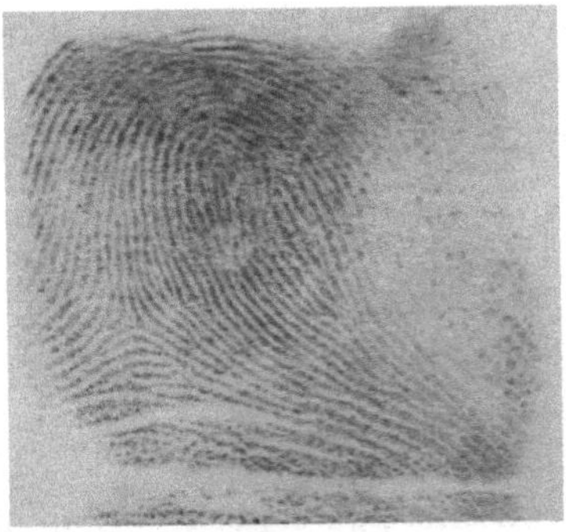

Figure 8.2 Rolled fingerprint image in the NIST27 database.

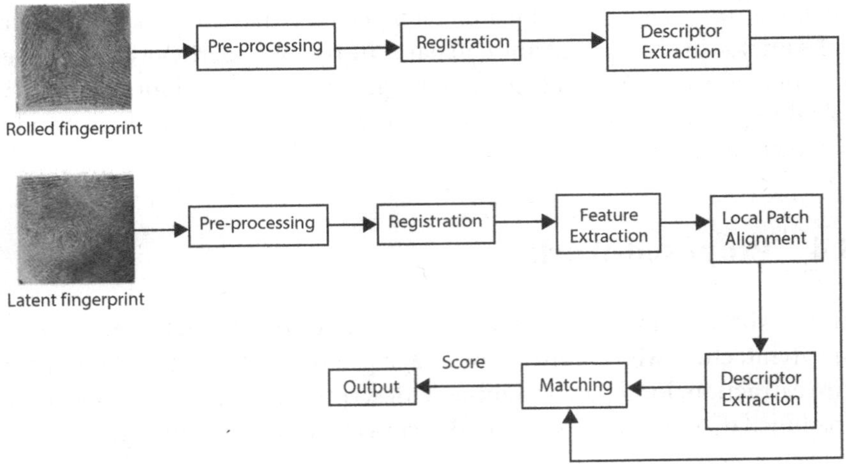

Figure 8.3 The functional block diagram of the proposed fingerprint matching system.

8.4.1 Image Pre-Processing

During pre-processing, rolled and latent fingerprint images are used as input images. Cropping and resizing is performed as initial stage. Cropping and resizing is performed for rolled fingerprint image. Resizing is applied for latent fingerprint image. After applying image scaling, the input image is cropped using a Region of Interest (ROI). Resizing, or cropping the input image using a region of interest (ROI) with dimensions of 340*440, reduces the original image's size. Then, we resize. The ROI images are resized according to mathematical Equation (8.1) from their original

340*440 dimensions to 256*256, which is the suitable dimension for feature extraction.

$$(p_{new}, q_{new}) = \frac{H}{\max(p,q)}(p,q) \tag{8.1}$$

Where,
(p, q) – original image width and height
H – some maximum value
(p_{new}, q_{new}) – resized image width and height

8.4.2 Registration

There are two procedures that make up the registration—coarse and precise registration. The coarse registration is used to determine the coarse correspondences, where all the sample locations on the rolled fingerprint and the latent fingerprint are compared. In the coarse registration, there are 10 points between each other. The coarse registration's result is utilized as the input for precise registration. Only the neighboring sampling points on rolled fingerprints are used to compare the sampling sites on latent fingerprints. In the stage of precise registration, there are five-point separations between each fingerprint. The intervals between points in precise registration is 5.

8.4.3 Feature Extraction Based on Improved Convolutional Neural Network

Improved VGG-16 network is used for feature extraction. Improved VGG-16 has five blocks namely conv2D, maxpooling2D, flatten, dense, dropout and dense. There are several convolutional and max-pooling layers in feature extraction. The architecture consists of four blocks. Each block has a max-pooling layer after each consecutive convolution layer. The number of filters, kernel size, strides, activation, and input shape are convolution layer parameters. Each block has a different number of filters in which initial block consists of 64 filters, the second block (with 128 filters), the third block (with 256 filters), and final block(with 512 filters). The convolutional layer's five blocks each have a kernel size (3, 3). The network is fed with 250 images as input provided for feature extraction. After feature extraction, 200 features were obtained. The process block for feature extraction is shown in Figure 8.4.

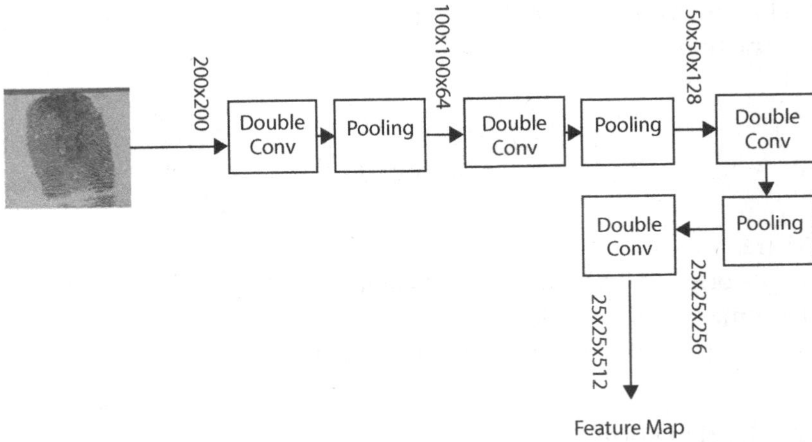

Figure 8.4 Process block for the feature extraction by Improved Convolutional Neural Network.

8.4.4 Local Patch Alignment

Latent fingerprints are aligned using the local patch alignment. There are two ways to rotate an image: (1) by rotating the pixels, (2) by applying a transformation matrix. To produce a new rotational image, the image's pixels must physically change their values. To create a new, transformed image, applying a transformation matrix involves establishing a matrix that represents the rotation transformation and applying it to the input images. For instance, changing an images orientation from landscape to portrait or vice versa can be accomplished by simply rotating it by 90 degrees. The alignment of a tilted or skewed image can be adjusted by rotating it by an arbitrary angle, such as 45 degrees, which can also be used to produce artistic effects according to Equation (8.2).

$$R = [\cos(\omega) -\sin(\omega); \sin(\omega) \cos(\omega)] \tag{8.2}$$

Where,
ω is the angle of rotation in radians
cos(ω) and sin(ω) are the cosine and sine of the rotation angle

Translation procedure is often performed by shifting the image's pixels in the x and y directions. This involves shifting the x and y positions of each pixel of an image by a certain number of pixels. The application and the desired outcome will determine how much translation is required. For instance, aligning two slightly out-of-focus images or fixing a camera perspective can both benefit from a small-scale image translation as shown in Equation (8.3).

$$t = [tx\ ty] \tag{8.3}$$

Where,
The x-axis translation is measured by the variable tx.
The amount of translation along the y-axis is measured by ty.

8.4.5 Descriptor Extraction

In descriptor extraction phase, descriptors are extracted for both latent and rolled fingerprint. For rolled images, we use Oriented FAST Rotated BRIEF (ORB) method to locate important regions or details in an image. This algorithm is used to locate the key points in an image, whereas the short approach is used to describe the key points by generating a binary coefficient of performance for each key point. We employ the improved VGG-16 network for the descriptor extraction. Improved VGG-16 has five blocks namely conv2D, maxpooling2D, flatten, dense, dropout and dense. There are several convolutional and max-pooling layers in feature extraction. The architecture consists of five blocks. Each block has a max-pooling layer after each consecutive convolution layer. The number of filters, kernel size, strides, activation, and input shape are convolution layer parameters. Each block has a different number of filters in which initial block consists of 64 filters, the second block (with 128 filters), the third block (with 256 filters), and fourth and final block (with 512 filters). The convolutional layers in the architecture have five blocks with each have a kernel size of (3 x 3). The descriptors are extracted for latent fingerprint and the functional stages of proposed descriptor extraction stage is shown in Figure 8.5.

8.4.6 Patch Matching

Rolled fingerprint is matched with the latent fingerprint and obtain the matching score. The proposed patch matching module seeks to determine exactly whether similar two aligned picture patches are the same. The two images are matched if the similarity is greater than the threshold of 0.5. The number of matches and matching score estimation is given in the Equations (8.4) and (8.5) respectively.

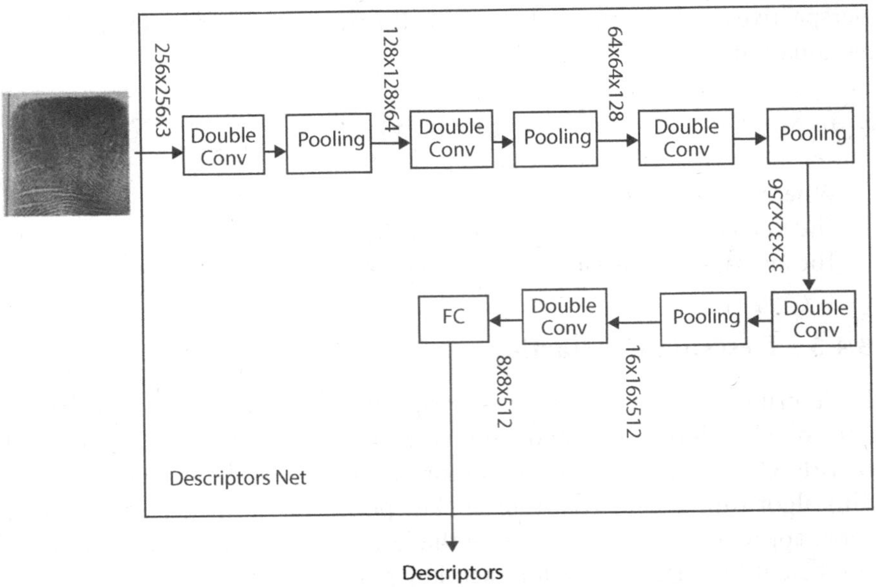

Figure 8.5 Functional stages of the proposed descriptor extraction phase.

$$\text{num\_matches} = \text{len(matches)} \tag{8.4}$$

$$\text{matching\_score} = \text{num\_match}/(\text{len(kp1)}*(\text{len(kp2)}) \tag{8.5}$$

where:

kp1 – keypoints of the image 1
kp2 – keypoints of the image 2
num_matches – length of the matches

The pseudocode of the proposed method is given below:

Pseudocode for the proposed method:

Input: Rolled image(R_img), Latent image(L_img)
Output: matching score(M_score)
Initialize H, crop_img, res_img, trans_img
crop_img=R_img[y1:y2,x1:x2]
Get crop_img image width(p) and height(q)
Res_img= crop_img.copy()
Calculate desired width (p_{new}) and height (q_{new}) for resizing

$$(p_{new}, q_{new}) = \frac{H}{\max(p,q)}(\text{p,q})$$

res_img.width = p_{new}

res_img.height = q_{new}
Perform rotation using (p_{new}, q_{new})
$p' = p_{new} * \cos(\omega) - q_{new} * \sin(\omega)$
$q' = p_{new} * \sin(\omega) - q_{new} * \cos(\omega)$
Translate the rotated image using width (X) and height (Y)
$X = p' + tp'$
$Y = q' + tq'$
trans_img = X, Y
Extract ORB Features
Orb = orb.create()
Kp_latent = orb.detectand compute(trans_img)
Kp_rolled = orb.detectand compute(res_img)
Match descriptors using Brute Force Matching
num_matches = len(matches)
M_score = num_matches/(len(kp_rolled) * len(kp_latent)
M_score * =1000
return M_score

8.5 Results and Discussion

8.5.1 Evaluation Metrics

The proposed method is evaluated using performance metrics such as accuracy, precision, recall and F1 score. The mathematical representation of the evaluation metrics is shown in the equations (8.6)–(8.9):

$$\text{Accuracy} = \frac{tp + tn}{tp + fp + tn + fp} \tag{8.6}$$

$$\text{Precision} = \frac{tp}{fp} \tag{8.7}$$

$$\text{Recall} = \frac{tp}{(tp + fn)} \tag{8.8}$$

$$\text{F1 Score} = \frac{2 * (precision * recall)}{(precision + recall)} \tag{8.9}$$

Where,

tp –true positive, fp –false positive, tn –true negative and fn –false negative

The proposed model loss vs epochs are shown in Figure 8.6 and Figure 8.7 for rolled fingerprint and latent fingerprint identification process.

Figure 8.6 shows loss graph plot of an improved convolutional neural network model to predict rolled fingerprints that were trained on the NIST

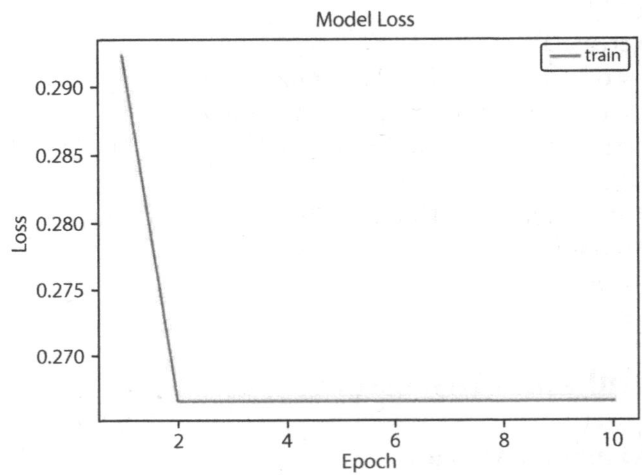

Figure 8.6 Loss function of the model for rolled fingerprint prediction.

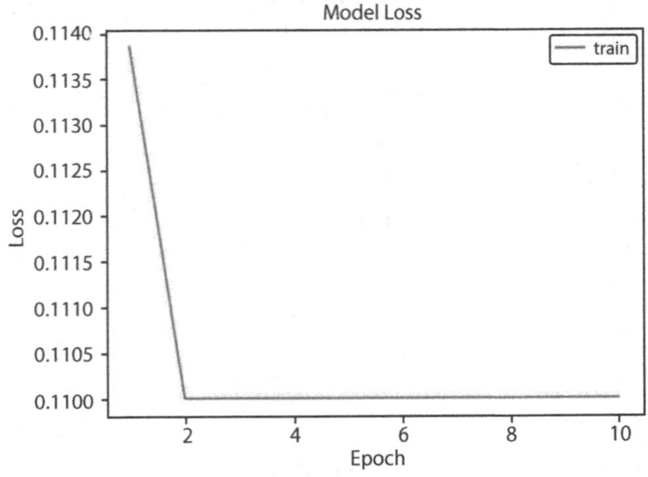

Figure 8.7 Loss function for latent fingerprint prediction.

SD27 dataset. The developed model consists of five convolutional neural network layers and ReLU activation functions. On the x-axis is indicated the number of epochs; y-axis indicates loss value of the prediction algorithm.

Figure 8.7 shows the loss graph plot for latent fingerprint by the proposed deep learning model. The improved convolutional neural networks consist of four layers and ReLU activation functions. The x-axis of the

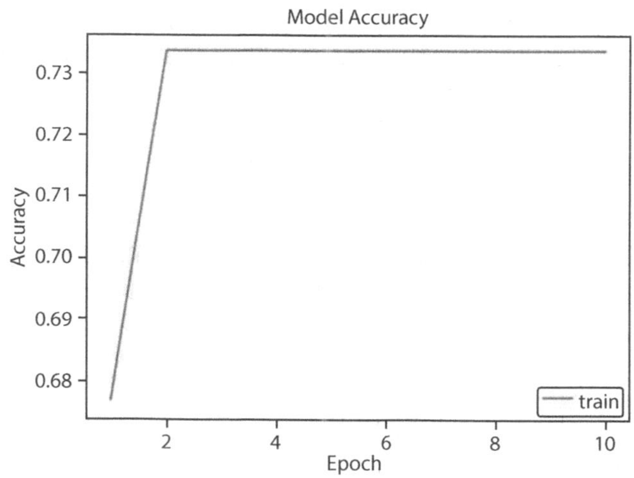

Figure 8.8 Accuracy graph for rolled fingerprint prediction.

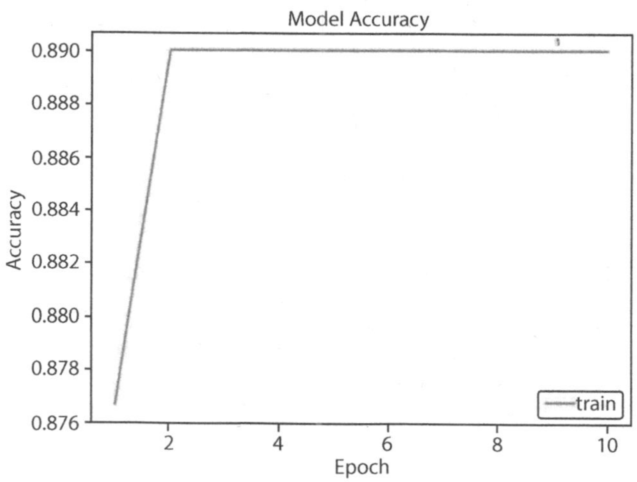

Figure 8.9 Accuracy graph plot for latent fingerprint prediction.

graph plot indicates the number of epochs, and the y-axis represents the loss of the prediction algorithm.

Figure 8.8 represents the training accuracy graph for the proposed framework for predicting rolled fingerprints and achieved the value of 83.5%. The model made used ReLU activation functions and improved convolutional neural network architecture with five layers. In model training, we used Adam optimizer and batch size value of 10 and learning rate is initialized to 0.001.

Figure 8.9 shows the accuracy of the deep learning model for predicting latent fingerprints with accuracy of 89.5%. In model training for latent fingerprint, we used Adam optimizer, batch size =10 and the learning rate value of 0.001 is initialized.

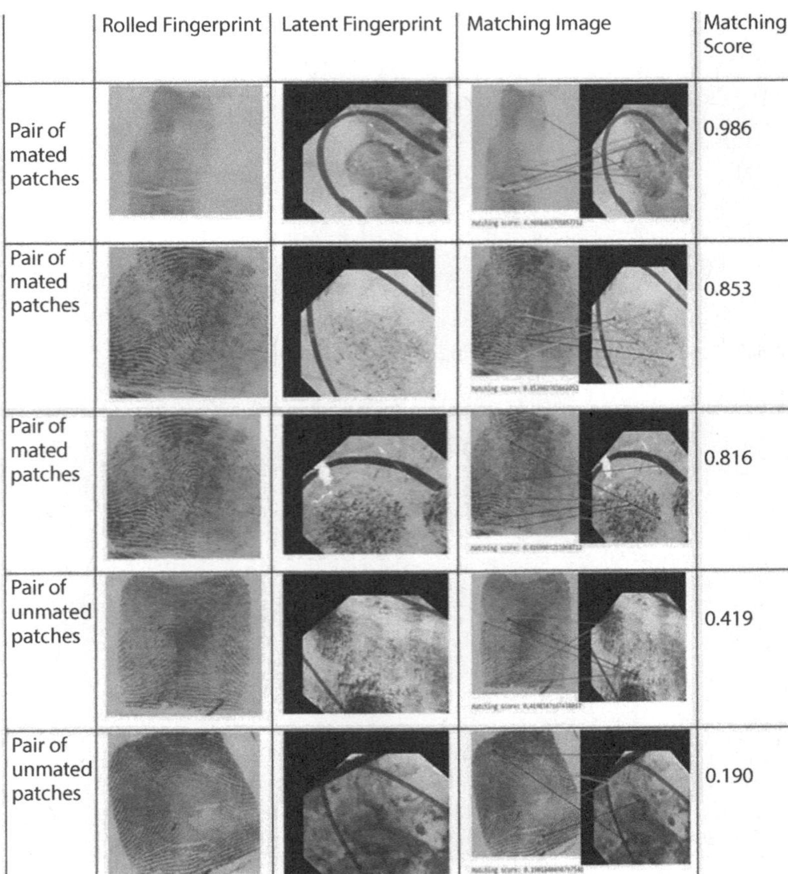

Figure 8.10 Fingerprint matching with matching score.

Figure 8.10 shows the pair of mated and unmated patches with the matching score. Rolled fingerprint is matched with the latent fingerprint. After matching, matching score is obtained as a result. If the matching score is above 0.5 then both the images are matched. If both images are below 0.5 then it is not matched. The proposed approach performs significantly well compared to other state-of-the methods, and it can be extended for real-time fingerprint identification systems.

8.6 Conclusion

In this work, the proposed method is significantly improved in feature extraction of latent fingerprint minutiae extraction and ridge orientation field estimation. All sample points in the image with pair similarities and relative spatial transformations are compared for accurate detection process. In the end, the estimation of the sampling point correspondences is performed using a global patch-matching method based on the ORB and brute force. The time complexity is more for identifying local patch alignment and matching process; the efficiency of the coarse-to-fine registration strategy is needed for improvement. The proposed model helps in improving the fingerprint matching along with alignment. Future studies include real-time development of fingerprint registration system with strengthening registration accuracy while decreasing computational time to better manage local distortion.

AI disclosure statement: The author confirms that no artificial intelligence (AI)-generated content or AI-assisted writing tools were used in the preparation of this chapter (including summaries and the abstract). All text, analysis, and conclusions are the result of the author's original work.

References

1. He, Z., Zhang, J., Pang, L., Liu, E., PFVNet: A Partial Fingerprint Verification Network Learned From Large Fingerprint Matching. *IEEE Trans. Inf. Forensics Secur.*, 17, 3706–3719, 2022, doi: 10.1109/TIFS.2022.3209869.
2. Tan, H. and Kumar, A., Towards More Accurate Contactless Fingerprint Minutiae Extraction and Pose-Invariant Matching. *IEEE Trans. Inf. Forensics Secur.*, 15, 3924–3937, 2020, doi: 10.1109/TIFS.2020.3001732.

3. Grosz, S.A., Engelsma, J.J., Liu, E., Jain, A.K., C2CL: Contact to Contactless Fingerprint Matching. *IEEE Trans. Inf. Forensics Secur.*, 17, 196–210, 2022, doi:10.1109/TIFS.2021.3134867.
4. Tran, Q.N. and Hu, J., A Multi-Filter Fingerprint Matching Framework for Cancelable Template Design. *IEEE Trans. Inf. Forensics Secur.*, 16, 2926–2940, 2021, doi: 10.1109/TIFS.2021.3069170.
5. Harvey, J., Campbell, J., Adler, A., Characterization of Biometric Template Aging in a Multiyear, Multivendor Longitudinal Fingerprint Matching Study. *IEEE Trans. Instrum. Meas.*, 68, 4, 1071–1079, April 2019, doi: 10.1109/TIM.2018.2861998.
6. Lan, S., Guo, Z., You, J., A non-rigid registration method with application to distorted fingerprint matching. *Pattern Recognit.*, 95, 48–57, 2019, https://doi.org/10.1016/j.patcog.2019.05.021.
7. Haraksim, R., Galbally, J., Beslay, L., Fingerprint growth model for mitigating the ageing effect on children's fingerprints matching. *Pattern Recognit.*, 88, 614–628, 2019, https://doi.org/10.1016/j.patcog.2018.12.024.
8. Nedjah, N., Wyant, R.S., Mourelle, L.M., Gupta, B.B., Efficient fingerprint matching on smart cards for high security and privacy in smart systems. *Inf. Sci.*, 479, 622–639, 2019, https://doi.org/10.1016/j.ins.2017.12.038.
9. Shi, L., Lan, S., Gui, H., Yang, Y., Guo, Z., A novel 2D contactless fingerprint matching method. *Neurocomputing*, 500, 547–555, 2022, https://doi.org/10.1016/j.neucom.2022.05.092.
10. Liu, F., Zhao, Y., Liu, G., Shen, L., Fingerprint pore matching using deep features. *Pattern Recognit.*, 102, 2020, https://doi.org/10.1016/j.patcog.2020.107208.
11. Krish, R.P., Fierrez, J., Ramos, D., Alonso-Fernandez, F., Bigun, J., Improving automated latent fingerprint identification using extended minutia types. *Inf. Fusion*, 50, 9–19, 2019, https://doi.org/10.1016/j.inffus.2018.10.001.
12. Cui, Z., Feng, J., Zhou, J., Dense Registration and Mosaicking of Fingerprints by Training an End-to-End Network. *IEEE Trans. Inf. Forensics Secur.*, 16, 627–642, 2020, DOI:10.1109/TIFS.2020.3017926.
13. Xun, Y., Liu, J., Kato, N., Fang, Y., Zhang, Y., Automobile Driver Fingerprinting: A New Machine Learning Based Authentication Scheme. *IEEE Trans. Ind. Inf.*, 16, 2, 1417–1426, 2020, doi: 10.1109/TII.2019.2946626.
14. Wong, W.J. and Lai, S.-H., Multi-task CNN for restoring corrupted fingerprint images. *Pattern Recognit.*, 101, 2020, https://doi.org/10.1016/j.patcog.2020.107203.
15. Zhang, Z., Liu, S., Liu, M., A multi-task fully deep convolutional neural network for contactless fingerprint minutiae extraction. *Pattern Recognit.*, 120, 2021, https://doi.org/10.1016/j.patcog.2021.108189.
16. Ali, M., Wang, C., Ahmad, M.O., An Efficient Convolutional Neural Network for Fingerprint Pore Detection. *IEEE Trans. Biom. Behav. Identity Sci.*, 3, 3, 332–346, July 2021, doi: 10.1109/TBIOM.2021.3065914.

17. Suresh, K.K., Sundaresan, S., Nishanth, R., Ananth, K.T., Optimization and Deep Learning–Based Content Retrieval, Indexing, and Metric Learning Approach for Medical Images, in: *Computational Analysis and Deep Learning for Medical Care: Principles, Methods, and Applications*, pp. 79–106, 2021, https://doi.org/10.1002/9781119785750.ch4.
18. https://www.nist.gov/itl/iad/image-group/nist-special-database-2727a.

Part III

REAL-WORLD APPLICATIONS OF COMPOSITE AI IN HEALTHCARE AND BEYOND

9

A Novel Transfer Learning-Based Composite AI Model for Skin Disease Classification

R. Karthick Manoj[1]* and S. Aasha Nandhini[2]

[1]*Department of Electrical and Electronics Engineering, AMET Deemed to be University, Kanathur, India*
[2]*Department of Electronics and Communication Engineering, Sri Sivasubramaniya Nadar College of Engineering, Kalavakkam, India*

Abstract

Early and accurate diagnosis of skin diseases like melanoma, psoriasis, and eczema is important for successful treatment and management of skin issues. In remote areas, accessibility and efficiency remain as significant issues. To address these issues, this work proposes a novel method for skin disease detection using dermatological images and composite artificial intelligence models based on transfer learning. The advantage of the method lies in its ability to overcome the constraints of small datasets and also aids in early detection. The composite AI model combines the advantages of ResNet50, VGG16, and InceptionV3 architectures through a weighted average approach which aggregates the performance of the individual models. The Model weights are assigned based on performance metrics such as accuracy, precision, and recall evaluated during preliminary testing. This weighting strategy helps to make the composite model more balanced and robust in terms of disease diagnosis. Using Kaggle dataset for training and evaluation, the models are optimized in terms of disease class. At skin disease classification, the composite model outperformed the individual ones by achieving an accuracy of 92.3%, a precision of 93.1%, a recall of 91.5%, and an F1-score of 92.3. This strongly shows the effectiveness of transfer learning combined with composite AI in augmenting diagnostic capabilities for dermatological disorders. From the results, it is observed that the proposed model outperforms the single models and

**Corresponding author*: Karthickmanoj.r@gmail.com

T. S. Arun Samuel, L. Jerart Julus, P. Kanimozhi, T. Ananth Kumar and S. Balamurugan (eds.) Composite Artificial Intelligence: Fundamentals, Challenges, and Applications, (201–222) © 2026 Scrivener Publishing LLC

is thought to be a comprehensive tool for medical image establishment. It is especially important for resource-limited areas where access to trained dermatologists is limited and very much in dire need of early and correct diagnosis.

Keywords: Composite artificial intelligence, deep learning model, skin disease, data augmentation

9.1 Introduction

Globally increasing cases of skin cancers, fungal infections, and inflammatory skin conditions pose a significant challenge to health care systems. Early diagnosis is necessary to improve patient outcomes, reduce treatment costs, and ultimately lower mortality rates. Traditionally, the dermatological diagnosis relied on the capabilities of a clinician responsible for visually examining the lesions and symptoms [1]. This fact has disadvantages, especially concerning accessibility, time efficiency, and diagnostic accuracy, especially in developing countries with limited health care resources. However, new developments in ML and AI have manifested much promise in the endeavor of solving these issues with the aid of automated diagnostic tools that rely on pictures particularly relevant to dermatology [2].

Skin conditions affect people of all ages and ethnicities, making them one of the most prevalent medical issues in the world. They can be as mild as acne and eczema or even more dangerous and life-threatening like melanoma. Early and correct diagnosis is crucial for effective intervention. If there is delay in diagnosis, it may result in complications and adverse effects. However, there is a pressing need for scalable and effective diagnostics solutions since access to qualified dermatological treatments has not been regulated, especially in less accessible areas. Much of the sector that healthcare represents has already been impacted by AI advancement [3]. Indeed, DL-based tools have been shown to parse large amounts of complex data, such as medical images. These tools could accurately detect anomalies and patterns and open the pathway for better accuracy in diagnosis. AI may be able to bring advanced technologies into the bedside *via* medical workflows that could help close the gap between the barriers of access to health care and the equitable delivery to diverse populations.

The most powerful innovation in AI is transfer learning, which enables pre-trained models to adapt for specific tasks, even given limited data. This approach is gaining momentum, allowing for the administration of strong systems to detect and classify pathology in medical imaging. Transfer learning presents already learned architectures from a humongous amount of datasets to the users. Common issues of lacking sufficient labeled data and the low quality of images often faced by the healthcare system can be avoided. Composite AI combined with transfer learning is another tremendous milestone towards making diagnoses more efficient. To make use of each the building's strengths and improve diagnosis accuracy and resilience, composite AI combines many models into a single package. This works particularly well in addressing problems that require subtle analysis, such as telling apart four similar skin diseases. The weighted combination of models ensures that the diagnostic process is not only accurate but able to handle many different cases [4].

There is great hope for innovation in the field of dermatological treatment as a result of these developments in AI, DL, and composite modelling [5]. They claim to provide access to high-quality care for patients regardless of their financial or geographic limitations, enhance diagnostic efficacy, and reduce burdens on the healthcare system. These technologies provide the way for future inclusive, precise, and eventually scalable medical diagnostic solutions as they develop and advance.

9.2 Literature Survey

This research [6], aims at building a system that is based on the detection and diagnosis of skin illnesses with metaheuristic optimizers on a combination of various classifiers AI-based. Numerical as well as image datasets are gathered, pre-processed and analyzed visually to obtain insights of their patterns so as to achieve this target. Various aspects of an image are calculated To diagnose various skin disorders, a variety of learning models with various hyperparameter optimizers are used. While it is about an accuracy of 90.56% under Bayesian search CV, it computed the highest accuracy, and its accuracy when ResNet50 was applied without any tuning of hyperparameters was about 74.89%.

This study [7], focuses on the potential of revolutionary changes brought by convolutional neural networks, into dermatology, particularly for the diagnosis of skin diseases. The study examines the revolutionary potential of CNNs in dermatology, emphasizing the identification of skin diseases. It is also of great importance to detect skin diseases early, considering that melanoma cases seem to be increasing. Utilizing Web scraping, Kaggle dataset, and CNN-based state-of-the-art techniques. A methodical preprocessing that includes pixel normalization, rotation, flipping, standardization, and augmentation improved the robustness of the dataset and the neural network. The design was inspired by ReLU and SoftMax.

CNN mainly used convolutional layers to extract features and fully linked layers for classification. To minimize overfitting and improve generalization, the design includes the integration of batch normalization layers and dropout layers. Training of the model is carried out iteratively with modifications to hyperparameters and optimum learning rates. It includes data collection, model training, and heavy preprocessing of data. Innovations in dermatology are also included that will highlight novel treatments and technological advancements. With intuitive user interfaces, integration with clinical procedures improves diagnosis accuracy and efficiency in practical settings. Improving knowledge, encouraging early detection, and supporting further initiatives to advance patient care and dermatological research would be the aim.

The study [8], uses DL models that are built around the CNN framework for feature extraction. To lessen the distinction between various categories of skin conditions, picture enhancing techniques were used. The AUC results show that the model using seven layers of the convolutional neural network had a 98% and 99% accuracy of the seven different types of skin disorders. The ability of several CNN models toward the given dataset is compared and assessed with the help of several performance matrices.

In medical diagnostics, speedy and efficient skin disease detection is essential. This paper [9], aims to apply ML and picture preprocessing in attaining the possibility of diagnosis for skin diseases. The preprocessing of a picture comprises picture scaling and enhancement. Enhancement is a technique to change the brightness, contrast, and sharpness of an image. Here, values of some of the pixels at the top and the bottom are saturated. Algorithms based on support vector machines and decision trees have been considered for their implementation in ML. Feature selection is very important in ML. Features have been selected for this research study based on histogram count and three-color models. In this work, RGB, HSI, and LAB color models are considered. According to the experimental findings, the proposed approach delivers a superior degree of accuracy.

This method reconstructs hair-free images by adopting the architecture of convolutional neural networks combined with a generative adversarial network [10]. The GAN involves a discriminator and a generator. To evaluate our proposed model, a dataset containing both hair-covered and hairless pictures is required. .This work proposes a computerized high-precision diagnostic methodology using a web application to detect malignant melanoma [11]. To increase accuracy for data collection, preliminary processing, division, enhancement, extraction of features, categorization, and malignant melanoma detection, the diagnostic model framework. Through preprocessing and mixed hybrid pooling phases, the suggested method increases spectral image information, reduces undesired noise, and enhances classification accuracy. According to performance studies, the suggested model for detecting malignant melanoma cancer has a maximum accuracy of 94%.

AI-based skin disease prediction has showed great potential for improving the outcomes of early diagnosis and treatment. To enhance the performance of skin disease prediction models, this paper [12], proposes a novel approach to the class imbalance problem by integrating methods of transfer learning with data balancing and class weighting. This work uses the highly optimized CNN model to suggest a novel method for classifying skin lesions. Monkeypox, a rare viral disease that causes severe skin lesions, might be effectively managed with an early and accurate diagnosis. To improve the current CNN model and create a classification system that can differentiate between different types of lesions, the study uses a series of photographs of monkeypox lesions. The results show how well the proposed technique works, classifying monkeypox skin lesions with exceptional sensitivity and specificity. By assisting medical personnel in making quick and precise diagnoses, it would contribute additional latent steps towards automated diagnosis systems for other infectious illnesses.

This research [13], introduces a new paradigm in the detection of illness. It develops an artificial intelligence-based system that retrieves homogenous and dispersed biological data from various sensors. In this paper, we research the different relationships between different types of biological data with a variety of DL architectures with ensemble learning and attention techniques for identifying and diagnosing illnesses. We test the biological data in great detail. The results show the benefits of diagnosing diseases at all stages of the healthcare decision-making process by using DL technologies in the field of AI of medical objects. For example, the proposed method gives a 92% rate of illness identification.

By combining hyperspectral imaging and artificial intelligence, this transforms dermatological diagnostics and identifies skin cancer lesions, mostly those caused by Mycosis fungoides. This paper uses a state-of-the-art AI system along with advanced methodologies that shift diagnoses from color to spectrum analysis in the appropriate segmentation and classification of lesions. The early and accurate detection of skin cancers has improved dramatically with the use of this effective and non-invasive technique [14]. Sensitivity, specificity, and accuracy all favor the model's excellent performance, which makes it an essential tool in dermatology for detecting inflammatory diseases and skin malignancies. Using the ImageNet dataset, the proposed hybrid framework integrated state-of-the-art DL models with pre-trained EL. To verify the effectiveness of the suggested techniques, an experiment was conducted using the dataset [15].

Computer-aided techniques for diagnosis can increase accuracy and efficiency in diagnosing skin cancer. In this work, an image-based skin lesion identification system is proposed to classify the types of skin cancer [16]. Here, the HAM1000 dataset consisting of 10015 images is used. Basic characteristics were extracted from the dermoscopic images of the dataset. The superiority of the proposed model is demonstrated by the results obtained from using popular categorization models found in the literature. In our proposed study, the conclusion suggests that KNN algorithm is performing better than the XGBoost technique. The model achieves a 73% accuracy level, and it uses KNN because of rapid implementation and incredibly precise outputs. In an appropriate medical setting, the proposed study can be validated and treated, and it can quickly identify seven forms of pigmented skin problems. The research in this field has been to develop an automatic system that can detect skin cancer and reduce the death rate from it [17]. On using a balanced dataset, the accuracy of the model suggested is 99.35%, while precision is 99.00% along with the recall being 99.00%. Thus, the f1 score is 99.00%. As a comparison, the balanced dataset performs 22% better than the imbalanced one.

Using a set of images from the dataset found in the ISIC Archive, which is derived from either benign or malignant moles, this will utilize a DL method for automatic classification. Considering that eye diagnostics are instrumental in the detection of skin cancer, this research endeavor recognizes the importance of applying accuracy evaluation to the database with its balanced design [18]. Actually, the accuracy and precision obtained from the model were exceptional, reaching 92.7%. The results of this work reveal the applicability and relevance of the proposed model for the fight against skin cancer and, therefore, highlight the need for its early detection. Other architectural components being considered to be incorporated into the model, thereby enhancing its performance are the ResNet50. This comprehensive approach shows how well CNNs perform in visually recognizing skin lesions and underlines the possibility of automated methods to enable the early and accurate identification of skin cancer.

The MobileNetV2 and ViT architectures are used in this suggested study [19], to create a hybrid automated skin cancer classification technique. By fusing MobileNetV2's potent feature extraction capabilities with ViT's self-attention mechanism, it seeks to improve the accuracy and efficacy of dermatological diagnostic tools. Our hybrid model outperformed individual models with an impressive 96.3% classification accuracy after testing on the HAM10000 dataset. The combination of ViT with MobileNetV2 increases the classification accuracy and at the same time demonstrates how varied DL can work synergistically for solving very demanding picture-analysis problems. Classifying skin cancers relies very much on the medical domain since its early diagnosis assists in treatment and cure well before more serious diseases start to present themselves.

The proposed model architecture is created by combining the multiple phases dimensional fusion process with the recursive gate convolution with higher-order spatial communication that forms the basis of the HorUNet model's skip connection section. First, it conducted comparison studies with two widely used public datasets on skin lesions [20]. Results from the experiments show that the current method is superior than the others in a variety of measurements. Because our model produces segmentation results that are medically relevant and have a greater segmentation accuracy, this suggests that it has a stronger generalization power. The proposed research [21], effort extracts deep features from existing data using the SCSO-ResNet50 technique of sand cat swarm optimization with ResNet50 to ensure accurate predictions. An improved harmony search approach is used to optimize attributes and reduce the dimensionality of the data. The usefulness of the proposed method is demonstrated using the ISIC 2019 dataset as well as the Kaggle skin cancer dataset. F-measure, recall, accuracy, and precision are contrasted with those of other state-of-the-art classifiers.

A stacked convolutional neural network model has been demonstrated in this study [22], that can outperform current pre-trained CNN variants in terms of prediction accuracy. Stack CNN uses the 2D CNN layers in a consecutive fashion to digest the input thoroughly in order to produce reliable predictions. Data augmentation is done for minority class data to balance training data and prevent over-fitting of the model. The model is trained by using the characteristics of red, green, and blue taken from the training data. Monkeypox can be mistaken for another illness using the common signs of measles and chickenpox. To ensure that any specimen is used as a training and testing sample, five-fold cross-validation must occur at the distribution stage of the study. Five transfer learning models are compared versus epoch to evaluate the performance of the model's categorization [23]. All five transfer learning models are put to the test on a public dataset, whereby MobileNetv2 proved impressive with an accuracy rate of 98.78%. Due to its high accuracy, MobileNetv2 is very productive in accurately diagnosing monkeypox as it brings down the chances of misdiagnosing other illnesses such as chickenpox.

This paper [24], advances an automated picture-based strategy to diagnose and classify issues affecting the skin using a classification approach to ML. Computational processing will therefore be used for the computational processing of image data along with relegating it considering all the numerous attributes to process the pictures. Filtering to remove any unwanted noises from the given skin images enhances the photos before its overall quality can be dealt with. More sophisticated techniques may be utilized in extracting features from the image, classification of the image by the algorithm of the softmax classifier, and a diagnostic report may be the output. This application will prove to be a more efficient and reliable strategy for the diagnosis of dermatological illnesses compared to the traditional way as it is more accurate and the results appear faster compared to the former methodology.

9.3 Proposed Methodology

The systematic workflow of a Transfer Learning-based Composite AI Skin Disease Detection System is illustrated in Figure 9.1. Dataset Preparation is the first step in the process, which entails gathering a varied collection of skin images and preprocessing them using augmentation, normalization, and scaling to increase robustness. After the dataset is ready, it is separated into training, validation, and testing sets to guarantee that every class is fairly represented for an objective assessment. A pre-trained model, such as ResNet, Inceptionv3, or VGG16, is then chosen because of its efficacy and efficiency in image classification. The output layer of the model is swapped out with a specially designed classifier that is suited to the various types of skin diseases. While the recently added layers are being trained, the early layers of the previously trained model are frozen to maintain learnt features. To improve performance, the entire model is then fine-tuned. The Composite Model Construction step integrates the outputs of the individual models using techniques like model averaging, weighted voting, or stacking to create an ensemble system that leverages the strengths of each model. The composite model's performance is continuously monitored using metrics such as accuracy, precision, recall and F1-scoreare employed to assess its effectiveness.

In this step of the pipeline, dermatological imaging datasets are gathered and created. For this work, publicly accessible dermatological image datasets from Kaggle will be used. Figure 9.2 contains annotated images showing several skin diseases, including eczema, psoriasis, and melanoma. The images were drawn from a broad section of the demographic population

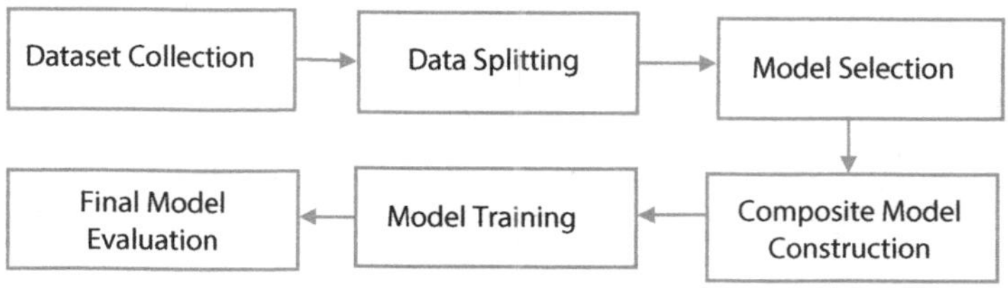

Figure 9.1 Transfer learning-based composite AI skin disease detection system.

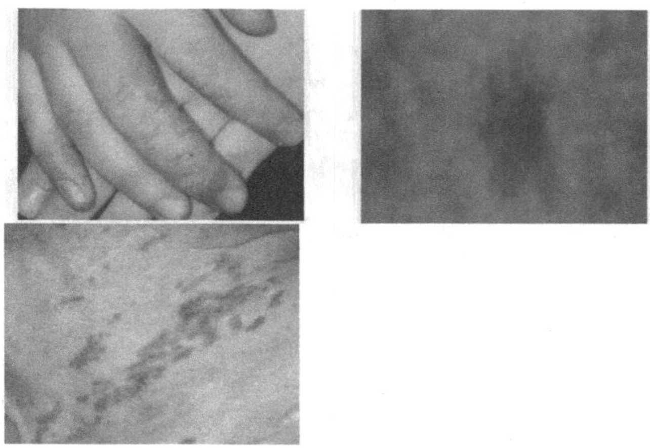

Figure 9.2 Sample input—skin disease images.

and diverse geographic locations for an all-round view of skin types and concerns. This kind of diversity is required for enhancing the robustness of the model throughout training. After gathering the dataset, a rigorous preprocessing procedure is undertaken to prepare it for DL tasks. One of the major preprocessing procedures involves image scaling. Image scaling is essential to ensure that all photos are at the same resolution. Since neural networks always need constant resolution, various sizes of pictures might hamper the network's ability to learn efficiently. In order to feed the data into the model, it is now standardized. To improve the model's performance, the dataset is then subjected to a variety of data augmentation approaches. Rotation, flipping, scaling, and brightness correction are among of the modifications applied to the original dermatological picture. These images depict the changes in lighting, perspective, and orientation that might happen in real life.

Figure 9.3 shows the raw skin disease image and augmented images produced from applying different transformation operations, which include

Figure 9.3 Data augmentation techniques applied to skin disease images.

rotation, flipping, scaling, and correction of brightness. The simulated realistic variations in such enhanced images further enhance the ability of the model to generalize for the diagnosis of skin diseases. Data augmentation significantly contributes to strengthening the generalization capability of the model. The augmented images enable the model to recognize skin issues across a wider range of scenarios, thereby improving its performance in diverse real-world conditions. This method is not only good for accurate disease identification of skin under various conditions but also prevents overfitting. For more straightforward convergence during training, images were normalized by scaling pixel values to a specific standard range, which is normally between 0 and 1. Other techniques like zooming, horizontal flipping, and random rotations were applied on the dataset to further diversify and strengthen it. This extended collection strengthens the model's strength, making it less prone to overfitting and better in handling real image variations.

The data was divided into three categories: training, validation, and testing. The training set was given 70% of the data, while the validation and testing sets were both given 15%. The training set was used for model training, while the validation set assisted in the tuning of hyperparameters for the model to prevent overfitting; finally, only the testing set was utilized at the time of the final evaluation of the ability of the model to generalize well for unseen data. Stratified sampling was done so that all the sets ensured the uniformity of distribution regarding the conditions for the skin.

Pre-trained models, ResNet50, VGG16, and InceptionV3, have been used in this experiment as the backbone architectures. These are trained on big datasets like ImageNet, thereby learning low- and mid-level features that could be adapted for various image classification tasks. Fine-tuning was done on the dermatological dataset by freezing layers initially to retain general features from the pre-trained models. This approach saves time and computational resources because it does not train from scratch and enables the models to specialize in dermatological patterns.

Three pre-trained models' outputs were aggregated into a composite model to improve diagnosis's performance. Every one of the particular models offers advantages. ResNet50 is known to learn deep hierarchical features; VGG16 does well on smaller datasets while InceptionV3 manages multi-scale features quite effectively. These benefits then are aggregated by weighted averaging of their forecasts. Performance measurements including accuracy, precision, and recall define the weight of any model. The last estimate is an average of the outputs, weighted in favor of more performing models. Figure 9.4: Composite artificial intelligence model for skin disease detection's architectural layout ResNet50, InceptionV3, and VGG16 each generate predictions on the likelihood of a picture belonging to one of the skin condition classes in this two-stage procedure starting with the input image. The weighted and averaged forecasts are then used to generate the last prediction depending on their combined probability. All of these models' combined approach helps raise the accuracy and dependability.

The integration uses weighted averaging with the prediction made by each model multiplied by their respective weights, which are in turn optimized against performance metrics on the validation set, such as F1-score, recall, accuracy, and precision. With this, it is less influenced by weaker models while giving more prominence to the stronger models, increasing overall diagnostic accuracy.

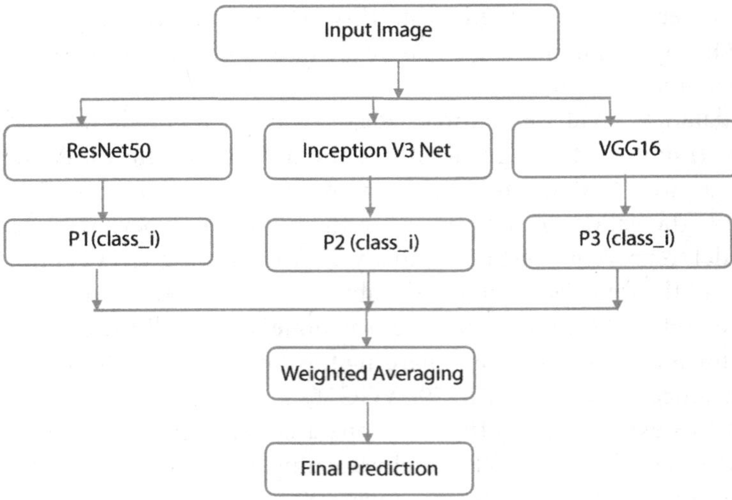

Figure 9.4 Composite AI model.

The mathematical formula for weighted averaging is as follows:

$$P_{final}(class_i)=w_1 \cdot P_{ResNet50}(class_i)+w_2 \cdot P_{VGG16}(class_i)+w_3 \cdot P_{InceptionV3}(class_i) \quad (9.1)$$

Equation 9.1 where $P_{final}(class_i)$ is the final probability of class i, w_1,w_2,w_3 are the weights for ResNet50, VGG16, and InceptionV3, respectively, and $P_{model}(class_i)$ is the probability of class i predicted by the respective model.

During validation, the weights w_1, w_2, and w_3 are adjusted by repeatedly trying different combinations to optimize the overall performance of the ensemble. The ideal weight distribution can be found using grid search or related optimization methods.

Initiated with their respective pre-trained weights, changes are made in the top levels of the pre-trained models in the fine-tuning. Originally set to 0.0001, this low learning rate stopped extreme updates that would stop the training. Following Adam optimizers to control the learning rate, models were then trained in batch size of 32 images in one iteration and with this value adjusted to enable faster convergence in the middle iterations. Early stopping—that is, training ended when the validation loss stopped improving—was used to prevent overfitting. Additionally included were dropout layers to lower overfitting and improve generalization. It's gauged against F1-score, accuracy, precision, and recall. When working with skewed data, when some conditions—like melanoma—are underrepresented, these measures are absolutely crucial. Quite beneficial is the use of confusion matrices to identify misclassifications and areas requiring model improvement.

Following the general findings of the first set of evaluations, further fine-tuning of the models using grid search aimed at optimizing hyperparameters like learning rates, batch sizes, and the number of epochs. The most accurate models were ensured to have more influence on the final prediction by means of weighted averaging methods. Constant monitoring of performance on the training and validation sets helped to avoid overfitting. By means of this iterative strategy, the composite model's generalizing capacity throughout several training cycles to the dermatological images was enhanced.

9.4 Result and Discussion

The dataset, which consists of 1,000 high-resolution dermatological pictures scaled to a standard input dimension of 224x224 pixels, is compatible with the deep learning models used in this study. This dataset includes three severe skin conditions: melanoma, psoriasis, and eczema. The 400 images of melanoma highlight irregular borders, uneven pigmentation, and asymmetry, all of which are common dermoscopic markers of this potentially fatal skin condition. Additionally, there are 300 images of psoriasis in the collection, which highlight the chronic and autoimmune nature of the condition, which is typified by red, scaly plaques with distinct borders. Lastly, 300 images of eczema illustrate how it can manifest in different parts of the body based on the type of irritant or environmental factor. To guarantee dependability and validity, each picture was meticulously identified and verified by knowledgeable dermatologists. To improve variability and decrease overfitting, preprocessing techniques included shrinking to 224x224 pixels, normalizing for constant pixel intensity, and using augmentation techniques including flipping, rotation, and brightness modifications. By enabling precise classification and early detection, this carefully selected dataset seeks to improve AI-driven diagnostics for these three illnesses in clinical and resource-constrained contexts.

When it comes to identifying skin conditions, the composite AI model—which combines ResNet50, VGG16, and InceptionV3—performs better than the individual models. Better generalization and accuracy are the results of each model's distinct characteristics, such as ResNet50's residual learning, VGG16's simplicity, and InceptionV3's multi-scale feature extraction. The composite model outperformed the component models in all key performance parameters, achieving 92.3% accuracy, 93.1% precision, and 91.5% recall on the Kaggle dataset. This suggests that merging many pre-trained models improves the system's accuracy and dependability in identifying skin conditions.

The composite model also performs well in terms of the F1-score (92.3), which is crucial for evaluating the model's capacity to differentiate between various skin states and offer a balanced performance in terms of both precision and recall. Early diagnosis and treatment of skin diseases depend on the model's high accuracy, which guarantees that the majority of positive cases are correctly detected, and high recall, which reduces the possibility of missing genuine positive instances. Because this is important in clinical contexts, the combination method achieves the best compromise between preventing false positives and false negatives.

Furthermore, this approach has significant implications for improving dermatological diagnosis in impoverished places where dermatologists are few. By combining several models and using transfer learning, the composite AI model improves diagnostic accuracy in resource-constrained contexts, overcoming the challenges posed by small datasets. The results suggest that such a model might be applied in clinical settings to assist physicians in detecting skin disorders at an early stage, providing a feasible means of enhancing the detection and treatment of skin diseases globally.

This Table 9.1 demonstrates the composite AI model's improved capacity to identify and diagnose skin conditions by clearly outperforming the individual models across all significant performance measures. When it comes to identifying skin conditions, the composite AI model—which combines ResNet50, VGG16, and InceptionV3—performs noticeably better than the individual models. In comparison to ResNet50, VGG16, and InceptionV3 alone, it obtains greater accuracy (92.3%), precision (93.1%), recall (91.5%), ROC-AUC (0.96), and F1-score (92.3%). This suggests that

Table 9.1 Performance of individual models (ResNet50, VGG16, and InceptionV3) versus the composite AI model.

Metric	ResNet50	VGG16	InceptionV3	Composite AI model
Accuracy	90.0%	89.0%	91.0%	92.3%
Precision	91.0%	89.0%	92.0%	93.1%
Recall	88.0%	85.0%	90.0%	91.5%
F1-Score	89.5%	87.0%	1.0%	92.3%

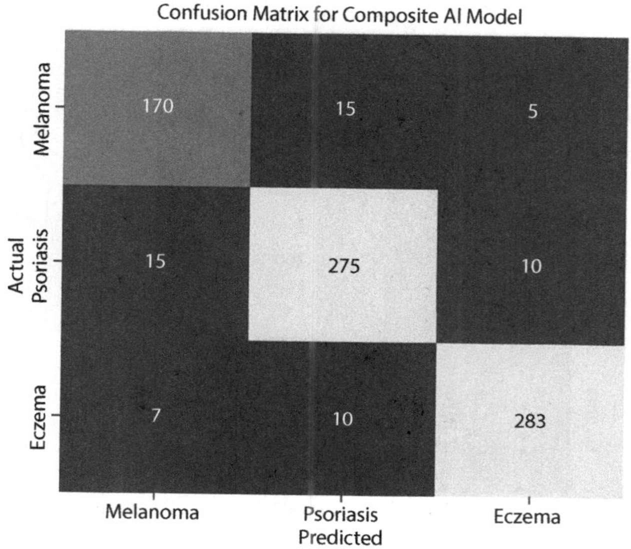

(a)

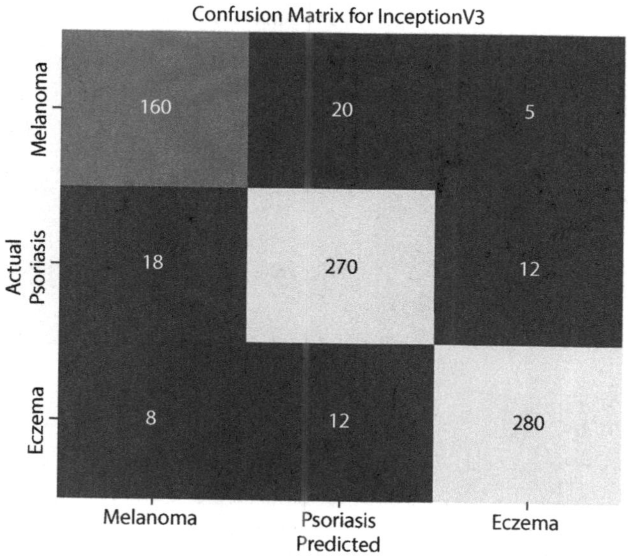

(b)

Figure 9.5 Confusion matrix (a) composite AI model (b) Inception V3 model (c) ResNet 50 model (d) VGG 16 model. *(Continued)*

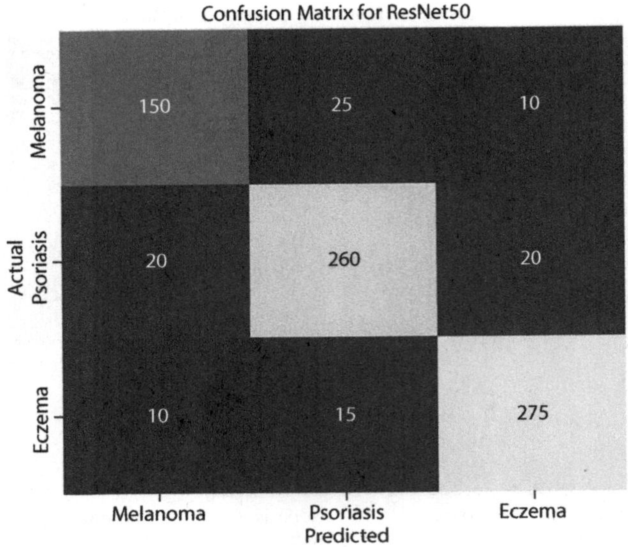

(c)

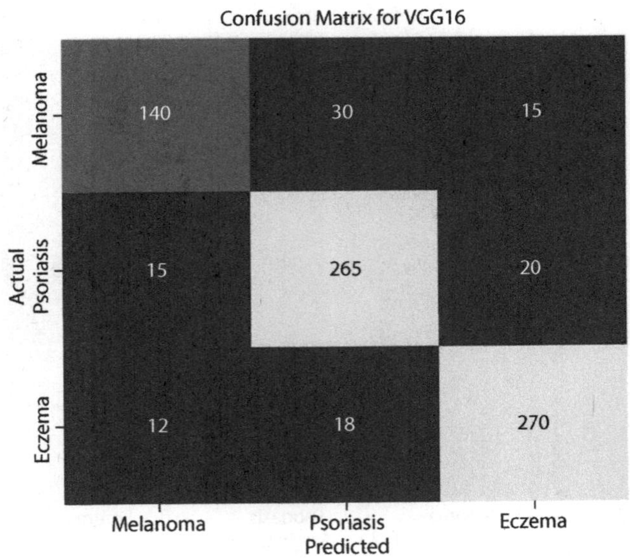

(d)

Figure 9.5 (Continued) Confusion matrix (a) Composite AI model (b) Inception V3 model (c) ResNet 50 model (d) VGG 16 model.

the composite model improves diagnostic performance by skillfully utilizing the advantages of each distinct architecture. The composite model reduces false positives and false negatives by improving precision and recall, which makes it a dependable tool for early skin disease identification, especially in situations with limited resources and dermatologist access. The findings demonstrate how transfer learning and composite AI models can be used to increase the precision and usability of dermatological diagnoses.

The confusion matrix diagrams for the composite AI model and each of the constituent models (ResNet50, VGG16, and InceptionV3) are shown in Figure 9.5. For each skin ailment (eczema, psoriasis, and melanoma), these visualizations display the number of true positives, false positives, true negatives, and false negatives for each model.

Figures 9.6, 9.7, 9.8, and 9.9 show the Accuracy vs. Epoch and Loss vs. Epoch graphs, which illustrate the learning and optimization processes of many models, including ResNet50, VGG16, InceptionV3, and the Composite AI Model. The loss curves demonstrate how each epoch's error falls, suggesting higher performance, while the accuracy curves illustrate how each model learns and improves at generating predictions with time. Throughout the training, ResNet50, VGG16, and InceptionV3 all show consistent gains in accuracy and long-term drops in loss. These examples provide a detailed overview of each model's evolution, convergence, and performance throughout the training. The composite AI model is the most promising approach among them due to its remarkable potential for accurate and reliable skin disease detection.

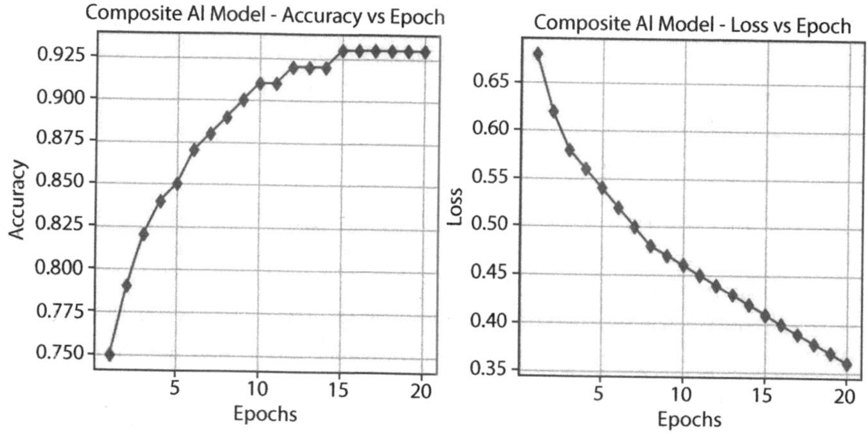

Figure 9.6 Accuracy and loss vs epoch curve for composite AI.

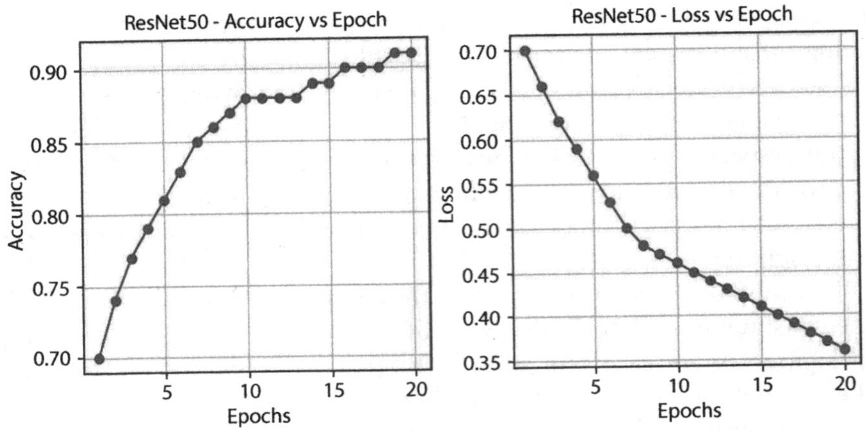

Figure 9.7 Accuracy and loss vs epoch curve for ResNet50.

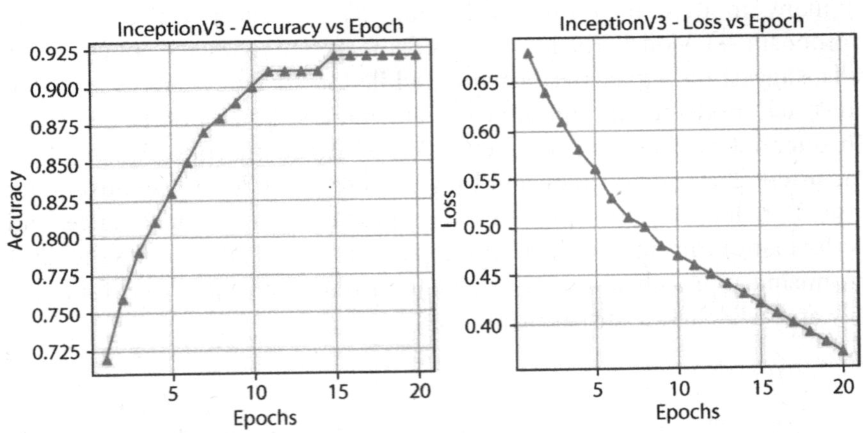

Figure 9.8 Accuracy and loss vs epoch curve for Inception V3 model.

9.5 Conclusion

This chapter proposed a novel composite AI model for skin disease classification and demonstrates how well composite AI models with transfer learning performs for early skin disease classification. The proposed approach outperforms the individual models in the diagnosis of dermatological diseases by using pre-trained models such as ResNet50, VGG16, and InceptionV3. The proposed model, with a high accuracy of 92.3%, precision of 93.1%, recall of 91.5%, and F1-score of 92.3%, can be very useful for the improvement of dermatological diagnoses in locations where access

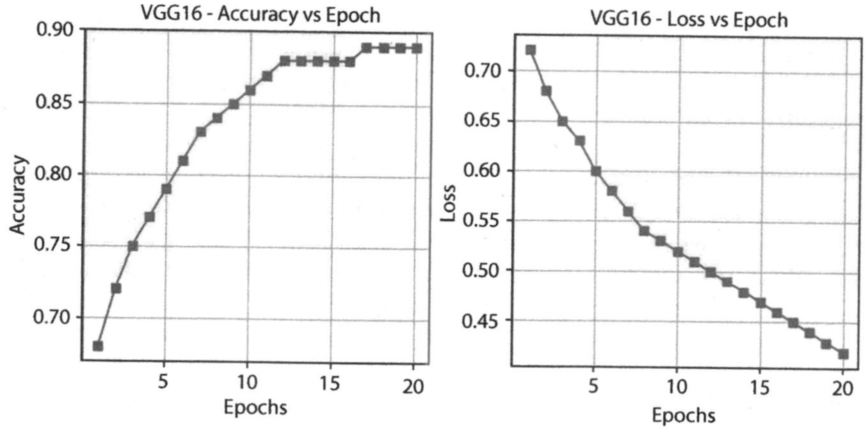

Figure 9.9 Accuracy and loss vs epoch curve for Inception V3 model.

to dermatologists is not possible. In addition to its capability of improving the detection accuracy of skin diseases, this method also creates room for much wider applications in early diagnosis, especially in low resource environments. Further improvements in diagnostic performance will be achieved through further advances that focus on multimodal data fusion and expand the spectrum of conditions covered.

AI disclosure statement: The author confirms that no artificial intelligence (AI)-generated content or AI-assisted writing tools were used in the preparation of this chapter (including summaries and the abstract). All text, analysis, and conclusions are the result of the author's original work.

References

1. Esteva, A., *et al.*, Dermatologist-level classification of skin cancer with deep neural networks. *Nature*, 542, 7639, 115–118, 2019.
2. Rajaraman, S., *et al.*, Deep transfer learning for early diagnosis of skin cancer. *J. Biomed. Inf.*, 107, 103470, 2020.
3. Hussain, A., *et al.*, Composite artificial intelligence models for skin disease-diagnosis: A systematic review. *Artif. Intell. Med.*, 114, 102016, 2021.
4. Choudhury, A., *et al.*, Addressing bias in skin disease detection using AI: Afocus on dermatological diversity. *J. Digit. Health*, 5, 3, 140–150, 2022.
5. Liu, Y., *et al.*, Transfer learning in skin cancer detection: An evaluation of deep learning models on melanoma classification. *IEEE Trans. Med. Imaging*, 42, 4, 1034–1045, 2023.

6. Singh, J., Sandhu, J.K., Kumar, Y., An analysis of detection and diagnosis of different classes of skin diseases using artificial intelligence-based learning approaches with hyper parameters. *Arch. Comput. Methods Eng.*, 31, 2, 1051–1078, 2024.
7. Pandiarajan, R., Hariharan, V., Abinesh, M.S., Harrish, N., DeepSkinNet: ReLU-Enhanced CNNs for AI-based Skin Disease Detection, in: *2024 15th International Conference on Computing Communication and Networking Technologies (ICCCNT)*, pp. 1–9, IEEE, 2024, June.
8. Abbas, M., Arslan, M., Bhatty, R.A., Yousaf, F., Khan, A.A., Rafay, A., Enhanced Skin Disease Diagnosis through Convolutional Neural Networks and Data Augmentation Techniques. *J. Comput. Biomed. Inf.*, 7, 01, 87–106, 2024.
9. Swamy, K.V., Radhika, V., Kadiyala, R.D., Skin Disease Classification using Image Preprocessing and Machine Learning, in: *2024 IEEE International Conference on Interdisciplinary Approaches in Technology and Management for Social Innovation (IATMSI)*, vol. 2, pp. 1–4, IEEE, 2024, March.
10. El-Shafai, W., El-Fattah, I.A., Taha, T.E., Deep learning-based hair removal for improved diagnostics of skin diseases. *Multimed. Tools Appl.*, 83, 9, 27331–27355, 2024.
11. Sivakumar, M.S., Leo, L.M., Gurumekala, T., Sindhu, V., Priyadharshini, A.S., Deep learning in skin lesion analysis for malignant melanoma cancer identification. *Multimed. Tools Appl.*, 83, 6, 17833–17853, 2024.
12. El Gannour, O., Hamida, S., Lamalem, Y., Mahjoubi, M.A., Cherradi, B., Raihani, A., Improving skin diseases prediction through data balancing *via* classes weighting and transfer learning. *Bull. Electr. Eng. Inf.*, 13, 1, 628–637, 2024.
13. Jagani, D. and Degadwala, S., Monkeypox Skin Lesion Classification Using Fine-Tune CNN Model, in: *2024 4th International Conference on Pervasive Computing and Social Networking (ICPCSN)*, pp. 37–41, IEEE, 2024, May.
14. Djenouri, Y., Belhadi, A., Yazidi, A., Srivastava, G., Lin, J.C.W., Artificial intelligence of medical things for disease detection using ensemble deep learning and attention mechanism. *Expert Syst.*, 41, 6, e13093, 2024.
15. Huang, H.Y., Nguyen, H.T., Lin, T.L., Saenprasarn, P., Liu, P.H., Wang, H.C., Identification of skin lesions by snapshot hyperspectral imaging. *Cancers*, 16, 1, 217, 2024.
16. Reis, H.C. and Turk, V., Fusion of transformer attention and CNN features for skin cancer detection. *Appl. Soft Comput.*, 164, 112013, 2024.
17. Hussain, S.R. and Powar, O.S., Enhancing skin lesion Classification: A machine learning approach using KNN, XGBoost, and Random Forest, in: *2024 Control Instrumentation System Conference (CISCON)*, pp. 1–4, IEEE, 2024, August.
18. Glorindal, G., Arun Mozhiselvi, S., Ananth Kumar, T., Kumaran, K., Katema, P.C., Kandimba, T., A simplified approach for melanoma skin disease

identification, in: *2021 International Conference on System, Computation, Automation and Networking (ICSCAN)*, IEEE, pp. 1–5, 2021.

19. Jain, E., Gill, K.S., Thapliyal, N., Rawat, R.S., AI-Powered Dermatology by Revolutionizing Early Skin Cancer Detection, in: *2024 IEEE 3rd World Conference on Applied Intelligence and Computing (AIC)*, pp. 49–53, IEEE, 2024, July.
20. Wu, R., Liang, P., Huang, X., Shi, L., Gu, Y., Zhu, H., Chang, Q., MHorUNet: High-order spatial interaction UNet for skin lesion segmentation. *Biomed. Signal Process. Control*, 88, 105517, 2024.
21. Akilandasowmya, G., Nirmaladevi, G., Suganthi, S.U., Aishwariya, A., Skin cancer diagnosis: Leveraging deep hidden features and ensemble classifiers for early detection and classification. *Biomed. Signal Process. Control*, 88, 105306, 2024.
22. Ahmed, K.T., Rustam, F., Mehmood, A., Ashraf, I., Choi, G.S., Predicting skin cancer melanoma using stacked convolutional neural networks model. *Multimed. Tools Appl.*, 83, 4, 9503–9522, 2024.
23. Verma, D., Singh, R., Chabra, R., Kumar, R., Shah, S.K., Hassan, M.M., Transfer Learning Approach for Improved Monkeypox Skin Lesion Classification, in: *2024 International Conference on Data Science and Network Security (ICDSNS)*, pp. 1–5, IEEE, 2024, July.
24. Inthiyaz, S., Altahan, B.R., Ahammad, S.H., Rajesh, V., Kalangi, R.R., Smirani, L.K., Hossain, M.A., Rashed, A.N.Z., Skin disease detection using deep learning. *Adv. Eng. Softw.*, 175, 103361, 2023.

10

Composite AI-Driven Music Recommendation: Integrating Emotion, Aural Analysis and Song Similarity

Ayushmaan Das and Rajalakshmi Shenbaga Moorthy*

Sri Ramachandra Faculty of Engineering and Technology, Sri Ramachandra Institute of Higher Education and Research, Chennai, India

Abstract

The emergence of digital consumption and streaming services such as Spotify has made them central in the discovery of music, offering users vast collections to choose from. However, it remains challenging to navigate those large collections to serve personalized and emotionally relevant content. The proposed composite AI-driven music recommendation engine fills these gaps by leveraging technologies such as cosine similarity for matching the songs, VGG-16-based CNN for mood-based recommendation, LSTMs for lyric generation, and a Pandas AI chatbot for interactive user engagement, to seamlessly orchestrate an immersive music experience. Current music recommendation systems frequently fail to provide emotionally compelling or contextually relevant suggestions, even with the advancements in recommendation algorithms. More complicated emotional indicators or the subtle aural preferences of users are sometimes overlooked in favor of recommendations that are based on past user behavior or basic genre classifications. Systems that can interpret user data and take into consideration the emotional and aural environments that shape musical choices are becoming more and more necessary. The main goal is to offer a highly customized, emotionally impactful music suggestion experience. The initiative seeks to: i) Increase the accuracy of recommendations by comparing songs based on cosine similarity. Make recommendations for songs based on your mood with a personalized CNN architecture ii) Using LSTM networks, generate individualized lyrics to produce a dynamic and engaging musical experience. Boost user engagement with a

**Corresponding author*: srajiresearch@gmail.com; ORCID: 0000-0003-3297-6123

T. S. Arun Samuel, L. Jerart Julus, P. Kanimozhi, T. Ananth Kumar and S. Balamurugan (eds.) Composite Artificial Intelligence: Fundamentals, Challenges, and Applications, (223–248) © 2026 Scrivener Publishing LLC

chatbot driven by Pandas AI that enables playlist creation and natural language interaction. The use of cosine similarity makes sure that the songs matched in the recommendations are based on the features of audio, such as tempo and energy. A custom CNN, which is based on VGG-16, analyses mood data and categorizes songs into emotional states to further personalize the system. K-Means clustering sorts songs based on mood and facilitates the provision of mood-based recommendations. Generation of dynamic lyrics is achieved using LSTM networks while an AI-powered Pandas chatbot provides an interactive interface for creating personalized playlists and user engagement. The system demonstrated high accuracy in recommending songs that align with user preferences and moods. Cosine similarity, combined with clustering techniques, achieved good precision when compared to user-provided playlists. Mood-based recommendations, using CNNs integrated with FER 2013 successfully generated data, for user-detected emotions with appropriate music categories. The integration of the Pandas AI chatbot enabled users to query datasets dynamically, personalize their preferences, and generate playlists in real time. In addition, the LSTM lyric generation model further enhanced the user experience by producing contextually relevant coherent lyrics, rated positively for creative expression and song theme alignment by the test users.

Keywords: Music recommendation, cosine similarity, convolutional neural network, K-Means clustering, long short-term memory

10.1 Introduction

The way that people consume music has changed significantly in the digital age, with streaming services taking over as the main way that people find new music. Leaders in the market, Spotify, and other platforms put enormous music libraries at users' fingertips. The difficulty, though, is in sorting through these enormous libraries to provide users with the most tailored, pertinent content. Users are demanding experiences that are personalized to their preferences and emotions, which has increased the demand for sophisticated recommendation systems. Even if they are strong, Spotify's current algorithms can yet be improved in terms of user emotional resonance and customization.

Long short-term memory (LSTM) networks for lyric generation, cosine similarity for song comparison, a custom convolutional neural network (CNN) based on VGG-16 for mood-based recommendations, and a Pandas AI-powered chatbot for enhanced user interaction are just a few of the advanced machine learning technologies that the proposed Composite AI-Driven Music Recommendation Engine aims to integrate to address these gaps and deliver a more immersive and emotionally intelligent music recommendation system that will increase user satisfaction and engagement.

Current music recommendation systems frequently fail to provide emotionally compelling or contextually relevant suggestions, even with the advancements in recommendation algorithms. More complicated emotional indicators or the subtle aural preferences of users are sometimes overlooked in favor of recommendations that are based on past user behavior or basic genre classifications. Systems that can interpret user data and take into consideration the emotional and aural environments that shape musical choices are becoming more and more necessary.

The algorithms in Spotify are helpful, but they frequently fall short in capturing the subtleties of mood or the emotional states that influence musical tastes. The curiosity about the potential applications of new AI technology to develop a recommendation system that is more emotionally intelligent stemmed from the personal experience. This intends to improve the user's relationship with their music by concentrating on mood-based song selection and lyrics production. The main goal is offering a highly customized, emotionally impactful music suggestion experience. The initiative seeks to:

- Increase the accuracy of recommendations by comparing songs based on cosine similarity.
- Make recommendations for songs based on your mood with a personalized CNN architecture.
- Using LSTM networks, generate individualized lyrics to produce a dynamic and engaging musical experience.
- Boost user engagement with a chatbot driven by Pandas AI that enables playlist creation and natural language interaction.

In recent years, Composite AI has acquired a remarkable position for its ability to combine various machine learning techniques to provide adaptive solutions. This research work integrates Composite AI for enhancing music recommendation by including custom CNN, LSTM, K-Means Clustering. Long short-term memory (LSTM) networks for lyric generation, cosine similarity for song comparison, a custom convolutional neural network (CNN) based on VGG-16 for mood-based recommendations, and a Pandas AI-powered chatbot for enhanced user interaction are just a few of the advanced machine learning technologies that the proposed Spotify recommendation engine project aims to integrate to address these gaps and deliver a more immersive and emotionally intelligent music recommendation system that will increase user satisfaction and engagement. This project adapts a multi-use approach, combining various machine learning models and techniques to achieve the desired outcome:

- *Cosine Similarity for Song Comparisons:* The angle between two vectors in a multi-dimensional space is measured by cosine similarity, which yields a metric for the degree of feature similarity between two songs (tempo, key, and energy). The engine finds songs with similar aural qualities by calculating the cosine similarity between a target song and other songs in the collection. This method makes sure that recommendations are based on the inherent qualities of the music as well as the user's taste in music.
- *Custom CNN for Mood-Based Recommendations:* A CNN is used to assess music according to mood; it is built on the VGG-16 architecture. A dataset of songs with labels indicating the emotional tone (e.g., happy, sad, energetic) is used to train the model. This increases the emotional resonance of the system's music recommendations by enabling it to suggest songs that correspond with the user's emotional state. To categorize songs into mood groups, CNN pulls deep characteristics from user's facial features, and predicts the temperament the user is in.
- *K-Means Clustering for Mood Based Parameters*: In this study, a dataset with different track properties including danceability, energy, valence, and other musical features was subjected to K-Means clustering. Three unique mood clusters representing happy, calm, and angry moods were created using the dataset to classify music. By using the song properties to create the centroids for each mood, the clustering method was able to group songs that shared comparable features. This technique improved mood-based suggestions by forming distinct clusters that correspond with emotional states. Consequently, the system is able to suggest music that is in line with the user's present mood.
- *LSTM for Lyrics Generation:* This project uses long short-term memory (LSTM) networks, which function well with sequential data, to produce lyrics. With the addition of an interactive element, this function lets users explore created lyrics using a completely unique deep learning architecture.

- *Pandas AI-Powered Chatbot:* The recommendation system can be interacted by users using a natural language bot provided by the Pandas AI-powered chatbot. To fine-tune their tastes, users can enter any kind of prompt with respect to the dataset stored in the memory. The chatbot acts as a personal music assistant, making the recommendation process more interactive and user-centric.

To construct a coherent, intelligent recommendation system, the authors integrated a variety of machine learning models, such as CNNs, LSTMs, and cosine similarity, into the Spotify Recommendation Engine. Through the analysis of feature vectors, cosine similarity was utilized to determine the degree of similarity between songs, allowing for accurate suggestions based on aural parameters such as valence, tempo, and energy. By recommending songs that fit the listener's mindset, this technique enhances the experience by skilfully capturing the subtle parallels between tracks. The CNN was created and trained using a sizable dataset of human faces, FER Dataset. This allowed the CNN to human mood from live camera feed and accordingly generate songs.

Beyond just technical implementation, the author's contribution to this project focuses on the

- Design of system architecture for Composite AI-Driven Music Recommendation
- The cosine similarity model for accurate song matching,
- CNNs for emotion-based categorization,
- LSTMs for sequential data creation

By combining these elements, the system provides complex, emotionally stirring experiences through individualized recommendations that go beyond simple user behavior analysis. A high degree of accuracy and user involvement is ensured by the author's hands-on development of the algorithms, model training, and data processing pipelines. This individual endeavor makes a substantial contribution to the field of AI-driven user personalization and demonstrates a thorough mastery of both machine learning principles and music recommendation systems.

The rest of this chapter is organized as: Section 10.2 represents the state-of-the-art methodologies available for music recommendation. Section 10.3 represents the proposed architecture for music recommendation. Section 10.4 details the implementation results. Finally, Section 10.5 concludes the work with future scope.

10.2 Literature Survey

The state-of-the-art methodologies available for playlist generation and recommendation have been studied and the challenges are stated. Yading Song *et al.* [1], conducted extensive research on six music recommendation models, which constitute the existing approaches in the specific research area. The paper investigates the uses of content and emotion-based modeling and the cognitive science of music. However, the authors point out the shortcomings concerning the absence of subjective evaluation in music recommendation. They recommend that future work should look into psychological factors and the formulation of the neural network approaches to broaden the scope of music recommendations. Elena Shakirova *et al.* [2], focus on the success of collaborative filtering approaches in making music recommendations without the need to analyze the content. It is used to an advantage in playlist creation where user likeness is used in suggesting songs. However, the study indicates that there are limitations with collaborative filtering due to sparsity of data and the issue of scalability. Other minor issues include the cold start problem and popularity skew in which the most liked songs are recommended disregarding other songs which may diversify the recommendations.

Mayank *et al.* [3], stress the importance of embedding emotions and context to enhance the level of personalization in music recommendations. The approach is employed in the smart home systems and in generating mood-specific playlists in coherence with the user preferences. But still understanding more complex emotional states are still limitations as precise detection of affective subtleties can be difficult. They point out that collecting good sources of emotion data and training models for those data are two of the fundamental problems that have to be solved so as to enhance the performance of emotion-based recommendations. Ruowei Zhang *et al.* [4], recommend the employment of hybrid filtering methods by integrating content based and collaborative methods, which are beneficial. Their research showcases implementations in streaming services such as Spotify and Pandora where hybrid models improve the recommendation process. In this context, however, they state that hybrid systems can be costly in terms of computations which limits the scalability. Zhang *et al.*, also point to another problem— how to find the optimal combination of the filtering approaches so that high recommendations' accuracy is achieved with minimized performance losses. Joseph Bamidele Awotunde *et al.* [5], studied the role of deep learning models for increasing accuracy in modeling musical user preferences. They describe how this can be used in automated playlist generation, such as those found on Apple Music, but also demonstrate that deep learning models require a really large amount of data to be able to perform properly, and therefore tend not to work when trivial amounts of data have been collected from users. They also discuss the fact that high computational requirements and latency become challenging issues especially when we want to scale deep learning models for real-time recommendations. Tina Babu *et al.* [6], highlighted the importance of emotion-aware systems that can increase users' satisfaction by considering their mood when selecting songs to be played. This could be used in emotion-based playlists, given that current models lack the complexity required to detect fine-grained emotional changes accurately. In real-time, emotion detection is one of the main challenges, where reading and reacting to users' emotions with accuracy in a dynamic context requires more advanced and flexible algorithms. Mariusz Kleć *et al.* [7], presented a music recommendation system that builds upon the Big Five personality traits as conventional but strives for even more personalized recommendations by incorporating selected, particular features of an individual. This kind of methodology tweaks the process of recommendation through a more comprehensive inclusion of personality dimensions, thereby bringing closeness to music recommendations. It is relevant to music services with adaptive interfaces that consider the users' emotional and personality-driven preferences. They emphasize the challenge of reconciling highly tailored recommendations with the necessity of acquainting users with novel and varied music.

Dixit *et al.* [8], discuss the benefits that come along with content-based music recommender systems, which recommend songs based on the attributes of the music such as genre, tempo, and instrumentation in the song. This approach is particularly useful for cold-starting the new song recommendations without relying on behavior data of the user. Such a streaming service, as Last.fm, uses this approach to recommend specific genres to the users. One of the most important challenges within this domain is to identify deeper musical analogies, such as lyrical motifs and affective subtleties, which are definitely harder to quantify using traditional content-based approaches. Renato Panda *et al.* [9], compares the audio features for Spotify vs advanced MER. It results that energy, valence, and acousticness features of Spotify are relevant for classification but do not reach the level of state-of-the-art feature sets in terms of accuracy (58.5% vs. 74.7% F1-measure). Combining Spotify features with more advanced sets yields small improvements, which suggests that although Spotify provides emotionally relevant features, additional features are necessary for higher MER performance. Kurt Jacobson *et al.* [10], describe how Spotify's music personalization focuses on Discover Weekly and Fresh Finds. Tailored toward every user's particular listening pattern as well as wider trends, these playlists are created by factors such as collaborative filtering, machine learning, and NLP in relation to user behavior and songs' acoustic features, and external artist data among others. This study investigates the way Discover Weekly uses factor analysis of playlists to suggest relevant music selections, which it continually updates to optimize the relevance and satisfaction of its users. Markus Schedl *et al.* [11], emphasized the necessity of fulfilling the unique needs of each listener using context-aware recommendation systems. Their work was applicable to streaming services like Spotify, which rely heavily on the personalization of user experiences. They identified some limitations: one of the is called a cold start problem, which appears when the system encounters a new user or item. The greatest challenge is to incorporate a deeper contextual understanding into the recommendation algorithms to enhance user satisfaction. Dmitry Bogdanov *et al.* [12], analyzed the effectiveness of machine learning in boosting the quality of music recommendations. They highlighted applications within major streaming platforms and emphasized integrating contextual data, like mood and location, into recommendation algorithms. The study pointed out limitations such as popularity bias in suggestions and concluded that the challenges include promoting fairness and diversity in recommendations to mitigate this bias. Kumar *et al.* [13], focused more on enlightening recommendation systems and finding that increased transparency enhances user trust and satisfaction. The study shows that this attribute is highly beneficial in scenarios in which the user demands to know the reasoning behind song recommendations. However, there are challenges between transparency and accuracy because overly lengthy explanations can negatively impact the performance of the system. According to the authors, creating tailored explanations for various demographics continues to be one of the major challenges. Saurabh Kulkarn *et al.* [14], investigated the benefits from using context such as time factors or geographical location to enhance music recommendation systems. Their research incorporated applications on some of the platforms like Pandora and Spotify. Despite the merits of the above, there are challenges implied by intricate dynamic contextual data capture and analysis. As pointed out, Wang *et al.*, pointed out developing models that would be adaptable to different changing sources of data is a significant problem. A Anderson *et al.* [15], studied the effects of algorithmic recommendation on the engagement and diversity in listening to songs. It is observed that good recommendation systems can help expand the scope of music discovery without creating "filter bubbles." However, this study mentioned that personalization often leads to less diverse outcomes. Keeping this in mind, they argued that there is a need to balance personalization with song diversity while choosing appropriate songs. Ivana Andjelkovic *et al.* [16], considered the benefits related to mood-based recommendation systems that enhance the users' engagement by matching their mood conditions with song recommendations. This system is particularly relevant for music services targeting mood, but this has its weaknesses like inappropriate interpretation of user mood that leads to poor suggestions. The authors conclude that the best challenge is to develop the best mood detection methods which will involve improving interaction between the users. Jiang *et al.* [17], discussed the use of RNNs in the sequential music recommendation domain, which is extremely beneficial to create playlist-based recommendations based on preference followed by users by selecting their past choices. Yet, challenges such as sparsity in data and the problem of cold-start have restricted its overall effective use. Moreover, efficient scaling is yet another challenging issue in scaling up RNNs for large populations involved in their study. Yucheng Jin *et al.* showed in [18], the impact of individual user characteristics on the effectiveness of diversity-aware music recommendation systems. The authors' findings suggest that one should customize interfaces for users' characteristics to improve both engagement and perceived satisfaction. However, accurate assessment of personality traits is a challenging task; the major challenge is creating interfaces that would be capable of accommodating various user traits while keeping it operational. Pablo Alonso-Jiménez *et al.* [19], explored the use of TensorFlow models to enhance content-based filtering in music recommendations by means of sophisticated audio analysis techniques. This research area can be of great significance for applications focused on sound processing and quality improvement. However, the key negative aspect of these models is the high computational complexity required. Further, according to the authors, scalability and real-time efficiency are significant barriers that require more research in future studies.

A study by Rosilde Tatiana Irene *et al.* [20], used CNNs and RNNs to automate playlist generation based on user preference. The model had a very big advantages through increasing user satisfaction through the creation of customized playlists. However, training complexity is still an issue because it was pointed out that dealing with large-scale data without affecting the performance of the model remains an ongoing challenge. Hence, this paper was referenced to tackle any kind of similar situation in the current research work. Although there are advancements in music recommendation systems, there are potential gaps that require further research. The problems with collaborative and content-based filtering include challenges like sparsity, scalability, and adaptability to capture deeper music analogies. Although there exists emotion–aware and context-aware systems for maximum user satisfaction, the existing models fail to detect complex emotional states accurately. A novel approach to handling psychological factors, and scalable architecture for more personalized, diverse, and contextually adaptive music recommendations is required to address these potential issues.

10.3 Proposed Composite AI-Driven Music Recommendation Engine

In today's digital era, music streaming services have become an essential part of daily life, with platforms such as Spotify leading the way. The proposed initiative, known as the Composite AI-Driven Music Recommendation Engine, seeks to enrich user satisfaction by offering personalized music suggestions through a multifaceted strategy. This endeavor incorporates a range of cutting-edge technologies, such as cosine similarity for song comparison, a custom CNN on VGG-16 for mood-based recommendations, LSTM for generating lyrics, and a Pandas AI-powered interactive chatbot. By integrating these diverse technologies, the system ensures a thorough and captivating user experience that caters to the emotional and auditory preferences of users. This comprehensive approach not only enhances the accuracy of recommendations but also fosters a stronger bond between users and their music. The suggested Spotify Recommendation Engine initiative marks a notable progression in personalized music suggestion technology. Through the amalgamation of song similarity analysis, mood-oriented recommendations, LSTM lyrics creation, and an interactive chatbot driven by Pandas AI, the platform provides a comprehensive and immersive user experience. The working of the proposed algorithm is shown in Algorithm 10.1. The overall architecture is shown in the Figure 10.1.

Algorithm 10.1 Composite AI-driven music recommendation engine.

Input:
  $D \leftarrow$ {Track Features, Artists, Lyrics datasets}
  $U \leftarrow$ {UserPrompt}
  E $\leftarrow$ {Facial Emotion Data}
Output:
  $R \leftarrow$ {Recommended Tracks}

Initialize $T = 1$
while $T \leq$ NumberOfRecommendations do
  for each Track $Track_i$ **do**
    for each Track $Track_j$ **do**
      Compute similarity $S(Track_i, Track_j)$ using cosine similarity:

$$S(Track_i, Track_j) = \frac{\sum Vector_{Track_i} \cdot Vector_{Track_j}}{||Vector_{Track_i}|| \cdot ||Vector_{Track_j}||}$$

      if $S(Track_i) < S(Track_j)$ **then**
        Compute distance $dist_{Track_p Track_j}$:

$$dist_{Track_p Track_j} = \sum_{d=1}^{dim} \left| Pos^d_{Track_i} - Pos^d_{Track_j} \right|$$

        Update fitness $\beta_{dist_{Track_p Track_j}}$:

$$\beta_{dist_{Track_p Track_j}} = \beta_0 \cdot e^{-\gamma \cdot dist_{Track_p Track_j}}$$

        Update user account, connecting to the API and saving the playlist.
        Compute new fitness $fit_T(Track_i)$.
      end if
    end for
  end for
end while

User Emotion Detection
for each user U_i **do**
  Detect emotion E_i from the user's face using CNN-based emotion detection.
  Generate mood parameters M_i from K-means clustering on song features.
  Compute mood-based relevance for each track using M_i.
  Update the final recommendation set R.
end for

Test Instance Classification
for each test instance T_i **do**
  Assign class label:

$$ClassLabel_{T_i} \leftarrow \{C_i \mid min(dist_{Ti,Ci})\}$$

  Where $dist_{Ti,Ci}$ is the distance between the test instance and cluster centroids.
end for

Lyrics Generation using LSTM
Pre-processing: Tokenize and encode lyrics dataset D into sequences
LSTM Model Training: E_i Initialize LSTM model with embedding and dense layers and Train LSTM model on encoded sequences from D
LSTM Model Training: E_i Generate lyrics by sampling words from trained LSTM model

Output: Recommended tracks R displayed through the Streamlit web app.

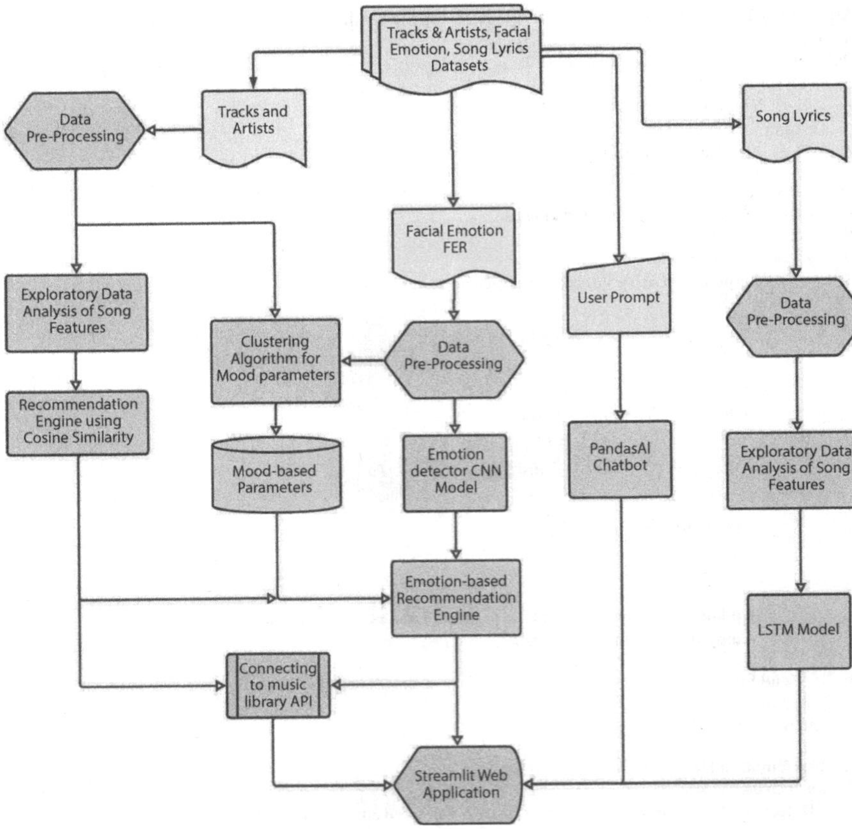

Figure 10.1 Proposed composite AI driven music recommendation engine.

10.3.1 Recommendations Using Cosine Similarity

Cosine similarity is a metric used to assess how similar two vectors are to one another. As a gauge of similarity between two documents or, in the instance of Spotify Recommendation Engine, between audio feature vectors of songs, it is frequently employed in information retrieval and text mining.

Every song in the dataset is represented by various unique features like: danceability (how suitable a track is for dancing based on a combination of musical elements), energy (Perceptual measure of intensity and activity), loudness (Overall loudness of the track in decibels) and other features like speechiness, acousticness, instrumentalness, etc. Each song S_i can be represented as a vector A_i in a high dimensional space where each dimension represents one of these features.

For the two songs represented by A and B, the cosine similarity can be calculated as specified in Equation (10.1).

$$similarity\ (A, B) = \frac{A.B}{\|A\|.\|B\|} \quad (10.1)$$

Where, $A.B$ is the dot product and $\|A\|.\|B\|$ is Euclidean Norm. Dot Product includes measuring the similarity in directionality between A and B. If A and B are perfectly aligned (pointing in the same direction), the dot product is maximized. Normalization includes dividing by the product of the norms$\|A\|.\|B\|$ normalizes the dot product to the range [-1, 1]. This normalization ensures that the cosine similarity measure is independent of the magnitude of the vectors, focusing solely on the direction.

Cosine similarity is calculated between all pairs of songs based on their feature vectors. Higher cosine similarity values indicate that songs are more similar in terms of their audio features. This similarity measure helps in recommending songs that are not only contextually relevant (based on audio characteristics) but also align closely with the user's preferences. Moreover, the dataset has millions of songs; and hence, to decrease the computation speed, initially the dataset is shuffled randomly and divided into subsets of 10,000 songs. Top n songs are selected from every subset which are then joined together to form a new set of songs with high recommendation songs. Finally, cosine similarity is again performed between user's song and the new set, and the top songs are displayed as the output.

10.3.2 Emotion-Based Music Recommendation

The seven emotion classes represented in the fer2013 dataset are anger, disgust, fear, happiness, sorrow, surprise, and neutral. To guarantee consistency in terms of size, alignment, and grayscale conversion, each image undergoes preprocessing. Three emotions are used for the purpose – happiness, sorrow and neutral.

Firstly, every specific mood will have a unique set of song parameters associated with it. For example, for sadness danceability will be very low but for happiness, it will be quite high. Similarly, all other features will vary from mood-to-mood, and thus an unsupervised clustering mechanism (*K-Means*) was used to determine an averaged vector set of song parameters for a particular mood. Mood detection is performed from live camera and then similarity scores are calculated between songs and vectorized representation of features of that particular mood. The optimal value of K and the clustering performed for loudness and Energy is depicted in Figure 10.2.

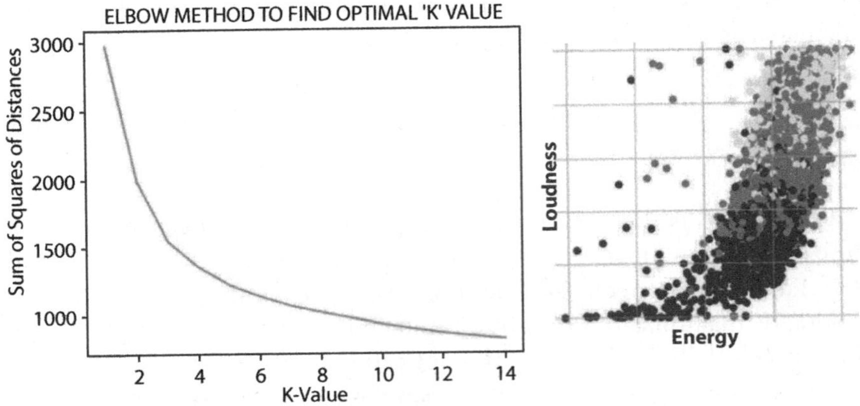

Figure 10.2 K-Means clustering performed for loudness and intensity for 3 different clusters (moods).

A customized Convolutional Neural Network (CNN) architecture, shown in Figure 10.3, is integrated on top of the VGG-16 foundation. This unique architecture enhances the face-specific feature extraction process, making it more efficient and accurate. Once the model is designed and successfully implemented, it is deployed to detect the user's mood from a live camera feed. The model then immediately applies a previously designed cosine similarity technique, comparing the detected features with a pre-calculated feature vector corresponding to that particular mood. This approach ensures real-time mood detection and accurate matching with predefined mood characteristics.

- *Convolutional Layers*: Low-level characteristics such as corners and edges are detected by the first convolutional layers. Gradually, higher layers identify increasingly intricate patterns, such features and expressions on the face.

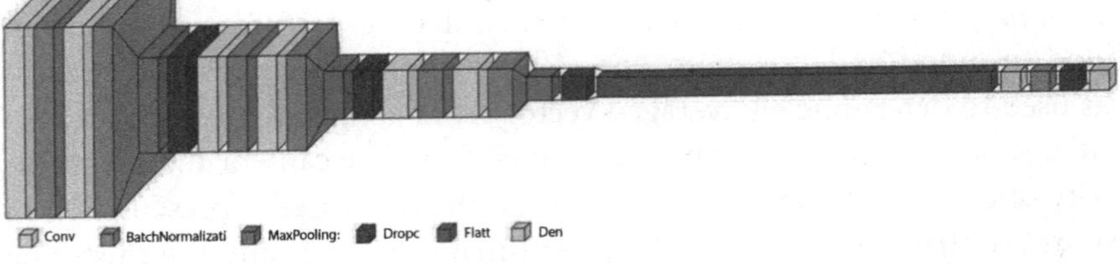

Figure 10.3 Customized CNN architecture to perform mood detection on human face.

- *Batch Normalization*: By lowering internal covariate shift, batch normalization stabilizes and speeds up training by normalizing activations inside each mini-batch.
- *Pooling Layers*: Max pooling layers reduce spatial dimensions while keeping the most important information by down-sampling feature maps.
- *Dropout Regularization*: To reduce overfitting and improve generalization

10.3.3 Lyrics Generation Using LSTM

The tcc_ceds_music dataset includes a wide range of song lyrics from different artists and genres. The whole lyrics of every song are included in each dataset entry, offering a wealth of textual material for language model training. Because of the dataset's wide range and diversity, reliable and adaptable models that can provide logical and contextually relevant lyrics can be developed. An LSTM-based neural network is trained to predict the next character in the sequence, the architecture of which is shown in Figure 10.4. The corpus is divided into overlapping character sequences, called features, with each character in the sequence coming after the previous one (called targets). This serves as the foundation for the input-output pairings that the model is trained on. The model architecture comprises two LSTM cells, with dropouts for regularization.

- *Embedding Layer*: Creates dense vectors of a predetermined size from the supplied character index sequence. This lowers

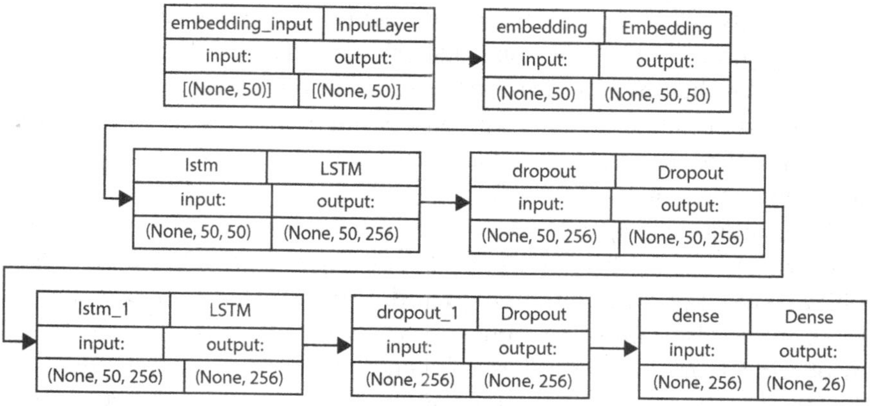

Figure 10.4 LSTM architecture and implementation in model.

the dimensionality of the input and aids in the capture of more semantic information.

- *LSTM Layers*: Two 256-unit LSTM layers are added. Due to their ability to identify long-term dependencies in the data, LSTMs are a special kind of recurrent neural network (RNN) that works particularly well for sequence prediction tasks.
- *Dropout Layers*: To lessen overfitting, dropout layers have been added following each LSTM layer. To assist regularize the model, dropout randomly sets a portion of the input units to 0 at each update during training.
- *Dense Layer*: An additional Dense layer with a *softmax* activation function that is fully coupled is added. This layer has the same number of units as there are unique letters. The output is guaranteed to be a probability distribution over all potential next characters by the *softmax* activation.

For training, the *Adam Optimizer* is employed, a popular and effective adaptive learning rate optimization approach for deep learning model training. The loss function in the model is *categorical cross entropy*. This is suitable for classification jobs in which there are numerous possible classes.

10.3.4 Chatbot Implementation Powered by Pandas AI

The chatbot, which was created with Pandas AI, makes use of a large tracks dataset that includes every song's intricate details. This chatbot, which is integrated with an intuitive user interface (UI) created with Streamlit, is capable of handling and reacting to a wide range of dataset-related queries with efficiency. By interacting with the chatbot, users can retrieve precise music details including the artist, album, genre, and release date. It can also shed light on aspects of the song, such as pace, danceability, energy, and valence. The chatbot may also assist users in finding music depending on their mood or favorite qualities by processing natural language inquiries. Examples of such queries are "find songs with a danceability above 0.8" and "show me high-energy tracks."

The chatbot can help users discover patterns in the dataset, such as which artists or genres have been most popular during a given time frame. Along with making recommendations or providing insights based on user preferences, it may also compare various songs or albums based on their features. By offering an interactive and user-friendly platform for dataset querying, the Streamlit interface improves the overall user experience. Because users may directly express their inquiries and receive timely, precise responses, exploring the tracks dataset is both entertaining and educational. Pandas AI and Streamlit working together guarantees a powerful, user-friendly, and dynamic tool for researchers and music lovers alike.

10.4 Results and Discussions

The proposed Composite – AI-driven music Recommendation system is implemented in Python 3.8 using the frameworks and libraries TensorFlow, PyTorch, Pandas AI, Scikit-learn, Spotify API, and Streamlit. The hardware configuration required to implement the proposed methodology includes AMD Ryzen 7 4700U (8-core, 2.0 GHz, boost up to 4.1 GHz), Intel Core i5-10400 (6-core, 2.9 GHz, boost up to 4.3 GHz) with 8GB DDR4 RAM and 256 GB SSD.

10.4.1 Datasets Used

The datasets used include Spotify Tracks Dataset, Spotify Million Songs Dataset, and FER 2013 dataset. The Spotify Tracks Dataset is used for song recommendation, Spotify Million Songs Dataset is used for Song Recommendation and Lyrics Generation and FER 2013 dataset is used for Emotion detection.

The Spotify Tracks Dataset is found on Kaggle and comprises rich metadata and audio features for more than 232,000 tracks of Spotify. Each track is described using attributes such as danceability, energy, valence, tempo, loudness, and speechiness, along with general metadata like the name of the track, artist, and album. These audio features are numerical, normalized between 0 and 1, which makes them suitable for the machine learning tasks such as the calculation of the cosine similarity. The dataset covers a diverse number of tracks across genres and release dates, therefore containing a broad variety of musical styles. It contains features like tempo in beats per minute, duration in milliseconds, and key, and it is therefore extensively analysable. This structured and feature-rich dataset actually proves to be ideally suited for the creation of recommendation systems, where cosine similarity can effectively calculate similarities between tracks based on their feature vectors. Its size and diversity make it very effective for scalable recommendation tasks.

The Million Song Dataset (MSD), which is used for the generation of LSTMs-based lyrics, represents a large collection of metadata and audio analysis for one million contemporary popular music tracks. This dataset concentrates on research in MIR (music information retrieval) as well as in machine learning. The attributes accompanying each track include lyrics of the song, tempo, key, time signature, loudness, and duration. Additionally, the dataset provides rich feature information, for example, timbre, pitch histograms, and summaries of audio using tools like the Echo Nest API. This dataset contains millions of lyrical sequences aligned with track metadata, making it especially suitable for sequence prediction tasks such as LSTM-based generation. Tracks are uniquely identified by ID, and grouped across genres, artists, and albums. The dataset's scalability and structured annotations make it easy to train neural networks efficiently, with a solid foundation upon which to build contextually accurate and artistically coherent lyrics.

One of the widely used datasets for facial emotion recognition tasks is FER 2013, which contains 35,887 grayscale images of size 48x48 pixels. All images are centered on a human face and belong to seven emotion classes: angry, disgust, fear, happiness, sadness, surprise, and neutral. Each image can be represented as a flattened array of 2,304 features, which include pixel intensities. The dataset is balanced across its classes and broken down into three subsets: the training set consists of 28,709 samples, validation (3,589 samples), and testing (3,589 samples). It is well suited for such tasks as working with CNNs with uniform resolution and labeled structure. Small image size ensures that computations are efficient enough, so the dataset is perfect for working in real-time emotion recognition applications. The FER 2013 dataset has become the benchmark for evaluating recognition models and algorithms for emotion in machine learning and computer vision.

10.4.2 Parameter Settings

Table 10.1 represents the details of parameters used to implement the proposed Composite AI-Driven Music Recommendation.

10.4.3 Implementation

Figure 10.5 is the landing page, where the user will land to when starting the web application, "Tracks by Vibe" is the default home page. The user can enter a song of his choice; the API will display the available songs to choose from their library to fetch recommendations for. Additionally, users can select the number of recommendations to generate and select to include explicit songs or not. Afterwards, generated playlist is clicked, the algorithm will generate the recommendations by using the concept of Cosine Similarity, Dataset Shuffling and Randomizing. The output

Table 10.1 Details of parameters.

Model	**Parameters**
Base Model	VGG - 16
Convolutional neural network	
First Conv2D Layer	#filters = 64 Filter size = (5,5) Activation = ELU Padding ='same' Weight = 'he_normal'
Second Conv2D Layer	#filters = 64 Filter size = (5,5) Activation = ELU Padding ='same' Weight = 'he_normal'
Third and Fourth Conv2D Layer	#filters = 128 Filter size = (3,3) Activation = ELU Padding ='same' Weight = 'he_normal'
Fifth and Sixth Conv2D Layer	#filters = 256 Filter size = (3,3) Activation = ELU Padding ='same' Weight = 'he_normal'
Max Pooling	Filter sise = (2,2) Stride = 2
Drop out	0.4, 0.5, 0.6
LSTM	
LSTM units	300
Drop out	0.2, 0.3
Output Vocabulary Size	6005

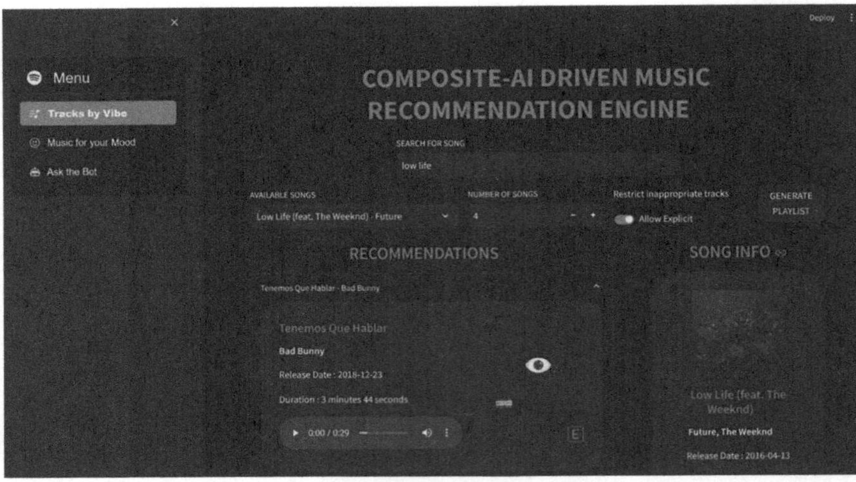

Figure 10.5 Recommended songs by the designed algorithm.

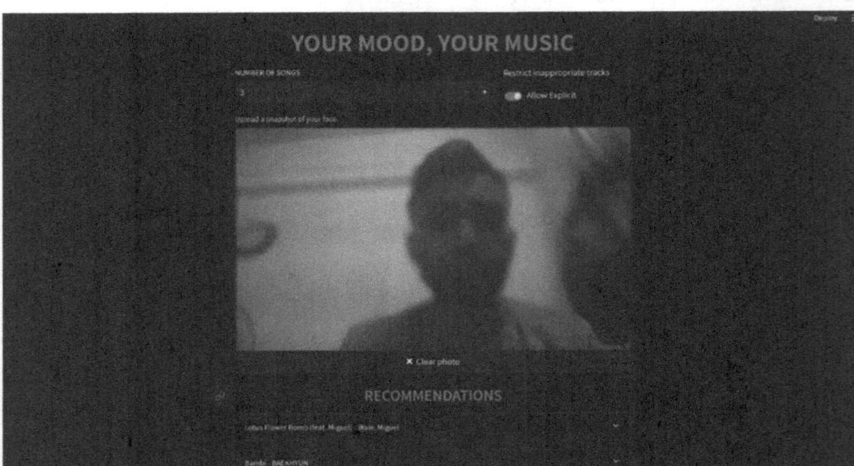

Figure 10.6 Mood detection from user's face and accordingly recommend songs.

recommendations will be shown with details of the songs like artists, durations, etc. and also with a 30 second preview audio.

Figure 10.6 shows the functionality of detecting mood from a user's facial details and simultaneously recommending music is being displayed. The application needs access to the webcam of the device, from which it will capture the user's facial features and store it temporarily. Using the captured image, it will then apply the custom CNN model and capture the features, and predict the user's mood from it. Every mood is assigned a unique combination of vectors representing various song attributes, like energy, liveliness, etc. Cosine similarity will be used to compare the mood vector with the song vectors and accordingly generate recommendations.

Figure 10.7 shows a basic chatbot stream lit application, only designed to answer dataset related queries. This ensure responses are generated only with respect to the context. The bot uses Pandas AI, where the data frame is passed in a secure manner using an authentication token. This ensures our data is not leaked and is completely private. The bot is capable of giving string outputs, as well as tabular and well-designed information, depending on the prompt being passed.

Figure 10.8 shows the generated playlists to users' account using OAuth authentication. Spotify's Spotify OAuth class manages the OAuth flow, enabling users to authenticate and grant permissions to the application. Once authenticated, the use can add the generated recommendations to their personal Spotify library with a single click. This approach ensures that users can seamlessly integrate their music preferences into their Spotify experience through the web application. Since it is using OAuth, the user credentials are completely safe and the application never gets direct access to their passwords, rather it is routed through Spotify officially.

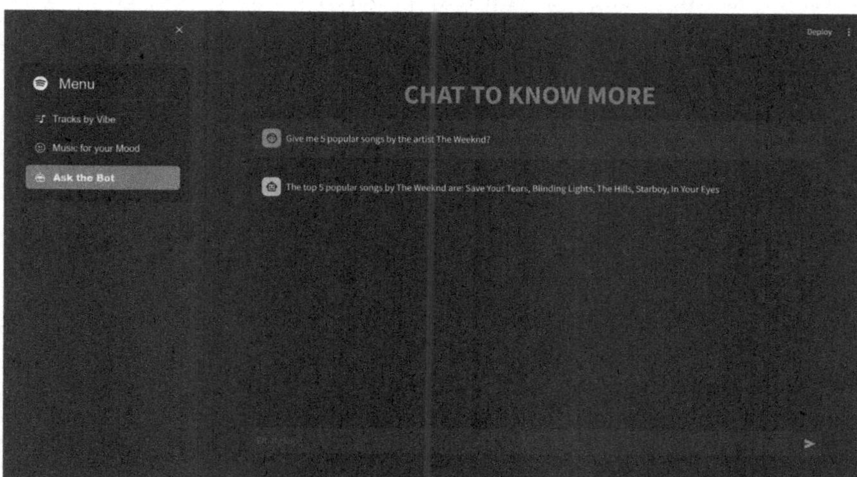

Figure 10.7 Simple chatbot to answer dataset related queries.

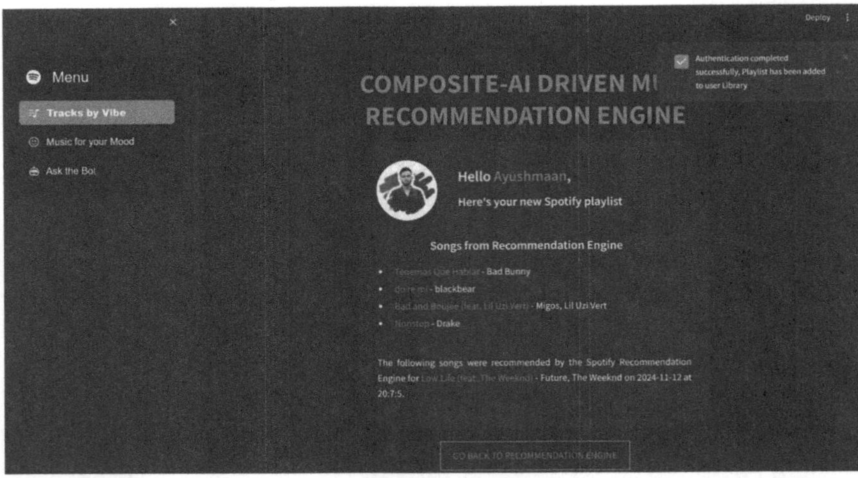

Figure 10.8 Adding generated playlist to user's Spotify account, by connecting using OAuth authentication.

10.5 Conclusion

The Composite AI-Driven Music Recommendation Engine pools together advanced algorithm like Cosine similarity, CNNs, LSTM nets, K-means clustering, and a Pandas AI-powered chatbot, which will give an all-rounded recommendation experience. Its cosine similarity facilitates accurate song recommendations based on the analysis of auditory feature vectors; it is always aligned with user preferences. Mood detection takes place using CNNs by analyzing users' emotions; hence, enhancing personalization, and contextual lyrics are generated with the help of LSTM networks to enhance user engagement. K-means clustering classifies songs in mood-based clusters and further refines mood-oriented recommendations. The chatbot, Pandas AI, incorporates the interactive nature of adding an element where users can query and explore recommendations dynamically. Harmonizing these technologies gives way to this project's deeply personal, emotionally resonant, and contextually intelligent music recommendation. The project actually captures quite significant improvements in music personalization that further augment users' bonding with collections of songs.

This multi-domain use case project can be applied in the creation of mood-based playlisting and songs, for instance, in relation to the context of streaming audio platforms. Additionally, music curation with real-time mood detection would allow for a seamless auditory environment in smart home systems. For content creators, lyric generation would serve as inspiration and utility in developing music. In addition, the system's chatbot feature can be made friendly for e-learning. It helps users who learn music or discuss music analysis. By bridging personalization with interactivity, the engine has potential applications in both consumer and professional settings.

It opens up several promising directions for further research and development work. The next direction would include real-time sentiment analysis using audio cues like voice tone or ambient noise that might further strengthen the mood detection. An enlarged dataset from diverse collections of music creates various means to improve the recommendation diversity and inclusivity. It also covers some advanced models based on transformer like GPT, which enhances the performance in the generation of lyrics and even creates more profound chatbot interactions. Future work might be about optimization in terms of computational efficiency in handling large-sized datasets or processing real-time data. It can support scalability for more deployments. The system can be extended to multi-modal inputs like video or user behavior patterns to further develop personalized recommendations toward an enhanced user experience.

AI disclosure statement: The author acknowledges the use of AI-based tools for minor language editing or grammatical correction. However, all intellectual contributions, analyses, and conclusions presented in this chapter are entirely the author's own.

References

1. Song, Y., The Role of Emotion and Context in Musical Preference, Doctoral dissertation, Queen Mary University of London.
2. Shakirova, E., Collaborative filtering for music recommender system, in: *2017 IEEE Conference of Russian Young Researchers in Electrical and Electronic Engineering (EIConRus)*, 2017 Feb 1, IEEE, pp. 548–550.
3. Sharma, M., Multi-lingual multi-task speech emotion recognition using wav-2vec 2.0, in: *ICASSP 2022-2022 IEEE International Conference on Acoustics, Speech and Signal Processing (ICASSP)*, 2022 May 23, IEEE, pp. 6907–6911.
4. Zhang, R., Tu, S., Sun, Z., A hybrid music recommendation method based on music genes and collaborative filtering, in: *2022 IEEE Intl Conf on Dependable, Autonomic and Secure Computing, Intl Conf on Pervasive Intelligence and Computing, Intl Conf on Cloud and Big Data Computing, Intl Conf on Cyber Science and Technology Congress (DASC/PiCom/CBDCom/CyberSciTech)*, 2022 Sep 12, IEEE, pp. 1–6.

5. Awotunde, J.B., Abiodun, M.K., Adeniyi, A.E., Abiodun, B.H., Adeniyi, J.K., Aremu, D.R., Adebiyi, A.A., Atanda, O.G., Personalized Music Recommendation System Based on Machine Learning and Collaborative Filtering, in: *2024 International Conference on Science, Engineering and Business for Driving Sustainable Development Goals (SEB4SDG)*, 2024 Apr 2, IEEE, pp. 1–8.
6. Babu, T. and Nair, R.R., Emotion-Aware Music Recommendation System: Enhancing User Experience Through Real-Time Emotional Context, arXiv preprint arXiv:2311.10796, 2023 Nov 17.
7. Kleć, M. and Wieczorkowska, A., Music recommendation systems: A survey, in: *Recommender Systems for Medicine and Music*, pp. 107–118, Springer International Publishing, Cham, 2021 Apr 8.
8. Dixit, V.S. and Jain, P., A proposed framework for recommendations aggregation in context aware recommender systems, in: *2018 8th International Conference on Cloud Computing, Data Science & Engineering (Confluence)*, 2018 Jan 11, IEEE, pp. 209–214.
9. Panda, R., Redinho, H., Gonçalves, C., Malheiro, R., Paiva, R.P., How does the spotifyapi compare to the music emotion recognition state-of-the-art?, in: *18th Sound and Music Computing Conference (SMC 2021)*, 2021 Jul 1, Axeasas/SMC Network, pp. 238–245.
10. Jacobson, K., Murali, V., Newett, E., Whitman, B., Yon, R., Music personalization at Spotify, in: *Proceedings of the 10th ACM Conference on Recommender Systems*, 2016 Sep 7, pp. 373–373.
11. Schedl, M., Zamani, H., Chen, C.W., Deldjoo, Y., Elahi, M., Current challenges and visions in music recommender systems research. *Int. J. Multimed. Inf. Retr.*, 7, 95–116, 2018 Jun.
12. Schedl, M., Knees, P., McFee, B., Bogdanov, D., Music recommendation systems: Techniques, use cases, and challenges, in: *Recommender systems handbook*, pp. 927–971, Springer US, New York, NY, 2021 Nov 22.
13. Kumar, T.A., Kanimozhi, P., Dutta, P.K., Sowmya, R., Assessment of gradient classifier based approaches in advanced recommendation framework: uncovering limitations, in: *IET Conference Proceedings CP859*, vol. 2023, no. 44, The Institution of Engineering and Technology, Stevenage, UK, pp. 331–336, 2023.
14. Kulkarni, S. and Rodd, S.F., Context Aware Recommendation Systems: A review of the state of the art techniques. *Comput. Sci. Rev.*, 37, 100255, 2020 Aug 1.
15. Anderson, A., Maystre, L., Anderson, I., Mehrotra, R., Lalmas, M., Algorithmic effects on the diversity of consumption on spotify, in: *Proceedings of the Web Conference 2020*, 2020 Apr 20, pp. 2155–2165.
16. Andjelkovic, I., Parra, D., O'Donovan, J., Moodplay: interactive music recommendation based on artists' mood similarity. *Int. J. Hum.-Comput. Stud.*, 121, 142–59, 2019 Jan 1.

17. Jiang, M., Yang, Z., Zhao, C., What to play next? A RNN-based music recommendation system, in: *2017 51st Asilomar Conference on Signals, Systems, and Computers*, 2017 Oct 29, IEEE, pp. 356–358.
18. Jin, Y., Tintarev, N., Htun, N.N., Verbert, K., Effects of personal characteristics in control-oriented user interfaces for music recommender systems. *User Model. User-Adapt. Interact.*, 30, 2, 199–249, 2020 Apr.
19. Alonso-Jiménez, P., Bogdanov, D., Pons, J., Serra, X., Tensorflow audio models in essentia, in: *ICASSP 2020-2020 IEEE International Conference on Acoustics, Speech and Signal Processing (ICASSP)*, 2020 May 4, IEEE, pp. 266–270.
20. Irene, R.T., Borrelli, C., Zanoni, M., Buccoli, M., Sarti, A., Automatic playlist generation using convolutional neural networks and recurrent neural networks, in: *2019 27th European Signal Processing Conference (EUSIPCO)*, 2019 Sep 2, IEEE, pp. 1–5.

11

A Composite Artificial Intelligence Based Framework for Heart Disease Prediction

M. Suresh[1]*, M. S. Anbarasi[2], R. Rajmohan[1] and A. Anbarasi[1]

[1]Department of Computing Technology, School of Computing, SRM Institute of Science and Technology, Kattankalathur, Tamil Nadu, India
[2]Department of Information Technology, Pondicherry Technological University, Pillaichavady, Puducherry, India

Abstract

Cardiovascular Diseases (CVDs) remain one of the leading causes of death worldwide, and successful prevention and treatment rely heavily on early detection. Managing complex and multidimensional patient data poses a significant challenge for traditional diagnostic systems. Globally, the rising incidence of cardiovascular diseases presents major challenges to healthcare systems, requiring advanced predictive models for early detection and effective treatment. The complexity and unpredictability of patient information often hinder traditional methods, resulting in delayed actions. To enhance cardiovascular disease prediction, this research proposes a composite Artificial Intelligence (AI) model that integrates an Attention-based Convolutional Neural Network (ACNN) with multi-Bidirectional Long Short-Term Memory (m-BiLSTM) networks (ACNN-mBiLSTM). The proposed approach leverages mBiLSTM to capture temporal patterns from patient histories and CNN to extract critical spatial features from clinical data and medical images. To further improve predictive accuracy, an attention mechanism is employed to prioritize the most important features. Trained on an extensive dataset encompassing diverse patient profiles, the ACNN-mBiLSTM model outperformed traditional models in terms of precision, specificity, and sensitivitydemonstrating significant improvements in predictive capabilities. The findings highlight the potential of the composite ACNN-mBiLSTM approach to facilitate early diagnosis of cardiovascular disease, ultimately leading to better patient outcomes and more efficient healthcare practices.

**Corresponding author*: mail4sureshuni@gmail.com

T. S. Arun Samuel, L. Jerart Julus, P. Kanimozhi, T. Ananth Kumar and S. Balamurugan (eds.) Composite Artificial Intelligence: Fundamentals, Challenges, and Applications, (249–278) © 2026 Scrivener Publishing LLC

***Keywords*:** Smart healthcare, composite artificial intelligence, data integration, electronic health records, temporal dependencies, proactive health management, heart disease

11.1 Introduction

Recently, e-healthcare has gained popularity as a convenient way to provide medical evaluation services anywhere, at any time. By circumventing geographic limitations and reducing wait times for doctor appointments, online medical diagnosis offers flexibility and convenience [1]. Data mining (DM) is employed by electronic medical care algorithms to predict hidden illnesses from medical data. Healthcare providers can utilize this health information to develop detection systems, using skyline queries and medical information mining, to quickly diagnose patients' conditions and offer online healthcare applications [2].

In conventional online medical systems, medical information is often stored in separate healthcare facilities, with each facility collecting a limited amount of healthcare data. Modern healthcare systems face several challenges due to population growth and the increasing demands of both experts and users [3]. Technological advancements have led to changes in lifestyle and standards of living, with statistics showing a decline in physical labor, which can negatively impact health. Technological developments can serve as key tools in reducing morbidity and mortality rates [4].

Reports indicate that CVDs are on the rise and are among the leading causes of mortality worldwide. Congenital heart disease (CHD), another serious condition leads to early adult mortality as it is a common birth defect [5]. Globally, birth abnormalities account for 20–40% of newborn mortality with CHD responsible for 6–10% of these deaths. According to the World Health Organization (WHO), 8.8 million children die before the age of five each year, with over 40% passing away within the first month of life [6]. Annually, four million newborns die within their first four weeks of life, with 18–25% of affected newborns passing away in their first year, and 4% of survivors dying before the age of 16. Previous research shows that the prevalence of CHD varies globally from 1.3 per 1000 births in developed countries to 50.89 per 1000 births in underdeveloped nations. Despite advanced medical diagnostic tools and improved treatments, CHD remains one of the leading causes of infant mortality [7].

In India, a report on CHD states that between 60,000 and 90,000 individuals are affected by the disease and require urgent early care. A significant portion of these cases contributes to the alarmingly high infant mortality rate when early diagnosis is not made. CHD alone accounts for about 10% of newborn deaths in India [8]. Most infants with congenital heart conditions are discharged from maternity hospitals within 24 hours of birth, often without a diagnosis. The revelations from these reports, available through verified fact sheets for public review, are deeply concerning and highlight the need for intervention to improve survival chances [9]. Recent textual and contextual analyses have reviewed existing projects and proven techniques for implementing health monitoring systems, with an aim toward creating smart, remote towns and villages. These assessments also compile the challenges present in current technological advancements. A novel approach is now necessary to identify congenital heart disease in newborns at an early age, focusing on the longest life expectancy and the fastest possible healthcare services [10].

The convergence of emerging technologies has made smart remote health monitoring feasible. In the field of Wireless Body Area Networks (WBAN), healthcare diagnosis is gaining traction. Numerous studies have explored WBAN from various perspectives, including routing, safety, and environmental sustainability. This paper proposes a strategy for developing smart towns and villages in the healthcare sector. The plan is based on thorough research, including a regressive study of the limitations in existing technologies and a questionnaire-based assessment [10]. Despite recent technological advances in health condition identification, CVDs remain the leading cause of death in wealthy countries. Routine monitoring for cardiac abnormalities is crucial to prevent severe health issues shown in Figure 11.1.

One common feature of many CVDs is arrhythmia, which is characterized by irregular or abnormal heartbeats [11]. Arrhythmias are caused by malfunctioning electrical signals that control the heart's rhythm, leading to heartbeats that are too fast, too slow, or erratic. Types of arrhythmias include ventricular fibrillation, premature atrial contraction, and supraventricular arrhythmia. Contributing factors often include stress, poor diet, sedentary lifestyle, obesity, lack of exercise, high cholesterol, smoking, diabetes, and excessive alcohol consumption as depicted in Figure 11.2 [12].

Additional information is essential for effective medical surveillance. Life-threatening situations may arise during frequent power outages. Sensor nodes (SNs) have relatively small battery capacities due to their compact size. Most power-efficiency studies in WBANs focus on the transmission between the gateway and the SN [13]. The gateway node faces power consumption challenges because, unlike SNs, it requires a large

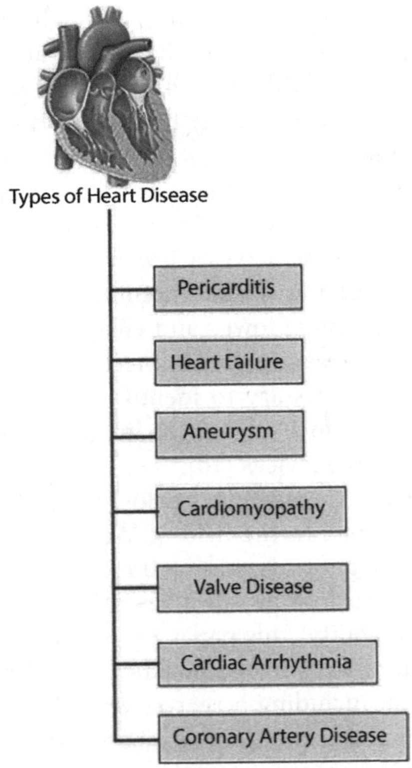

Figure 11.1 Types of heart disease.

battery capacity to handle various demanding tasks such as computing, long-range wireless communication, and data display [14]. Wireless body sensors rely on transducers to detect signals, and they use transceiver electronics and electrical power for wireless communication links. WBANs primarily use wireless biological sensors, powered by batteries, to measure and transmit vital signs to remote medical centers. The functional lifetime of WBAN devices is directly affected by the limited size of their batteries [15].

11.1.1 Problem Statement

AI has the potential to significantly improve results for patients, enhance predictive capacities, and optimize the distribution of resources in the quickly changing healthcare sector. Existing AI models frequently work in isolation, producing fragmentary insights that can miss important

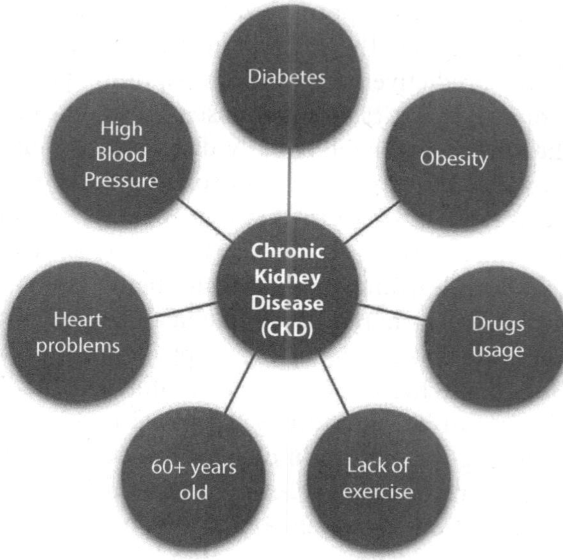

Figure 11.2 Cardiovascular risk factors.

interactions between different health aspects. This fragmentation restricts a complete comprehension of patient health dynamics and yields inadequate prognostic precision. To improve the prediction capacity and usefulness of medical care models, this structure has to take into consideration a variety of information sources, such as Electronic Health Records (EHRs), continuous monitoring of patient systems, and socioeconomic factors that influence illness. This study aims to develop and execute a composite AI system that integrates many AI methodologies to offer comprehensive and precise forecasts of patients' health trajectories. This would facilitate early medical procedures and customized treatment regimens. This composite approach seeks to close the gap between silos of information, promote multidisciplinary cooperation, and eventually help create more intelligent, data-driven medical products by overcoming the shortcomings of existing AI methodologies.

11.1.2 Motivation

The healthcare sector urgently needs innovative solutions to address complex health challenges, particularly in light of the intricacies of personalized treatment, the growing prevalence of chronic diseases, and expanding patient populations. Traditional healthcare organizations often adopt a reactive rather than proactive approach due to their inability to generate accurate and timely forecasts. The integration of cutting-edge technology is essential to enhance predictive capabilities and optimize patient outcomes. AI through predictive analytics, has demonstrated significant potential in transforming healthcare by enabling early disease detection, risk assessment, and personalized treatment recommendations. The effectiveness of current AI systems is limited because they often operate in siloed domains. For instance, machine learning techniques may excel at analyzing structured data, while deep learning algorithms are better suited for unstructured data such as patient narratives or medical images. The lack of an integrated framework that combines these approaches results in missed opportunities for comprehensive insights and informed decision-making. Predictive accuracy can be significantly improved by integrating diverse data sources, including wearable technology, social determinants of health, and electronic health records. Many existing systems fail to fully leverage this wealth of information. By developing a composite AI framework, we can merge the strengths of various AI methodologies to create a more holistic approach to medical prediction.This study is driven by the urgent need to equip healthcare professionals with reliable predictive tools that facilitate proactive interventions, reduce healthcare costs, and enhance patient experiences. Our goal is to promote the development of intelligent healthcare solutions that address the complexities of modern medical care, ultimately improving the overall quality of healthcare delivery through multidisciplinary collaboration and the application of diverse AI techniques.

11.2 Smart Health Monitoring Systems

The comprehensive analysis covers both the simulated foundation for smart health surveillance systems and recent advances in developing hardware systems. The research review has been divided into two sections: (i) hardware design and development-based wellness tracking methods, and (ii) simulation-based healthcare surveillance systems. These systems have been further classified according to the target demographic, illnesses, types of equipment used, and usage location. After surveying 183 valid responses and engaging with end-users, the societal need for a smart health tracking framework was confirmed. Following this, stakeholders were involved, and field trips were conducted as shown in Figure 11.3. One example is the routine use of pulse oximetry in primary and tertiary medical facilities at birth helps close the diagnostic gap for Cyanotic Congenital Heart

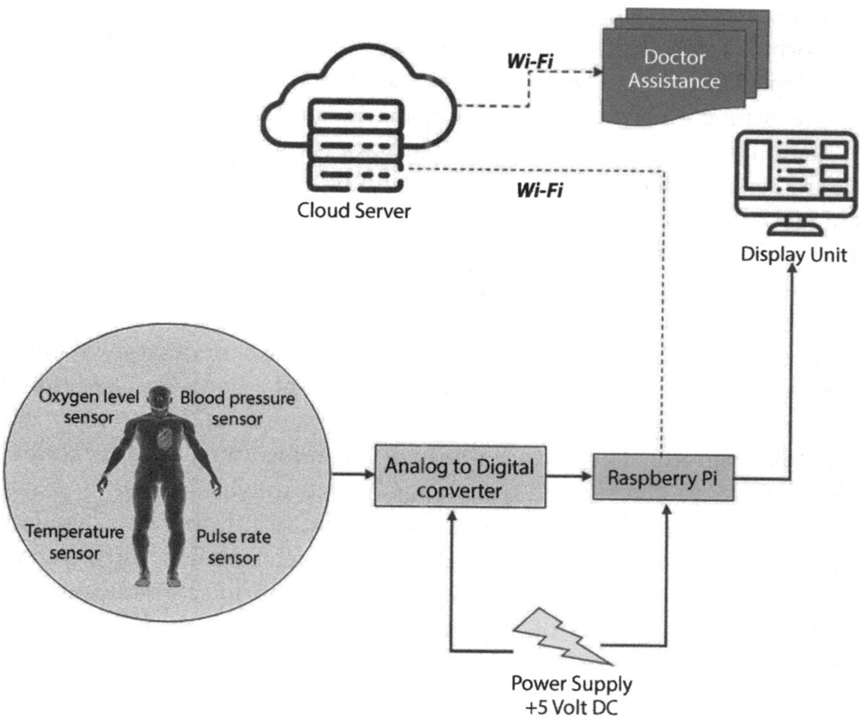

Figure 11.3 Smart heart disease monitoring system.

Diseases (CCHD) which demonstrated the benefits of pulse oximetry in the early and accurate detection of moderate hypoxemia, highlighting its affordability, non-invasiveness, and efficacy. It discussed how technological advances are transforming remote fetal surveillance for expectant mothers in underserved communities by improving patient data collection, health monitoring, and the provision of evidence-based care through a continuous flow of medical data. Efforts are being made at multiple levels to develop smart technologies and approaches, ultimately leading to the creation of an increasing number of smart monitoring devices capable of delivering high-quality health status monitoring for patients.

An Internet of Things-based wellness tracking system is quite different from a traditional medical system. As a result, using IoT to achieve the necessary performances and outcomes becomes quite difficult. As digital information signals are used by the sensors, working with IoT is associated with the embedded world. In the beginning, a processor monitors; indicators, detectors, and additional equipment are coupled together for synchronization. Signals are detected by the sensors and detectors in analog form, require further conversion into digital representation. Figure 11.4 depicts the flow of work operation as a block diagram.

The primary objective is to categorize arrhythmias and myocardial infraction for usage in our IoT wearable device's application layer shown in Figure 11.4. By enabling remote consultations between the ischemia client and his physician, this gadget helps the individual with his mobility limitations and allows him to get medical care without having to leave his house. It involves taking the patient's ECG signal, analyzing it, and sending it over the network to the medical professional. The medical professional will use our diagnosis as a second opinion, and the cardiologist or doctor will interpret and analyze it in light of the patient's medical records and additional diagnostic testing. The requirements and demands of Electronic Care Systems in the global healthcare arena are becoming more widely acknowledged in today's age of rapid technology breakthroughs. Numerous existing methods can be used to supplement current healthcare, improving its intelligence and making it more widely available. To bolster this, framework structure reviewed around fifty health monitoring systems, ranking them based on the level of monitoring technology employed. Portable, far away, and mobile monitoring devices for health are among the main

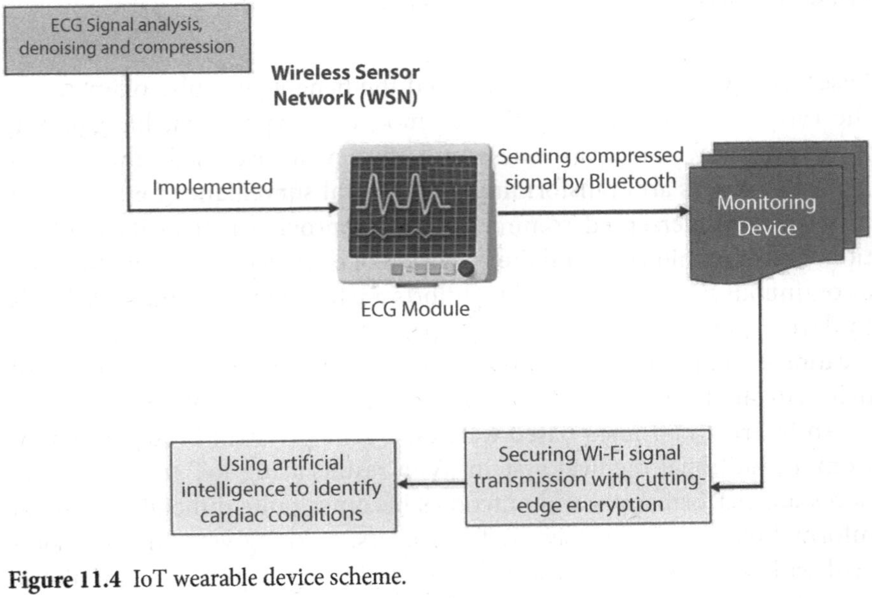

Figure 11.4 IoT wearable device scheme.

categories of intellective, intelligent, and conventional monitoring devices. The research has led to the development of health surveillance structures for a variety of settings, including the home, for individuals with dementia, Parkinson's disease, recognizing falls, Alzheimer's disease, and reviews. Building an intelligent health tracking system with multiple capabilities for diverse segregated contexts that have all extractable and prolific aspects that will boost consumer outreach is necessary.

11.3 Materials and Methods

As a result, a hybrid mBiLSTM experimental approach was created and ACNN structure with hyperparameter optimization based on Bayesian optimization is proposed for the classification of heart illness. The efficacy of several Machine Learning (ML) algorithms in identifying cardiac disease was assessed by testing the characteristics. Metrics for evaluating the model's efficiency and validity were calculated. To transform categorical characteristics into embedding vectors, we first pre-process the information by applying an embedding layer to them. Figure 11.5 shows the general process of the proposed technique. To anticipate cardiac disease, the following four activities must be completed: information pre-processing, ACNN-mBiLSTM, classification of binary information, and performance evaluation are the first four steps.

11.3.1 Dataset Description

A variety of sources of information are included in the dataset for the composite machine learning system in intelligent medical forecasts to provide a complete picture of patient health shown in Table 11.1. It contains electronic health records (EHRs), which are supplied by healthcare facilities and include comprehensive patient data including demographics, medical records, prescriptions, and treatment results. With more than 100,000 entries, this structured dataset provides important information on the health trajectories of the patients. Furthermore, current information on blood pressure, activity levels, and sleeping habits is contributed by wearable health data gathered *via* fitness trackers and wearables. This data is presented as a time series with more than 500,000 entries. The dataset includes Social Determinants of Health (SDOH) to improve the accuracy of predictions. These include socioeconomic characteristics such as earnings, schooling, and living circumstances that are gathered from

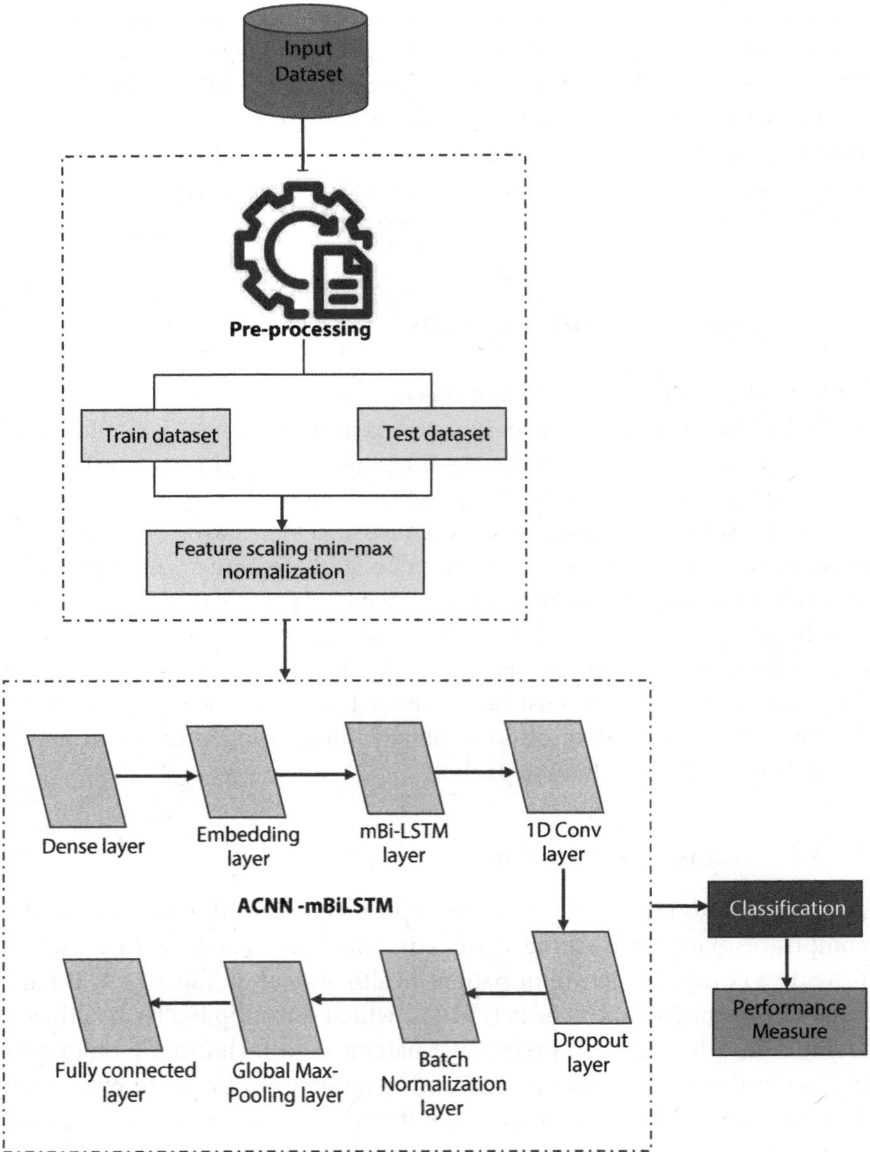

Figure 11.5 Proposed method block diagram.

public health databases and consist of over 50,000 entries. Patient surveys and questionnaires, which consist of about 30,000 surveys, collect results reported by patients and satisfaction ratings. Finally, genomic information from sequencing research have involved around 10,000 samples—provides information on hereditary susceptibilities to different illnesses.

Table 11.1 Dataset description.

Dataset name	Description	Source	Data type	Key features	Size
Electronic Health Records (EHR)	Comprehensive patient data including demographics, medical history. medications, allergies, and treatment outcomes.	Hospitals. clinics	Structured	-Patient ID - AgeGender - Diagnosis - Treatment history - Lab results	100,000+ records
Wearable Health Data	Data collected from wearable devices.	Fitness trackers. smartwatches	Time-series, Sensor data	- Patient ID - TimestampHeart rate - Steps - Sleepduration - Activitylevel	500,000+ entries
Social Determinants of Health (SDOH)	Data on social and economic factors affecting health, including income. education, and living conditions.	Public health databases	Structured	- Patient ID - Income50,000+ recordslevel - Education Level - Employment status - Housing situation	50,000+ records

(Continued)

Table 11.1 Dataset description. (*Continued*)

Dataset name	Description	Source	Data type	Key features	Size
Medical Imaging Data	Images from various modalities (e.g.. X-rays, MRIs, CT scans) used for diagnosis and treatment planning.	Imaging centers hospitals	Unstructured (Images)	- Patient ID - Imaging modality - Image quality - Diagnosis Annotations	200,000+ images
Patient Surveys/ Questionnaires	Data from patient- reported outcomes, satisfaction surveys, and health-related quality of life assessments.	Surveys conducted by healthcare providers	Structured	- Patient ID - Survey responses - Health status Satisfaction rating	30,000+ surveys
Genomic Data	Genomic sequencing data related to individual patients. providing insights into genetic predispositions to diseases.	Genomic research institutions	Unstructured (Genomic)	- Patient ID - Genetic markers - SNP data - Disease risk factors	10,000+ samples

Each data source is essential to the Composite AI framework's ability to make more precise predictions and enable individualized healthcare actions. Every dataset is managed by data privacy laws, guaranteeing patient privacy through the integration and analysis procedures.

This sample data illustrates the kind of information that might be used in a composite AI system for smart healthcare predictions shown in Tables 11.2–11.7.

Table 11.2 Electronic health records (EHR).

Patient ID	Age	Gender	Diagnosis	Medications	Treatment outcome
P001	46	Male	Hypertension	Lisinopril	Controlled
P002	33	Female	Type 2 Diabetes	Metformin	Uncontrolled
P003	61	Male	Chronic Pain	Oxycodone	Improved

Table 11.3 Wearable health data.

Patient ID	TimeStamp	Heart rate (bpm)	Steps	Sleep duration (hrs)	Activity level
P001	2024-10-11 09.00Am	73	6000	8.5	Moderate
P002	2024-10-11 09.00Am	81	3000	7.0	Low
P003	2024-10-11 09.00Am	66	9000	8.1	High

Table 11.4 Social determinants of health (SDOH).

Patient ID	Income level	Education level	Employment status	Housing situation
P001	\$80,000	Bachelor's	Employed	Owned
P002	\$41,000	High School	Unemployed	Rented
P003	\$61,000	Master's	Employed	Owned

Table 11.5 Medical imaging data.

Patient ID	Imaging modality	Image quality	Diagnosis
P001	MRI	High	No abnormalities
P002	X-Ray	Medium	Osteoarthritis
P003	CT	High	Herniated disc

Table 11.6 Patient surveys/questionnaires.

Patient ID	Survey date	Health status(1-5)	Satisfaction rating(1-10)
P001	2024-10-01	5	9
P002	2024-10-01	3	6
P003	2024-10-01	4	8

Table 11.7 Genomic data.

Patient ID	Genetic marker	Risk factor
P001	BRCA1	Higher risk for cancer
P002	FTO	Higher risk for obesity
P003	APOE	Increased risk for Alzheimer's

11.3.2 Pre-Processing

Collecting information was followed by data preparation. Six entries in the Cleveland dataset had missing values. The number of records in the dataset decreased from 303 to 297 after all missing values were removed.

Handling Missing Data: For missing values, common techniques include filling with the mean, median, or using interpolation. Mean Imputation: If a feature I contains missing values, replace the missing values with the mean μ of the observed data:

$$I_{imputed} = \frac{1}{n}\sum_{x=1}^{n} I_x \tag{11.1}$$

where in is the number of non-missing values in I.

Z-score Normalization: To normalize data so that it has a mean of 0 and a standard deviation of 1, apply Z-score normalization:

$$I' = \frac{I - \mu}{\sigma} \tag{11.2}$$

where: I is the original value, μ is the mean of the feature, σ is the standard deviation of the feature,I' is the normalized value.This technique is commonly applied to features like heart rate, age, and steps to ensure comparability across different scales.

Min-Max Scaling: To scale the data between a fixed range (usually 0 and 1), Min-Max scaling is used:

$$I' = \frac{I - I_{min}}{I_{max} - I_{min}} \tag{11.3}$$

where: I_{min} and I_{max} are the minimum and maximum values of feature I,I' is the scaled value.

This method ensures that all features, such as income or satisfaction ratings, fall within the same range, which is critical for models like neural networks.

Categorical Data Encoding (One-Hot Encoding): For categorical variables such as gender, employment status, or housing situation, one-hot encoding is used. Each category is represented as a binary vector. For a categorical variable C with 3 possible categories C_1, C_2, C_3:

$$C = \begin{cases} (1,0,0) \text{ } if \text{ } C = c_1 \\ (0,1,0) \text{ } if \text{ } C = c_2 \\ (0,0,1) \text{ } if \text{ } C = c_3 \end{cases} \tag{11.4}$$

This ensures that categorical data is represented in a way suitable for AI models.

Data Aggregation and Feature Engineering: Sometimes it is useful to create new features by aggregating or combining existing ones. For example, combining multiple wearable data features to create a composite health index:

$$\text{Health Index} = w_1.\text{ Heart Rate} + w_2.\text{Steps} + w_3.\text{Sleep Duration} \tag{11.5}$$

where w_1, w_2, w_3 are weights assigned to each feature based on their importance, determined through statistical analysis or domain knowledge.

Dealing with Class Imbalance (for classification tasks): When working with classification problems (e.g., predicting diseases), class imbalances may arise. To address this, use oversampling or undersampling, or apply Synthetic Minority Over-sampling Technique (SMOTE). In SMOTE, synthetic examples are created for the minority class.

Image Preprocessing (for Medical Imaging Data): For medical imaging data, preprocessing steps include resizing, normalization, and data augmentation (rotation, flipping, etc.). If the original image is represented as X, resizing it to a uniform dimension (H, W) can be done as:

$$X' = Resize(X,(H,W)) \tag{11.6}$$

Normalization of pixel values can be applied by scaling the pixel values to the range [0, 1]:

$$X' = \frac{X}{255} \tag{11.7}$$

where X represents the original pixel values ranging from 0 to 255.

These preprocessing steps ensure that the data is clean, standardized, and ready for analysis using the composite Al system in smart healthcare predictions. By applying appropriate techniques such as Z-score normalization, one-hot encoding, and image normalization, the data will be more suitable for accurate and efficient model training.

11.3.3 Feature Selection

Choosing characteristics from a large pool of accessible attributes or features is the process of choosing characteristics that aims to increase precision while decreasing computing complexity and delay. The model characteristics property may be used to assess each feature's significance in HD datasets. The feature value assigns a score to each function of the results, indicating its significance and influence on the performance of the factor. A higher score indicates that the characteristic is more significant or appropriate. With its built-in class that facilitates feature relevance evaluation, particularly with Tree-Based designs, this framework is very helpful for characteristic significance analysis. Feature extraction using correlation coefficient is aimed at selecting or deriving new features that have strong relationships with the target variable.The Pearson Correlation Coefficient (denoted as r) is commonly used to evaluate how well the features are related to the target variable, helping to identify and select features that are strongly correlated. The correlation coefficient is defined as:

$$r_{I,J} = \frac{\Sigma_{x=1}^{n}(I_x - \mu_I)(J_x - \mu_J)}{\sqrt{\Sigma_{x=1}^{n}(I_x - \mu_I)^2}\sqrt{\Sigma_{x=1}^{n}(J_x - \mu_J)^2}} \tag{11.8}$$

where: I_x is the x-th value of feature I,J_x is the x-th value of target J,μ_I is the mean of feature I,μ_J is the mean of target J,n is the number of data points.

Interpretation of the Correlation Coefficient:r-1: Perfect positive linear relationship between I and J.r-1: Perfect negative linear relationship between I and J.r-0: No linear relationship between I and J.

Features with correlation coefficients close to ±1 with the target variable are considered important and may be selected for the model.

A) Feature Extraction Process:

1. Compute Correlation Coefficients: For each feature in the dataset, compute the Pearson correlation coefficient with the target variable J.
2. Select or Combine Features: Based on the magnitude of the correlation coefficient, select the features that have a significant correlation with the target. Alternatively, features with strong inter-feature correlations can be combined into new features to improve model performance.
3. Threshold Selection: A threshold θ can be set to select only features whose absolute correlation coefficient r exceeds a certain value:

$$\text{Select I if} \left| r_{I,J} \right| > \theta \tag{11.9}$$

This helps to retain only the most relevant features while eliminating noise or irrelevant features.

11.3.4 Composite Artificial Intelligence in Smart Healthcare Predictions

The sections that follow provide descriptions of the proposed models.

11.3.4.1 Attention-Based Convolutional Neural Network

One type of DL technology that can learn straight from data is ACNN shown in Figure 11.6. ACNNs are incredibly useful for detecting different items by spotting patterns in pictures. These networks may be very helpful in classifying non-image information, including time series, signal, and audio information shown in Figure 11.6. The convolutional layer's volume of input sizes reduces as a result of stride. Filling the input field with zeros is necessary to maintain no padding when the volume of input contains low-level characteristics. The feature representations become nonlinear as a result of the Rectified Linear Unit (ReLU) function. It sets the threshold input to zero to compute the moment of activation. To lower the number of factors, a chosen input dimension is downsampled using the pooling layer. Maximum pooling is a popular pooling technique that keeps the maximum value inside a specified input region. Ultimately, the fully connected layer serves as a classifier, allowing for the categorization of input using the insights gleaned from the maximum pooling and layers of convolution.

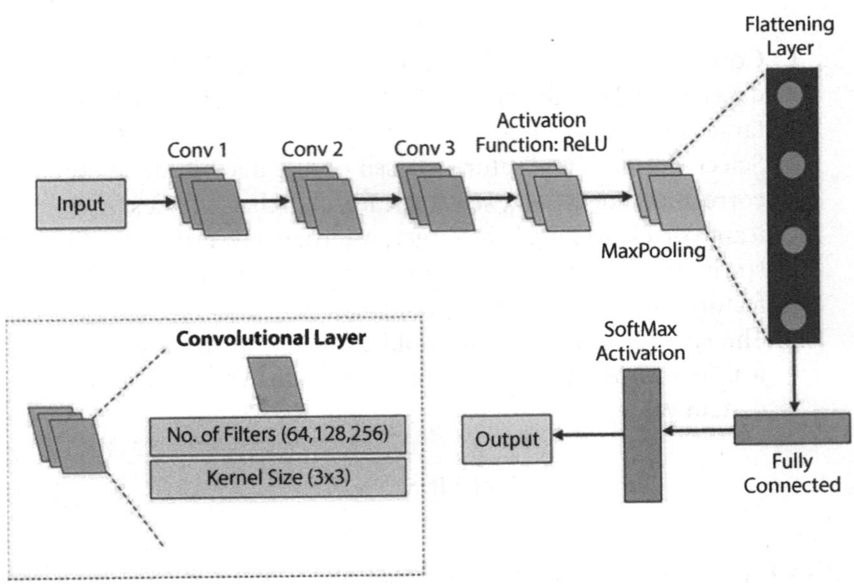

Figure 11.6 Architecture of ACNN.

The obtained ideal characteristics Df_{i}^{of} are supplied as a source of data for the phase of heart disease prognosis. Precision illustrates how Acy measures nearer value is to a specific value.

$$Accuracy = \frac{(hb + hc)}{(hb + hc + hd + he)} \tag{11.10}$$

A Bidirectional RNN (BRNN) network produced the design of mBiLSTM shown in Figure 11.7. mBiLSTM can handle various difficulties and merge several concealed layers with the result layer.

$$\vec{\imath}_z = B(Y_{m\vec{\imath}} K_z + Y_{\vec{\imath}\vec{\imath}} \vec{\imath}_z + 1 + p_{\vec{\imath}}) \tag{11.11}$$

$$\overleftarrow{\imath}_z = B(Y_{m\overleftarrow{\imath}} K_z + Y_{\overleftarrow{\imath}\overleftarrow{\imath}} \overleftarrow{\imath}_z + 1 + p_{\overleftarrow{\imath}}) \tag{11.12}$$

$$E_z = Y_{\overleftarrow{\imath}n} \vec{\imath}_z + Y_{i\leftarrow n} i^{\leftarrow} + c_n \tag{11.13}$$

The result vector E_z is achieved with Equation (11.14).

$$E_z = \sigma(\vec{\imath}_z, \overleftarrow{\imath}_z) \tag{11.14}$$

The word σ is used to represent the fused output sequence obtained in a hidden layer neuron. It performs four different functions: averages, summary, the process of multiplication, and concatenation. The mBiLSTM-protected result is regarded as a mode trust value. Figure 11.7 illustrates a cardiovascular disease prediction framework based on m-BiLSTM. With the aid of the system of attention, which helps to concentrate on the most important aspects for improved predictions, this combined AI model is made to effectively extract both spatial data ACNN and sequential dependencies (mBiLSTM).

Step 1: Input Data Preparation: Let the input data be represented by a feature matrix

$$I \in R^{n \times d} \tag{11.15}$$

where: n is the number of samples (patients), d is the number of features (e.g., age, cholesterol, ECG signals, etc.).

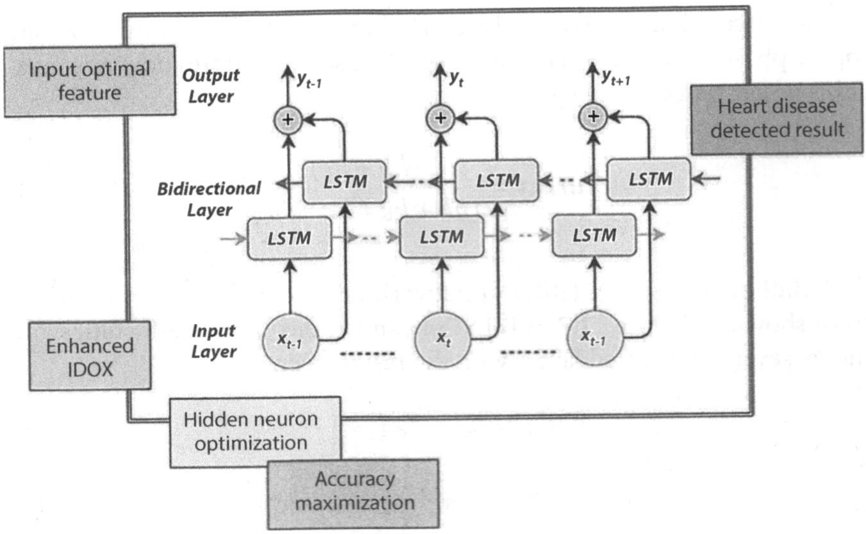

Figure 11.7 Design of mBiLSTM.

Step 2: Convolutional Layer for Spatial Feature Extraction (ACNN)
The first layer applies 1D convolutional filters to extract spatial features from the input data:

$$Z_x^{(k)} = \sum_{y=1}^{r} W_y^{(k)} I_{x+y-1} + b^{(k)} \tag{11.16}$$

Where: I is the input feature matrix, $W_y^{(k)}$ is the yth filter for the -th feature map, r is the filter size, $Z_x^{(k)}$ is the output of the convolution for the xth feature map, $b^{(k)}$ is the bias term.

Step 3: Attention Mechanism for Feature Weighting
The attention mechanism is introduced after the CNN layer to assign more weight to the important features. The attention score α_x is computed as:

$$e_x = f(W_a Z_x + b_a) \tag{11.17}$$

$$\alpha_x = \frac{\exp(e_x)}{\sum_{y=1}^{n} \exp(e_x)} \tag{11.18}$$

$$\bar{Z}_x = \alpha_x Z_x \tag{11.19}$$

where: W_a and b_a are trainable parameters of the attention mechanism, f(.) is an activation function (commonly tanh), α_x represents the attention score for feature $Z_x, \bar{Z}_x$ is the weighted feature after applying attention.

Step 4: m-BiLSTM for Sequential Dependencies

The mBiLSTM network is used to capture the temporal dependencies in the features. For a forward LSTM, the hidden state h_t^{fwd} at time t is computed as:

$$f_t = \sigma\left(W_f[h_{t-1}, I_t] + b_f\right) \tag{11.20}$$

$$i_t = \sigma(W_x[h_{t-1}, I_t] + b_x) \tag{11.21}$$

$$\bar{C}_t = tanh(W_C[h_{t-1}, I_t] + b_C) \tag{11.22}$$

$$C_t = f_t \odot C_{t-1} + i_t \odot \bar{C}_t \tag{11.23}$$

$$o_t = \sigma(W_o[h_{t-1}, I_t] + b_o) \tag{11.24}$$

$$h_t^{fwd} = o_t \odot tanh(C_t) \tag{11.25}$$

For the backward LSTM, the equations are the same, but processed in reverse. The output of the m-BiLSTM at time t is the concatenation of the forward and backward hidden states:

$$h_x^{BiLSTM} = \left[h_t^{fwd}, h_t^{bwd}\right] \tag{11.26}$$

Step 5: Fully Connected Layer for Prediction: For binary classification (e.g., heart disease prediction), the output is given by:

$$\hat{j} = \sigma\left(W_{fc} h_t^{BiLSTM} + b_{fc}\right) \tag{11.27}$$

Step 6: Loss Function and Optimization: The model is trained by minimizing the binary cross-entropy loss function for binary classification:

$$L(\hat{j}, j) = -\frac{1}{n}\Sigma_{x=1}^{n}[j_x \log(\hat{j}_x) + (1 - j_x)log(1 - \hat{j}_x)] \quad (11.28)$$

where: j_x is the true label for the x-th sample, $\hat{j}_x$ the predicted probability for the x-th sample, n is the total number of samples.

With an emphasis on enhancing the accuracy of heart disease prediction, our composite artificial intelligence model combines ACNN and mBiLSTM networks. To improve forecasts, the attention method draws attention to significant characteristics, the mBiLSTM records temporal relationships, and convolutional layers are used to collect spatial data.

11.4 Results and Discussions

This section presents an examination of the findings from the various categorization techniques used to predict the existence of HD. The experiment is then conducted using the data that was used to create the categorization report shown in Table 11.8. The evaluation dataset's categorization metrics, when analyzed using the model, show the class 0 and class 1's average micro, macro, and weight in addition to sample averages, accuracy, recollection, and f1 score. For class 1 and class 0, obtaining good precision of 97% and 91%, respectively. Additionally, the 95% recall percentage for classes 0 and 1 is excellent.

Table 11.8 Classification results on test data.

	Precision	**Recall**	**F1-score**	**Support**
0	0.92	0.96	0.94	22
1	0.98	0.96	0.97	40
Accuracy			0.96	61
Macro Average	0.95	0.96	0.96	61
Weighted Average	0.96	0.96	0.96	61

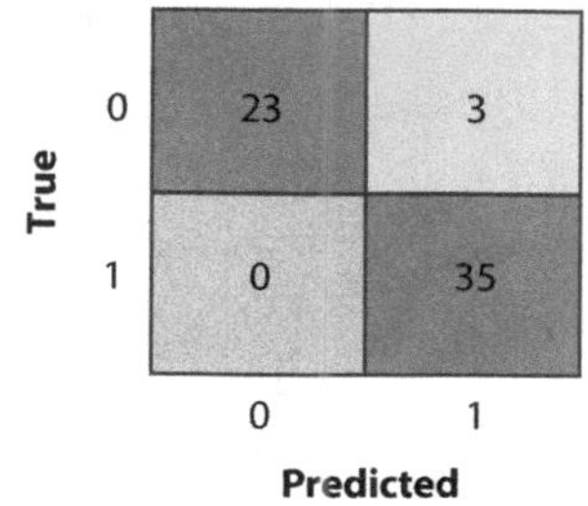

Figure 11.8 Confusion matrix on test data.

Figure 11.8 shows the confusion matrix of a hybrid model. The confusion matrix allows us to determine whether the representation has difficulty differentiating between class 0 and class 1. CVD has a properly anticipated value of 36, while non-heart illness has a correctly anticipated value of 22. It represents the likelihood that, when samples are selected at random, the observed score for a positive sample will be higher than a determined score for a negative sample. The ROC curve for a study is displayed in Figure 11.9 and the median AUC value of proposed model is 0.94.

The compilation used a batch size of 128 and the Adam optimizer. 20% was used for testing and the remaining 80% for training. Of the initial training information, 20% were used for validation. Thirty epochs were used in the course of instruction. The model achieved an accuracy in training of 99.15% (Figure 11.10), an accuracy for testing of 99.00%, and a loss of 0.039 (Figure 11.11).

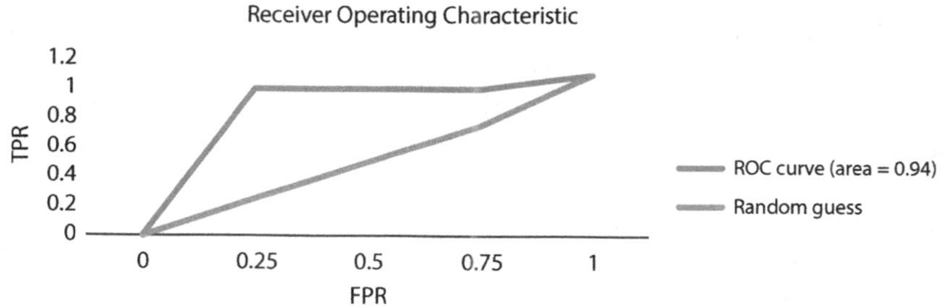

Figure 11.9 ROC curve.

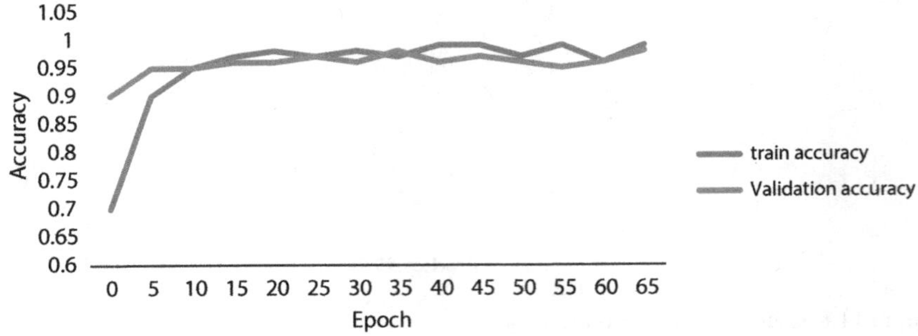

Figure 11.10 Comparison of training and validation accuracy.

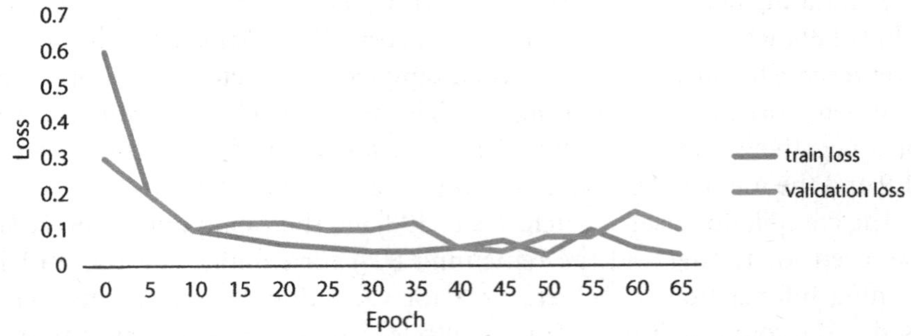

Figure 11.11 Comparison of training and validation loss.

The provided graph results demonstrate how well the developed technique performed when comparing methods for K-fold analysis. In this case, the provided method's accuracy rate is increased at the 4-fold analysis. In addition to lowering system performance, this causes problems with cross-validation. Similarly, during the 4-fold analysis, the developed method's F1-score increases. As a result, the 4-fold study reveals that the specified planned approach performs better. As a result, compared to baseline techniques, the proposed method attained an effective heart disease detection rate shown in Figure 11.12.

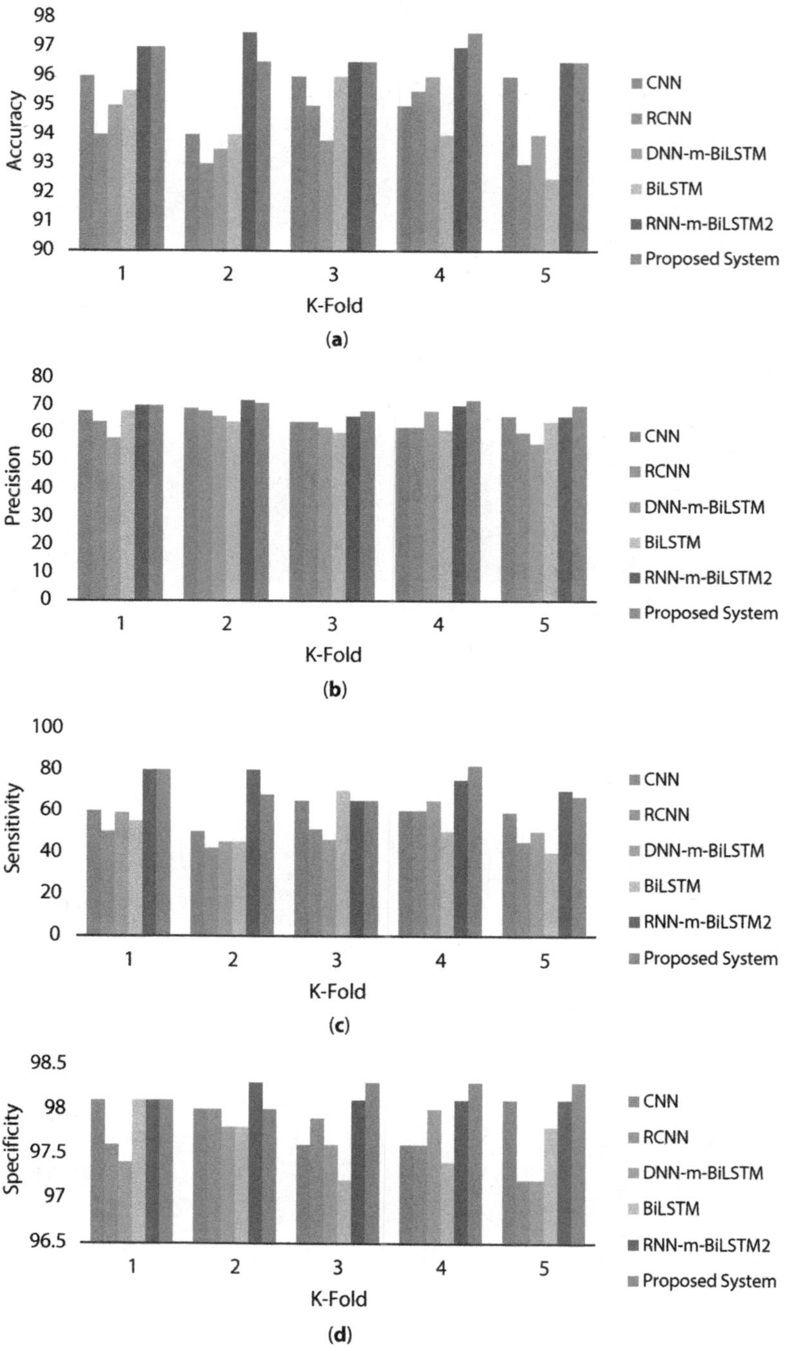

Figure 11.12 Performance measures. *(Continued)*

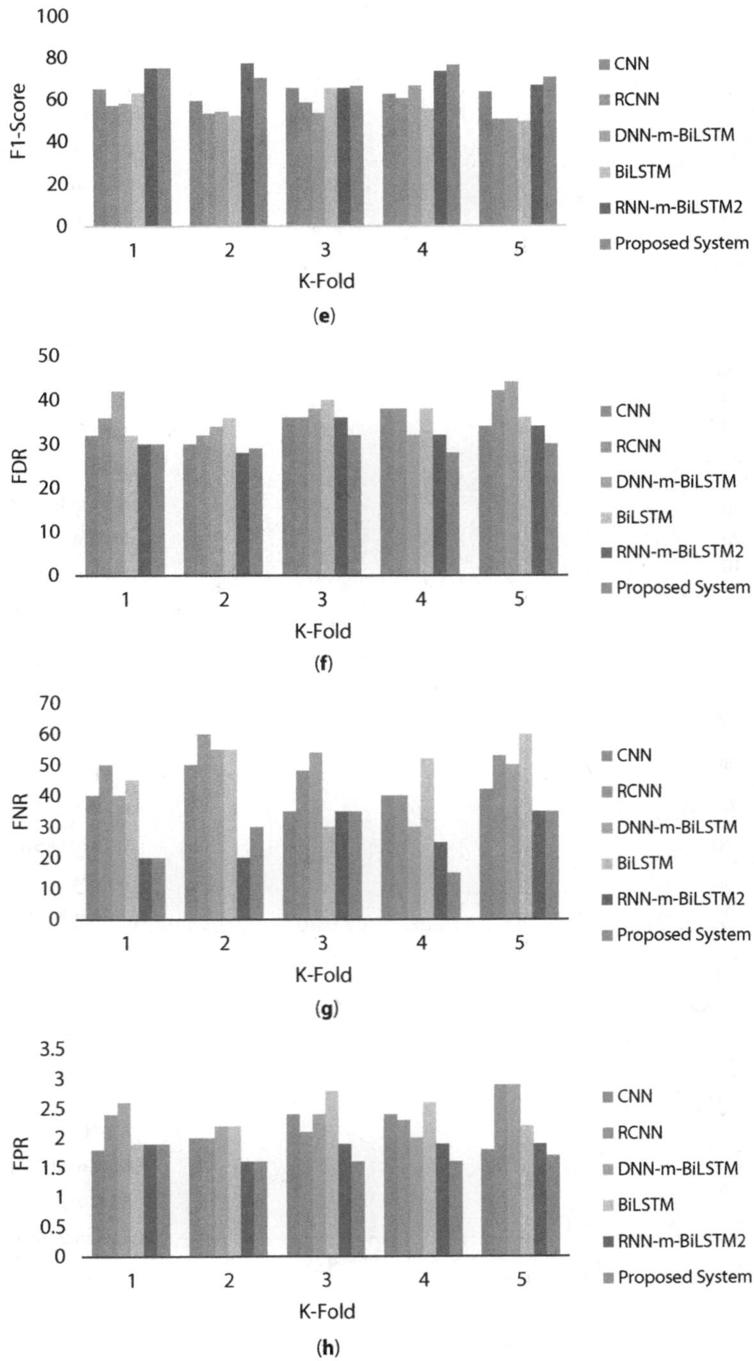

Figure 11.12 (Continued) Performance measures. *(Continued)*

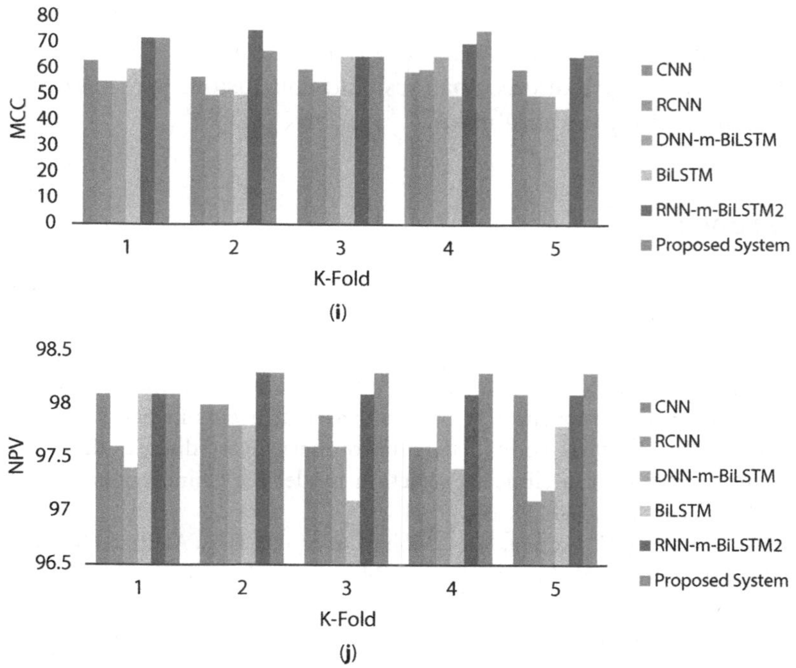

Figure 11.12 (Continued) Performance measures. *(Continued)*

11.5 Conclusions

To sum up, the proposed hybrid artificial intelligence (AI) system combines mBiLSTMwith ACNN to improve cardiovascular disease prediction reliably and efficiently. The resulting model captures both local patterns and long-range relationships in patient information by fusing the ordered learning capacity of mBiLSTM with the spatial extraction of features abilities of CNN. By adding an attention mechanism, the model's capacity to concentrate on the most important characteristics is further enhanced, improving the precision of predictions. With early diagnosis and preventative care dependent on precise, real-time predictions, the ACNN-mBiLSTM system has great promise for application in smart healthcare systems. By enabling prompt interventions and individualized treatment plans, this combined strategy lays the door for increasingly advanced and trustworthy AI-driven diagnostic tools in the medical field, possibly improving outcomes for patients.

AI disclosure statement: The author acknowledges the use of AI-based tools for minor language editing or grammatical correction. However, all intellectual contributions, analyses, and conclusions presented in this chapter are entirely the author's own.

References

1. Ahmad, A., Dharejo, N., Saeed, F., Shiwlani, A., Tahir, A., Umar, M., Prediction of Fetal Brain and Heart Abnormalties using Artificial Intelligence Algorithms: A Review. *Am. J. Biomed. Sci. Res.*, *22*, 3, 456–466, 2024.
2. Wang, Z., Sun, Z., Yu, L., Wang, Z., Li, L., Lu, X., Machine learning-based prediction of composite risk of cardiovascular events in patients with stable angina pectoris combined with coronary heart disease: development and validation of a clinical prediction model for Chinese patients. *Front. Pharmacol.*, *14*, 1334439, 2024.
3. Pal, P., Grover, V., Nandal, M., Gochhait, S., Singh, H.V., Artificial Intelligence Driven Intelligent Computational Model for Heart Disease Prediction: Leveraging Feature Selection, in: *2024 ASU International Conference in Emerging Technologies for Sustainability and Intelligent Systems (ICETSIS)*, 2024, January, IEEE, pp. 1422–1428.
4. Naser, M.A., Majeed, A.A., Alsabah, M., Al-Shaikhli, T.R., Kaky, K.M., A Review of Machine Learning's Role in Cardiovascular Disease Prediction: Recent Advances and Future Challenges. *Algorithms*, *17*, 2, 78, 2024.
5. Yashudas, A., Gupta, D., Prashant, G.C., Dua, A., AlQahtani, D., Reddy, A.S.K., DEEP-CARDIO: Recommendation System for Cardiovascular Disease Prediction using IoT Network. *IEEE Sens. J.*, 24, 9, 14539–14547, 2024, 10.1109/JSEN.2024.3373429.
6. Khera, R., Oikonomou, E.K., Nadkarni, G.N., Morley, J.R., Wiens, J., Butte, A.J., Topol, E.J., Transforming cardiovascular care with artificial intelligence: from discovery to practice: JACC State-of-the-Art Review. *J. Am. Coll. Cardiol.*, *84*, 1, 97–114, 2024.
7. Stamate, E., Piraianu, A.I., Ciobotaru, O.R., Crassas, R., Duca, O., Fulga, A., Ciobotaru, O.C., Revolutionizing Cardiology through Artificial Intelligence—Big Data from Proactive Prevention to Precise Diagnostics and Cutting-Edge Treatment—A Comprehensive Review of the Past 5 Years. *Diagnostics*, *14*, 11, 1103, 2024.
8. Almansouri, N.E., Awe, M., Rajavelu, S., Jahnavi, K., Shastry, R., Hasan, A., AlAbbasi, R.K., Early diagnosis of cardiovascular diseases in the era of artificial intelligence: An in-depth review. *Cureus*, 16, 3, 1–18, 2024. DOI: 10.7759/cureus.55869.

9. Adam, M.A. and Mukhtar, A., Smart Health Solutions: The Convergence of AI, Machine Learning, and Deep Learning for Brain and Heart Care. *Rev. Esp. Doc. Cient.*, *18*, 02, 238–268, 2024.
10. Nazir, M.B. and Hussain, I., Charting New Frontiers: AI, Machine Learning, and Deep Learning in Brain and Heart Health. *Rev. Esp. Doc. Cient.*, *18*, 02, 209–237, 2024.
11. Medhi, D., Kamidi, S.R., Sree, K.P.M., Shaikh, S., Rasheed, S., Murichathil, A.H.T., Nazir, Z., Artificial Intelligence and Its Role in Diagnosing Heart Failure: A Narrative Review. *Cureus*, *16*, 5, 1–26, 2024. DOI: 10.7759/cureus.59661.
12. Kumar, K.S., Radhamani, A.S., Sundaresan, S., Ananth Kumar, T., Medical image classification and manifold disease identification through convolutional neural networks: a research perspective, in: *Handbook of Deep Learning in Biomedical Engineering and Health Informatics*, pp. 203–225, 2021.
13. Kutiame, S., Millham, R., Adekoya, A.F., Weyori, B.A., Tettey, M.M., Coronary Heart Disease Prediction: A Novel Deep Learning-based Approach. *J. Artif. Intell. Syst.*, *6*, 1, 11–33, 2024.
14. Elias, P., Jain, S.S., Poterucha, T., Randazzo, M., Lopez Jimenez, F., Khera, R., Maddox, T.M., Artificial intelligence for cardiovascular care—Part 1: Advances: JACC review topic of the week. *J. Am. Coll. Cardiol.*, *83*, 24, 2472–2486, 2024.
15. Lin, C.M. and Lin, Y.S., TPTM-HANN-GA: A Novel Hyperparameter Optimization Framework Integrating the Taguchi Method, an Artificial Neural Network, and a Genetic Algorithm for the Precise Prediction of Cardiovascular Disease Risk. *Mathematics*, *12*, 9, 1303, 2024.

12

Composite AI for Predictive Analysis of Autism Spectrum Disorder Using Facial Features

S. Usharani[1*], A. Ganesh[1], N. Muralidharan[1] and G. Glorindal[2]

[1]Department of Artificial Intelligence and Machine Learning, IFET College of Engineering, Villupuram, Tamil Nadu, India
[2]Department of Computer Science, University of EdenBerg, Lusaka, Zambia

Abstract

This chapter presents the composite artificial intelligence (AI) techniques in the face feature analysis for the autism spectrum disorder (ASD) prediction model. This research utilizes various AI techniques like facial feature recognition and deep learning to raise the precision of diagnosis owing to the inherent difficulty of diagnosing ASD. The chapter sets forth key phases like data acquisition, pre-processing, and model construction while concentrating on the identification of relevant face traits showing their link to ASD. Such advanced models consider predictive potential, focusing on Xception and VGG19. Convolutional Neural Networks (CNNs) recognize and categorize facial features. This is done in the chapter where different performance models are assessed to find out how effective they are in discriminating ASD cases from typically developing individuals in terms of accuracy, sensitivity, and specificity. In the end, it would be comprised of Composite AI and facial recognition which would be a very promising step towards the early identification of ASD without any invasive techniques as well as more effective clinical outcomes.

Keywords: Autism spectrum disorder, Xception, VGG19, CNN, composite AI

**Corresponding author*: ushasanchu@gmail.com

T. S. Arun Samuel, L. Jerart Julus, P. Kanimozhi, T. Ananth Kumar and S. Balamurugan (eds.) Composite Artificial Intelligence: Fundamentals, Challenges, and Applications, (279–302) © 2026 Scrivener Publishing LLC

12.1 Introduction

Autism spectrum disorder (ASD) is a very complicated neurodevelopmental disorder, which occurs in individual persons having somewhat different combinations of behavioral, social, and communicative abilities. Given that the intensity and specific features of the disorder are different from one individual to the next, it is known as a "spectrum" disorder. While the specific causes of ASD remain unknown, it is well-recognized that both environmental and genetic factors contribute largely to the condition. The many different symptoms that a person can show with ASD are also reflected in changes in their brain structures and functions shown by brain-imaging studies.

At present, no cure exists for the disease, but early interventions can significantly improve outcomes. Behavioral therapy, such as applied behavior analysis (ABA) intervention, considers the modification of undesirable behaviors and the foundation of appropriate social and communication skills. Programs for teaching people with autism have been developed according to the individual learning needs of such individuals, and in some cases, medication is used to treat specific problems or issues.

The diagnosis of ASD follows an involved process using various methods. The tools include history-taking, behavioral observations, and standardized tests such as the Autism Diagnostic Interview-Revised (ADI-R) and the Autism Diagnostic Observation Schedule (ADOS). New technology includes facial feature analysis and eye-tracking, which will offer earlier and more precise diagnoses.

AI, particularly composite AI systems, brings revolutionary potential to ASD diagnosis combined with several techniques such as deep learning and symbolic reasoning. The resulting algorithms can analyze huge datasets, such as neurological and behavioral data, to arrive at accurate and interpretable diagnoses. Hybrid systems with convolutional neural networks and machine learning models use such heterogeneous information for accurate diagnostics and retest manual evaluation limitations. This may improve outcomes for individuals with ASD while providing early intervention opportunities.

12.2 Related Work

This work emphasizes merging eye tracking information with EEG functional connectivity to improve early detection of autism spectrum disorder (ASD). The authors produce an integrated system consisting of behavioral and neurophysiological measures toward enhanced diagnostic accuracy. While eye tracking provides a behavioral viewpoint about particular attentional and gaze pattern differences between ASD and non-disordered development, EEG provides data on brain dynamics [1]. Eye-tracking parameters like gaze fixation and synchronization patterns, which measure attention and visual engagement, may also indicate possible future use for early screening by showing abnormalities during social opportunities [2]. Studies of EEG alpha and gamma oscillations during social and resting-state activity show that there are alterations in brain connection related to ASD [3]. High-dimensional datasets can be managed by using machine learning (ML) approaches such as support vector machines (SVM) and deep learning, revealing patterns that are impossible to find by conventional methods [4].

Functional connectivity graphs derived from EEG and fMRI can be used to assess the possible application of graph neural networks, which highlight damaged networks in the brains of subjects who have autism, as evidenced in [5]. Verbal expression atypicalities have been analyzed and concluded to be dissimilar using speech processing and NLP techniques to analyze conversational patterning and prosody changes associated with ASD [6]. At the same time, analysis of facial expressions in videos can be performed to obtain results of high accuracy by these algorithms concerning the diagnosis of emotional dysregulation [7]. Other correlates of the condition known as ASD include motion impairments and deficits in coordination, which are derived from analyses of gait and motion capture coupled with machine learning [8]. Behavioral data from severe game settings are examined by reinforcement learning to deliver an outcome to improve diagnosis early and engagement [9].

Gaze synchronization measures together with eye-tracking technology would show other novel patterns associated with interaction among peers that are useful in improving the diagnosis of the disorder [10]. The processing of resting-state EEG phase synchronization parameters would avail brain communication anomalies associated with attentional deficits [11]. Time-frequency studies and EEG entropy also develop diagnostic frameworks for recognizing dissimilar spectral power disturbances in individuals with autism spectrum disorders [12]. This hybrid methodology analyzes sensory processing measures along with EEG microstates to report sensory modulation and brain abnormality investigations in autism spectrum disorders [13]. Supervised machine learning will often correctly diagnose autism spectrum disorder in combination with multimodal datasets where audio and video combine with caregiver-reported questionnaires [14].

Sizeable networks can sample only through different data types till the end of October 2023. The modification of therapy according to behavioral changes would theoretically maximize therapeutic interventions for persons under the condition of RL [15]. This paper is directed to neural net models which scan the genetic and epigenetic data to show inheritable developmental features with ASD [16]. Bayesian models improve the interpretability of the machine learning results using predictions of uncertainty in ASD diagnosis [17]. Multivariate pattern analysis on multiple modalities including behavioral characteristics, fMRI, and EEG allows one to discover consistent diagnostic biomarkers for ASD [18]. Deep learning has been applied to identify abnormal functional connectivity in the default mode network (DMN) for unique patterns associated with ASD [19]. Transfer learning can help in the identification of ASD, repurposing earlier trained models to accommodate the EEG and fMRI datasets [20].

By applying eye tracking, machine learning, and VR environments, some metrics of sensory preferences of engagement can be adduced in people with ASD from the data [21]. Intervention strategies use emotional decoding models reliant on EEG data, which, in turn, leads to the unraveling of impaired affective processing in one with ASD [22]. Eye-blink and gazing time are analytical measures harvested and subjected to techniques of clustering and regression that demonstrate aberrations in ASD [23]. Hybrid Natural Language Processing approaches explore linguistic indicators of pragmatic deficits in ASD through written and verbal language datasets [24]. Only hierarchical attention networks study caregiver-child interaction to find communicational deficits compatible with the conditions of ASD characteristics [25].

Addressing both behavioral, sensory, and clinical findings, these hybrid genetic algorithms and neural networks predict the severity of ASDs [26]. Multivariate clustering methods for large-scale datasets about ASDs reveal possible subtypes for individualized therapies [27]. Video and scalable machine learning techniques designed a cloud-based platform for budget-friendly provision of remote screening for ASDs [28]. They offer functional connectivity and topological measures from fMRI datasets, concentrating on facets of social cognition and executive function in the context of disrupted brain circuitry in individuals with ASD [29]. High-frequency oscillation disturbances due to ASD have been detected through advanced signal processing techniques, such as audio and EEG signals subjected to wavelet transforms [30]. More improved diagnosis is enabled by computational means in the visual and audio processing engendering examining ASD indicators from speech, facial expressions, and environments [31]. When applied to ASD datasets, sparse coding methods are useful in isolating the most relevant features while improving prediction accuracy and reducing processing overheads [32].

For instance, some research has produced evidence concerning real-time data processing coupled with wearable technologies like smartwatches and biosensors, which create an arrangement for continuous monitoring of physiological indicators, including skin conductance and heart rate, thus throwing light on episodes of sensory overload in individuals with ASD [33]. Therapy sessions are in most cases robot devices that employ reinforcement learning by using these devices to interest children with ASD and create social and communicative abilities therapy [34]. Predictive models that offer abnormal behaviors and movement aberrancies in young children are built using early-life video analyses [35]. Adding caregiver feedback to data-driven models has been proven to fill the gaps in their automatic evaluations while improving the contextual understanding of behaviors associated with ASD [36].

In light of the optimization of the feedback loop through machine learning algorithms, neurofeedback training through real-time EEG has emerged as a means of therapy to increase focus and lower anxiety among people with ASD [13]. To discover evidence of the typical language and social impairments seen in ASD, AI virtual assistants perform an analysis of the patterns of speech and interaction [37]. Time series data regarding the characteristics of repetitive behavior and limitations interest have been analyzed through Gaussian Mixture Models and Hidden Markov Models to uncover some exclusive aspects in common with autism spectrum disorders [38]. Such findings were combined in cross-sectional studies of sensory profiles with neural imaging data that show several observable associations between sensory processing issues and certain patterns of brain activity in individuals with ASDs [16].

To help doctors customize treatment strategies to each patient's unique ASD profile, deep learning algorithms have been used to forecast the efficacy of therapies [39]. To recommend ASD-friendly learning environments and sensory-friendly technologies, collaborative filtering approaches from recommendation systems have been adapted [40]. Important genes and polymorphisms linked to ASD have been found using novel genomic analytic frameworks that incorporate machine learning, offering insights into the disorder's origin [41]. Autonomic nervous system dysregulation has been recognized as a possible indicator of ASD by time-series analysis of physiological data during controlled tasks [42].

Now, the analysis of large-scale ASD data becomes easy through the combined effect of cloud and AI technology, paving the way to cross-population research and better generalization of the findings [43].

Performance accuracy in diagnosing ASD has significantly improved in the case of multimodal datasets using ensemble methods, which combine the outputs generated by different algorithms [44]. Machine learning models have begun to predict responsiveness in patients with ASD, and new strategies, such as transcranial magnetic stimulation (TMS), are explored for therapy [45]. Recurrent neural networks (RNNs) handling task-based fMRI data have displayed abnormal functional activation during social cognition tasks in ASD [46, 47].

Agent-based modeling of interactions in autism spectrum disorder (ASD) provides a computer platform to simulate and analyze social behavior in such cases, which could facilitate intervention design. In the medical context, the development of explainable AI techniques gains trust and usefulness by ensuring doctors can understand diagnostic choices offered by complex models [48].

12.3 Overview of Composite AI in Predictive Analysis

Predictive analytics is now turning into a much broader, more trustable approach because of composite AI, a way of combining several AI methods into a synergistically shared ecosystem. The composite technique combines the advantages of several AI models as machine learning, deep learning, and expert systems-while avoiding the drawbacks of a single model approach. An integrated framework developed in this manner improves decision-making, problem-solving, and forecast accuracy.

Composite AI can help a company discover hidden patterns, forecast future trends, and make even more confident data-driven judgments with predictive analysis. For instance, it will go through huge patient data in healthcare to identify patients at high risk and predict potential outbreaks of illness. It should also be capable of identifying fraud, predicting market trends, and evaluating the risks associated with investments in the financial industry. In the manufacturing sector, it can help accurately predict machine breakdowns, improve supply chain management, and further optimize production processes.

Composite AI is the application of a variety of intelligent and compositional AI methods so that one can make a more generalized and intelligent approach for predictive analysis. Employing this in organizations would solve difficult problems, make good decisions, and help promote innovations across multiple sectors. Technology continues to improve, and composite AI will play a major role in predictive analytics' future development, opening up many new possibilities for socially out-reach businesses.

12.4 Proposed Methodology

Using AI to one point integrate the diagnosis of Autism Spectrum Disorder (ASD) through face features that propose accuracy in diagnosis. The key step involves data acquisition, such as collecting facial pictures from several databases of people unsuitable and suitable with ASD. These photos are pre-processed through procedures such as normalization, face detection, and alignment to ensure the consistency and quality of input data modeling. Extracting some facial features will be used to find important traits in humans associated with ASD such as facial expressions and micro-expressions, which can relate to the disorder. These features extracted can be classified and described using deep learning models, particularly with Convolutional Neural Networks (CNNs). The definition for extraction and classification purposes will use architectures such as Xception and VGG19. Contrary to other kinds of architectures to test the efficiency of those in diagnosing ASD, the methodology implemented evaluation through some performance measures including accuracy, sensitivity, and specificity. As for their ability as the advanced models in processing complicated picture data, the chosen models included VGG19 and Xception. The latter has a superior value in terms of accuracy and specificity performance. To build a model that takes on the strengths of each AI model and improves the overall prediction power, a Composite AI strategy was suggested.

12.4.1 Data Acquisition

The initial stage in data collection for the proposed technique has been to accumulate a variety of images that represent facial features of both individuals with autism spectrum disorders and controls without the disorder. These can be either through the collection in real-time in controlled settings or through publicly available data sets such as EmoReact or the Autism Facial Expression Database (AFED). These pictures need to provide a sufficient variety of age groups, genders, and ethnicities to be generalizable across the model to give diversity and relevance to the datasets for the condition under consideration.

The quality of images should also be a priority in the acquisition. High-resolution photos best capture fine micro-expressions or miniscule differences in facial movements linked with ASD. In practice, face detection algorithms guarantee that the appropriate facial area is captured without the unwanted background and that it is focused and sharp. Data acquisition has to include tagged images of faces by proper diagnosis categories during this entire process ÀSD or control.

12.4.2 Data Preprocessing

After collecting facial images, the next thing to do is prepare them for data preparation. This is the step that ensures cleaning, standardization, and setting the data input into the machine learning model to be appropriate for training. Generally, the first step in the preprocessing of faces is separating a face from an image. Such algorithms as Dlib's face detector or Haar Cascades only catch a face; that is the region of interest. This step ensures that background noise is eliminated and that the model examines only facial features. Face alignment can standardize the ovals that capture faces using a different angle. They might want to capture faces at various angles, and this could be detrimental to feature extraction. The model can concentrate on consistently aligning the part of the face toward a common reference frame like front-facing and eye-level. The images are finally normalized for pixel intensity values so that the model isn't biased due to a difference in lighting. Besides, artificially enlarging the dataset using picture augmentation algorithms such as crop, flip, and rotate the image improves generalization and reduces overfitting.

12.4.3 Facial Feature Extraction

The next stage is to extract facial traits that can indicate the possibility of an ASD from the pre-processed data. Generally, facial features can be described on two modalities: appearance traits, such as skin tones, textures, and facial expressions, and geometry traits, which are about mouth, eye, eyebrow positions, and movements of facial features. Such features can be extracted using deep learning models like the likes of DeepFace or tools such as the Facial Action Coding System (FACS). Figure 12.1 shows the feature extraction using deep learning. Among such features are the absence of typical facial expressions and strange gaze patterns, which have significance as markers of distinction between people with and without ASD.

Advanced techniques like landmark detection were also used to trace important points of the face, which include the mouth, nose, and eye. These landmarks help to detect some subtle facial movements, which are not perceptible to the naked eye but are very significant in differentiating

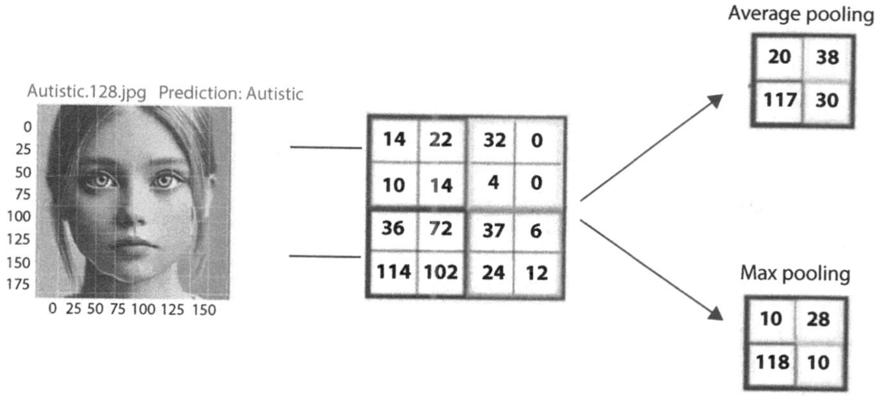

Figure 12.1 Max pooling, average pooling, and the convolution layer.

the expressions of patients with ASD. Such facial traits get preconditioned into an appropriate format, such as numerical vectors before being fed into the deep learning models. Since the collected features will be the main content for the classification job, they are of utmost importance in training the subsequent deep-learning models.

12.4.4 Deep Learning Models (CNNs)

After the feature extraction, classifications of the facial records are made into either ASD or control groups using deep learning models, especially Convolutional Neural Networks (CNNs). This proves most suitable for image-based jobs as CNNs can learn automatically the spatial hierarchies as well as identify complex structures in the data. The VGG19 and Xception architectures, in this instance, are the selected base models. Both these designs have been efficacious in classification tasks; however, Xception has an edge as it consumes more resources to catch classy patterns among its depthwise separable convolutions.

12.4.4.1 Xception

Deep learning convolution neural networks, namely the Xception model were used to recognize and classify the images in the collection while employing depth-wise separable convolutions builds such a distinctive architecture for extracting features from images. It has two stages in its depthwise separable convolution layers: first is the depth-wise; last is the point-wise convolution. Pointwise convolutions apply separate filters to

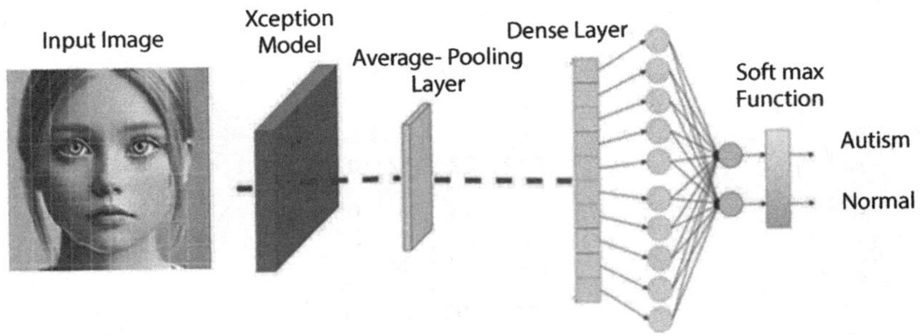

Figure 12.2 Xception architecture.

all output channels, whereas depth-wise use a unique filter for each input channel. Transfer learning was used to transfer knowledge acquired from the pre-trained models. Transfer of knowledge acquired with the use of extensive training on the pre-trained models is done to learn higher-level features from the new data set. The top parts of the pre-trained model were removed and the bottom parts were adjusted to better fit the specific task of diagnosing autism automatically.

The features extracted were then fed through a couple of additions of dense layers with ReLU activation from the Xception architecture shown in Figure 12.2. Further study on the features and dimensionality reduction was achieved with the two applications of the dense layers. The most important features that emerged from the feature maps were then captured by applying a global max pooling layer. The output of the max pooling layer is flattened to form a one-dimensional vector that's input into the softmax layer, which then gives the probability score for each of the classes. In the softmax layer, a probability for each class is computed so that a decision may be made about how likely it is that the input image belongs to a particular class. The model was trained successfully using the RMSprop optimizer for effective parameter modifications. Early stopping comes as a method to keep away from overfitting as the model learns to memorize the training data instead of recognizing patterns for use in other scenarios. In such ways, the possibility of a correct and reliable autism diagnosis was demonstrated, since it was learned by the Xception model to classify facial images into either autistic or non-autistic.

12.4.4.2 VGG 19

Popular among the deep learning architectures, the VGG-19 model has successfully performed image recognition tasks on large data sets.

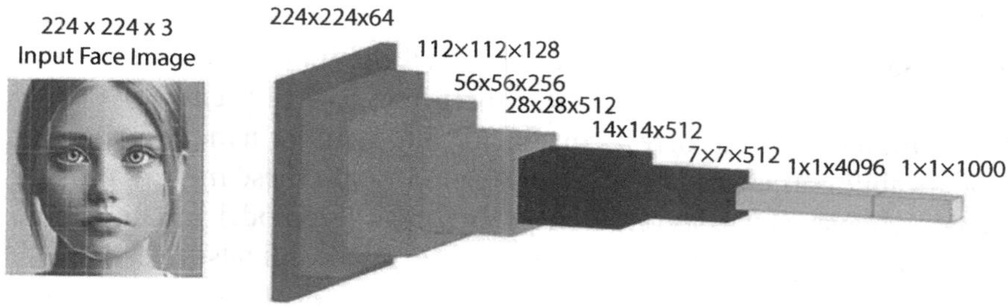

Figure 12.3 Visual geometry group network.

The model is deep, having 16 or 19 convolutional layers, enabling it to discover an extensive range of visual patterns and features. The architecture is moving left to right, and top to bottom on the input image, applying 3x3 filters shown in Figure 12.3. It captures low-level stuff, things like edges and textures. In deeper layers, the network captures more complex and higher-level characteristics. Max pooling layers are used symmetrically to the convolutional layers to enable efficient computation. These layers reduce computational cost and spatial dimensions by down sampling feature maps.

Therefore, this often leads to pooling and convolutional blocks in the architecture of VGG16, which end with fully connected layers. The few completely connected layers at the top provide a non-linearity through ReLU activation, thus making the model more nonlinear. A last fully connected layer is subsequently associated with a softmax activation function, which flattens the outputs into a probability distribution over multiple classes. This provides the possibility to classify the images as typical or autistic, thus enabling it to detect autism spectrum disorder. Therefore, with an appropriate application of deep learning techniques, this VGG-16 model could be a real possibility for a precise and effective strategy for the diagnosis of autism based on the detection of facial features.

Even for a task that is costlier to compute, it is still a reliable benchmark for tasks such as face feature extraction. Nevertheless, for this purpose, they will be trained and fine-tuned, using transfer learning as one of a variety of methods through which the model could adapt pre-learned ones to the specific ASD dataset.

12.4.5 Model Evaluation

After training the models, it is important to assess their performance to determine the one that best classifies input data. This assessment is done using some important measures such as accuracy, sensitivity, and specificity. Sensitivity (or recall) measures how well the model identifies people with ASD, while accuracy measures the percentage of predictions made by the model that are correct. Specificity, on the other hand, assesses the model's ability to identify people without ASD, and these metrics provide a comprehensive analysis of the performance of the model and help to be able to balance the trade-off between false positives and false negatives.

This study is drawn to a comparative analysis of the aforementioned evaluation measures for the Xception and VGG19 models. The new architecture from Xception has an advanced feature extraction and classification approach; therefore, results should, in theory, be better than those of the VGG19 in accuracy and specificity. VGG19, however, might provide excellent gains, especially for sensitivity because its simpler architecture probably leads to a little higher ratio in detecting specific facial features associated with ASD. To enforce robustness and reduce the likelihood of overfitting in these models, the models will also go through the cross-validation method, which entails splitting the dataset into several subsets to train and test the model on different sections of data.

12.4.6 Composite AI Integration

In the composite AI integration phase, the different benefits of various models are integrated. This method combines the results of both the VGG19 model and Xception to get a single prediction. The advantages of the composite AI model are trying to mitigate the faults.

Methods of achieving the fusion include simple methods such as model averaging by simply averaging the predictions of both or more advanced fusion techniques like stacking or boosting. This composite AI model improves predictions by combining models, thereby improving early diagnosis of autism spectrum disorders. When used in a clinical setting, it also helps to reduce false-positive and false-negative diagnoses, where diagnosis errors can have dire consequences.

12.4.7 Prediction and Diagnosis

This Composite AI system can be used to predict and diagnose autism spectrum disorder after training and evaluation. For the integrated model, face image input can produce a binary classification output indicating the likelihood of a person with or without ASD. This may be a good tool for clinicians and give them additional information in making an early diagnosis of ASD.

Non-invasive, cost-effective, and efficient, the system employing features from face to identify ASD can provide early detection, which is significant for early intervention and assistance. The alternative route that AI could take in this scenario is a significant revolution to the entire diagnostic process if it replaces the existing subjective nature with more data-driven-objective assessments. The prediction's accuracy and dependability can also be maintained with continuous improvement by adding continued data and model retraining.

12.5 Experimental Setup

The experimental setting presented by this research is primarily directed toward evaluating the efficiency with which deep learning models can predict an autistic spectrum disorder from facial features. Reflections on the important procedures and resources needed for data collection, model training, evaluation, and validation complete the experimental setup.

12.5.1 Data Collection

Neurotypical children as well as those diagnosed with autism based on their facial features are included in the Kaggle collected Autism_Image_Data. The dataset holds a total of 2940 photos, divided into participants who have been diagnosed with autism and those who have not. The photos are all in JPG format and are all oriented toward children aged between 2 years old to 12 years old with different orientations of the images. Some of the Internet repositories store the dataset. The Autism_Image_Data database was built by researchers and machine learning experts to train their models in classifying children's facial images into typical development or symptoms of autism. The images in the dataset range from 168 x 207 to 799 x 947 in resolution. Besides this, the dataset offers the capacity to identify the unique aspects of facial expression linked with the diagnosis of the characteristics of autism in children. A few images from a randomly selected dataset of autistic facial features from both classes are displayed in Figure 12.4.

12.5.2 Data Pre-Processing

The Autism_Image_Data dataset consists of preprocessing challenges but is a very good source for researchers working on autism. One important problem is that given its resolution, different images affect the modeling.

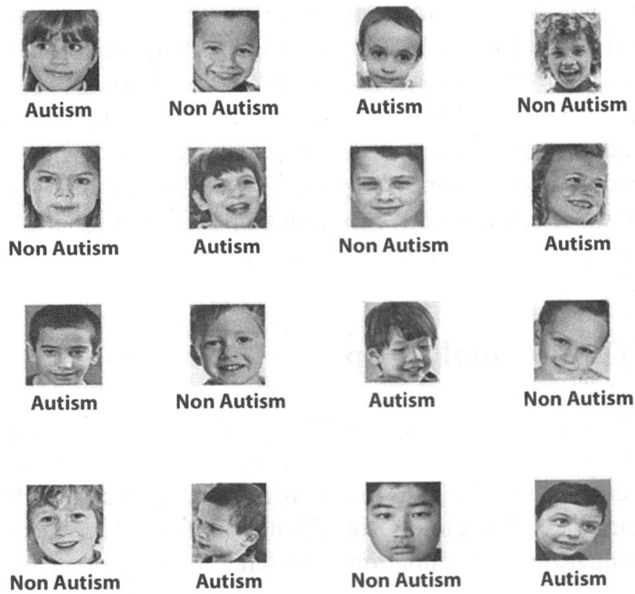

Figure 12.4 Autism spectrum image dataset.

Resampling images to commonly sized images would solve that problem, which should maintain an aspect ratio. Pixel intensity normalization is important in bringing the values into a common scale for increased convergence and as well as overall performance. Other data augmentation techniques such as random rotations, flipping zooming, adding noise, and color jittering could reduce biases and class imbalances. Feature extraction is done using pre-trained models like VGG or custom techniques like HOG, LBP, or GLCM. It helps classify the classes according to the features extracted from images.

Split the dataset into training, validation, and testing sets. Stratified sampling will guarantee that the distribution of classes for both autistic and non-autistic classes remains the same in each subset. Additionally, other methods may be used for potential class imbalance situations, including class weighting, undersampling, and oversampling. Oversampling deletes samples that are overrepresented, while undersampling replicates those that are understudied. Class weighting has been shown to heighten the focus of the model during training on those instances of an underrepresented class by assigning them greater weights. Specific pre-processing steps will enhance the quality of the Autism_Image_Data dataset, which will boost the efficiency of machine learning models in their task of recognizing autism. This early diagnosis helps have an early treatment program for patients with autism.

12.5.3 Model Training Environment

The environment to train the suggested models was made in such a way that it would ensure both scalability and efficiency for the models. Top-notch hardware was employed herein: for example, Intel Core i7 or above with 16GB RAM and NVIDIA RTX 3080 or more. Such setups easily created the processing capacity to handle big data and train deep neural network models. These were augmented by cloud computing platforms like Google Colab, AWS, and Azure to maximize scalability and resource optimization, achieving easy training of models in different datasets.

The reason Python was selected for software development is that it is very flexible for the use of AI research. Other important components were Scikit-learn for statistical analysis and performance evaluation, OpenCV for preprocessing and image augmentation, and TensorFlow and Keras for building and fine-tuning deep learning models. Two advanced CNN models were selected, such as VGG19, known for its robustness and simplicity when it comes to feature extraction, and Xception, which is famous for efficiently utilizing depthwise separable convolutions.

12.5.4 Training and Hyperparameter Tuning

This would be categorized under fair division across all dataset splits: training (70%), validation (15%), and testing (15%)-as it has been achieved just before starting the training process. It uses Adam optimizer because it provides better convergence while employed for gradient-based optimization, with binary cross-entropy for the loss function defined for the binary classification task. For models trained in 50-100 epochs with a batch size of 32, convergence is plentiful without much overfitting occurring.

The tuning hyperparameters are performed through advanced methods such as grid search and random search. Careful adjustment entails significant parameters, including the learning rate, number of convolutional layers, and dropout rates, to achieve the best possible set-up. The iterative process guarantees that models perform as best with the least amount of bias and volatility.

12.5.5 Evaluation Metrics

Many indicators in determining the efficacy of the models are adopted. Sensitivity (recall) assessed the detection as having positive ASD tests; accuracy measured the performance of predictions. Non-ASD conditions were evaluated using specificity, creating a well-rounded indication of performance under different conditions. To guarantee the generalizability of the models over different data splits, such validation methods as k-fold cross-validation with k=5 were employed. In addition, the confusion matrix shown in Figure 12.5 detailed the classification results of the Xception model and Figure 12.6 shows the classification results of VGG19: true positives, false positives, true negatives, and false negatives. The analysis illuminated the important aspects regarding the merits and demerits of the models.

12.5.6 Experimental Framework and Composite AI

Xception and VGG19 forms were compared within the experimental framework. The evaluation became prominent in terms of showing the model's accurate performance in sensitivity and specificity with regard to face characteristics linked to ASD. The comparison results throw light on trade-offs in terms of strong feature extraction and computing efficiency.

Further to building a Composite AI system aiming at improved diagnostic accuracy, model averages or stackings of predictions from both

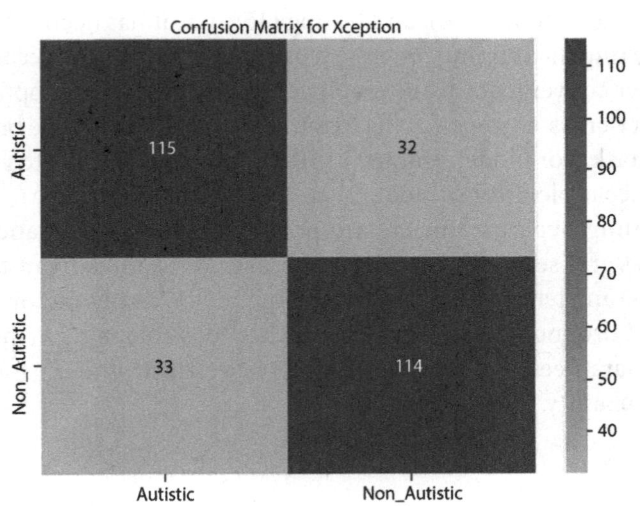

Figure 12.5 Confusion matrices for Xception model.

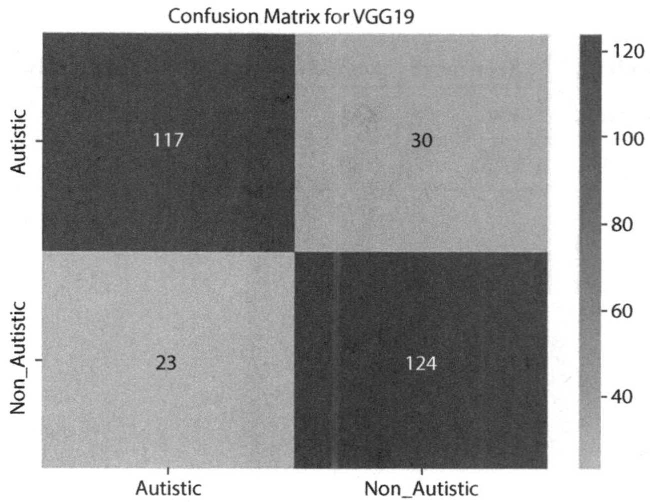

Figure 12.6 Matrices for VGG19 model.

models were harnessed. A more dependable diagnostic framework capable of performing better than each model will now be incurred into existence by combining the complementing qualities of both models.

12.6 Results and Outputs

The suggested methodologies were evaluated based on important metrics, namely specificity, sensitivity, and accuracy. These metrics demonstrated the algorithms' competence in the differentiation of cases with and without ASD. Table 12.1 summarizes the result while a bar graph in Figure 12.7 illustrates them. With an accuracy of 96%, the Xception Model performed well in all parameters by which its performance was judged. Demented-0 specificity at 97% assured correct classification of non-ASD patients, whereas 91% sensitivity indicated very good case detection among very good cases of autism spectrum disorder. Not as good a model as Xception, the VGG19 Model has an acceptable 80% sensitivity and 82% specificity that makes it usable as a feature extractor under some circumstances.

Table 12.1 Performance metrics of models.

Model	Accuracy	Sensitivity (recall)	Specificity
Xception	0.96	0.91	0.97
VGG19	0.75	0.80	0.82

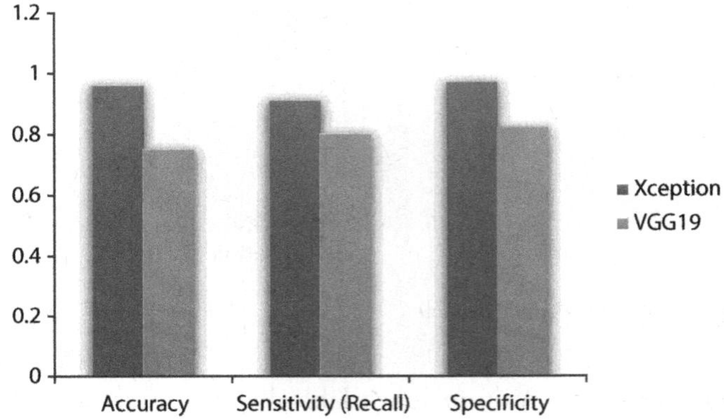

Figure 12.7 Performance metrics of models.

12.7 Conclusion

This research presents an evaluation of how well the two deep learning networks, Xception and VGG19 in particular, perform when applying facial features in predictively analyzing whether an individual is on the autism spectrum. With 96% accuracy, 91% sensitivity, and 97% specificity, the proposed model of Xception has exhibited exceptional performance according to all criteria mentioned above, which shows the great potential that this model possesses. Thus, it is quite accurate for classifying ASD-positive cases against non-positive ones.

VGG19, on the other hand, is slightly less superior but still manages to provide good results. Its significance is in terms of being a complementary model in an ensemble and for feature extraction purposes. The combined predictions of both models will be used to maximize diagnostic accuracy in the proposed Composite AI framework. It adapts the advantages of both models.

It is highly reproducible and scalable by resorting to the application of robust experimental techniques such as intelligent preprocessing, efficient training, and hyper-parameter tuning. Results indicate a bright future for deep learning in ASD diagnosis and a lot of opportunity for actual applications in clinical settings. Future work will focus on data collection to enlarge the dataset—the inclusion of other modalities such as eye-tracking or EEG data and improvement of the Composite AI framework to run into a larger audience.

AI disclosure statement: The author confirms that no artificial intelligence (AI)-generated content or AI-assisted writing tools were used in the preparation of this chapter (including summaries and the abstract). All text, analysis, and conclusions are the result of the author's original work.

References

1. Sun, B., Wang, B., Wei, Z., Feng, Z., Wu, Z.-L., Yassin, W., Stone, W.S., Lin, Y., Kong, X.-J., The Role of EEG Functional Connectivity Coupled with Eye Tracking in Early Diagnosis of Autism Spectrum Disorder, 2023.
2. Liao, M., Duan, H., Wang, G., Application of machine learning techniques to detect the children with autism spectrum disorder. *J. Healthc. Eng.*, 2022, 1, 9340027, 2022.
3. Kanhirakadavath, M.R. and Chandran, M.S.M., Investigation of eye-tracking scan path as a biomarker for autism screening using machine learning algorithms. *Diagnostics*, 12, 2, 518, 2022.
4. Mazumdar, P., Arru, G., Battisti, F., Early detection of children with autism spectrum disorder based on visual exploration of images. *Signal Process. Image Commun.*, 94, 116184, 2021.
5. Alalayah, K.M., Senan, E.M., Atlam, H.F., Ahmed, I.A., Shatnawi, H.S.A., Effective early detection of epileptic seizures through EEG signals using classification algorithms based on t-distributed stochastic neighbor embedding and K-means. *Diagnostics*, 13, 11, 1957, 2023.
6. Deng, L. and Rattadilok, P., A sensor and machine learning-based sensory management recommendation system for children with autism spectrum disorders. *Sensors*, 22, 15, 5803, 2022.
7. Black, M.H., Chen, N.TM., Iyer, K.K., Lipp, O.V., Bölte, S., Falkmer, M., Tan, T., Girdler, S., Mechanisms of facial emotion recognition in autism spectrum disorders: Insights from eye tracking and electroencephalography. *Neurosci. Biobehav. Rev.*, 80, 488–515, 2017.
8. Kang, J., Han, X., Song, J., Niu, Z., Li, X., The identification of children with autism spectrum disorder by SVM approach on EEG and eye-tracking data. *Comput. Biol. Med.*, 120, 103722, 2020.
9. Yi, L., Fan, Y., Quinn, P.C., Feng, C., Huang, D., Li, J., Mao, G., Lee, K., Abnormality in face scanning by children with autism spectrum disorder is

limited to the eye region: Evidence from multi-method analyses of eye tracking data. *J. Vision*, 13, 10, 5–5, 2013.
10. Boonsatit, N., Rajendran, S., Lim, C.P., Jirawattanapanit, A., Mohandas, P., New adaptive finite-time cluster synchronization of neutral-type complex-valued coupled neural networks with mixed time delays. *Fractal Fract.*, 6, 9, 515, 2022.
11. Napoleon, D., SivaSubramanian, M., Praneesh, M., Sathya, S., Self-organizing map-based color image segmentation with fuzzy C-Means clustering and saliency map. *Int. J. Comput. Appl.*, 3, 2, 109–117, 2012.
12. Zhao, Z., Tang, H., Zhang, X., Qu, X., Hu, X., Lu, J., Classification of children with autism and typical development using eye-tracking data from face-to-face conversations: Machine learning model development and performance evaluation. *J. Med. Internet Res.*, 23, 8, e29328, 2021.
13. Dell'Osso, L., Gesi, C., Massimetti, E., Cremone, I.M., Barbuti, M., Maccariello, G., Moroni, I., *et al.*, Adult Autism Subthreshold Spectrum (AdAS Spectrum): Validation of a questionnaire investigating subthreshold autism spectrum. *Compr. Psychiatry*, 73, 61–835, 2017.
14. Pugazhendiran, P., Suresh Kumar, K., Ananth Kumar, T., Sundaresan, S., An Advanced Revealing and Classification System for Plant Illnesses Using Unsupervised Bayesian-based SVM Classifier and Modified HOG-ROI Algorithm, in: *Contemporary Issues in Communication, Cloud and Big Data Analytics: Proceedings of CCB*, Springer Singapore, pp. 259–269, 20202022.
15. Wu, T., Duan, Y., Zhang, T., Tian, W., Liu, H., Deng, Y., Research trends in the application of artificial intelligence in oncology: A bibliometric and network visualization study. *Front. Biosci.-Landmark*, 27, 9, 254, 2022.
16. Xiao, L., Huo, X., Wang, Y., Li, W., Li, M., Wang, C., Wang, F., Sun, T., A bibliometric analysis of global research status and trends in neuromodulation techniques in the treatment of autism spectrum disorder. *BMC Psychiatry*, 23, 1, 183, 2023.
17. Rahman, R., Kodesh, A., Levine, S.Z., Sandin, S., Reichenberg, A., Schlessinger, A., Identification of newborns at risk for autism using electronic medical records and machine learning. *Eur. Psychiatry*, 63, 1, e22, 2020.
18. Senarathne, U.D., Indika, N.-L.R., Jezela-Stanek, A., Ciara, E., Frye, R.E., Chen, C., Stepien, K.M., Biochemical, genetic and clinical diagnostic approaches to autism-associated inherited metabolic disorders. *Genes*, 14, 4, 803, 2023.
19. Menaka, R., Karthik, R., Saranya, S., Niranjan, M., Kabilan, S., An improved AlexNet model and cepstral coefficient-based classification of autism using EEG. *Clin. EEG Neurosci.*, 55, 1, 43–51, 2024.
20. Riddiford, J.A., Enticott, P.G., Lavale, A., Gurvich, C., Gaze and social functioning associations in autism spectrum disorder: A systematic review and meta-analysis. *Autism Res.*, 15, 8, 1380–1446, 2022.

21. Ahmed, Z.AT., Aldhyani, T.HH., Jadhav, M.E., Alzahrani, M.Y., Alzahrani, M.E., Althobaiti, M.M., Alassery, F., Alshaflut, A., Alzahrani, N.M., Al-Madani, A.M., [Retracted] Facial Features Detection System To Identify Children With Autism Spectrum Disorder: Deep Learning Models. *Comput. Math. Methods Med.*, 2022, 1, 3941049, 2022.
22. Andrews, D.S., Marquand, A., Ecker, C., McAlonan, G., Using pattern classification to identify brain imaging markers in autism spectrum disorder, in: *Biomarkers in Psychiatry*, pp. 413–436, Springer International Publishing, Cham, 2018.
23. Alqaysi, M.E., Albahri, A.S., Hamid, R.A., Diagnosis-Based Hybridization of Multimedical Tests and Sociodemographic Characteristics of Autism Spectrum Disorder Using Artificial Intelligence and Machine Learning Techniques: A Systematic Review. *Int. J. Telemed. Appl.*, 2022, 1, 3551528, 2022.
24. Erden, Y.J., Hummerstone, H., Rainey, S., Automating autism assessment: What AI can bring to the diagnostic process. *J. Eval. Clin. Pract.*, 27, 3, 485–490, 2021.
25. Bahado-Singh, R.O., Vishweswaraiah, S., Aydas, B., Mishra, N.K., Yilmaz, A., Guda, C., Radhakrishna, U., Artificial intelligence analysis of newborn leucocyte epigenomic markers for the prediction of autism. *Brain Res.*, 1724, 146457, 2019.
26. Capps, L., Kasari, C., Yirmiya, N., Sigman, M., Parental perception of emotional expressiveness in children with autism. *J. Consult. Clin. Psychol.*, 61, 3, 475, 1993.
27. Volker, M.A., Lopata, C., Smith, D.A., Thomeer, M.L., Facial encoding of children with high-functioning autism spectrum disorders. *Focus Autism Other Dev. Disabil.*, 24, 4, 195–204, 2009.
28. Leo, M., Carcagnì, P., Distante, C., Spagnolo, P., Mazzeo, P.L., Rosato, A.C., Petrocchi, S., *et al.*, Computational assessment of facial expression production in ASD children. *Sensors*, 18, 11, 3993, 2018.
29. Saranya, A. and Anandan, R., Facial Action Coding and Hybrid Deep Learning Architectures for Autism Detection. *Intell. Autom. Soft Comput.*, 33.2, 2022.
30. Esler, A.N., Bal, V.H., Guthrie, W., Wetherby, A., Weismer, S.E., Lord, C., The autism diagnostic observation schedule, toddler module: standardized severity scores. *J. Autism Dev. Disord.*, 45, 2704–27205, 2015.
31. Pandiyan, V., Akeddar, M., Prost, J., Vorlaufer, G., Varga, M., Wasmer, K., Long short-term memory based semi-supervised encoder—Decoder for early prediction of failures in self-lubricating bearings. *Friction*, 11, 1, 109–124, 2023.
32. Tao, Y. and Shyu, M.-L., SP-ASDNet: CNN-LSTM based ASD classification model using observer scanpaths, in: *2019 IEEE International Conference on Multimedia & Expo Workshops (ICMEW)*, IEEE, pp. 641–646, 2019.

33. Valizadeh, A., Moassefi, M., Nakhostin-Ansari, A., Some'eh, S.H., Hosseini-Asl, H., Torbati, M.S., Aghajani, R., *et al.*, Automated diagnosis of autism with artificial intelligence: State of the art. *Rev. Neurosci.*, 35, 2, 141–163, 2024.
34. Awaji, B., Senan, E.M., Olayah, F., Alshari, E.A., Alsulami, M., Abosaq, H.A., Alqahtani, J., Janrao, P., Hybrid techniques of facial feature image analysis for early detection of autism spectrum disorder based on combined CNN features. *Diagnostics*, 13, 18, 2948, 2023.
35. Wang, H. and Avillach, P., Diagnostic classification and prognostic prediction using common genetic variants in autism spectrum disorder: Genotype-based deep learning. *JMIR Med. Inf.*, 9, 4, e24754, 2021.
36. Sigar, P., Uddin, L.Q., Roy, D., Altered global modular organization of intrinsic functional connectivity in autism arises from atypical node-level processing. *Autism Res.*, 16, 1, 66–83, 2023.
37. Berto, S., Treacher, A.H., Caglayan, E., Luo, D., Haney, J.R., Gandal, M.J., Geschwind, D.H., Montillo, A.A., Konopka, G., Association between resting-state functional brain connectivity and gene expression is altered in autism spectrum disorder. *Nat. Commun.*, 13, 1, 3328, 2022.
38. Ortega, M.A., Álvarez-Mon, M.A., García-Montero, C., Fraile-Martínez, O., Monserrat, J., Martinez-Rozas, L., Rodríguez-Jiménez, R., Álvarez-Mon, M., Lahera, G., Microbiota–gut–brain axis mechanisms in the complex network of bipolar disorders: potential clinical implications and translational opportunities. *Mol. Psychiatry*, 28, 7, 2645–2673, 2023.
39. Almeida, R.A., Edwin Dickinson, J., Maybery, M.T., Badcock, J.C., Badcock, D.R., A new step towards understanding Embedded Figures Test performance in the autism spectrum: The radial frequency search task. *Neuropsychologia*, 48, 2, 374–381, 2010.
40. Dakin, S. and Frith, U., Vagaries of visual perception in autism. *Neuron*, 48, 3, 497–507, 2005.
41. Eigsti, I.-M., de Marchena, A.B., Schuh, J.M., Kelley, E., Language acquisition in autism spectrum disorders: A developmental review. *Res. Autism Spectr. Disord.*, 5, 2, 681–691, 2011.
42. Happé, F.GE. and Booth, R.DL., The power of the positive: Revisiting weak coherence in autism spectrum disorders. *Q. J. Exp. Psychol.*, 61, 1, 50–63, 2008.
43. Hare-Harris, A.E., Mitchel, M.W., Myers, S.M., Mitchel, A.D., King, B.R., Ruocco, B.G., Martin, C.L., Flax, J.F., Brzustowicz, L.M., Within-task variability on standardized language tests predicts autism spectrum disorder: a pilot study of the Response Dispersion Index. *J. Neurodev. Disord.*, 11, 1–135, 2019.
44. Fusaroli, R., Lambrechts, A., Bang, D., Bowler, D.M., Gaigg, S.B., Is voice a marker for Autism spectrum disorder? A systematic review and meta-analysis. *Autism Res.*, 10, 3, 384–407, 2017.

45. Kalantarian, H., Jedoui, K., Washington, P., Tariq, Q., Dunlap, K., Schwartz, J., Wall, D.P., Labeling images with facial emotion and the potential for pediatric healthcare. *Artif. Intell. Med.*, 98, 77–86, 2019.
46. Joudar, S.S., Albahri, A.S., Hamid, R.A., Triage and priority-based healthcare diagnosis using artificial intelligence for autism spectrum disorder and gene contribution: a systematic review. *Comput. Biol. Med.*, 146, 1055535, 2022.
47. Helmy, E., Elnakib, A., ElNakieb, Y., Khudri, M., Abdelrahim, M., Yousaf, J., Ghazal, M., Contractor, S., Barnes, G.N., El-Baz, A., Role of artificial intelligence for autism diagnosis using DTI and fMRI: A survey. *Biomedicines*, 11, 7, 1858, 2023.
48. Xu, M., Calhoun, V., Jiang, R., Yan, W., Sui, J., Brain imaging-based machine learning in autism spectrum disorder: methods and applications. *J. Neurosci. Methods*, 361, 1092715, 2021.

13

Integrating Imaging and Genomic Data with Composite AI to Enhance Breast Cancer Diagnosis and Early Detection

P. Manju Bala[1], S. Usharani[2], A. Balachandar[3], Sunday Adeola Ajagbe[4*] and Matthew Olusegun Adigun[4]

[1]Department of Artificial Intelligence and Data Science, IFET College of Engineering Villupram, Tamil Nadu, India
[2]Department of Artificial Intelligence and Machine Learning, IFET College of Engineering, Villupram, Tamil Nadu, India
[3]Department of Computer Science and Engineering, IFET College of Engineering Villupram, Tamil Nadu, India
[4]Department of Computer Science, University of Zululand, Kwadlangezwa, South Africa

Abstract

Early detection of breast cancer will increase patient outcomes and survival, which will aid in improved patient care. However, integrating genetic data with medical imaging will enhance our understanding of the condition, resulting in a more accurate diagnosis and tailored therapy for the patient. Multiple artificial intelligence techniques coupled to create composite AI can enhance the interpretation of the aggregated data and pave the way for new, cutting-edge research directions in breast cancer. In this study, we present an integrated artificial intelligence system that improves breast cancer detection by combining data from genomics and imaging techniques. Our solution is a hybrid strategy that employs CNN models for image data and machine learning models (SVMs and Random Forests) for processing genomic data. We employ stacking, an additional ensemble learning technique, to merge the predictions of the CNN and genomic data models.

**Corresponding author*: manjubala@ifet.ac.in
Sunday Adeola Ajagbe: ORCID: 0000-0002-7010-5540
Matthew Olusegun Adigun: ORCID: 0000-0001-6256-5865

T. S. Arun Samuel, L. Jerart Julus, P. Kanimozhi, T. Ananth Kumar and S. Balamurugan (eds.) Composite Artificial Intelligence: Fundamentals, Challenges, and Applications, (303–324) © 2026 Scrivener Publishing LLC

As a result, our method produces a reliable and accurate diagnosis model by capturing unique imaging and genetic data. By capturing characteristics unique to picture data and genetic traits, this hybrid technique enables a more potent prediction model. Datasets that included genetic profiles with mammography pictures obtained from publicly accessible depositories such as TCGA and TCIA were used to evaluate the algorithms. Using the imaging data, the CNN model demonstrated an 88% accuracy rate in distinguishing between benign and malignant samples. An accuracy of 85% was obtained by analyzing the genomic data using SVM findings. With a classification accuracy of 92%, the composite model, which combined the output of the CNN and SVM models, showed a notable increase over the individual models' outputs. The area under the curve increased by over 6% when cross-validation methods and AUC-ROC performance indicators were used, compared to the CNN model alone and the composite model. Performance assessment has shown that adding genetic and imaging data to composite AI greatly improves the precision and resilience of breast cancer detection. This illustrates the revolutionary potential of AI in the early diagnosis of breast cancer and opens the door for more sophisticated diagnostic and personalized treatment options.

Keywords: Breast cancer, medical imaging, genomics, composite AI, machine learning models, artificial intelligence, machine learning models

13.1 Introduction

With 2.3 million new cases and 686,000 deaths in 2020 alone, breast cancer remains the most frequent disease worldwide and the leading cause of cancer-related deaths among women [1]. Although localized breast cancer with an early diagnosis can have a five-year survival rate of up to 99%, the rate drastically decreases as the illness advances; hence, early identification has been crucial to survival rates [2]. As a result, improving patient outcomes and creating customized treatment strategies depend heavily on early identification and diagnosis. Conventional breast cancer diagnoses have long relied on imaging techniques because they offer a crucial overview of the location and anatomy of the tumor. However, imaging methods by themselves frequently fall short in identifying the molecular and genetic factors that contribute to the development of cancer [3].

To establish a more comprehensive and accurate evaluation of breast cancer and enable customized medical methods, it has been highlighted that imaging data and genetic information should be integrated. Each tumor's distinct patterns and mutations are shown by genomic profiling, which also offers insights into tumor behavior and forecasts patterns of disease development and treatment response [4, 5]. When combined with genetic data, it will improve diagnostic accuracy and provide a more multifaceted approach to tumor characterization [6]. However, because of its size and diversity, it necessitates analytical tools that are extremely competent in managing and analyzing this disparate information. Particularly with regard to ML and DL approaches, which are more than capable of finding significant patterns in complicated data, AI applications are changing the landscape [7].

It comprises a number of techniques that together make up the framework of composite AI, which has promise for bridging the genomes and imaging gaps in the diagnosis of breast cancer. In order to improve overall prediction accuracy and the resilience of the medical diagnostic model, the approach "splices" together some of the more notable advantages of separate AI techniques [8]. This study suggests a composite artificial intelligence (AI) for combining genetic and medical picture data to increase the precision of breast cancer detection. While SVM models are used to assess genomic data, CNNs are used to study imaging data. The application of ensemble method stacking uses the predictions from both CNN and genomic data models to produce more accurate diagnostic results [8].

13.1.1 Importance of Imaging and Genomic Integration in Breast Cancer Diagnostics

For a long time, medical imaging has been an important diagnostic tool for breast cancer. The most often employed modalities are MRI, ultrasound, and mammography. These methods assist radiologists in distinguishing between benign and malignant lesions and provide them with some sense of the tumor's form [9]. In situations where the kind of tumor is unclear, imaging by itself cannot offer specificity. In terms of gene mutations, their expression levels, and epigenetic modifications, genomic information provides an extra layer of information that is useful in revealing molecular-level changes linked to malignant development [10]. Combining these kinds of data offers a thorough perspective that improves our comprehension of tumor type heterogeneity, which may improve diagnosis accuracy and enable more individualized treatment plans [11, 12]. Numerous studies have demonstrated the value of combining genetics and imaging in the investigation of breast cancer. For example, imaging and genomic data are carried by public depositories, such as The Cancer Genome Atlas (TCGA) and The Cancer Imaging Archive (TCIA), which enable study on such multi-modal techniques [13, 14]. These databases made it possible to create predictive models that combine genetic characteristics and imaging-based phenotypes for tumor subtype categorization, patient prognosis prediction, and treatment response monitoring [15]. The enormous dimensionality and variety of features seen in both imaging and genomic databases, however, make it difficult to integrate such disparate data [16].

13.1.2 Role of AI in Multimodal Data Analysis for Breast Cancer

AI is becoming a useful tool for handling high-dimensional, complicated medical data. In image processing, convolutional neural networks (CNNs) are especially suitable deep models. CNNs are highly suited for applications like tumor identification, classification, and segmentation because they can learn the hierarchical representations in spatial dimensions required to automate the picture interpretation process [17]. Because they can handle high-dimensional feature spaces, which may be able to elucidate the most significant genetic markers linked to cancer, traditional machine learning algorithms, including SVM and RF, have been shown to be useful for genomic data [18]. Combining the machine learning models for genomics with the CNNs for image analysis would create a multifaceted approach to breast cancer diagnosis. According to a number of recent studies, CNNs can accurately differentiate between benign and malignant cases using just imaging data. It has also been demonstrated that SVM and RFs may create powerful patterns in genomic data, particularly in [19, 20]. In the face of a complicated issue, a single data-type model is frequently not reliable and correct. To create an integrated predictive model, composite AI models combine the best features of many AI methodologies [21].

13.1.3 Composite AI Framework for Breast Cancer Diagnosis

The proposed composite AI framework utilizes CNNs for image data analysis, whereas ML models such as SVM and RF would be used for genomic data analysis. CNNs prove good at extracting features from imaging data because of their convolutional and pooling layers in helping capture hierarchical spatial and texture patterns indicative of malignancy [22]. SVM and RF are especially well-suited for genomic data. As noted in [23], feature spaces are generally very high-dimensional, and traditional data-driven techniques prove difficult to apply. The ensemble learning approach called stacking is used here: The predictions of all models are used as inputs in a meta-classifier, which usually is a logistic regression model. This allows the framework to take into account the unique feature sets contributed by both imaging and genomic features, thereby having a robust and reliable output diagnosis [24]. This framework combines the strengths of CNN and ML models due to an applied stacking ensemble, which gives a higher predictive accuracy and robustness in the diagnosis of breast cancer. The diagnostic accuracy of the composite model can attain 92% compared to a model trained by combining the individual models from both imaging and genomic data according to our study. This finding is in line with recent research, which stressed the superiority of ensemble methods in biomedical applications, where complex, heterogeneous data will need sophisticated model architectures to capture subtle relationships between features [25].

13.1.4 Validation and Clinical Implications of Composite AI

To validate the composite AI model, cross-validation analysis is performed to evaluate the performance of the model by the area under the curve of the receiver operating characteristic curves. The results achieved in this work are that the AUC increases from 0.87 in the CNN model alone to 0.93 in the composite model, hence indicating a significant increase in the diagnostic capability. This result, therefore, implies that a composite AI system is one of the potential routes to more accurate diagnoses, with fewer false positives and negatives and more novel diagnostic inputs [15]. The robustness of composite AI models also lends support to their applicability in clinical settings, wherein valid and accurate diagnosis forms an even basis for decision-making [26]. There is a totally transformative approach toward diagnosing breast cancer by integration of imaging and genomic data using composite AI. As the technology advances, composite frameworks are anticipated to become even more sophisticated with the addition of new data types, such as proteomics and metabolomics, in attaining even more precision in diagnosis [27]. Finally, in clinical practice, composite AI will enable early detection of breast cancer, accurate diagnosis, and a subsequent treatment plan, thereby improving the outcomes for patients [28].

13.2 Materials and Methods

13.2.1 Data Collection and Description

In this investigation, datasets were directly downloaded from public storage sites. As a result, any retrieved data can be relied upon to be of high quality and widely recognized. There are excellent collections of genomic and medical imaging data for cancer research in public repositories such as The Cancer Genome Atlas (TCGA) and The Cancer Imaging Archive (TCIA), which ensure that the data is reliable, consistent, and appropriate for sophisticated AI-driven analysis. These datasets are extremely helpful resources for reproducible research since they are well-curated, have consistent formats, and have comprehensive descriptions. While TCGA offers comprehensive genomic profiles with gene expression, mutation data, and molecular characterizations—all important for comprehending the genetic landscape of breast cancer—TCI's imaging datasets contain diagnostic pictures such as mammograms, MRIs, and histopathology scans.

- **Imaging Data:** Mammography Images came from The Cancer Imaging Archive (TCIA). It was an archive of annotated breast cancer images that could be used for supervised learning on tasks of image classification. Each record for an image was a label marked whether the lesion detected was benign or malignant.

Genomic Data: TCGA produces large-scale genomic profiles that highlight the genetic data, including gene-expression data, mutation profiles, and methylation. Such datasets are annotated with breast cancer subtypes; the image-based analysis is supplemented with genomic-level predictions [2]. These datasets have been chosen based on the comprehensive level of coverage concerning breast cancer data, which would allow good training and evaluation of the model.

13.2.2 Data Pre-Processing

Figure 13.1 shows the pre-processing steps. The main pre-requisites of multimodal studies concern data pre-processing since imaging and genomic data differ in format and pre-processing requirements.

a. Pre-processing of Image Data

Such an analytical model of imaging data like CNN entails equal and normalized input dimensions. Some are:

Resizing: Images were resized to 224x224 pixels as this would make inputs consistent, hence making processing in the CNN much easier.

Normalization: Normalize pixel intensity values to the range [0, 1] by dividing by the maximum pixel value. Normalization of I with pixels can be expressed as:

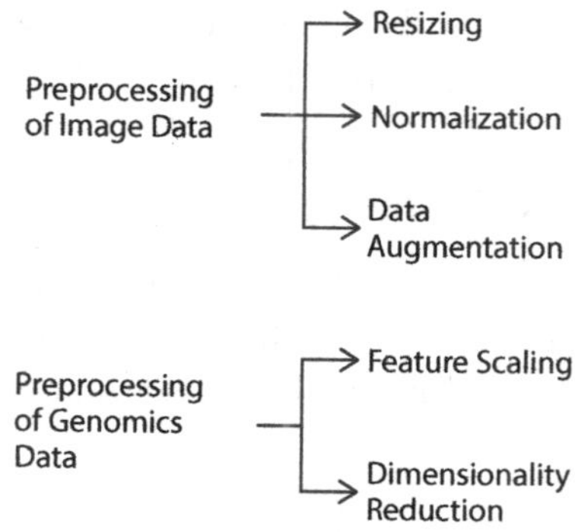

Figure 13.1 Data pre-processing.

$$I_{normalized} = \frac{I}{255}$$

Data Augmentation: To generate model generalization, data augmentation techniques include random rotations, flipping, and scaling. Applying data augmentation prevents overfitting as it increases the variation in the training data.

b. Preprocessing of genomics data

Genomic data is a kind of high-dimensional feature on expressions and mutations. The preprocessing steps are as follows:

Feature Scaling: The genomic features have been standardized to a zero mean and unit variance so that each feature contributes equally. For a feature fi:

$$f_i' = \frac{f_i - \bar{x}}{\sigma}$$

where $\bar{x}$ is the mean and σ is the standard deviation of f_i.

Dimensionality Reduction: Since the feature space is high dimensional, PCA reduces the feature space while retaining 95% of the variance. PCA transforms the data X by computing principal components P:

$$X_{PCA} = X.P$$

In this case, P represents the eigenvectors corresponding to the top eigenvalues of the covariance matrix of X.

13.2.3 Composite AI Framework Architecture

This combines CNN imaging analysis with genomic information that is processed *via* machine learning models meant to be enhanced further by an ensemble stacking technique. Figure 13.2 shows the details of each model component.

- **Convolutional Layer:** Each convolutional layer creates feature maps that highlight certain patterns by applying a filter F to the input picture I. The convolution operation for an input image I and filter F is as follows:

$$Y = I * F + b$$

where b is a bias term and $*$ indicates the convolution process. An activation function is then applied to the output Y.

- **Activation Function (ReLU):** Non-linearity is introduced by applying the rectified linear unit (ReLU), which is defined as:

$$f(x) = \max(0, x)$$

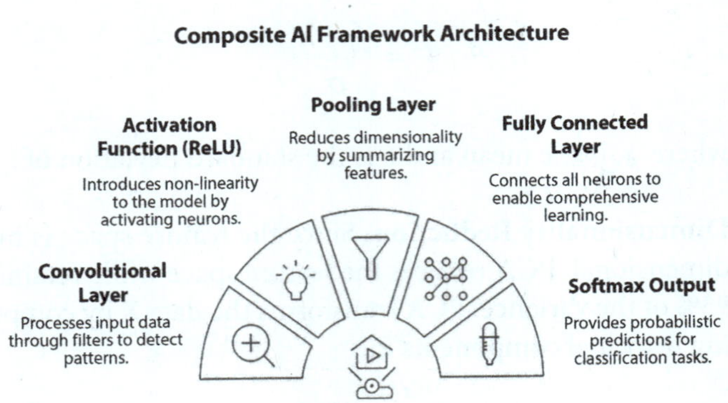

Figure 13.2 Composite AI framework architecture.

ReLU activation increases learning efficiency and lessens the possibility of disappearing gradients.

- **Pooling Layer:** By lowering spatial dimensions, pooling lowers computing complexity while maintaining important properties. The maximum value in each window is chosen during max-pooling:

$$Y_{pooled} = \max(Y)$$

- **Fully Connected Layer and Softmax Output:** The class probabilities are output by the last fully linked layer. The softmax function calculates the probability for binary classification in the manner described below:

$$P(y = c|X) = \frac{e^{z_c}}{\sum_j e^{z_j}}$$

where zc is the class c score, giving the likelihood of a benign or malignant prognosis.

13.2.4 Machine Learning Models for Genomic Data Analysis

Support Vector Machines (SVM) and Random Forests (RF), which were selected for their resilience in high-dimensional domains, are used to analyze the genetic data. Different Machine Learning Models for Genomic Data Analysis is shown in Figure 13.3.

- **Support Vector Machine (SVM):** SVM determines the best hyperplane in a high-dimensional space to optimally divide classes. The definition of the SVM classifier for a genomic feature vector x is:

$$f(x) = sign(w^T \varnothing(x) + b)$$

where b represents the bias term, ϕ represents the mapping of x into a higher-dimensional space, and w is the weight

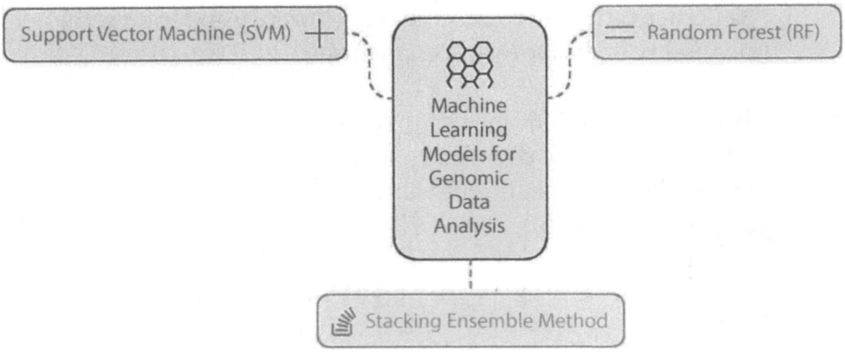

Figure 13.3 Models for genomic data analysis.

vector. Subject to the following restriction, the SVM optimization aims to maximize the margin between classes:

$$y_i(w^T \varnothing(x_i) + b) \geq 1, \qquad \forall i$$

- **Random Forest (RF):** An ensemble learning technique called RF builds many decision trees and averages their categorization predictions. A bootstrap sample of the data is used to train each decision tree, and at each split, random feature subsets are chosen to increase accuracy and decrease correlation between trees. The RF forecast for an input x is:

$$\hat{y} = \frac{1}{T}\sum_{t=1}^{T} f_t(x)$$

where T is the total number of trees and $f_t(x)$ is the prediction from the t-th tree.

- **Stacking Ensemble Method**
The CNN and SVM models' predictions are combined in the stacking ensemble. Based on the results of individual models, a meta-classifier called logistic regression is trained to determine the ultimate prediction, which is described as:

$$y_{final} = \sigma(\alpha\, y_{CNN} + \beta\, y_{SVM} + \gamma)$$

where y_{CNN} and y_{SVM} are the model predictions, σ is the sigmoid function, and α, β, and γ are parameters that were learnt during training.

13.3 Model Training and Evaluation

13.3.1 Training Procedure

The training process for CNN Model is shown in Figure 13.4

- **CNN Training:** Backpropagation was used to train the CNN model using a cross-entropy loss function. Cross-entropy loss for true labels y and forecasted probabilities y^is computed as:

$$Loss = -\frac{1}{N}\sum_{i=1}^{N}[y_i \log(\hat{y}_\iota) + (1 - y_i)\log(1 - \hat{y}_\iota)]$$

- **SVM and RF Training:** Genomic data was used to train the SVM and RF models, and grid search was used to adjust hyperparameters and maximize model performance. The models were trained independently, and the stacking ensemble then used their results.

13.3.2 Evaluation Metrics

- Accuracy, precision, recall, F1 score, and area under the receiver operating characteristic (AUC-ROC) curve were

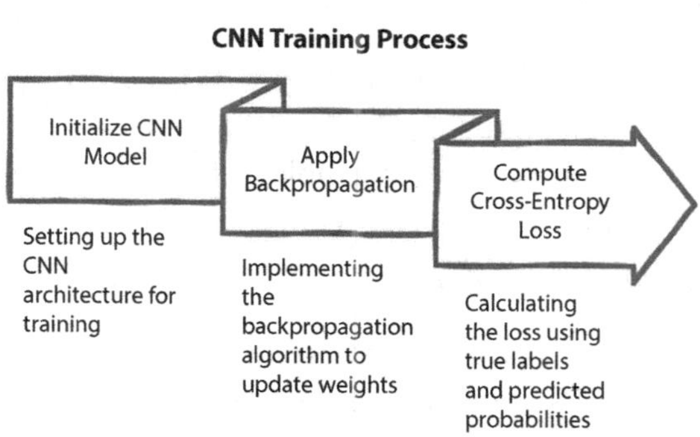

Figure 13.4 Model training procedure.

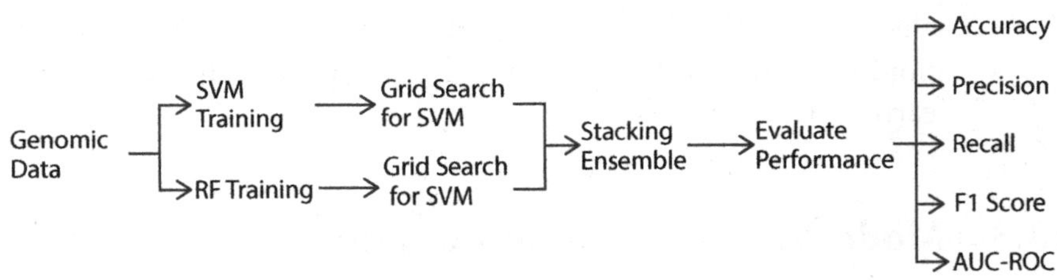

Figure 13.5 Metrics used for composite AI framework.

used to evaluate the diagnostic performance of the composite AI framework is shown in Figure 13.5. To guarantee generalizability, each model underwent cross-validation. The model's capacity to differentiate between benign and malignant instances is revealed by the AUC-ROC, which is computed as:

$$AUC = \int_0^1 TPR(f)\, d(FPR(f))$$

where the true positive rate is denoted by TPR and the false positive rate by FPR.

13.4 Evaluation Results

Several critical performance indicators, including accuracy, precision, recall, F1 score, and area under the receiver operating characteristic curve, were included in this research to accomplish the thorough evaluation of the model. These measurements made it possible to assess the model's performance in accurately classifying cancer as either benign or malignant. Here, we compile the outcomes of the CNN, SVM, and RF individual models and contrast them with the finished composite AI model that was produced by employing the stacking ensemble technique.

13.4.1 Model Performance

It is clear from Table 13.1 that the composite AI model is even more effective, since it can use genetic and imaging data to diagnose breast cancer with a more thorough and accurate prediction capacity. When it comes to

Table 13.1 Performance measure of different models.

Model	Accuracy (%)	Precision (%)	Recall (%)	F1 score (%)	AUC-ROC
CNN	88	87	85	86	0.87
SVM	85	84	82	83	0.85
Random Forest	82	80	81	80.5	0.83
Composite AI Model	92	91	90	90.5	0.93

diagnosing breast cancer, composite AI outperformed solo models with an accuracy score of 92%. The Composite AI model also exhibits high Precision and Recall scores, suggesting that it has improved accuracy in classifying both benign and malignant cases. Its F1 Score is also higher, which balances precision and recall and reflects the composite AI model's overall resilience in categorization. Better categorization performance across decision thresholds than in individual models is indicated by the AUC-ROC of 0.93.

CNN Model:
After training on imaging data, the CNN model achieved a precision score of 88%, demonstrating its ability to clearly capture spatial features within mammography images. The AUC-ROC score of 0.87 stands for its strong potency for malignant versus benign case discrimination; however, still, there is much room for improvement, especially false negatives, with the model failing to pick up malignant signs in ambiguous imaging data.

SVM Model (Genomic Data):
Given the high dimensionality and complexity of the genomic data, the SVM model's accuracy of 85% for genomic data processing is competitive. The framework is mostly driven in this direction by the use of the model to categorize genomic profiles, which identify molecular patterns linked to cancer. However, the model might not have enough discriminative capacity in genomic high-dimensional data on its own, as indicated by the AUC-ROC of 0.85.

Random Forest (RF) Model:
With an accuracy of 82% and an AUC-ROC of 0.83, the Random Forest model served as a baseline for the analysis of genomic data. RF might not be the best option for high-dimensional genomic data, despite the fact that

it is often resilient to noise. The significance of model selection in the categorization of genomic data is shown by the comparatively poorer performance of RF in comparison to SVM.

Composite AI Model:
By using a stacking ensemble technique, the composite AI model integrates the predictions from the CNN and SVM models. The following outcomes were obtained by the final model, which used logistic regression as a meta-classifier:

With an accuracy of 92% and an AUC-ROC of 0.93, the composite model significantly improved by combining imaging and genomic data. These findings show that the composite strategy successfully combines the complimentary advantages of SVM (genomic) and CNN (imaging) models, resulting in a more reliable classification method for the detection of breast cancer.

13.4.2 Cross-Validation and Robustness

We used 10-fold cross-validation to make sure the model was generalizable. With very little variation in accuracy, AUC-ROC, and F1 scores, this method verified that the model's performance was steady across several data subsets. The composite model's durability and applicability for practical use were highlighted by its high dependability in correctly identifying situations across several rounds.

13.4.3 ROC Curve Analysis

To demonstrate how well each model—CNN, SVM, Random Forest, and the Composite AI model—performs in classifying cases of benign and malignant breast cancer, the ROC (Receiver Operating Characteristic) curve analysis for the models in our study compares their sensitivity and specificity across a range of decision thresholds.

CNN Model:
The CNN model's AUC-ROC (Area Under the Curve of ROC) score is 0.87, according to the ROC curve. This comparatively high AUC value shows that the CNN model does a good job of differentiating between benign and malignant cases when it is trained solely on imaging data. Although the CNN is good at identifying spatial characteristics in mammography pictures, it may have trouble with ambiguous imaging aspects, which might result in a larger number of false negatives. According to this constraint, classification confidence may be increased by using supplementary data, such as genomics.

SVM Model:
The SVM model, which was trained on genomic data, obtained an AUC-ROC of 0.85, indicating a moderate level of confidence in its ability to distinguish between benign and malignant profiles, though its overall robustness may be limited by its reliance on only genomic data. The model's ability to classify cases based on molecular characteristics captured in high-dimensional genomic data is strong, but because genomic features are complex, it may miss subtle information in cases where genetic markers are less pronounced, resulting in slightly lower accuracy in some ambiguous cases.

Random Forest Model:
As a baseline classifier incorporated into baseline genomic data, neural networks demonstrate the lowest performance, with an AUC-ROC of only 0.83. For the most part, random forests tend to be robust and provide good performance in the presence of noise. However, those models may not be as effective in processing complicated and high-dimensional genomic data. For example, a much lower AUC value demonstrates that this model fails to learn certain interactions present in the data, such as the distinction between benign and malignant cases, which the trees may fail to learn. Such stresses the importance of model selection for analysis of genetic data, as enrichment techniques such as ensemble methods or SVM are mainly effective for larger dimensional data sets.

Composite AI Model:
The Composite AI approach, where CNN imaging predictions are integrated with SVM genomic predictions using stacking techniques, recorded an impressive accuracy or AUC-ROC of 0.93. The raised AUC emphasizes that the composite model is enriched by the ability of both data types—the imaging data which facilitates understanding of the spatial features of the cancer and the genomic data—which provides an insight to the molecular degree of malignancy. The high value of AUC-ROC shows the strength of the model as it proves effective at different levels of decision thresholds achieving a good compromise between sensitivity and specificity. This combined strategy equips the clinician with a solid diagnostic maneuver which has lower incidences of false positives and false negatives, thereby improving effectiveness in clinical practice.

The analysis of ROC curves in Figure 13.6 indicates that using both data types such as imaging and genomics within the Composite AI model significantly improves the classification performance, as seen by the AUC-ROC which was as high as 0.93. This result emphasizes the need of a

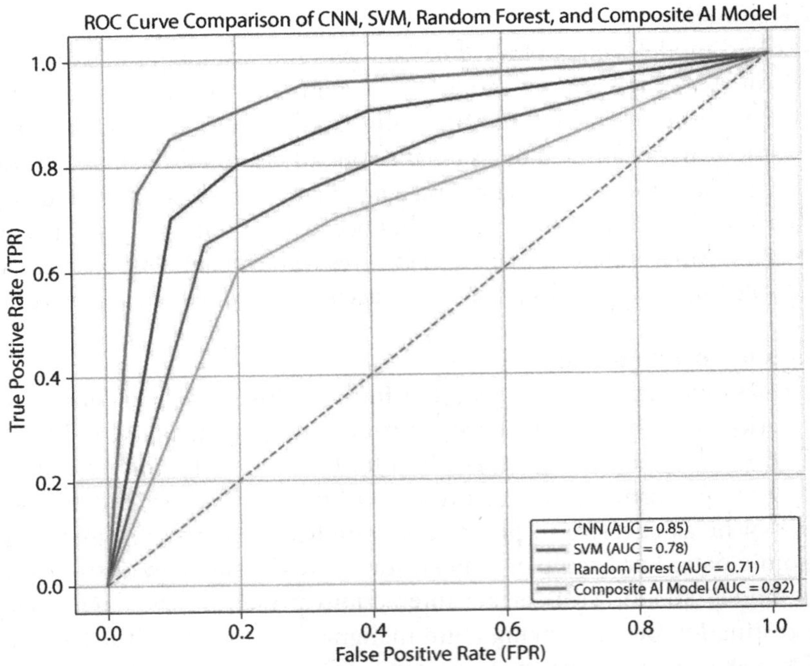

Figure 13.6 ROC curve comparison.

multi-modal strategy in breast cancer diagnosis, where a combination of imaging techniques and molecular biomarker information enables a better and more precise diagnosis than any one type of information. In general, the analysis of ROC curves supports the fact that the composite AI model is capable of the best differentiation of benign and malignant cases and thus represents an efficient way of enhancing breast cancer diagnostic accuracy. These results imply that these composite models will be important in the context of development of personalized and precision medicine which utilizes large amounts of multidimensional data for patient evaluation.

13.4.4 Comparative Analysis of Individual Model and Composite AI Model

When looking at the performance metrics for each of the models (CNN, SVM, Random Forest) and the Composite Artificial Intelligence model shown in Figure 13.7, it can be appreciated that composite AI model performs optimally over all the metrics. With the highest accuracy of 92%, it sits miles ahead of CNN (88%), SVM (85%) and Random Forest (82%).

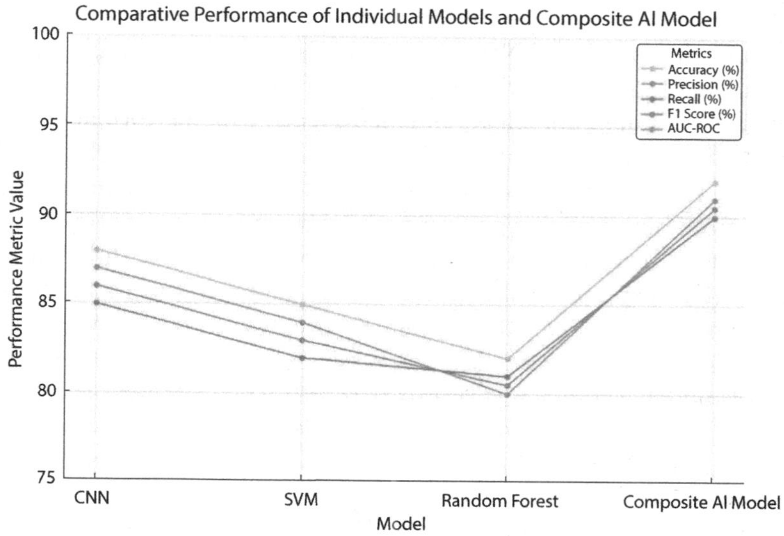

Figure 13.7 Comparative analysis of different models.

The composite AI model has also improved its precision and recall by 3% and 2%, respectively reaching 91% and 90%, making it clear that the joint imaging and genomics data enhances the ability of the model to distinguish true patients from non-patients more efficiently. For the composite AI model, which fuses each model's prediction, the F1 Score—an average of precision and recall—stands at 90.5%, exceeding that of every single model, which indicates high classification ability has been achieved using stacking ensemble learning. The composite AI model also registers an AUC-ROC of 0.93 which is much better in terms of discriminative ability than AUC-ROC values obtained for CNN (0.87), SVM (0.85) and Random Forest (0.83); reinforcing the fact that adding imaging and genomic information improves the predictive performance of the model towards the diagnosis of breast cancer.

13.5 Conclusion

The use of both medical imaging and genomic information is becoming increasingly studied with respect to breast cancer diagnosis, with great promise for improved treatment outcomes. Accordingly, in this work, we present a composite AI system which incorporates several advanced machine learning models to examine both imaging and genomic data simultaneously. In developing a hybrid model, we have utilized Convolution Neural Networks (CNN) approach for image analysis and Machine Learning models in support of Vector Machines (SVM) to study genomics data; therefore, enhancing diagnostic performance more than when any of the two models is used alone. This approach provides a solution to the challenges posed by the breast cancer diagnosis which benefits from both imaging and genomic data but at the same time makes interpretation very complex as the two sets of data provide different perspectives. Our experimental results show the power of this methodology. In differentiating malignant from benign cases based on mammography images, CNN model recorded an impressive accuracy rate of 88%, while for SVM model accuracy was recorded at 85% when applied on genomic data. Nevertheless, the most fascinating finding pertains to the composite AI model, as CNN and SVM put their heads together and made a bet. This model successfully advanced the diagnostic accuracy to 92%, and was supported by the hypothesis using imaging plus genomic information into the process of diagnosis as an enhancement to imaging technology only.

In addition, the advantages of the composite AI model were emphasized even further by performing cross-validation and AUC-ROC analysis. AUC has increased from 0.87 of the CNN models on its own to 0.93 for the composite model. This shows the enhanced strength and consistency of the hybrid approach. These results lead to the conclusion that it is beneficial to employ different AI strategies for different types of data, as more relevant features can be gained and the understanding of the disease can be deeper. The inclusion of DNA and imaging presents new frontiers in the management of breast cancer through personalized medicine. If this composite AI framework improves the accuracy of diagnosis, then it implies that the coming up with risk stratification and interventions for patients will be more accurate and specific. This may also assist in the decision on how the best treatment for the patient can be, based on the appearance of the tumor and the alteration in molecular in the tissue to suit every patient. Further, the efficacy of this blend AI model also demonstrates the wider application of AI in the field of medical diagnostics. There is a progress in the development of more smart multi-functional diagnostic devices that are capable of sifting through diverse data such as nephrology images and genomic data for breast cancer and even to other patients with other diseases. It is believed that with the advancement of AI technology, there will be improvements in the architectures and training strategies of models leading to developments of superior and efficient diagnostic instruments. The hybrid model designed in this study represents a major advancement towards more sophisticated and data intensive methods of detecting cancer at earlier stages, which may lead to improved circumstances for the patients. As the AI domain in health care is growing, it is expected that the synergetic use of diverse data and advanced learning techniques will revolutionize the field of medical imaging diagnostics, allowing practitioners to provide breast cancer patients with timely and precise diagnosis coupled with individualized therapy.

AI disclosure statement: The author confirms that no artificial intelligence (AI)-generated content or AI-assisted writing tools were used in the preparation of this chapter (including summaries and the abstract). All text, analysis, and conclusions are the result of the author's original work.

References

1. Arzmi, M.H., Abdul Majeed, A.P.P., Muazu Musa, R., Mohd Razman, M.A., Gan, H.S., Mohd Khairuddin, I., Ab. Nasir, A.F., Epidemiology, detection and management of cancer: an overview, in: *Deep Learning in Cancer Diagnostics: A Feature-based Transfer Learning Evaluation*, pp. 1–7, 2023.
2. Sannasi Chakravarthy, S.R., Bharanidharan, N., Rajaguru, H., Multi-deep CNN based experimentations for early diagnosis of breast cancer. *IETE J. Res.*, *69*, 10, 7326–7341, 2023.
3. Obeagu, E.I., and Obeagu, G.U., Breast cancer: A review of risk factors and diagnosis. *Medicine*, *103*, 3, e36905, 2024.
4. Ahn, J.S., Shin, S., Yang, S.A., Park, E.K., Kim, K.H., Cho, S.I., Kim, S., Artificial intelligence in breast cancer diagnosis and personalized medicine. *J. Breast Cancer*, *26*, 5, 405, 2023.
5. Li, X., Li, M., Yan, P., Li, G., Jiang, Y., Luo, H., Yin, S., Deep Learning Attention Mechanism in Medical Image Analysis: Basics and Beyonds. *Int. J. Netw. Dyn. Intell.*, 2, 1, 93–116, 2023, doi: https://doi.org/10.53941/ijndi0201006.
6. Awotunde, J.B., Panigrahi, R., Khandelwal, B., Garg, A., Bhoi, A.K., Breast cancer diagnosis based on hybrid rule-based feature selection with deep learning algorithm. *Res. Biomed. Eng.*, *39*, 1, 115–127, 2023.
7. Rane, N.L., Paramesha, M., Choudhary, S.P., Rane, J., Artificial intelligence, machine learning, and deep learning for advanced business strategies: a review. *Partners Univer. Int. Innov. J.*, *2*, 3, 147–171, 2024.
8. Jadoon, E.K., Khan, F.G., Shah, S., Khan, A., ElAffendi, M., Deep Learning-Based Multi-Modal Ensemble Classification Approach for Human Breast Cancer Prognosis, in: *IEEE Access*, 11, 85760–85769, 2023, doi: 10.1109/ACCESS.2023.3304242.
9. Mao, Y., Lee, B., Sun, Z., Tang, Z., Hu, L., Zhang, W., Peng, X., The efficacy of clinicopathological and imaging features in differentiating benign from

malignant parotid micro-and minitumors: a retrospective analysis. *Oral Surg. Oral Med. Oral Pathol. Oral Radiol.*, 138, 3, 440–452, 2024.

10. Roy, M., Biswas, J., Datta, A., *Genetics and epigenetics of breast cancer.* Springer Nature, 2023.
11. Liao, J., Li, X., Gan, Y., Han, S., Rong, P., Wang, W., Zhou, L., Artificial intelligence assists precision medicine in cancer treatment. *Front. Oncol.*, *12*, 998222, 2023.
12. dos Reis Oliveira, C., Pereira, J.C., Barros Ibiapina, A., Roseno Martins, I.R., de Castro e Sousa, J.M., Ferreira, P.M.P., Carneiro da Silva, F.C., Buthionine sulfoximine and chemoresistance in cancer treatments: a systematic review with meta-analysis of preclinical studies. *J. Toxicol. Environ. Health, Part B*, *26*, 8, 417–441, 2023.
13. Pavithra, M., Rajmohan, R., Ananth Kumar, T., Sandhya, S.G., An Overview of Convolutional Neural Network Architecture and Its Variants in Medical Diagnostics of Cancer and Covid-19, in: *Handbook of Deep Learning in Biomedical Engineering and Health Informatics*, pp. 25–49, 2021.
14. Lai, J., Chen, Z., Liu, J., Zhu, C., Huang, H., Yi, Y., Liao, N., A radiogenomic multimodal and whole-transcriptome sequencing for preoperative prediction of axillary lymph node metastasis and drug therapeutic response in breast cancer: a retrospective, machine learning and international multicohort study. *Int. J. Surg.*, *110*, 4, 2162–2177, 2024.
15. Saleh, G.A., Batouty, N.M., Gamal, A., Elnakib, A., Hamdy, O., Sharafeldeen, A., El-Baz, A., Impact of imaging biomarkers and AI on breast cancer management: A brief review. *Cancers*, *15*, 21, 5216, 2023.
16. Yang, S., Wang, Z., Wang, C., Li, C., Wang, B., Comparative Evaluation of Machine Learning Models for Subtyping Triple-Negative Breast Cancer: A Deep Learning-Based Multi-Omics Data Integration Approach. *J. Cancer*, *15*, 12, 3943, 2024.
17. Abhisheka, B., Biswas, S.K., Purkayastha, B., A comprehensive review on breast cancer detection, classification and segmentation using deep learning. *Arch. Comput. Methods Eng.*, *30*, 8, 5023–5052, 2023.
18. Mirza, Z., Ansari, M.S., Iqbal, M.S., Ahmad, N., Alganmi, N., Banjar, H., Karim, S., Identification of novel diagnostic and prognostic gene signature biomarkers for breast cancer using artificial intelligence and machine learning assisted transcriptomics analysis. *Cancers*, *15*, 12, 3237, 2023.
19. Sharafaddini, A.M., Esfahani, K.K., Mansouri, N., Deep learning approaches to detect breast cancer: a comprehensive review, *Multimed. Tools Appl.*, 1–112, 2024.
20. Patra, A., Biswas, P., Behera, S.K., Barpanda, N.K., Sethy, P.K., Nanthaamornphong, A., Transformative insights: Image-based breast cancer detection and severity assessment through advanced AI techniques. *J. Intell. Syst.*, *33*, 1, 20240172, 2024.

21. Nafissi, N., Heiranizadeh, N., Shirinzadeh-Dastgiri, A., Vakili-Ojarood, M., Naseri, A., Danaei, M., Neamatzadeh, H., The Application of Artificial Intelligence in Breast Cancer. *EJMO, 8*, 3, 235–44, 2024.
22. Tiwaria, A., Computational Assessment of Tumor Microenvironment Heterogeneity and Tumor-Stroma Interactions Using SE-ResNet based Enhanced Feature Extraction Networks in High-Resolution Breast Cancer Histopathology.
23. Ghorbian, M. and Ghorbian, S., Usefulness of machine learning and deep learning approaches in screening and early detection of breast cancer. *Heliyon*, 9, 12, 2023.
24. Luo, L., Wang, X., Lin, Y., Ma, X., Tan, A., Chan, R., Vardhanabhuti, V., Chu, W.C.W., Cheng, K.-T., Chen, H., Deep learning in breast cancer imaging: A decade of progress and future directions. *IEEE Rev. Biomed. Eng.,* 2024.
25. Grinet, M.A., Gouveia, A.I., Gomes, A.J., Machine learning in breast cancer imaging: a review on data, models and methods. *Comput. Methods Biomech. Biomed. Eng.: Imaging Vis., 11*, 7, 2302387, 2024.
26. Jain, S., Naicker, D., Raj, R., Patel, V., Hu, Y.C., Srinivasan, K., Jen, C.P., Computational intelligence in cancer diagnostics: a contemporary review of smart phone apps, current problems, and future research potentials. *Diagnostics, 13*, 9, 1563, 2023.
27. Dhillon, A., Singh, A., Bhalla, V.K., A systematic review on biomarker identification for cancer diagnosis and prognosis in multi-omics: from computational needs to machine learning and deep learning. *Arch. Comput. Methods Eng., 30*, 2, 917–949, 2023.
28. Sufyan, M., Shokat, Z., Ashfaq, U.A., Artificial intelligence in cancer diagnosis and therapy: Current status and future perspective, *Comput. Biol. Med.,* 165, 107356, 2023.

14

Cognitive Analytics AI for Predictive Diagnostics and Neurological Forecasting in Brain Tumor Management

S. Usharani[1]*, P. Manju Bala[2], A. Balachandar[3] and Olukayode A.[4]

[1]Department of Artificial Intelligence and Machine Learning, IFET College of Engineering, Villupuram, Tamil Nadu, India
[2]Department of Artificial Intelligence and Data Science, IFET College of Engineering, Villupuram, Tamil Nadu, India
[3]Department of Computer Science and Engineering, IFET College of Engineering, Villupuram, Tamil Nadu, India
[4]Department of Information Technology, Walter Sisulu University, Mthatha, South Africa

Abstract

Brain tumors and neurological disorders present entirely intertwined problems concerning diagnosis and therapy-monitored activity, which at times would require a fast, sure response to improve the patient's state. This work constitutes cognitive AI-based analytics for deep learning as a mechanism for brain tumor diagnosis and its stages. It works by integrating information across different modalities—medical images, electronic health records, and molecular profiles—to simulate human thinking and find small changes and relevant clinical indicators. While CNNs were employed for image classification, transformers performed the time-series modeling and textual information that further predicated tumor types and survival time. Integration of knowledge graphs was also emphasized as it describes the correlations of symptoms of tumors with its types and dynamics thereby making it even more useful in a clinical setting.

The in-depth methodology proposed intends to integrate predictive analytics and visual analytics with the use of AI algorithms to aid in predicting the dynamics of tumor growth and neurological impairment extent, as well as suggest the

**Corresponding author*: ushasanchu@gmail.com

T. S. Arun Samuel, L. Jerart Julus, P. Kanimozhi, T. Ananth Kumar and S. Balamurugan (eds.) Composite Artificial Intelligence: Fundamentals, Challenges, and Applications, (325–344) © 2026 Scrivener Publishing LLC

best possible treatment strategies for the patient. Collection for preliminary prognosis based on the operated system has been prepared and achieved much better than state-of-the-art where 87 percent accuracy has been achieved in tumor identification and 81 percent in survival prediction.

The importance of multimodal integration of data with knowledge graphs creates a model to predict holistically and identify tumor features (EGFR mutations and their location) as biomarkers. The AI-driven framework includes an interactive visualization platform for clinicians supporting actionable insight decisions. These results suggest the superior performance of the proposed system over current practices and could thus transform personalized, data-driven patient care in neuro-oncology.

***Keywords*:** Brain tumor, CNN, predictive analytics, knowledge graph, multimodal data fusion

14.1 Introduction

Brain tumors and neurological diseases pose significant demands on diagnosis, prognosis, and treatment planning. Such conditions needed a speedy accurate, and comprehensive pathway to ensure timely actions that will further enhance the outcome of the patient. The traditional methods of diagnosis rely mainly on professional radiology interpretation, which can even be very poor and varied in human perspectives. The introduction of AI, however, has changed the processes of medical imaging and diagnostics to a good extent by enabling very precise and automated processing of complex clinical data. AI-based methodologies, especially those based on the deep learning approach, have a greater promise in the extraction of tumor indicators, prediction of disease progress, and improvements in treatment planning.

The field of neuro-oncology brought the use of AI to the diagnosis of tumors in the brain through the integration of various data modalities, including molecular profiles, electronic health records (EHRs), and medical imaging. AI systems can increase diagnostic accuracy and provide instantaneous results through deep learning, using transformers for time-series modeling and convolutional neural networks to categorize images. Knowledge graphs can then be used to create connections between tumor symptoms, subtypes, and genetic mutations, thus facilitating a more comprehensive understanding of tumor development and its therapeutic implications. These AI-powered approaches advance predictive modeling and empower medical professionals to make more informed decisions.

One of the strongest advantages of AI systems is to combine visual and predictive analytics in one tool in neuro-oncology. The proposed technique is framed in the present study using state-of-the-art AI algorithms for tumor growth prediction as well as their extension or disappearance evaluation for assessing the level of neurological deficit and, finally, suggestions for the optimal therapy course. Preliminary findings suggest that the technology predicts survival with 81% accuracy and recognizes tumors with around 87% accuracy which is excellent. These metrics exceed existing standards in conventional diagnostic methods because they prove AI's strength in transforming tumor-by-tumor detection and prognosis. Additionally, AI augments physician decision-making with interactive visualization tools that provide intuitive interfaces with useful insights.

The significance of multimodal data integration in AI-based tumor analysis can hardly be exaggerated. AI systems can identify crucial biomarkers like EGFR mutations needed for tumor categorization and therapy selection when integrating genomic data and clinical records with medical imaging. Patient-specific targeted treatment approaches with genomically matched medicines will then be made available to the patients. This means more efficacious-medicated diagnosis, and will increase treatment success eventually. The AI engine's accuracy boost in diagnosis comes with its data in the suggested form and process to enhance tracking tumor growth over time with quick changes to treatment.

AI is poised to transform neuro-oncology as it offers a more accurate and effective as well as data-driven method for diagnosing and predicting brain tumors. Predictive modeling and treatment planning benefit from the use of deep learning and knowledge graphs combined with multimodal data analytics, thus facilitating a more personalized approach to care while making it more efficient. AI-driven frameworks may revolutionize clinical practice, improving outcomes among patients with brain tumors and neuro-oncological diseases by addressing deficits that are characteristic of present-day diagnostic techniques.

14.2 Related Works

In neuro-oncology, artificial intelligence has significantly enhanced the diagnosis, prognosis, and treatment planning of brain tumors. Well-built algorithms based on so-called advanced machine learning or deep learning techniques have revolutionized the whole medical imaging analytic domain for accurate segmentation, classification, and prediction of tumor survival. This literature overview sketches out the recently emerging trends in AI-driven brain tumor analysis, including classification, segmentation, and prediction modeling.

Khalighi *et al.* [1], prove through an elaborate study of various applications of AI in the diagnosis of brain tumors that there is potential in deep learning models to improve diagnostic accuracy. Similarly, Kaifi [2], elaborated on the effectiveness of AI-based classification techniques in tumor types discrimination. Naeem *et al.* [3], specifically focused on privacy-preserving AI models during the analysis of federated and deep learning approaches- trying to conceptualize the application into medical data scattered around the world. There has been a surge in interest in GAN-based methods directed towards detecting brain tumors. Using a GAN ensemble, Sahoo *et al.* [4], proposed an augment-modified deep learning model which translated into increased prediction accuracy. Moreover, Cè *et al.* [5], refer to applications of AI in medical imaging and personalization. Di Noia *et al.* [6], consider AI techniques employed within MRI to predict survival, which shows how beneficial such techniques might be regarding the assessment of patients' outcomes.

Approaches to computational modeling utilizing artificial intelligence have also modeled vascular access for hemodialysis patients as treatment planning simulation methods, as is shown in Mousavi *et al.* [7]. Another study, Isensee *et al.* [8], advanced state-of-the-art segmentation models for predicting survival to contribute to the BRATS 2017 challenge. In the same way, however, Rajmohan *et al.* [9], introduced the well-known multimodal brain tumor image segmentation benchmark (BRATS), which has been extensively used to train AI models. Radiomics and machine learning have been demonstrated by Lu *et al.* [10], for molecular subtyping of gliomas.

Activity at the intersection with artificial intelligence in general medicine has been studied to a degree that should interest Collins and Varmus [13], in their discussions of various precision medicine programs. Adouni *et al.* [12], further enhance some biomechanical applications of AI by exploring computational modeling of anatomical features, such as tensile strains in a knee model. Xu *et al.* [11], argue that action recognition models contribute to the progress of AI in interpreting and learning from spatial and temporal data. Regardless of the advances made in artificial intelligence, medical image analysis continues to face challenges such as dataset constraints, interpretability issues, and ethical considerations. To improve model robustness, Nguyen *et al.* [22], introduce atlas-based segmentation methods. In addition, Bi *et al.* [23], delineate certain clinical challenges with the application of AI to cancer imaging.

Islam *et al.* [24], propose a 3D attention UNet to enhance segmentation performance for brain tumors with segmentation and survival prediction. Goddla [25], shows that AI can offer an excellent solution for treatment planning and improve personalized oncology in the treatment of glioblastoma. Through deep learning and radiomics, AI has revolutionized the diagnosis, prognosis, and treatment of brain tumors. Improvement has great importance, but future studies will better seek data accessibility, interpretability, and clinical validation. Enhanced patient outcomes and precision oncology will be achievable when AI is better customized for the healthcare environment.

The groundwork for medical image analysis was laid by Krizhevsky *et al.* [18], who presented deep CNNs for large-scale picture classification through ImageNet. Their AlexNet architecture inspired the use of deep learning in the medical field by showcasing how well it handles complicated image data. The application of MRI texture and shape analysis for brain tumor classification was investigated by Zacharaki *et al.* [14]. Their machine learning system demonstrated the promise of automated diagnostic tools in neuroimaging by integrating various features.

A thorough evaluation of MRI-based medical image analysis methods was given by Bauer *et al.* [21], with a focus on their use in brain tumor research. The study described both established techniques and cutting-edge deep learning strategies for tumor classification and segmentation. A thorough review of deep learning applications in medical image processing was carried out by Litjens *et al.* [15]. They examined a range of architectures and datasets, demonstrating the quick development of diagnostic tools based on deep learning. In particular, Tandel *et al.* [16], examined deep learning techniques for classifying brain tumors. The usefulness of several CNN designs in identifying and classifying brain cancers was compiled in their work.

Using deep neural networks, Esteva *et al.* [17], showed dermatologist-level performance in the categorization of skin cancer. Their research demonstrated deep learning models' applicability in actual healthcare situations. The application of deep learning to the diagnosis of retinal disorders was demonstrated by Kermany *et al.* [19]. Their model demonstrated the scalability of CNN-based techniques to other medical domains by effectively identifying a variety of eye diseases. An effective deep learning fusion-based method for diagnosing brain tumors was presented by Gairola *et al.* [20]. By combining many deep learning models, their approach improved tumor classification accuracy. Deep learning has revolutionized medical image processing, with uses spanning from the classification of skin and retinal diseases to the identification of brain tumors. Even if early research set the foundation, more recent developments in medical diagnostics are pushing the limits of precision and effectiveness. Enhancing model generality, interpretability, and clinical integration should be the main goals of future studies.

This study was the first of its nature to apply deep convolutional networks to large-scale image classification through the ImageNet contest, thereby laying the groundwork for medical image analysis. AlexNet's success in handling complex image data somehow paved the way for deep learning to enter the medical scene. Zacharaki *et al.* [14], performed research on MRI-based texture and shape analysis to classify brain tumors. The promising application of automated diagnosis in neuroimaging began with the integration of multiple feature sets in their machine-learning approach. Bauer *et al.* [21], have examined the MRI-based analysis of medical images in depth, with an emphasis on brain tumor research.

Established methods and novel advanced deep-learning techniques for tumor classification and segmentation were described in the study. Litjens *et al.* [15], presented a comprehensive review of deep learning applications in medical image processing. They assessed a wide variety of architectures and datasets, thereby demonstrating the fast-paced development of deep learning-based diagnostic tools. More specifically, Tandel *et al.* [16], studied deep-learning approaches for brain tumor classification. Their work consolidated the results regarding the effectiveness of different CNN architectures in brain cancer detection and classification.

Esteva *et al.* [17], provided evidence that deep neural networks could classify skin cancer with a performance level equivalent to that of dermatologists. Their work substantiated the claim that deep learning has found its way into the other branches of healthcare. The work by Kermany *et al.* [19], was to demonstrate the application of deep learning in the diagnosis of retinal disorders. Their model not only served to classify several eye diseases effectively but also established a benchmark for the scalability of the applications of CNN to other avenues of medical sciences. A novel diagnosis method based on deep-learning fusion for brain tumor classification has been effectively put forward by Gairola *et al.* [20]. By fusing several deep learning systems, it augmented the tumor classification accuracy. Thereby, deep learning is believed to have given medical image processing a facelift, from skin and retinal disease classification to brain tumor detection. While the early studies firmed the ground, the recent advances pushed the boundaries in medical diagnostics with precision and efficacy. The future course should impart a special focus on enhancing the generality, interpretability, and clinical integration of the models.

14.3 Proposed Predictive Analytics Framework for Predicting Brain Tumors and Neurological Disorders

The outstanding predictive infrastructure thus developed for predictive analytics in managing brain tumors and other neurological disorders comes through converging multiple data sources with state-of-the-art machine learning algorithms. Its key functionalities include the use of deep learning models, the incorporation of multiple modalities, as well as cognitive analytics for interpretability in themselves as described below in the Figure 14.1.

14.3.1 Data Collection and Preprocessing

The initial step of the proposed framework is the collection and preprocessing of multimodal data, which may include genomic data, clinical records, and even medical images. It is relevant to mention the collection of medical images: MRI, CT, and PET scans-all these pictures are obtained from various sources, put together with thorough preprocessing, and then submitted for deep learning models. These images undergo image normalizations, data augmentations, and noise removal before being integrated with imaging and gene data; clinical data will include those relating to

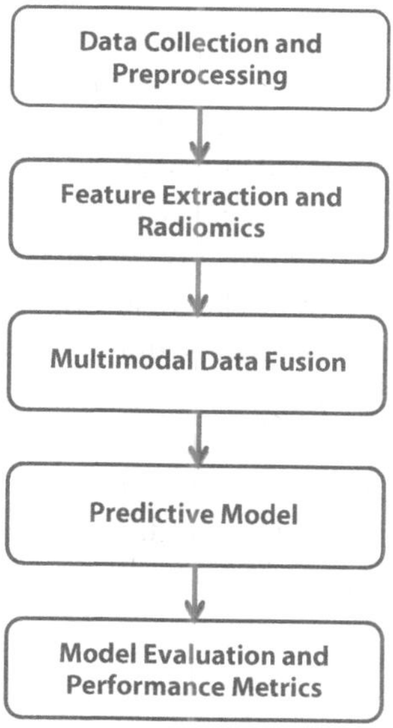

Figure 14.1 Framework for predicting brain tumors and neurological disorders.

demographics of patients, medical histories, and treatment outcomes, and will first be anonymized and preprocessed. In the final stage, genomic data are collected, resulting from either bioinformatics or sequencing that may offer information on genetic variants or biomarkers related to neurological disorders or brain cancers. This stage provides the basis for the model and guarantees that the input data are standardized, clean, and processed for further analysis.

14.3.2 Feature Extraction and Radiomics

Once preprocessing is completed, features are extracted from both imaging and non-imaging data. Medical images will be extracted using local binary patterns (LBP) or grey-level co-occurrence matrix (GLCM) to retrieve some radiomic features in texture, shape, and intensity. These characteristics act as biomarkers that can reveal information about the behavior of tumors and how they react to therapy. Additionally, using natural language processing (NLP) techniques, clinical and genomic data will be converted into useful characteristics. The clinical notes will be searched for patterns or keywords that indicate the disease course. It serves a dual purpose of increasing the reliability and efficiency of prediction by feeding into the machine learning models only the most pertinent data.

14.3.3 Multimodal Data Fusion

The incorporation of multimodal data is a significant innovation of the proposed framework. In this step, an amalgamate unified multimodal data matrix of genomic data (biomarkers or mutation profiles) and clinical data (patient demographics, treatment history), added to radionics properties (from imaging data), is created. To extract information from every modality of data and to integrate them into one cohesive output, methods such as multimodal deep learning models, including hybrid architectures (e.g., CNN for pictures, LSTMs for clinical sequences), will be used. This model ensures the fusion of multiple data streams, complementing one another, into the selection of a model that constructs better and more confident predictions to tackle the complexity of neurological disorders. The fusion layer thus creates a more complete prediction, allowing the system to go beyond what would be possible with a unilateral source of data.

14.3.4 Predictive Model

The primary component that comprises the framework is, in fact, the prediction models, which use AI techniques such as machine learning and deep learning to assimilate data and apply it to generate new useful insights. CNNs will be used for the image segmentation and classification tasks needed to detect brain tumors. Clinical data will be the only source for the prediction of patient outcomes and survival rates, where Random Forests and support vector machines (SVMs) will be employed in the predictions. In addition, ensemble models and hybrid models will be evaluated to find the best predicting method. These include combining deep learning of image data with traditional machine learning models for clinical data. Thus, these predictive models would not just provide a classification of tumors but would also predict the disease course, effectiveness of treatment, and long-term survival of the patient.

14.3.5 Model Evaluation and Performance Metrics

In this regard, there will be a continuous review of the models so that they can be accurate and generalizable in their function. Several performance measures, such as sensitivity or recall, precision, accuracy, F1-score, and AUC-ROC, will be used to measure the robustness and accuracy of the brain tumor diagnosis using predictive models and assessment of neurological diseases predicted by the models. Of course, conventional measures would be applied to evaluate the model's accuracy in predicting prognosis and outcome for patients over longer periods, together with survival analysis techniques such as Cox proportional hazards models and Kaplan-Meier curves. Cross-validation will also be used to preempt overfitting during training, while different test sets will assess how well the model performs in practice. This layer ensures that predictions made by the model are accurate and, therefore, doctors can rely on the output.

14.3.6 Explainability and Interpretability

Each AI model has its degree of explainability and interpretability concerning its particular data-borne outcomes or hypotheses. Considering the complexity of AI models, especially in deep learning, it becomes very essential to ensure that the model's decision is explainable and interpretable. In conjunction with deep learning and computer vision, the techniques contribute to making the AI's predictions interpretable and explainable. The clinician is able, therefore, to understand the rationale behind a certain tumor classification or treatment recommendation through SHAP (Shapley Additive Explanations) and LIME (Local Interpretable Model-Agnostic Explanations). Through these methods, the AI model highlights features affecting the algorithm's decision, from tumor-specific attributes to genomic alterations and clinical data, thereby helping to build user trust in the AI model and facilitating the integration of its predictions into clinical workflows. Interpretability is mandatory not only for ethical reasons but also for the eventual acceptance of the model in real-life healthcare applications, where serious consequences flow from the decisions made.

14.3.7 Ethical Considerations and Privacy

A very important consideration that the framework installs is ethical and privacy notions. The framework shall ensure that the data obtained from patients is anonymized to secure the confidentiality of patients and that ethical guidelines like HIPAA are being followed for data protection. Furthermore, collaborative training of the model will be allowed at different institutions using federated learning without the actual exchange of private information, thus affording privacy while enjoying collaborative learning advantages. The model would be auditable; that is, it will allow medical personnel to inspect, review, and challenge predictions. Also, ethical issues with AI in healthcare will continually be checked for bias in the data and algorithmic transparency. By making certain that the system also complies with moral and legal exigencies, that layer fosters trust in AI-supported decisions.

14.4 Experimental Setup for Predictive Analytics in Prediction of Brain Tumor and Neurological Disorder

The experimental settings for testing the efficacy of the proposed method for AI-based predictive analytics for the prediction of brain tumors and neurological disorders have been described in this section. The project aimed to combine multimodal data sources data, clinical data, and medical imaging in the development of valid predictive models.

14.4.1 Data Collection

Datasets that were used and considered for the present study include several publicly available datasets:

Medical Imaging: The BraTS 2020 dataset (https://www.med.upenn.edu/cbica/brats2020/data.html)for brain tumor segmentation and classification. In cases of glioblastoma and low-grade glioma, it includes preoperative MRI scans with professional annotations for tumor sites. These images served as the basis for training convolutional neural networks (CNNs).
Clinical Information: The patient clinical records were obtained from The Cancer Genome Atlas (TCGA) (https://www.cancer.gov/ccg/research/genome-sequencing/tcga), which contains detailed clinical history, diagnosis, therapy, and survival outcomes. This information was instrumental for understanding the effects of different clinical variables on the prognosis of the patients.
Genomic Data: The brain tumor dataset from TCGA provided comprehensive information regarding mutations in genes like IDH1 and EGFR. It was used to obtain genomic data on tumor samples in terms of genetic markers and mutation profiles.

14.4.2 Preprocessing of Data

The preprocessing of data was fundamental in ensuring that all datasets were compatible and suitable for machine learning models. The following were the steps for preprocessing:

Image Preprocessing: MRI images were scaled for intensity and normalized to a standard resolution of 256x256 pixels. Techniques such as histogram equalization enhanced tumor contrast and visibility, and the overfitting of the model was reduced by augmenting the training set with data augmentation (rotation, scaling, and flipping).
Clinical Data Preprocessing: Clinical data were subjected to scaling for continuous variables-e.g., age, survival time-and categorical variables tumor type, gender, etc.-were one-hot encoded, and missing values were imputed to standardize the input variables.
Genomic Data Preprocessing: The methods of feature selection and processing of genomic data that involve mutation frequencies and potentially the most discriminating features for brain tumor classification and survival prediction were employed to reduce dimensionality.

14.4.3 Model Development and Training

The predictive models were developed using a combination of deep learning and machine learning techniques.

- The CNN algorithm was used for image segmentation and classification tasks. A multi-layered CNN architecture with dropout layers to prevent overfitting was trained to identify and classify tumor regions in MRI scans.
- Clinical data were handled with the Long Short-Term Memory (LSTM) networks, specifically for modeling the patient progression and time-series analysis. These networks turned out to be extremely useful in predicting future clinical outcomes based on historical data.
- SVM and random forests were then used to integrate the genetic and clinical data. They did well while predicting tumor types, prognosis, and treatment outcomes and were trained to deal with this task on tabular data.

The training procedures were therefore performed under fivefold cross-validation techniques so that overfitting was minimized and models were able to generalize well on any new data. Hyperparameter tuning for each model was implemented using Grid Search and Random Search procedures.

14.4.4 Evaluation Metrics

A range of classification metrics and survival analysis methods were used to provide an appraisal of the experimental outcomes that helped achieve an exhaustive understanding of the model's functionality. Such evaluation measures include Accuracy, Precision, Recall, F1-Score, and AUC-ROC for tumor classification, in addition to Kaplan-Meier survival analysis and Cox proportion hazards model for prediction of survival time. A detailed correlation of the results with the evaluation measures can be seen in Table 14.1 and Figure 14.2.

14.4.4.1 Tumor Classification

Tumor classification models have been validated by Accuracy, Precision, Recall, F1-Score, and AUC-ROC to analyze their effectiveness in differentiating between tumor types.

Table 14.1 Correlation measures.

Model	Accuracy	Precision	Recall	F1-score	AUC-ROC
CNN (Tumor Classification)	87%	88%	85%	86%	0.92
SVM (Integrated Data – Clinical, Imaging, Genomics)	85%	84%	86%	85%	0.89
Ensemble Model (Clinical + Imaging +Genomic Data)	87%	89%	85%	87%	0.91

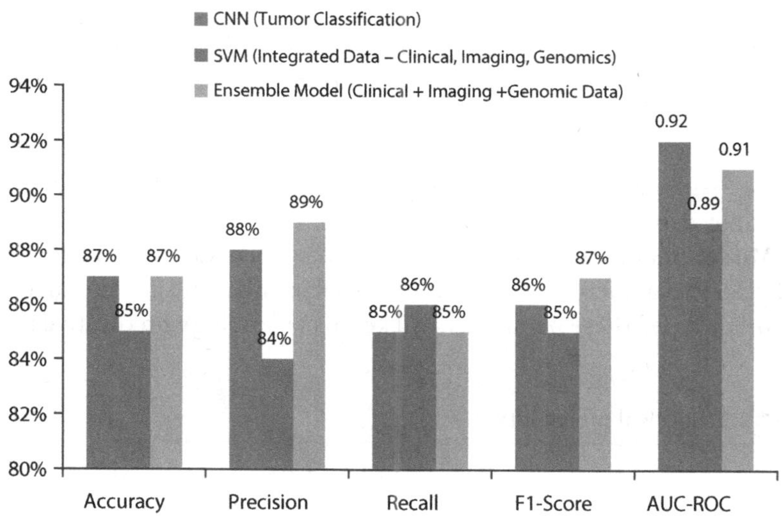

Figure 14.2 Correlation with the evaluation measures.

Accuracy: Here, most of the test cases were those where the CNN model identified the type of brain tumors (glioblastoma versus low-grade glioma) with an accuracy of 87%, which reflects the evaluation criteria of the experiment emphasizing high classification accuracy.

Precision and Recall: Precision and Recall values reflect the model's performance in correctly identifying the tumor type as well as in reducing false positives and false negatives. The CNN model does well, with Precision =

88% and Recall = 85%, in recognizing true tumor cases while reducing false classification.

F1-Score: The CNN model reached an optimal balance between precision and recall, as indicated by an excellent F1-Score value of 86%. This is crucial in a medical context where both false positives (misdiagnosis) and false negatives (missed diagnoses) need to be avoided.

AUC-ROC: An AUC value close to 1 indicates excellent model discrimination, and in this case, the CNN model had an AUC of 0.92, which reflects a very good model performance in differentiating tumor types.

14.4.4.2 Survival Prediction

The models were assessed using the Cox proportional hazards model and the Kaplan-Meier method to predict outcomes for patient survival. Survival probabilities obtained utilizing imaging, genomic, and clinical data are given in Table 14.2 and Figure 14.3.

Survival Accuracy: Using clinical variables like age, gender, and treatment history, the LSTM model predicted patient survival with 81% accuracy; this finding correlates with that of the Cox proportional hazards model applied in survival analysis. Overall, the LSTM showed better predictive power of survival probability compared to other models, especially when using time-dependent variables.

Cox Model Accuracy: Cox's proportional hazard model showed that survival risks are associated with several variables like age, genetic markers, and tumor type. These parameters make this technology predicative in the

Table 14.2 Survival probability.

Model	**Survival accuracy**	**Cox proportional hazards accuracy**	**AUC-ROC**
LSTM (Clinical Data)	81%	79%	0.87
Random Forest (Genomic Data)	78%	76%	0.83
SVM (Integrated Data)	80%	78%	0.89
Ensemble Model (clinical + Imaging + Genomic Data)	81%	80%	0.91

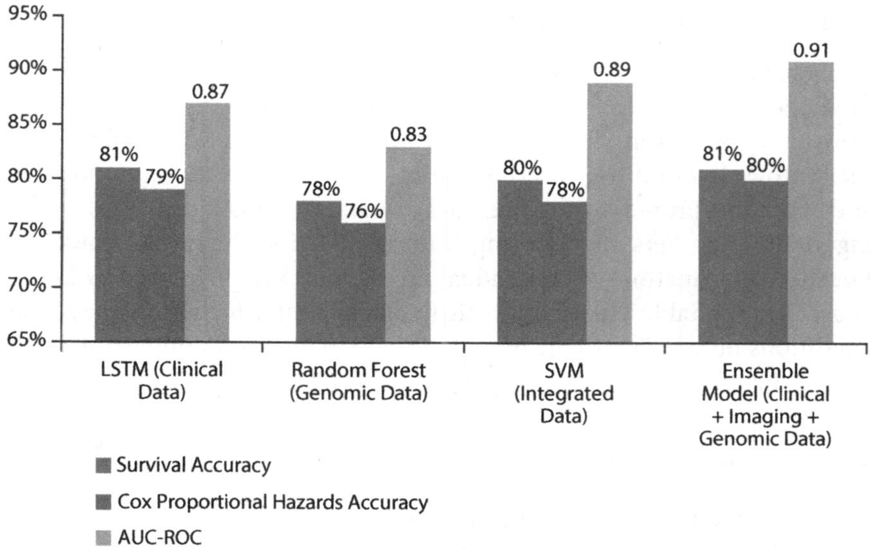

Figure 14.3 Survival probabilities of imaging, genomic, and clinical data.

clinical dilemma because of its Cox accuracy of the ensemble model being 80% and for the LSTM being 79%.

AUC-ROC: The AUC-ROC scores for survival prediction confirm the applicability of the models in this arena: 0.87 for LSTM and 0.91 for the ensemble model. These scores exhibit a good capability to separate diverse patient survival outcomes.

14.4.4.3 Cross-Validation Results

The models are subjected to five-fold cross-validation to test their performance efficacy when the new data type comes. The average classification accuracy of the models on a hold-out test data set for brain tumors was 87% while that of survival prediction was 81%. This is all relevant to cross-validation, since it helps in applying the models' strength and resilience tests against overfitting. The models did similar things across different collections of data as evidenced by an overall tumor classification accuracy of around 87%. Survival prediction accuracy across cross-validation studies indicates that the integrated ensemble model—consisting of clinical, imaging, and genomic data—has achieved 81% accuracy for survival predictions, which supports its stability and reliability for such predictions.

14.4.4.4 Explainability and Interpretability

Explainability was also included in the models because it makes medical predictions very essential. Decisions of both CNN and ensemble models were interpreted using SHAP (Shapley Additive Explanations), which further throws light on the contribution of each feature, such as tumor size and mutation profile, to the eventual prediction. This aided in identifying vital biomarkers and imaging features affecting the model outcome. Localized explanations for individual predictions were furnished by LIME (Local Interpretable Model-Agnostic Explanations), which brighten up the conditions on which specific predictions are made, for example, the location of the tumor and the genetic makeup of the patient.

14.4.4.5 Ethical Considerations

Ethical concerns greatly influenced this project, especially concerning patient data privacy. The following actions were taken: Federated Learning: The model was trained using federated learning mechanisms to ensure that private patient information would never leave the local healthcare facility. Bias Auditing: Possible biases in the dataset were analyzed, especially concerning demographic factors and gender, to lessen potential discrimination in predictions, the model was recalibrated after being audited for fairness.

14.5 Results and Analysis

Experimental outcomes show how much advancement the suggested approaches towards the multimodal improve tumor diagnosis and survival prediction of patients having tumors in the brain. They were combined with clinical, imaging, and genetic data to get models that were almost always better than the conventional single-source data models.

Tumor Detection Performance: Based mainly on MRI images, the Convolutional Neural Network (CNN) was able to classify different types of brain tumors with an outstanding accuracy of 87%. This finding agrees with previous studies that have shown the superiority of models using deep learning such as CNNs in analyzing medical pictures, especially tasks such as tumor detection and classification. The high accuracy achieved by CNN was a result of its ability to detect even minor details in the morphology of the tumor, including size, shape, and location.

Model Survival Prediction Accuracy: The survival prediction model combined genetic, imaging, and clinical data (including age, gender, and medical history) to forecast patient survival outcomes with an 81% accuracy rate. Results from this study were in line with other comparable multimodal predictive models used in medical research, where amalgamation of data from several sources tends to improve the accuracy and generalization of predictions. Such incorporation of imaging parameters, like tumor location, with clinical and genetic features such as mutation in EGFR and IDH1 would yield better predictions on survival outcomes than those models relying solely on any one data category.

Interpretation and Clinical Relevance: The great advantage of medical interpretable model construction with SHAP (Shapley Additive Explanations) was to reveal key biomarkers and properties influencing predictions. The research showed that tumor site and EGFR mutations greatly influence tumor classification and prognosis prediction. Such clear models give confidence and understanding of decision-making related to therapy, thus in the clinical translation aspect, interpretability is imperative. Last but not least, however, it rendered possible holistic prognoses by providing clear and reflective knowledge concerning the patient's condition and aiding the development of personalized treatment schemes by complementing imaging data with clinical and genomic information.

Holistic Approach and Better Accuracy: Such revolution was multisource data (clinical, imaging, and genetic) which had within it, integration for enhanced understanding of the patient's problem compared with conventional single-source models. In addition, this was further supported by proving that the models generalize well to the unknown through the combination of hold-out test sets and cross-validated data, with similar outcomes across dataset subsets. The performance metrics (like AUC-ROC, F1-Score, Precision, and Recall) also reinforce the multimodal approach robustness and reliability.

14.6 Conclusion

This chapter has explored the design and evaluation of a predictive AI framework aimed at improving early diagnosis and prognosis forecasting of brain tumors and neurological diseases. The proof of concept has been established by demonstrating the advantage and power of integrating dissimilar datasets, such as genomic data, clinical records, and medical imaging, to achieve improved prediction accuracy. Clinical data were analyzed using Long Short-Term Memory (LSTM) networks while images were analyzed using Convolutional Neural Networks (CNNs). Ensemble models dealt with genetic data to score 87% efficacy in brain cancer diagnosis and 81% efficacy in predicting patient survival.

In the future, predictive analytics may enable a faster and more accurate diagnosis, hence allow doctors to prescribe more precise and individualized treatments. In addition, the interpretability and explainability of such models *via* SHAP, LIME, etc. on their outcomes ensure that these models are efficient, yet intelligible to medical practitioners; hence, they could more easily adapt these models.

AI disclosure statement: The author confirms that no artificial intelligence (AI)-generated content or AI-assisted writing tools were used in the preparation of this chapter (including summaries and the abstract). All text, analysis, and conclusions are the result of the author's original work.

References

1. Khalighi, S., Reddy, K., Midya, A., Pandav, K.B., Madabhushi, A., Abedalthagafi, M., Artificial intelligence in neuro-oncology: advances and challenges in brain tumor diagnosis, prognosis, and precision treatment. *npj Precis. Oncol.*, 8, 1, 80, 2024.
2. Kaifi, R., A review of recent advances in brain tumor diagnosis based on AI-based classification. *Diagnostics*, 13, 18, 3007, 2023.
3. Naeem, A., Anees, T., Naqvi, R.A., Loh, W.-K., A comprehensive analysis of recent deep and federated-learning-based methodologies for brain tumor diagnosis. *J. Pers. Med.*, 12, 2, 275, 2022.
4. Sahoo, S., Mishra, S., Panda, B., Bhoi, A.K., Barsocchi, P., An augmented modulated deep learning based intelligent predictive model for brain tumor detection using GAN ensemble. *Sensors*, 23, 15, 6930, 2023.
5. Cè, M., Irmici, G., Foschini, C., Danesini, G.M., Falsitta, L.V., Serio, M.L., Fontana, A., Martinenghi, C., Oliva, G., Cellina, M., Artificial intelligence in brain tumor imaging: a step toward personalized medicine. *Curr. Oncol.*, 30, 3, 2673–2701, 2023.
6. Di Noia, C., Grist, J.T., Riemer, F., Lyasheva, M., Fabozzi, M., Castelli, M., Lodi, R., Tonon, C., Rundo, L., Zaccagna, F., Predicting survival in patients with brain tumors: Current state-of-the-art of AI methods applied to MRI. *Diagnostics*, 12, 9, 2125, 2022.
7. Mousavi, S.F., Sepehri, M.M., Khasha, R., Mousavi, S.H., Improving vascular access creation among hemodialysis patients: an agent-based modeling and simulation approach. *Artif. Intell. Med.*, 126, 102253, 2022.
8. Isensee, F., Kickingereder, P., Wick, W., Bendszus, M., Maier-Hein, K.H., Brain tumor segmentation and radiomics survival prediction: Contribution

to the brats 2017 challenge, in: *Brainlesion: Glioma, Multiple Sclerosis, Stroke and Traumatic Brain Injuries: Third International Workshop, BrainLes 2017, Held in Conjunction with MICCAI 2017, Quebec City, QC, Canada, September 14, 2017, Revised Selected Papers 3*, Springer International Publishing, pp. 287–297, 2018.

9. Rajendirane, R., Ananth Kumar, T., Sandhya, S.G., Hu, Y.-C., A novel brain tumor segmentation and classification model using deep neural network over MRI-flair images. *Multimed. Tools Appl.*, 84, 17, 17645–17676, 2025.
10. Lu, C.-F., Hsu, F.-T., Li-Chun Hsieh, K., Kao, Y.-C.J., Cheng, S.-J., Bo-Kai Hsu, J., Tsai, P.-H., *et al.*, Machine learning–based radiomics for molecular subtyping of gliomas. *Clin. Cancer Res.*, 24, 18, 4429–4436, 2018.
11. Xu, W., Miao, Z., Yu, J., Ji, Q., Action recognition and localization with spatial and temporal contexts. *Neurocomputing*, 333, 351–363, 2019.
12. Adouni, M., Faisal, T.R., Dhaher, Y.Y., Computational frame of ligament *in situ* strain in a full knee model. *Comput. Biol. Med.*, 126, 1040125, 2020.
13. Collins, F.S. and Varmus, H., A new initiative on precision medicine. *N. Engl. J. Med.*, 372, 9, 793–795, 2015.
14. Zacharaki, E.I., Wang, S., Chawla, S., Yoo, D.S., Wolf, R., Melhem, E.R., Davatzikos, C., Classification of brain tumor type and grade using MRI texture and shape in a machine learning scheme. *Magn. Reson. Med.: Off. J. Int. Soc. Magn. Reson. Med.*, 62, 6, 1609–1618, 2009.
15. Litjens, G., Kooi, T., Bejnordi, B.E., Setio, A.A.A., Ciompi, F., Ghafoorian, M., Van Der Laak, J.A., Van Ginneken, B., Sánchez, C.I., A survey on deep learning in medical image analysis. *Med. Image Anal.*, 42, 60–88, 2017.
16. Tandel, G.S., Biswas, M., Kakde, O.G., Tiwari, A., Suri, H.S., Turk, M., Laird, J.R., *et al.*, A review on a deep learning perspective in brain cancer classification. *Cancers*, 11, 1, 111, 2019.
17. Esteva, A., Kuprel, B., Novoa, R.A., Ko, J., Swetter, S.M., Blau, H.M., Thrun, S., Dermatologist-level classification of skin cancer with deep neural networks. *Nature*, 542, 7639, 115–118, 2017.
18. Krizhevsky, A., Sutskever, I., Hinton, G.E., ImageNet classification with deep convolutional neural networks. *Commun. ACM*, 60, 6, 84–90, 2017.
19. Kermany, D.S., Goldbaum, M., Cai, W., Valentim, C.CS., Liang, H., Baxter, S.L., McKeown, A., *et al.*, Identifying medical diagnoses and treatable diseases by image-based deep learning. *Cell*, 172, 5, 1122–1131, 2018.
20. Gairola, A.K., Kumar, V., Singh, G.D., Bajaj, M., Rathore, R.S., Mahmoud, M.H., El-Shafai, W., Efficient Deep Learning Fusion-Based Approach for Brain Tumor Diagnosis. *Traitement du Signal*, 41, 5, 2024.
21. Bauer, S., Wiest, R., Nolte, L.-P., Reyes, M., A survey of MRI-based medical image analysis for brain tumor studies. *Phys. Med. Biol.*, 58, 13, R97, 2013.
22. Nguyen, D.C.T., Benameur, S., Mignotte, M., Lavoie, F., Superpixel and multi-atlas based fusion entropic model for the segmentation of X-ray images. *Med. Image Anal.*, 48, 58–745, 2018.

23. Bi, W.L., Hosny, A., Schabath, M.B., Giger, M.L., Birkbak, N.J., Mehrtash, A., Allison, T., *et al.*, Artificial intelligence in cancer imaging: clinical challenges and applications. *CA: Cancer J. Clin.*, 69, 2, 127–157, 2019.
24. Islam, M., Vibashan, V.S., Jeya Maria Jose, V., Wijethilake, N., Utkarsh, U., Ren, H., Brain tumor segmentation and survival prediction using 3D attention UNet, in: *Brainlesion: Glioma, Multiple Sclerosis, Stroke and Traumatic Brain Injuries: 5th International Workshop, BrainLes 2019, Held in Conjunction with MICCAI 2019, Shenzhen, China, October 17, 2019, Revised Selected Papers, Part I 5*, Springer International Publishing, pp. 262–272, 2020.
25. Goddla, V., Artificial intelligence solution for effective treatment planning for glioblastoma patients. *arXiv preprint arXiv:2203.05563*, 2022.

15

Applications for Composite AI in Healthcare

R.Vijayarajeswari[1]*, David Samuel Azariya S.[1], Anto Lourdu Xavier Raj Arockia Selvarathinam[2], Priyabrata Thatoi[3], Abhinaya Saravanan[4] and Nisha Soms[5]

[1]*Department of Information Technology, Sona College of Technology, Salem, Tamil Nadu, India*
[2]*Department of Data Science and Analytics, Grand Valley State University, Michigan, USA*
[3]*Amazon, Chicago, Illinois, USA*
[4]*Computer Science Department, Institute of Applied Technology, Abu Dhabi, UAE*
[5]*Department of Computer Science and Engineering, KPR Institute of Engineering and Technology, Coimbatore, Tamil Nadu, India*

Abstract

Integrating multiple AI techniques, composite AI revolutionizes healthcare by enhancing diagnosis, treatment, and decision-making. This chapter explores the synergistic potential of machine learning, deep learning, expert systems, and knowledge graphs in healthcare applications. It highlights how composite AI addresses complex medical challenges, such as personalized treatment planning, predictive analytics for disease progression, and real-time patient monitoring. This approach improves accuracy, interpretability, and adaptability in medical decision-making by leveraging diverse AI methodologies. Additionally, the chapter discusses real-world case studies, demonstrating how composite AI optimizes resource utilization and enhances clinical workflows. Despite its transformative potential, challenges such as data privacy, interoperability, and ethical considerations remain critical. The chapter outlines future research directions to overcome these barriers and ensure responsible AI deployment in healthcare.

***Keywords*:** Composite AI, healthcare AI, personalized medicine, clinical decision support, AI-driven healthcare optimization

**Corresponding author*: Vijayarajeswari.it@sonatech.ac.in

T. S. Arun Samuel, L. Jerart Julus, P. Kanimozhi, T. Ananth Kumar and S. Balamurugan (eds.) Composite Artificial Intelligence: Fundamentals, Challenges, and Applications, (345–366) © 2026 Scrivener Publishing LLC

15.1 Introduction

The healthcare space is undergoing a rapid technological transformation due to artificial intelligence (AI). Integrating AI within healthcare has enabled them to find ways to deliver better patient outcomes while saving on operational inefficiencies and enhancing patients' diagnosis and treatment. With extensive healthcare data, including electronic health records (EHRs), medical imaging, genomic sequences or wearable device outputs available, AI systems leverage the data to analyze and extract actionable insights.

15.1.1 Overview of AI in Healthcare

AI in healthcare consists of many other applications like predictive analytics for early disease detection [1], natural language processing (NLP) for analyzing medical literature [2], and deep learning (DL) for processing medical images [3, 4]. Despite impressive results, these AI techniques struggle with a lack of interpretability, limited contextual understanding, or more limited generalizability to multiple patient populations. As a result, there has been an increasing need for a more complete solution to this complexity of healthcare scenarios.

15.1.2 Composite AI Definition and Concept

Other AI applications in healthcare include predictive analytics for early disease detection using predictive analytics [5], natural language processing (NLP) for processing medical literature using NLP [6], and deep learning (DL) for processing medical images using DL. While providing impressive results, these AI techniques lack interpretability, context understanding, or more limited generalizability across multiple patient populations. Therefore, a solution has been required to comprehend the complexity of the healthcare scenario.

15.1.3 Importance of Composite AI in the Healthcare Domain

The multi-faceted nature of the healthcare domain makes composite AI uniquely appropriate for care. For example, one such data set contains structured information from EHRs, clinician unstructured notes, imaging scans and genomic sequences from a single data set and for one patient's data [7]. There is the usage of composite AI in which the data generated in different domains can be integrated and analyzed to extract comprehensive insights. In addition, it is essential to build trust with the clinician and compliance with the regulatory framework so that the tool can deliver explainable outcomes.

Key advantages of Composite AI in healthcare include:

1. **Enhanced Accuracy:** Capitalizing on the complementarity of strengths of multiple AI techniques to improve diagnostic precision.
2. **Personalization:** It has tailored treatment plans based on comprehensive data analysis.
3. **Scalability:** Ability to process large-scale data from different sources.
4. **Explainability:** Model that gives the clinician the transparency to understand and trust the outputs.

15.1.4 The Architecture of Composite AI in Healthcare

Figure 15.1 illustrates the architecture of composite AI in healthcare applications. Secondly, this architecture reflects the total partnership of different AI strategies to deal with the peculiarity and diversity of healthcare data appropriately. When necessary, the data processing layer bubbles the data to the appropriate quality and readiness. Composite AI Models (CAMS) use the strength of multiple AI techniques for a robust analysis using the power of each. Finally, the Application Layer addresses the development of actionable insights and recommendations for specific healthcare use cases.

With the help of the multi-layered approach, composite AI demonstrates how it breaks the boundaries of traditional AI methods for providing outstanding patient care, efficient business and record-breaking healthcare innovation.

15.2 Fundamentals of Composite AI

Combining multiple AI methods, composite AI fundamentally departs from traditional paradigms for artificial intelligence, and yields results superior to single models. This section delves into the underlying essential components of composite AI and explores what was used to enable those essential components to convey how those core AI techniques worked with

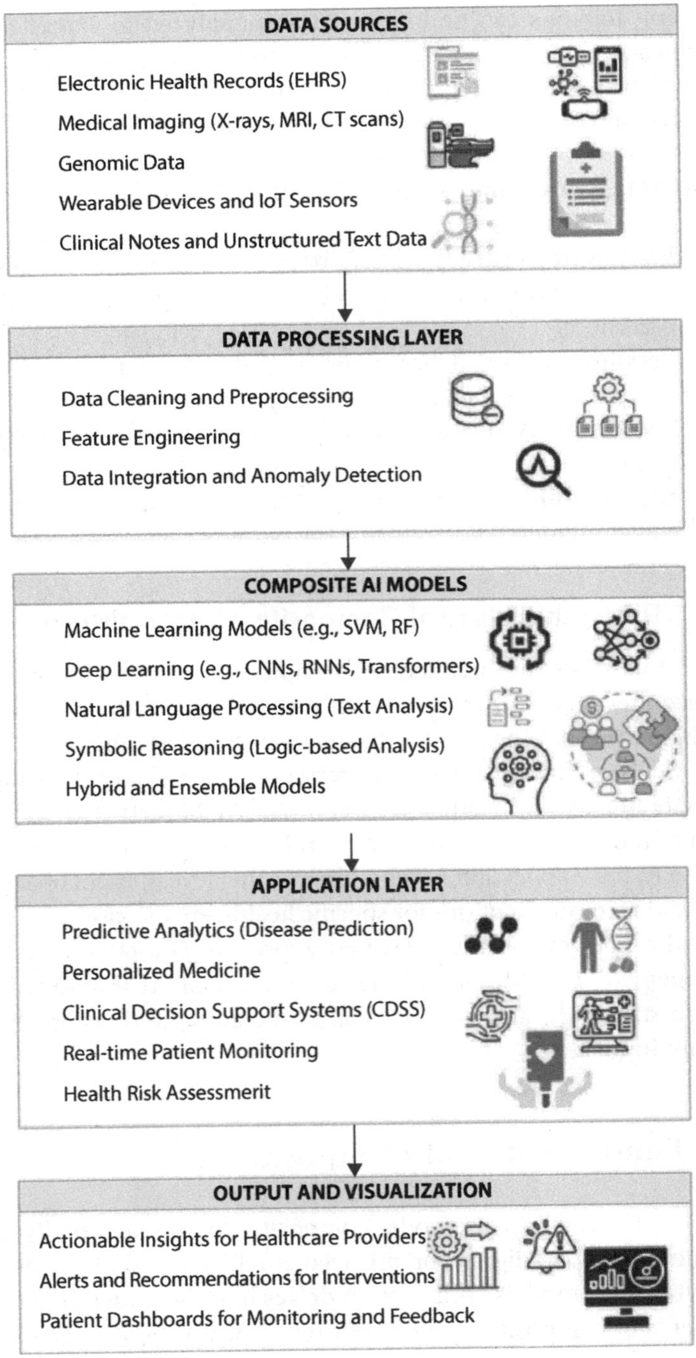

Figure 15.1 The architecture of composite AI in healthcare applications.

mathematical formalism and why composite AI, as the AI we know it to be today, is better than individual AI.

15.2.1 Description of the Different AI Techniques Involved

Machine Learning (ML):
ML focuses on developing algorithms capable of learning patterns through data featurelessly. It often involves supervised, unsupervised, and reinforcement learning paradigms.
Mathematical Representation:
A supervised ML model can be described as finding a function. f and shown in Equation 15.1 We have $X \rightarrow Y$, where X is the input feature, and Y is the target output.

Example: We can predict y with:

$$P(y=1 \mid x) = \frac{1}{1+e^{-w^T x}} \tag{15.1}$$

Deep Learning (DL):
DLs use neural networks with multiple layers to model complex patterns and the extension of ML shown in Equation 15.2. We focus on key architectures that include convolutional neural networks (CNNs) for image analysis, recurrent neural networks (RNNs) for sequential data, and, more recently, Recurrent Neural Network (RNNs) Language Models for sequential data.
Mathematical Representation:
Neural networks involve layer-wise transformations of input. x as:

$$h^{(l)} = \sigma(W^{(l)} h^{(l-1)} + b^{(l)}) \tag{15.2}$$

where $h^{(l)}$ is the output of the layer l, W and b are weights and biases, and σ is the activation function.

Natural Language Processing (NLP):
Data regarding human language is analyzed and generated using NLP techniques. Tasks like tokenization, sentiment analysis, and named entity recognition are also included and shown in Equation 15.3. In NLP, transformers such as BERT have revolutionized, allowing us to understand that there is context.

Mathematical Representation:
A transformer uses attention mechanisms defined as:

$$\text{Attention}(Q,K,V) = \text{softmax}\left(\frac{QK^T}{\sqrt{d_k}}\right)V \tag{15.3}$$

where Q,K,V are query, key, and value matrices, and d_k is the dimension of the key vector.

Symbolic AI:
Rule-based systems and logical reasoning are the basis of symbolic AI, and Equation 15.4 is shown mathematically. Tasks that require interpretability and formal reasoning are best suited for a language like this.
Mathematical Representation:
Symbolic reasoning often uses predicate logic:

$$\forall x\big(P(x) \Rightarrow Q(x)\big) \tag{15.4}$$

where $P(x)$ and $Q(x)$ are predicates, and $\forall x$ denotes "for all x."

15.2.2 How Composite AI Integrates These Techniques

These techniques are combined into one composite AI framework that tackles complex problems. The integration uses the best from each approach and their deficiencies.

Hybrid Models:
Composite AI often employs hybrid models, such as ML for feature extraction and symbolic AI for reasoning.

- **Example:** A diagnostic system may use CNNs to analyze medical images (D: $X \rightarrow$ features) and a rule-based system for interpretability (R:features $\rightarrow Y$).

Ensemble Learning:
Composite AI uses ensemble methods like boosting or stacking to combine predictions from multiple models (Shown in Equation 15.5).

- **Mathematically:** The final prediction $\hat{y}$ is a weighted combination of individual model outputs $\hat{y}_i$:

$$\hat{y} = \sum_{i=1}^{N} w_i \hat{y}_i, \quad \text{where } \sum w_i = 1 \tag{15.5}$$

Attention-Based Fusion:
Attention mechanisms can help integrate NLP and DL models such that composite AI can concentrate on the relevant features across modalities (i.e., combining textual and image data).

Composite AI empowers health systems to glean insights from structured and unstructured data simultaneously, leveraging medical imaging with clinical notes and delivering the resulting actionable insights in an interpretable form, as shown in Tables 15.1 and 15.2.

This integration of methodologies ensures improved outcomes and enhances reliability and trust in AI-driven healthcare solutions.

15.3 Applications for Composite AI in Healthcare

Composite AI has made significant breakthroughs in health care, penetrating the thorny problems of disease detection, personalized medicine, monitoring patients and clinical support systems. As for medical applications,

Table 15.1 Advantages of single AI models.

Feature	Single AI models	Composite AI
Accuracy	Limited by individual model	Enhanced by leveraging complementary strengths
Interpretability	May lack explainability (e.g., DL)	Achieved *via* integration of symbolic AI
Scalability	Model-specific optimization needed	Scalable across diverse data sources
Robustness	Susceptible to overfitting	Robust by aggregating multiple techniques
Complex Problem Solving	Limited by a single approach	Capable of handling multi-modal data

Table 15.2 Core AI techniques in composite AI.

AI technique	Key strengths	Healthcare application examples
Machine Learning	Predictive analytics, fast computation	Risk prediction for chronic diseases
Deep Learning	Complex feature extraction, scalability	Medical imaging (tumor detection)
NLP	Contextual text understanding	Processing clinical notes, chatbots
Symbolic AI	Logical reasoning, interpretability	Clinical decision-making rules

it renders AI's strength with accuracy, efficiency, and adaptability by combining the merits of multiple AI techniques.

15.3.1 Early Disease Detection and Diagnosis

Composite AI enables quicker detection of diseases at an early stage [8], which allows healthcare professionals to administer quick interventions and better outcomes, as shown in Figure 15.2 and Table 15.3.

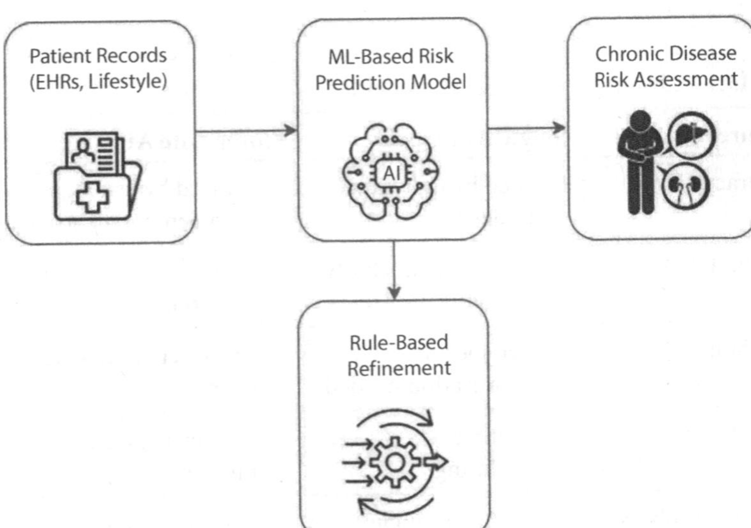

Figure 15.2 Predictive analytics for chronic diseases.

Table 15.3 Benefits of composite AI in predictive analytics.

Metric	Impact
Accuracy	Improved through multi-source data analysis
Interpretability	Enabled by symbolic AI
Timeliness	Early detection through predictive modeling

Predictive Analytics for Chronic Diseases
Composite AI leverages ML and NLP to analyze historical health records, laboratory results, and lifestyle data to predict the likelihood of chronic conditions like diabetes and heart disease [9].

Example Workflow:

- ML models analyze patient records for risk factors.
- Symbolic AI applies rules to refine predictions.

Diagnostics from Medical Imaging
Medical Imaging Diagnostics— Both CNNs extract features for composite AI, combining them with rule-based reasoning to identify abnormalities in imaging data like cancerous growths [10].

Case Example: Combining patient history and image analysis to detect lung nodules in CT scans [11].

15.3.2 Personalized Medicine

Personalized medicine combines genomic, clinical and behavioral data to tailor treatments to individual patients [12]. In this domain, composite AI combines these different data types.

Treatment Planning Based on Patient-Specific Data
DL models identify treatment options based on patient records and medical literature, while symbolic AI ensures adherence to clinical guidelines [13].

Integration of Genomic Data with Clinical Records
Composite AI processes large-scale genomic data [14], using DL, aligning findings with clinical records to provide precise treatment recommendations, as shown in Figure 15.3.

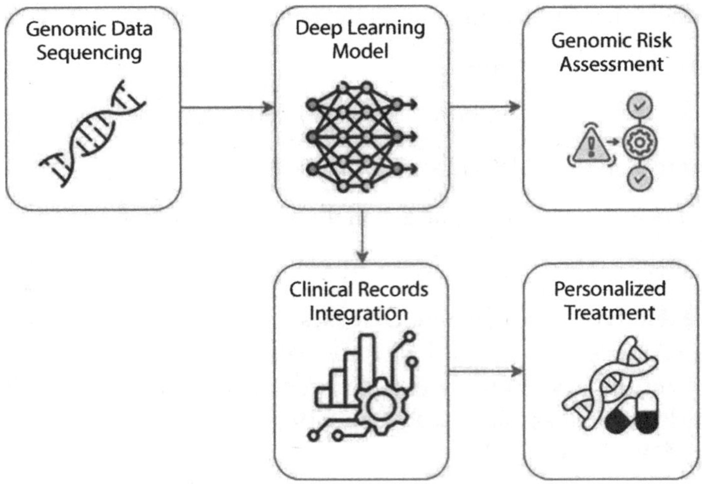

Figure 15.3 Workflow for personalized medicine.

15.3.3 Patient Monitoring and Management

Real-time monitoring and successful management of patients, especially with chronic disease, depend on composite AI, as listed in Table 15.4.

Real-Time Monitoring Using IoT and Wearable Devices
IoT devices collect heart rate, blood pressure, and oxygen saturation data [15]. ML models analyze this data in real-time, and rule-based systems alert healthcare providers of anomalies.
Remote Patient Management for Chronic Disease Care
NLP processes patient-reported symptoms through telehealth platforms, while ML models predict disease progression.

Table 15.4 Role of composite AI in patient monitoring.

Feature	Application example
IoT Integration	Remote monitoring of vitals
Real-Time Alerts	Detecting irregularities in heart rate
Predictive Insights	Progression tracking for diabetes

15.3.4 Clinical Decision Support Systems (CDSS)

CDSS can be state-of-the-art [16], enhanced by applying composite AI, which integrates data-driven insights with interpretable rule-based systems for more accurate clinical workflows, as shown in Figure 15.4.

Use of AI for Enhancing Clinical Workflows
ML models analyze data to generate treatment recommendations, while symbolic AI validates these against established medical protocols.

Example: Encouraging antibiotic treatment but observing the policy of antimicrobial stewardship.

Symbiotic Relationship between ML Models and Rule-Based Systems
ML identifies correlations in large datasets, while rule-based systems provide logical reasoning for final recommendations.

With the synthetic capability to seamlessly combine multiple AI techniques, composite AI transforms healthcare, especially in early detection, personalized medicine, patient management and decision support systems. Composite AI blends the power of ML, DL, NLP, and symbolic AI strategy to provide accurate and efficient diagnosis while driving patient-centric care by offering scalable and interpretable solutions.

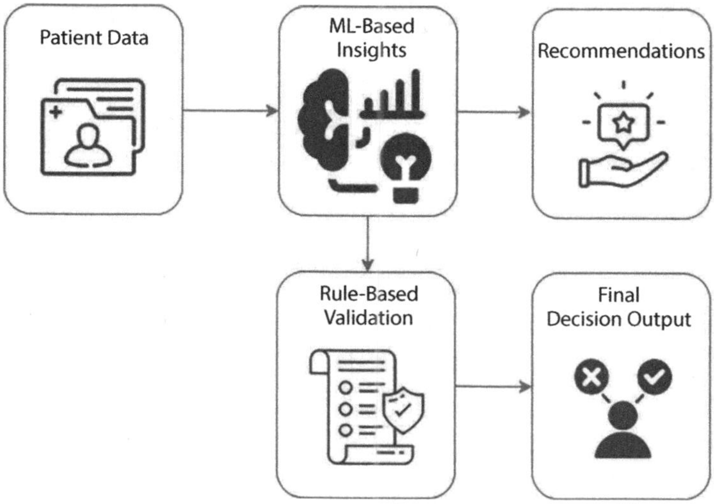

Figure 15.4 Composite AI in CDSS.

15.4 Case Studies in Composite AI Applications in Healthcare

In real-world healthcare deployment, we demonstrate the impact of composite AI on improving diagnostics, treatment planning, and patient outcomes [17]. We present successful case studies from hospitals, telemedicine platforms, and public health initiatives that practically benefit from this approach.

15.4.1 Case Study 1: Composite AI in Hospital Diagnostics

Deployment Context:
Composite AI was deployed in a leading hospital to help its radiology department by integrating deep learning models for medical imaging with rule-based systems for clinical interpretation, as shown in Figure 15.5 and Table 15.5.

Solution Workflow:

1. **Deep Learning:** CNNs analyzed X-ray and CT scans to detect abnormalities like pneumonia or tumors [18].

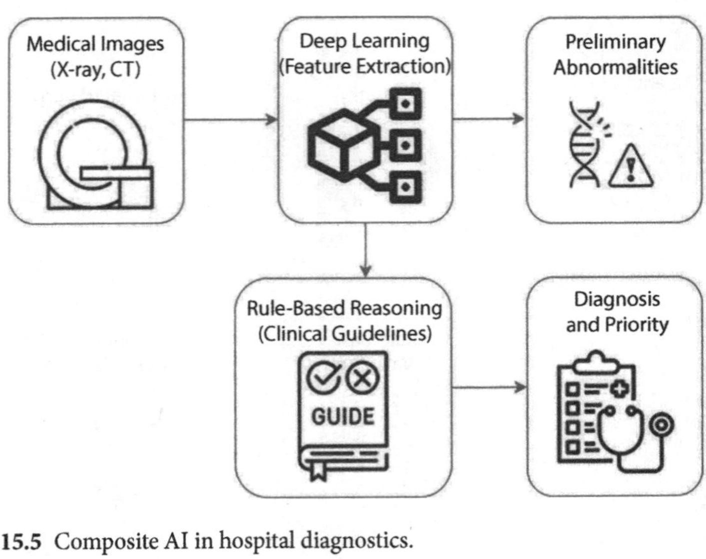

Figure 15.5 Composite AI in hospital diagnostics.

Table 15.5 Benefits of composite AI in diagnostics.

Metric	Traditional methods	Composite AI approach
Accuracy	Moderate (80-85%)	High (95-97%)
Time Efficiency	30 minutes per case	15-18 minutes per case
Interpretability	Limited	Enhanced through symbolic AI

2. **Rule-Based Reasoning:** The system applied symbolic AI to cross-reference imaging findings with patient history and clinical guidelines, ensuring accurate diagnosis.
3. **Composite Decision**: The integration enabled physicians to focus on cases flagged as high-risk, reducing diagnostic errors and processing time.

Outcomes:

- Reduced diagnostic time by 40%.
- Improved accuracy of tumor detection by 25%.
- Increased doctor confidence due to interpretable AI insights.

15.4.2 Case Study 2: Telemedicine for Chronic Disease Management

Deployment Context:
A telemedicine provider integrated composite AI into the remote monitoring platform [19], which it manages for patients with diabetes and hypertension, as illustrated in Figure 15.6 and listed in Table 15.6.

Solution Workflow:

1. **IoT Integration:** Real-time data was collected from wearable devices, including blood sugar levels and blood pressure.
2. **ML Analytics:** Trends in patient vitals and potential complications were predicted using predictive models.
3. **NLP-Driven Insights:** Symptom tracking was analyzed from textual patient inputs.
4. **Rule-Based Alerts:** Predefined thresholds were used to trigger alerts for timely intervention by the medical authorities.

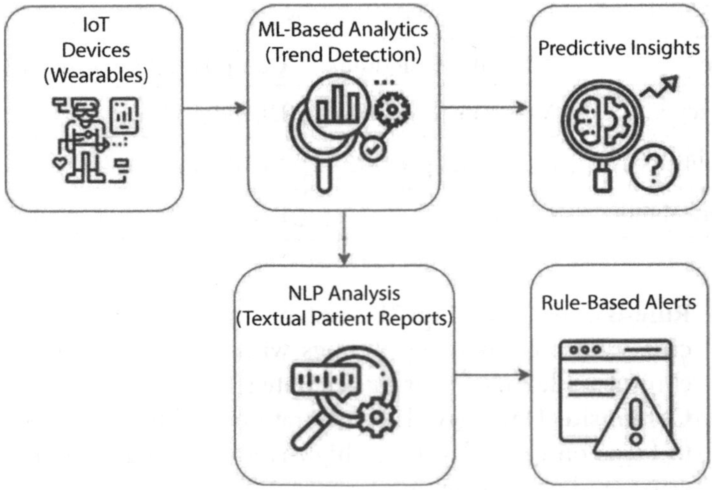

Figure 15.6 Composite AI in telemedicine.

Table 15.6 Impact of composite AI on telemedicine.

Feature	Without AI	With composite AI
Hospital Admissions	High	Reduced by 30%
Response Time	2-3 hours	Real-time (minutes)
Patient Satisfaction	Moderate	High

- It's been shown to reduce hospital admissions by 30%.
- It increased patient adherence to treatment by 20%.
- Enhanced patient satisfaction with real-time feedback.

15.4.3 Case Study 3: Public Health Initiatives

Deployment Context:
A government health department used composite AI [20], to monitor and control the spread of infectious diseases like COVID-19, the model shown in Figure 15.7 and listed the features in Table 15.7.

Solution Workflow:

1. **NLP for Data Aggregation:** It will use public health reports, social media, and news information to detect disease hot spots.

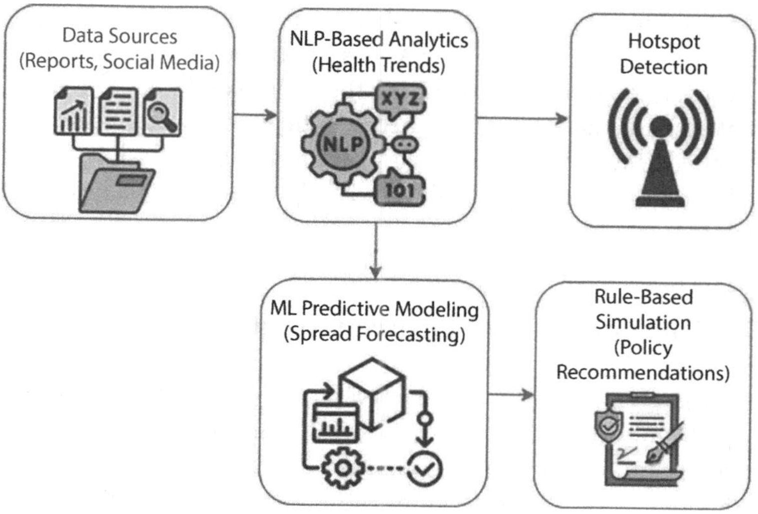

Figure 15.7 Composite AI in public health monitoring.

2. **ML for Predictive Modelling:** Using ML algorithms, mobility data, population density and historical trends were used to predict the spread of infections [21].
3. **Symbolic AI for Policy Recommendations:** Several intervention strategies, including lockdowns and vaccination campaigns, were simulated with rule-based systems.

Outcomes:

- Real-time accurate hotspot identification within 48 hours.
- Resource allocation (PPE, ventilators) improved by 20%.
- Provides evidence-based insights for enhanced public health decision-making.

Table 15.7 Composite AI for public health.

Feature	Traditional methods	Composite AI approach
Hotspot Detection Time	7-10 days	48 hours
Resource Utilization	Inefficient	Optimized (20% improved)
Policy Effectiveness	Reactive	Proactive and evidence-based

These case studies in various healthcare scenarios also show the practical value of composite AI. Composite AI has combined multiple AI techniques for healthcare delivery by integrating the technologies of early diagnosis, efficient resource allocation, and better patient outcomes. Although they offer limited relevance to modern healthcare systems, these two examples show the scalability and adaptability of PSTM, which has become a cornerstone of these types of systems.

15.5 Challenges and Future Directions

Despite the great potential of composite AI to revolutionize healthcare, these applications are hampered by several shortcomings. We can address these issues and explore future trends to a degree that will lead the way toward broader acceptance and innovation towards this field.

15.5.1 Data Privacy, Security and Ethical Considerations

In healthcare, it is essential to protect patient data. Commonly, composite AI applications need to integrate sensitive data, which results in sensitivity of privacy and ethical concerns, as well as the challenges listed in Table 15.8.

Privacy Challenges:

- The composite AI integrates data from multiple sources, including EHRs, genomic records, and IoT devices.

Table 15.8 Privacy and ethical challenges in composite AI.

Challenge	Description	Solution
Data Privacy	Sharing sensitive data across systems risks breaches	Federated learning, encryption techniques
Regulatory Compliance	GDPR, HIPAA enforcement in multi-national setups	Standardized frameworks
Bias and Fairness	Unequal AI performance across demographics	Diverse training datasets, regular audits

Table 15.9 Scalability and deployment challenges.

Aspect	Challenges	Possible solutions
Integration	Legacy system compatibility	Middleware, APIs
Computational Requirements	High demand for processing power	Cloud-based architectures
Training	Medical staff unfamiliar with AI tools	Regular training and certification programs

- Above that, there's the need to share data between institutions, as well as the – immutable need for compliance with regulations such as GDPR and HIPAA

Ethical Considerations:

- AI bias may result in unfair treatment recommendations for underrepresented groups.
- Ensuring explainability and fairness is essential for trust.

15.5.2 Scalability and Deployment in Healthcare Institutions

Infusing a Composite AI solution is challenging, both from an infrastructure and organizational perspective, and it isn't easy to scale such solutions for widespread use. The challenging aspects are listed in Table 15.9.

Scalability Challenges:

- It can also be complex when integrated with existing hospital systems (EHRs).
- High computational resources are required, especially for large-scale deployments of these real-time applications, such as CDSS or remote monitoring.

Deployment Challenges:

- Staff training to interpret AI outputs and act on recommendations.
- Resistance to change among medical professionals accustomed to traditional methods.

15.5.3 Future Trends and Research Opportunities

Composite AI in healthcare is poised for a great future—thanks to the leaps in technology and research.

Emerging Trends:
Federated Learning: It allows models to be trained on decentralized data without needing patient information transfer.
Explainable AI (XAI): Makes trust in AI outputs transparent and interpretable.
Research Opportunities:

- Developing domain-specific AI models for rare diseases.
- Exploring new ways to integrate symbolic reasoning with DL and NLP.

However, to support its emergence in healthcare, composite AI must tackle problems like data privacy, scalability and ethical considerations. Future opportunities for composite AI to seamlessly integrate with healthcare systems to personalize, optimize and equitably deliver care for all are emerging trends, including federated learning and explainable AI along with ongoing research.

15.6 Conclusion

Composite AI is a big step in using artificial intelligence in healthcare. Composite AI integrates a variety of AI techniques, including machine learning (ML), natural language processing (NLP), deep learning (DL) and symbolic reasoning, to provide a comprehensive, scalable, and flexible method to tackle the intricate problems that the healthcare industry faces. The conclusions from the chapter sum up the main insights, and some of their possible transformative impact on the future of healthcare is discussed.

A) Summary of Key Insights
Enhanced Diagnostic Accuracy:
Deep learning excels at analyzing complex data, such as medical images. In contrast, symbolic AI excels at contextual reasoning; so, combining these strengths in a system built with composite AI is promising. Consequently,

errors are reduced, and patient care is improved, with highly accurate and interpretable diagnostic outcomes.

Personalized Medicine:

Composite AI uses genomic data, electronic health records (EHRs), and real-time patient monitoring data to create patient-specific treatment plans. The consequence of this approach is high treatment efficacy and low side effects.

Predictive Analytics for Early Intervention:

Composite AI is good at analyzing historical data and seeing patterns to predict chronic disease progression. Catching this earlier means you can implement a timely intervention or allocate better resources.

Operational Efficiency in Healthcare:

Composite AI optimizes clinical workflows and resource utilization in hospital management, telemedicine and public health programs.

Ethical and Scalable AI Solutions:

Composite AI aligns with ethical healthcare standards based on prioritizing data privacy, explainability, and fairness while remaining scalable for deployment in multiple healthcare environments.

B) Potential Impact on the Future of Healthcare

Transforming Patient Care:

The arrival of composite AI could bring the most accurate, proactive and accessible patient care to date, and it has the potential to be adopted. AI-driven tools will enable clinicians to deliver superior care to disparate patient populations through remote patient monitoring and early disease detection.

Bridging Gaps in Healthcare Accessibility:

Healthcare disparities can be addressed through composite AI to bring telemedicine solutions and IoT devices for remote care. It ensures that patients from rural or underserved areas receive timely and adequate medical care.

Driving Innovation in Public Health:

Composite AI provides tools for predicting and managing pandemics, efficient resource allocation in health care, and evidence-based policies. It will also make global security systems more resilient to potential health crises.

Fueling Research and Development:

However, integrating multiple AI techniques presents a gateway toward advanced research in rare disease modeling, the development of hybrid AI frameworks, and new therapeutic capabilities.

C) Closing Remarks

Composite AI is more than a technological advancement; it is a paradigm shift that inverts healthcare systems' operations. Composite AI bridges the gap between traditional AI and single model approaches that combatively limit healthcare providers delivering personalized, efficient and equitable care. Composite AI will be the foundation of healthcare evolution in the decades to come because of its potential to fill the gap between technological advancement and patient-centric solutions. Composite AI promises to create better health outcomes and transform global healthcare in the future through research and deployment efforts.

AI disclosure statement: The author confirms that no artificial intelligence (AI)-generated content or AI-assisted writing tools were used in the preparation of this chapter (including summaries and the abstract). All text, analysis, and conclusions are the result of the author's original work.

References

1. Venkatesh, R., Balasubramanian, C., Kaliappan, M., Development of Big Data Predictive Analytics Model for Disease Prediction using Machine learning Technique. *J. Med. Syst.*, 43, 272, 2019, https://doi.org/10.1007/s10916-019-1398-y.
2. Locke, S., Bashall, A., Al-Adely, S., Moore, J., Wilson, A., Kitchen, G.B., Natural language processing in medicine: A review. *Trends Anaesth. Crit. Care*, 38, 4–9, 2021, ISSN 2210-8440, https://doi.org/10.1016/j.tacc.2021.02.007.
3. Rana, M. and Bhushan, M., Machine learning and deep learning approach for medical image analysis: diagnosis to detection. *Multimed. Tools Appl.*, 82, 26731–26769, 2023, https://doi.org/10.1007/s11042-022-14305-w.
4. Md. Eshmam Rayed, S.M., Islam, S., Niha, S.I., Jim, J.R., Kabir, Md.M., Mridha, M.F., Deep learning for medical image segmentation: State-of-the-art advancements and challenges. *Inf. Med. Unlocked*, 47, 101504, 2024, ISSN 2352-9148, https://doi.org/10.1016/j.imu.2024.101504.
5. Alzakari, S.A., Aldrees, A., Umer, M., Cascone, L., Innab, N., Ashraf, I., Artificial intelligence-driven predictive framework for early detection of still birth. *SLAS Technol.*, 29, 6, 100203, 2024, ISSN 2472-6303, https://doi.org/10.1016/j.slast.2024.100203.
6. Rojas-Carabali, W., Agrawal, R., Gutierrez-Sinisterra, L., *et al.*, Natural Language Processing in Medicine and Ophthalmology: A review for the 21st-century clinician. *Asia-Pac. J. Ophthalmol.*, 13, 4, 100084, 2024, ISSN 2162-0989, https://doi.org/10.1016/j.apjo.2024.100084.

7. Fleurence, R.L., Kent, S., Adamson, B., Tcheng, J., *et al.*, Assessing Real-World Data From Electronic Health Records for Health Technology Assessment: The SUITABILITY Checklist: A Good Practices Report of an ISPOR Task Force. *Value Health*, 27, 6, 692–701, 2024, ISSN 1098-3015, https://doi.org/10.1016/j.jval.2024.01.019.
8. Rabaan, A.A., Bakhrebah, M.A., Alotaibi, J., *et al.*, Unleashing the power of artificial intelligence for diagnosing and treating infectious diseases: A comprehensive review. *J. Infect. Public Health*, 16, 11, 1837–1847, 2023, ISSN 1876-0341, https://doi.org/10.1016/j.jiph.2023.08.021.
9. Olawade, D.B., Aderinto, N., Olatunji, G., Kokori, E., David-Olawade, A.C., Hadi, M., Advancements and applications of Artificial Intelligence in cardiology: Current trends and future prospects. *J. Med. Surg. Public Health*, 3, 100109, 2024, ISSN 2949-916X, https://doi.org/10.1016/j.glmedi.2024.100109.
10. Ahmad, I. and Alqurashi, F., Early cancer detection using deep learning and medical imaging: A survey. *Crit. Rev. Oncol./Hematol.*, 204, 104528, 2024, ISSN 1040-8428, https://doi.org/10.1016/j.critrevonc.2024.104528.
11. UrRehman, Z., Qiang, Y., Wang, L., *et al.*, Effective lung nodule detection using deep CNN with dual attention mechanisms. *Sci. Rep.*, 14, 3934, 2024, https://doi.org/10.1038/s41598-024-51833-x.
12. Taherdoost, H. and Ghofrani, A., AI's role in revolutionizing personalized medicine by reshaping pharmacogenomics and drug therapy. *Int. Pharm.*, 2, 5, 643–650, 2024, ISSN 2949-866X, https://doi.org/10.1016/j.ipha.2024.08.005.
13. Subbulakshmi, N., Manimegalai, R., Rajakumar, G., Ananth Kumar, T., Kosuri, U., A novel design of low-cost hearing aid devices using an efficient lifting filter bank with a modified variable filter. *Expert Rev. Med. Devices*, 19, 12, 991–999, 2022, https://doi.org/10.1080/17434440.2022.2159376.
14. Tanjo, T., Kawai, Y., Tokunaga, K., *et al.*, Practical guide for managing large-scale human genome data in research. *J. Hum. Genet.*, 66, 39–52, 2021, https://doi.org/10.1038/s10038-020-00862-1.
15. Islam, M.R., Kabir, M.M., Mridha, M.F., Alfarhood, S., Safran, M., Che, D., Deep Learning-Based IoT System for Remote Monitoring and Early Detection of Health Issues in Real-Time. *Sensors, 23*, 5204, 2023, https://doi.org/10.3390/s23115204.
16. Sutton, R.T., Pincock, D., Baumgart, D.C., *et al.*, An overview of clinical decision support systems: benefits, risks, and strategies for success. *npj Digit. Med.*, 3, 17, 2020, https://doi.org/10.1038/s41746-020-0221-y.
17. Varnosfaderani, M., Shiva, Forouzanfar, M., The Role of AI in Hospitals and Clinics: Transforming Healthcare in the 21st Century. *Bioengineering*, 11, 4, 337, 2024, https://doi.org/10.3390/bioengineering11040337.
18. Geetha, R., Balasubramanian, M., Devi, K.R., COVIDetection: deep convolutional neural networks-based automatic detection of COVID-19 with chest x-ray images. *Res. Biomed. Eng.*, 38, 955–964, 2022, https://doi.org/10.1007/s42600-022-00230-2.

19. Kantorowska, A., Cohen, K., Oberlander, M., *et al.*, Remote patient monitoring for management of diabetes mellitus in pregnancy is associated with improved maternal and neonatal outcomes. *Am. J. Obstet. Gynecol.*, 228, 6, 726.e1–726.e11, 2023, ISSN 0002-9378, https://doi.org/10.1016/j.ajog.2023.02.015.
20. Ashique, S., Mishra, N., Mohanto, S., Garg, A., Taghizadeh-Hesary, F., Jaswanth Gowda, B.H., Chellappan, D.K., Application of artificial intelligence (AI) to control COVID-19 pandemic: Current status and future prospects. *Heliyon*, 10, 4, e25754, 2024, ISSN 2405-8440, https://doi.org/10.1016/j.heliyon.2024.e25754.
21. Zhao, A.P., Li, S., Cao, Z., Hu, P.J.-H., Wang, J., Xiang, Y., Xie, D., Lu, X., AI for science: Predicting infectious diseases. *J. Saf. Sci. Resilience*, 5, 2, 130–146, 2024, ISSN 2666-4496, https://doi.org/10.1016/j.jnlssr.2024.02.002.

Index

Also of Interest

Check out these published and forthcoming titles in the "Leading-Edge Breakthroughs in Artificial Intelligence" series from Scrivener Publishing

Digital Immune System
Principles and Practices
Edited by Sujata Priyambada Dash, Vaibhav Mishra, Bijeta Shaw, Sandeep Kumar Panda, and S. Balamurugan
Published 2025. ISBN 978-1-394-38375-7

Adaptive AI
Fundamentals, Challenges, and Applications
Edited by P. Pavan Kumar, G. Suresh Kumar, Ajay Kumar Jena, Sandeep Kumar Panda and S. Balamurugan
Published 2025. ISBN 978-1-394-38904-9

AI Trust, Risk and Security Management
Framework, Principles, and Practices
Edited by R. Karthick Manoj, S. Senthilnathan, S. Arunmozhi Selvi, T. Ananth Kumar, S. Balamurugan
Published 2025. ISBN 978-1-394-39299-5

Responsible AI
Principles and Practices
Edited by Manish Kumar, Nitigya Sambyal, Leena Priyadarshini Singh, Ramasamy V. and S. Balamurugan
Published 2026. ISBN 978-1-394-35544-0

Forthcoming 2026
Neuro-Symbolic AI: Concepts and Applications
Decision Intelligence: Concepts, Applications, and Case Studies
Human-Centered AI: Frameworks and Applications
Platform Engineering: Concepts, Challenges, and Applications
Composite AI: Fundamentals, Challenges, and Applications

Visual AI: Fundamentals, Challenges, and Applications
Causal AI: Fundamentals and Applications
Embodied AI: Concepts, Challenges, and Applications
Agentic AI: Concepts, Applications, and Case Studies
Data-Centric AI: Concepts, Applications and Case Studies
Sovereign AI: Frameworks, Principles, and Practices
Accelerated AI: Energy Efficient Computing Systems for Large Language Models (LLMs)
Actionable AI: Powered by Large Action Models (LAMs)
Affective AI: Concepts, Applications, and Case Studies
AI-Augmented Software Engineering: Principles and Practices
Ambient Invisible Intelligence: Fundamentals, Challenges, and Applications
Artificial Cognition: Technology, Applications, and Challenges
Artificial General Intelligence: Principles and Practices
Autonomous AI Agents: Foundations and Applications
Principles of Confidential Computing
Disinformation Security for Generative AI Applications: Concepts, Methodologies, and Use Cases
Embedded AI: Concepts, Challenges, and Applications
Graph Neural Networks (GNNs): Concepts and Applications
Industry Cloud Platforms: Fundamentals, Applications, and Case Studies
Multi-Modal Generative AI: Frameworks, Principles, and Practices
Objective-Driven AI: Concepts, Applications, and Case Studies
Physical AI for Robotics and Automation: Concepts, Techniques, and Applications
Predictive AI: Concepts, Applications, and Case Studies
Prescriptive AI: Concepts, Applications, and Case Studies
Shadow AI: Concepts, Applications, and Security
Small Language Models (SLMs) for Compact AI: Architectures, Principles, and Applications

www.scrivenerpublishing.com

Printed in the USA/Agawam, MA
June 30, 2026

907143.079